Inequalities of Love

INEQUALITIES OF LOVE

College-Educated Black Women and the
Barriers to Romance and Family

AVERIL Y. CLARKE

DUKE UNIVERSITY PRESS
Durham & London 2011

Printed in the United States of America on acid-free paper ∞
Designed by Jennifer Hill
Typeset in Adobe Warnock Pro by Tseng Information Systems, Inc.

Library of Congress Cataloging-in-Publication Data
appear on the last printed page of this book.

For Mom, Dad, Greer, Hilton, Aunty, and
those you have made my family—

Rachel, Domi, Kyle, Jordy, Courtney,
Jonas and Drew

CONTENTS

In the Chapters

In the Appendix

In the Chapters

In the Appendix

ACKNOWLEDGMENTS

ALMOST A YEAR before I was ready to submit this manuscript, I watched the Quill awards honoring books and writers on television. At the end of the show, the award for the most popular novelist was given to Nora Roberts, and she began her acceptance speech by pointing out how many of her predecessors on the stage had thanked their spouses and children. She then asserted that her spouse had not written the book and went on to make it clear that no one had written the book but her. And listening in my living room, up to my elbows in paper versions of one or another chapter of my baby that was still too long and complicated, I was overwhelmed with feelings of empathy. Writing a book (at least for me and, I suppose, Nora Roberts) is a lonely journey, and even now, as close as I feel to the end, I feel a distinct sense of longing for the moment that I can return to interacting with the world like the me I am when I am not writing a book. But having established that the writing of this book—the stringing together of words to make meaning, the omissions, misrepresentations, and mistakes that create confusion or offense—is all mine, I must also say that I don't think I could have taken or completed this lonely journey without the support and contributions of others.

As will probably be most obvious to anyone who reads the book, I owe much to my sample of anonymous informants (and to those who were not informants but who referred me to their friends and associates who were eligible for the study). The words of the college-educated black women who were willing to be interviewed and who graciously shared the private, public, mundane, extraordinary, esteem-worthy, and "shameful" details of their lives fill many of the pages of this book. I hope I have represented them well, for they have assisted me in answering the research questions that began my study and in unearthing the answers to questions I did not know that I had. I regard the conversations that we had as a privilege. It is because I do not take their disclosures lightly that I have remained committed to writing in a way that fully represents their realities even as it illuminates the broader social questions about inequality, marriage, and family that I am attempting to address.

I am also thankful to my intellectual colleagues. This is a broad group. It includes all those people who have been available to me for conversations about this project during the many years that I have been reading, collecting and analyzing data, writing, and revising. To those faculty and students in my immediate, everyday work life—Rachel, Julia, Hannah, Andrew, Elizabeth A., Emilie T., Adrian, Michael Y., Shoham, Tamiko, Cynthia S., to name a select few—I appreciate your insights and encouragement, as well as the reading of chapter drafts that you did that informed those conversations. Moreover, those of you who helped me with the project in other ways, including introducing me and the project to the editors at various academic publishing organizations (yes, this includes you, Leslie) and helping me to fulfill the requirements of those publishers (yes, this means you, Themba and Damon), have made the text in its final form possible. The development of a relationship with a publisher, as well as the review process that Duke University Press has put me through, has brought important focus and direction to the manuscript.

I am also fortunate to have the support of colleagues in and out of academia and in and out of sociology who have taken an interest in the project. Thanks to email, I was able to send out draft work to these colleagues over the years, and many have responded with both comments and encouragement. They have done the homework of reading and responding under the auspices of our shared membership in writing groups and anonymous or public review processes, and they have done this work just because I asked and they were both available and generous with their time. I thank the members of MAJAC (Jacqui O., Niki, Judith, Maggie, Stacey, Katherine, Lance, Jackie J., Chrishana, Belkus, Darrick, Kesha) and the members of my very first writing group (Kesha, Maggie, Judith, Sherri), as well as those who have at one time or another participated as virtual reading group members (Keith, Tara, Monique, Kerry). I am also extremely grateful to my reviewers. The anonymous reviewers from Duke University Press sent copious notes, questions, and criticisms, each of which helped to expand my vision for the book beyond its demographic roots. Sam Preston, Doug Massey, and Mary Pattillo also had occasions to review different versions of the text and they too offered the kind of comments that enabled me to see the potential of the work and motivated me to get closer to that potential. I am a social learner: I depend upon conversations with others—even others who are in stark disagreement with me—in order to figure out what I know and don't know, what I am saying clearly and what I am obscuring, and what I am agreeing to and fighting against. Thanks for reading, for listening, and reflecting me into articulateness. As the engaged and vocal witnesses on my lonely journey, you have been the book's first audience. You have helped me to develop the imagination to write to multiple audiences at once and to communicate to students, scholars, and lay readers with diverse backgrounds and interests.

There are some witnesses to my journey who have been more than intellectual colleagues. For they have engaged me in this process beyond its academic aspects. They have been in my life for those conversations in which emotions like frustration, fatigue, and disappointment at the slow pace at which I was able to complete the analyses for new tables or sections of chapters clouded the vision I had for a particular literature summary. Kesha, you have read most of this book in almost all of its iterations. You have patiently counseled me through any number of intellectual missteps, writing blocks, missed deadlines, and failed attempts at communicating my ideas. You have helped me to negotiate the emotionally precarious terrain of writing about material that is close to my own life. You have been there for the love and the money. Although granting you co-authorship feels like too much, thanking you in my acknowledgements feels far too small. Since the differences that we bring to our friendship consistently challenge me intellectually and spiritually, I will offer you this: I will try to continue to live and work in a way that makes you proud. And since your generosity to me and this project has known few bounds, I will say that you continue to inspire a generosity of spirit in me.

Diana, Brooke, and Tara, it has been wonderful to have friends who have accommodated both the cognitive and emotional struggles that completing this book has implied. Your efforts to be there for my emotional highs and lows mean that you have become conversant in the book's theses and typologies and in the argument's inconsistencies and weaknesses. Moreover, you have discussed them with me in ways that have challenged and inspired me to push through the writing difficulties but also to take a break and to care for myself. Diana, you have suggested, lobbied for, coaxed, facilitated, and accompanied both work sessions and breaks. Brooke and Tara, you are both brilliant and skilled in your manipulation of the fine line. You both have called and you have beckoned, always demanding that I remain faithful to the task of telling authentic, respectful, true, and illuminating stories of college-educated black women's experiences and always insisting that it is self-love, self-care, and nurturance of bonds with the likes of persons like you that make me worthy of that awesome task. As far away as you three might be from me, you never forget to reach out and to send love my way or to invite and welcome me into your spaces. All I have to offer to you is the long-awaited finish line that is this book. I hope the prize makes you proud of your connection to it.

Since I believe in neither self-made people nor one-stop shopping, I could go on like this forever. Toren, Valencia, Keith, Vilna, Archie, Pastor McArthur, Professor Hildebrand, and Sandy (the dancer who first told me when I was on the cusp of becoming a college-educated black woman that "we"—as in college-educated black women—don't reproduce), I know that in many ways you may feel like my past. But you need to know that I have forgotten neither those who nurtured me and this project during its infancy nor the lessons you have taught me about myself and my work. Even if our contact is more limited than it once was, I continue to employ these lessons every day. Those of you who filled my life and supported my work in Durham, North Carolina—Karolyn, Phil, Reynolds, Eduardo, Linda, Brenda, and my Sunday School class leaders and members—may feel like the more recent past. But I talk about you all the time and marvel at how the very short and abbreviated experience I had there made such an impact on me the writer and the person. North Carolina was where I reframed the book and completed a brand new introduction. These experiences (that oh-so-important conversation with Linda among them) occasioned the new birth that turned what was "Child Sacrifice" into *Inequalities of Love*. Just because the book is done doesn't mean that these relationships with my "past" are over. Indeed, I hope that finishing it and employing the lessons that finishing it have taught me will enable me to be a better friend and/or colleague in our future relationships.

And then there are those who have most advanced this project by being friends to me. I have a list of writing buddies who not only checked in with me but opened spaces to me and at times even brought their work and worked alongside me so that I could get the writing done. As many of you know, a lot of writing is just that—writing, reading, and rewriting, setting time aside for writing, putting time into writing, sitting in front of the computer and writing, enclosing oneself in a circle of piled paper and books, and writing. Yeah, I know, it sounds pretty boring, and truth be told, it often is—not to mention frustrating, slow-going, and downright painful. Niki, Jacqui, Judith, Lois, Maggie, and Daphne: the spaces, the company, the checking in, the study break conversations are much appreciated gifts. For those who offered much needed reprieves at important moments (including Faith, Robin, Rodney, Kenneth, Pat, Anjelica, Anna, Tene, and Tim and Ellen, as well as many I have already mentioned) thanks for the spa days, weekend getaways, fluff parties, Vineyard retreats, outlet shopping, fasts, and all those respites that made returning to the book task possible. And to those who have continued to call me "professor," making the final year of decision-making, editing, proofing, and mostly waiting bearable—Michael B., Raffi, and Aki: I thank you for being there and reminding me of who I am and what my teaching and writing has been to you and others.

Mom, Dad, Greer, Hilton, Aunty, and those you have made my family (Drew, Jonas, Courtney, Jordyn, Kyle, Dominique, and Rachel): what I most fear is disappointing you, being unworthy of the tremendous love and support that you have provided to me, doing less than the absolute best that you have done for me. This book cannot make up for the moments I did not spend with you, the late cards and birthday presents, and all the good intentions toward you not realized. However, it represents a significant portion of the energy, spirit, thought, and expression that is my life. I dedicate it to all of you because at this moment, it is what I have to give.

Inequality

What's Love Got to Do with It?

STORIES ABOUT inequality tend to open with the sad news of famine-starved children, rodent-infested tene-ments, or a woman incarcerated for killing her batter-ing spouse. Textbooks about inequality discuss rates of joblessness, health disparities, and the tragic dilemmas of individuals trying to care for families through some combination of illegal activity, borrowing or sharing among extended kin and friends, and stretching insuf-ficient funds from a stingy welfare state. But here, in this book, inequality looks more like a "chick flick."[1] For example, the book's argument includes juicy details of the ill-fated romances that led up to Ashley's[2] climac-tic encounter with "Mr. Right," the tale of her quick engagement and eventual wedding, and the narrative of her six-year wait to pregnancy. It paints a picture of Ashley's journey from girlhood in a small southern town through life as a single "yuppie" in a midwestern city to marriage in a suburban home—a picture that reads like a glossy, touched-up photograph. Then there is the birth of Ashley's daughter coming after struggles with infertility, and a family business finally turning profit-able—two more events that might just as well be the raw material for one of Hollywood's romantic movies. And yet this book uses what often sound like soap-opera story lines to describe processes intrinsic to the maintenance of inequality.

Ashley is a pseudonym for an actual woman. Since she chose it, perhaps it does represent the name she would have given herself in a romance novel or a television sit-com being constructed about her life. She is thirty-five years old, black, and college educated. The story lines are data collected from her and fifty-seven other middle-class (that is, college-educated) black women of reproductive age (that is, under fifty) during interviews that covered their educational backgrounds, their careers, and their romantic, sexual, and reproductive experiences. In this book, these tabloid-like details of Ashley's upbringing, of her sexual and romantic life, and of her efforts to have a baby are the central components of an argument about an inequality of reproductive relations.

The book considers the origins and consequences of individual women's decisions about their educational and professional lives and about their sexual and family formation behavior. It interrogates the decision making of college-educated black women in particular—asking whether their status as African American females has led to experiences or placed them in relationships that constrain the choices they can make about school, work, and family or that motivate them to make some educational, professional, or family formation choices over others. College-educated black women are then compared to women of other races with college degrees and to black women with less education. These comparisons indicate the degree of similarity or the extent of difference that exists between their sexual and reproductive decision making and that of women who occupy different positions in social hierarchies than they do.

The description of middle-class black women's decision making in this book has the glitz and glamour of a "chick flick" because of the two features that differentiate it from much scholarly work on inequality: first, love, romance, and baby making are given centrality; and second, the cast of characters are in a class of college-educated professionals. With respect to this first point, scholars describing individuals' status attainment, social mobility, or the reproduction of racial and class hierarchies from one generation to the next have not typically been concerned with things like Ashley's struggle to have a child or the connection between her desire to preserve her marriage and her decision to relinquish her $80,000 per year salary and become a homemaker. Since women were not seen as the primary earners in households, neither their class attainment processes nor their romantic and childbearing behaviors were seen as consequential to the maintenance of economic hierarchy.[3] In contrast, women's involvement in reproductive labor (that is, the performance of tasks and the forging and building of relations that support the birth of the next generation and the physical and emotional care of past, present, and future role players in the world economy) is a central topic in this study's analysis. Explanations of women's decision making with respect to romance and reproduction and descriptions of race and class similarities and differences in sexual and reproductive behavior form the evidence in this book's argument about inequality. Indeed, one of the two major arguments that this book makes is that *degreed black women are deprived and maligned in sexual and reproductive relations*; their romantic and family formation life trajectories provide examples of the way *the combination of experience and action in both reproductive and productive arenas can be constitutive of race, class, and gender inequities.*

With respect to the second point, the intensive analyses of the specific motivations, decisions, and circumstances that support elites' achievement of their economically superior outcomes is another distinctive feature of this book, since such a focus on elites is also quite rare in studies of inequality.[4] Unlike the world of popular television shows, magazines, and movies, which are virtually obsessed with the middle and upper classes,[5] academicians concerned with looking at the decision making of individuals and how that relates to stratification and class outcomes have focused almost exclusively on analyses of individuals in disadvantaged groups. Textbooks may make arguments about the activities of elites, but mainly in their roles as employers, managers, teachers, or other kinds of caretakers (for example, social workers, medical professionals) of those in the lower class. Because there is little analysis of the circumstances, motivations, decisions, and activities that allow their educational, professional, and personal life trajectories to unfold, a dynamic in inequality study has developed in which the highly scrutinized activities of lower-class and minority-raced individuals are contrasted with what more advantaged individuals "seem," based on their consistently superior outcomes, to be thinking and doing.[6]

This book examines inequality through the lens of college-educated black women, and in so doing, it looks simultaneously at advantage (class) and disadvantage (race and gender). Ashley's humble beginnings in a small southern town and her escape to her professional, middle-class, suburban life are moved from the realm of fairy tale and folklore, and here they are united with her experiences of racial isolation and feminine surrender in a description of the ways that the decisions of both the advantaged and the disadvantaged (or the simultaneous decision making from positions of advantage and disadvantage) maintain unequal relations. Here, the book makes its second argument, one about *the importance of Ashley's statuses within multiple hierarchical systems to the maintenance of inequality.* In short, this argument makes a claim about the relevance of theories of "intersectionality" to descriptions of how and why inequality is maintained over time. Intersectionality theory argues for the interconnectedness of different systems of inequality, maintaining that the continuity of class difference depends upon processes of racialization and racist practices (and vice versa), that the maintenance of racial hierarchy relies upon gender-sex inequality (and vice versa), and that gender hierarchy and patriarchal relationships persist with the assistance of class differentiation (and vice versa). In effect, inequality maintenance proceeds (and is often challenged) based on the actions of persons constrained and motivated by the interlocking (rather than side-by-side or additive) nature of their race, class, and gender statuses.

Below, this introduction outlines the book's two major arguments. The first argument about the importance of sex, marriage, and baby making to inequality maintenance hinges on a description and demonstration of African American women's romantic deprivation. And the second argument about the ways race, class, and gender stratification systems depend upon, support, and at times conflict with one another suggests that this race-based romantic deprivation has implications for degreed black women's gender and class identity performance. The introduction explains how the qualitative data on degreed black women's lives and the quantitative comparisons of sex and childbearing across racial and class groups figures into these arguments. And it demonstrates how research on the love stories of middle-class women develops the demographic study of race and class differences in family formation and the sociological literature on inequality in critical ways.

It Ain't All about Money

I interviewed the thirty-four-year-old Christian elementary school teacher whom I call Wanda in the apartment of the housing project in which she and her mother reside. There I learned that she had withdrawn from the first university she attended. When I asked why, she described feelings of isolation, cold temperatures, and a large, rural campus that was far away from family, a black neighborhood, and urban life. After dropping out, Wanda landed in a community program that focused on teaching local women in her mostly poor and all-black neighborhood how to economize when cleaning, making household repairs, and shopping for food for the family. I remember wondering how participation in such a program could possibly have led her back to university education, but it did, and she eventually graduated from a city university less than five miles from her home.

Wanda's interview also provided me with details about her family life growing up: she was the only girl child in a family of three children. Although her parents had lived together when she was very young and their home was in South Carolina, only her mother and brother were with her in the northeastern city where she began the third grade and still lives to this day. Except for the first abbreviated college experience and her two years of service in the Peace Corps, Wanda has resided in this city, in the same neighborhood in which she spent the bulk of her childhood. She met her oldest and best friend as well as the one significant man in her romantic relationship history in this neighborhood.

Since there was just the one relatively important man, it did not take me long to get the details about Wanda's love life. Even though this man (I call him Justice) has been around for many years and Wanda cares for him a great deal, he has only managed to make intermittent romantic appearances in her life. She gave me the impression that he was one she would like to settle down with if the opportunity for a long-term committed relationship presented itself, but she also seemed doubtful that it would.

As was the case for all of my fifty-eight interview subjects, I collected at least two hours' worth of data from Wanda. A stratification scholar perusing the transcribed interview would likely have found this lengthy conversation and some of my questions a bit excessive, but given the type of data with which these scholars work and the kind of analyses in which they typically engage, Wanda's transcript would have still inspired commentary from them. More specifically, stratification scholars might have made note of the inconsistency between Wanda's relatively high education level (for example, her college degree) and her relatively low wages. In this branch of inequality scholarship, a concern with low wages is part and parcel of scholars' overall goal of using quantitative methods of data analysis to explain differences in things like individual and household income, wealth, employment, and occupational status.[7] Inequities in these areas associated with economic productivity become in this research the very definition of unequal lives, and since these scholars have built a myriad of models showing that increases in a person's education level tend to improve her earnings,[8] Wanda's low income provides such a researcher with a certain conundrum that requires a solution.

Many Wandas and Their Unequal Work Lives

Stratification researchers do not look solely to Wanda for the answer to their conundrum. Instead they rely on data from many people like Wanda (that is, other black women with college degrees) and from even more people who are not like Wanda (that is, people who differ from her in terms of age, sex, race, educational achievement, residence geography, family status, and occupational status). Then they sort these data in a way that enables them to compare Wanda to other individuals who appear just like her except for one of these variables. In one instance this varying variable may be age, in another it may be sex, and in still another it may be marital status, and so on. When they make these comparisons, they usually discover that what seems like a random bunch of unequal lives is really systematic variance in employment or income by age (for example, younger white electricians have lower occupational statuses than older white electricians),[9] by sex (for example, women with high-school diplomas earn less than men at the same education level),[10] or by family status (for example, childless women move up the career ladder faster than women with children).[11] In the stratification researcher's world, Wanda is rarely alone in her high-education-low-income situation: rather, she shares some quality with other research subjects—a quality that likely affects her activities in the productive sector and consequently lowers all of their wages. The key for this kind of inequality researcher is to find this quality.

When stratification researchers uncover areas of systematic variance, they are in a position to identify the important quality that causes Wanda's conundrum, and this is how they add to our knowledge of how inequality comes about. The variance allows them to confirm or reject the inequality theories that inform their work—those that pertain to individuals' productive capacities and behaviors.[12] For example, variance in occupation by sex would help them to determine whether Wanda's low income is related to the fact that her career opportunities are confined to areas of the labor market dominated by women.[13] Or variance in employment by race would permit them to make an assessment about whether racial antagonism and consequent discrimination in labor markets is at its worst in areas where the concentration of African Americans is high and consequently in regions where Wanda and most black people live.[14] Similarly, if racial groups are clustered in the same regions and/or corporations, these researchers might use the data to support claims about racism restricting Wanda's social network and her access to persons who have information about higher-paying jobs.[15] And alternatively, some stratification scholars might even frame Wanda's residence in the housing project and work in a helping profession as a choice: if the systematic variance is based on the fact that social group members share values or preferences and make similar choices, then the low wages become an outcome Wanda desires, one that just may be associated with a decision to use her educational resources and her capacity for high labor market productivity in service to her community.[16]

Now the data on individuals that stratification researchers use can come from different regions of the United States, from nations with very different social and economic systems, from eras in which individuals and nations are experiencing greater or fewer of the conditions associated with economic depression or recession, and from sampling processes that may be more or less restrictive with respect to gender, age, occupation, and education levels. This variability, as well as different ways of measuring or not measuring the concepts of interest to them, produces some disagreement in their answers to the question of how inequality comes about.[17] In some studies age and education level differences are the most important reasons that sampled individuals are living such unequal lives while in others race and gender discrimination appear to separate employed from unemployed and high earners from low earners. Notwithstanding the importance of these distinctions, the distinction between unequal outcomes that are chosen and those over which individuals have little or no control are foundational to debates in stratification research as well as in general discussions of inequality that take place in intellectual and political circles.

Inequality and individuals' unequal experiences usually become social problems in need of remedy when the systematic variance in economic outcomes that stratification researchers uncover is not viewed as the result of individual choice. Those interested parties that are resistant to the redistributive and ameliorative programs that would equalize individuals' lived experiences tend to be unsupportive of these programs because they interpret variance by education level, by age, by employment experience, and even by occupational status as the consequence of personal freedom. Here, unequal outcomes are understood as the unproblematic feature of a social structure characterized by relative equality for all those willing to apply appropriate effort in school and on the job (and who have the talent and interest to focus their efforts on particular career fields). In contrast, consistently lower than average education, employment, wages, or wealth on the part of a group of persons sharing a social status can be touted as the very definition of social group inequality and as the distinctive characteristic of a social structure that serves the interests and needs of one group while exploiting and devaluing the contributions that others make. One of the main driving forces spurring on inequality study, then, is scholars' interpretation of Wanda's own role in creating her high-education, low-income situation. As strange as it sounds, if Wanda has the opportunity to be rich and chooses to be poor because she finds the life agendas and tasks of the wealthy unappealing, then poverty may not be such a bad thing.[18]

Few Wandas and Their School Choices

There is a group of inequality scholars that would have been concerned to look more directly at Wanda's choices and the situations over which she did and did not have control. These qualitative investigators of inequality or inequality ethnographers would have been more appreciative of the two-hour conversation that I had with Wanda and the time that I took to ask her about the feelings, motivations, and interpretations that surrounded the events in her life. They would have wanted to analyze the settings and situations that created the context for her decision making, and they would have endeavored to describe the way in which her various possibilities for action in such situations would have been read and understood in these settings. Such scholars have a concern equivalent to that of stratification scholars with regard to answering the question of how inequality comes about, but they use "thicker" data on what is typically a smaller number of respondents to answer this question. The "how" in their how-inequality-comes-about question remains interested in assessing the degree to which social structures beyond individuals' control limit choice and the self-determination of one's own outcomes. But here structural limitations are demonstrated by descriptive details of the conditions faced by women like Wanda and of the way such research subjects understand their options and make choices[19] (rather than on observations of the social variables that Wanda shares with large numbers of persons who similarly have high education levels and low incomes).

As was the case in stratification research, economic production and the productive capacities and behaviors of individuals are given centrality in a qualitative investigation of inequality. Thus when inequality ethnographers collect the more extended life histories on Wanda's life or dedicate hours, weeks, months, or years to observing her activities and interactions, they hone in on places, spaces, and interactions in which economic production occurs and in which economic production capacities are built. Much like the stratification researcher who puts the data on Wanda into a table that will include columns on her years of schooling, her occupation, her work experience, and her income, these qualitative scholars observe in school settings,[20] in workplaces,[21] and shadow or otherwise collect data from people on their work and school lives and on the interactions (for example, job interviews) and experiences (for example, parental involvement in homework) that are distinctly connected to their work and school experiences.[22] This would mean paying close attention to the isolation Wanda felt on the large, cold campus of the college she would eventually leave and analyzing her discussion of activities and interactions that led to her making such an inappropriate choice of schools for herself.

Of course some inequality ethnographers would argue that analysis of the qualitative data on Wanda indicates that she had little if any school choice. They would describe her high school, noting that it lacked college counselors who advertised college fairs and met with high-achieving students to make recommendations about colleges that meet their particular needs. They might then argue that the lack of information and guidance led to her decision to apply to only one school—the one that actively solicited her application and waived the application fee. This large, cold, predominantly white university that was far away from Wanda's family and from urban life sent a representative to a Saturday program (separate from the public high school) that Wanda attended: it was the only school that so aggressively recruited the lower-class black attendees of this Saturday program. The inequality ethnographers might then go on to make the point that individuals at different positions in the socioeconomic hierarchy (for example, whites and blacks, poor and wealthy) have different experiences in schools: inequities in everything from curriculum and campus to coaching and college counseling ensure that the children of elites will be offered the highest-paying and most stable jobs and that less advantaged children (like Wanda) will leave school with so few credentials that they will have little choice but to work under and for this new elite.[23] In this way, a qualitative investigator of inequality makes the point that educational and economic institutions are set up by dominant social groups in ways that protect their privileged status: the poor individual and those in other disadvantaged groups essentially have no control over the arrangements in schools and workplaces and consequently are not choosing their low economic outcomes.

Inequality scholars may split between an interest in collecting quantitative data on individuals' experiences and qualitative data on their understandings of events and interactions, but they agree on the importance of focusing on data on Wanda's school and labor market experiences: they agree that inequities in the capacities and behaviors associated with economic productivity are constitutive of inequality. Stratification scholars and inequality ethnographers may engage in different kinds of sampling and analytical techniques, but they agree on the centrality of the task of assessing how it is that individuals come to be living unequal lives. Thus, as in the case of stratification research, the multiplicity of qualitative investigations of this question leads to some dissension about the degree to which individuals like Wanda face structural limitations in moving out of the disadvantageous circumstances of their childhoods.

Qualitative investigators that argue that Wanda's high-education, low-income outcome reflects some self-expression and choice might maintain that she and others like her are not so unaware or so easily manipulated as those who describe school-based, inequality-producing processes might indicate. Indeed, they explain that some lower-class girls and boys do their best to disrupt the smooth functioning of the school and resist dominant group control of that institution by acting out and interrupting teachers' lectures or completing assignments in a chaotic way that subverts the instructors' intentions. They point out that black, Hispanic, and other communities of color whose history of residence in the United States involved conquering, colonization, and/or forced migration deliberately enact an oppositional culture—one that devalues compliant behavior and high levels of achievement in a school and a labor market that will nevertheless discriminate against and marginalize those persons.[24] Many argue that it is these very countercultural behaviors (for example, lower-class males' valorization of the masculinity of factory work and rejection of feminized intellectual labors) that represent the choices that disadvantaged individuals make about their lives. Here the human agency of the disadvantaged matters: marginalized persons and groups may act in ways that reproduce their subordinate status, but they are not simply engaging in predetermined responses to the actions and manipulations of the dominant group members that control schools and workplaces. Wanda and others like her may choose substantial social mobility (for example, choosing to return to school and choosing to be the first in their families to complete college) and a low-wage job that puts them in a position to help other disadvantaged persons to resist and surpass hurdles erected by those in control of dominant group institutions (for example, choosing to work in the Peace Corps in a developing nation).

Wanda's Love

This book is concerned with a fundamental question of inequality scholarship—the question of how inequality comes about. And as is the case in the writings of stratification researchers and inequality ethnographers, this investigation of that question makes assessments about whether and to what degree an individual like Wanda can be seen as an active agent or a manipulable pawn in the creation of the outcomes that place her experience beneath that of others in her social world. But while the text follows the traditions established by a broad range of inequality scholars in this and a number of other ways, it nonetheless shifts the terms of the discussion. It does so by placing the focus on inequities in reproductive capacities and behavior rather than productive ones. Or, in less imposing, less academic speak, *it changes the matter from which unequal lives are constituted from money to love.* Here, a fascination with solving the high-education, low-income conundrum and an interest in identifying the causes and consequences of a circuitous journey to degree attainment and professional status are made secondary to providing an explanation for Wanda's stalled family formation trajectory.

At first glance, the movement of the thirty-four-year-old Wanda's never-had-a-child, never-been-married, never-had-sex state to center stage makes this book seem less like an academic investigation of inequality and more like a dramatization of events complete with a list of complaints worthy of a "drama queen." After all, isn't it the "drama queen"—and the "chick flick" for that matter—that gets caught up in the meaningless and insignificant details of which girl does not have a date to the senior prom and what color bridesmaid's dress looks best when there are real problems in the world? Inequality researchers take pains to write about childbearing, marriage, and the labors done for love rather than money only insofar as these events and activities can be made important by their connection to inequities in the productive arena. Thus, demographers use the data and models of stratification researchers to engage in debates about whether women in poorer classes and poorer countries are poor because of the level, timing, and/or marital status associated with their childbearing behavior.[25] Similarly, students of the labor market changes that contracted the supply of urban jobs available to working-class males argue that declines in marriage rates and increases in the numbers of children born to single mothers are a consequence of these changes in economic production.[26] This book differs from such work in its insistence on examining the inequities in individuals' reproductive activity and in their love and sex lives on their own terms. Furthermore, the analysis lets the data on family status inequality speak for itself. It allows for a discussion of how an inequality of reproductive relations emerges—

of how inequities in sex, marriage, and childbearing come about—even if such things are unrelated to the productive arena.

The research tasks and questions associated with this book represent a departure from inequality research not only in their shift from money study to love study but also in the degree to which they question the value of money. Typically, even the research that does not focus on explaining money differences serves to underscore the importance of those differences. It does so by drawing links between economic inequality and the outcomes and experiences in other spheres of life. An example here would be health disparities research, an arena in which inequality scholars connect race and class inequality to disease incidence and mortality. These scholars show that the large differences in health and wellness reflect the fact that those with greater economic resources can use their resources to reduce their vulnerability to disease: they might point out the benefits of purchasing or renting a home in a neighborhood where air and water are relatively free of pollutants or toxins; they might discuss the health advantages of eating regular healthy meals that maintain one's nutritional status and immune system; or they might attribute differences in disease experience and death from disease to the fact that those who have greater education and income are also more likely to have the knowledge and money to access medical treatments that heal or prolong life in the case of illness or injury. Such health scholarship discusses health inequality and directs attention back to arguments about the importance of money inequality.[27]

The same can be said of criminology studies that compare individuals with higher and lower occupational status, with higher and lower wages, and with greater or lesser regularity in employment. When such scholarship goes on to conclude that economically disadvantaged persons are more vulnerable to victimization by a criminal offender, surveillance and arrest by the police, conviction for a crime, and stringent punishment for criminal conviction, it also supports the central role that inquiries into the inequities associated with economic production play in inequality study more broadly speaking. By leaving room for the possibility that money may be of only minor relevance in the generation of advantage with respect to sexual, romantic, marital, and reproductive relations, this book tries to make substantive changes in the ways inequality scholars think about how unequal lives, unequal experiences, advantage, and disadvantage are constituted.[28]

Demographers have typically studied love inequality in much the same way that scholars have approached health, crime, and justice system inequality. Connecting differences in birthrates and the ages at which women marry and start families to economic and racial inequality, they have invariably described, confirmed, and at times rejected hypothesized connections between love and money. The salient theme of their theoretical and empirical work in the United States and abroad and in historical and contemporary eras is that of an inverse relationship between a woman's fertility and her schooling and work—that is, a relationship that says much love equals little money or much money means little love. Thus women who delay marriage and childbearing and have fewer kids improve their educational and economic outcomes relative to those who have larger numbers of children or who give birth early in the life course. Similarly, poor women's education and earning potential is curtailed by their voluntary or involuntary involvement in motherhood.[29] Note then that in the context of demographic study of love inequality, Wanda's stalled family formation trajectory is framed as advantageous.[30] In the concluding arguments of some studies it becomes the reason for Wanda's upward mobility—the reason that she earns the college degree that her parents and the sexually active teen mothers in her neighborhood did not.[31]

I consider excellent health and zero time spent in jail to be good examples of the point being made by the type of investigation that connects money inequality to outcomes in arenas like health or crime or love—the point that those that dominate in the relations of economic productivity can use their resources in this arena to create more advantageous circumstances for themselves in these other spheres of life. However the arguments in this book begin with the notion that Wanda's childlessness and nonexistent sex life constitute a more ambiguous example of this point. It is not entirely clear that having no sex, no marriage, and no child constitute advantages in love in the same way that it is clear that having no disease and no jail time respectively indicate advantage in health and in relations with the justice system.

The arguments in this book maintain that Wanda's money cannot necessarily buy her the love of an attractive spouse, the marital sexual relationship that she wants with that spouse, and the children that she had hoped to have in marriage. The book also argues that the low-fertility, high-education inverse relationship outcome is not one of Wanda's choosing: rather, specific race, class, and gender constraints limit her access to the marriage that she believes needs to precede the rest of these "goods" in the reproductive arena. Or, put in a way that more accurately reflects Wanda's feelings and motivations, race-class-gender constraints limit her access to the marriage that would make the sex and childbearing into "goods" she can enjoy rather than evidence of a moral and religious fall. Finally, this book's arguments maintain that Wanda's unrealized family formation aspirations put her at a disadvantage relative to other women at her age and station in life[32] and that *these disadvantages in love are the result of the fact that love (like money) is unequally distributed along specific social group lines.*[33]

This book allows women's experiences of their sexual and family formation outcomes to determine how advantageous those outcomes are. Furthermore, descriptions of the lack of choice women experience in determining such outcomes and identification of the social group differences in the processes through which these outcomes are determined are the analytical techniques used to demonstrate the point that love matters in the generation and maintenance of social inequality. This contrasts with a pattern in inequality research in which we assume that those with economic advantages are in the best position to choose the outcomes that are desirable to them. Although largely unspoken, this assumption emerges from a compilation of literature in which stratification researchers make no direct observations of the moments in which individuals make the decisions that lead to their outcomes or of the individuals' perceptions of the limitations and options that they face in these moments, while qualitative researchers have largely restricted such direct observations to the poor or economically disadvantaged.[34] We thus learn about the ways that the poor are limited in their choices and about the reasons that they behave in these "illogical" ways that seem to reproduce their poverty. At the same time, we conclude that Wanda has choices and that her fertility control reflects her higher status—perhaps even her lack of need to create an identity around mothering and caretaking or to rely on men and marriage for food and shelter.

My assertions about this book's exploration of a love inequality that is not necessarily related to productive sector inequality are grounded in data collection and analyses that directly observe Wanda's perceived limitations in the reproductive arena, that demonstrate that white and His-

panic women with college degrees do not experience these limitations
to the same degree, and that explore the continuities and discontinuities
between lower- and middle-class black women's experience of deprivation with respect to romantic love, sexual relations, and the marital and
familial bonds that arise from these emotional and physical exchanges.
In sum, a compendium of inequality research that privileges investigation of the relations and individual behaviors and capacities associated
with economic production have led to the unexamined conclusion that
Wanda's stalled family formation trajectory reflects her social advantage and greater choice. This book challenges this notion with Wanda's
own testimony about her limited opportunities in love and with description of the social inequities in the specific romantic processes that lead
to women's fertility outcomes. It uses the techniques of stratification and
qualitative inequality researchers and follows their traditional line of inquiry into how inequality comes about. But its analyses of the degree to
which individuals choose or are limited to the experiences that constitute
their unequal lives reference their romantic and family formation experiences to a greater extent than they do their school and work lives.

A Book about Love Inequality

The explanation of this book's claims about a racial inequality in reproductive relations begins in chapter 2, where I describe systematic variance
in family formation outcomes. I use the techniques of stratification researchers and national data generated from a random sample of women
who vary widely on a whole host of social variables and family formation
behaviors.[35] Here, I show that family formation outcome differences are
at times related to women's productive capacities (for example, their education levels) and at other times related to their racial status. Furthermore, I argue that even those situations that indicate that black, Hispanic,
and white women with college degrees have similar family formation outcomes mask stark racial differences in the means by which fertility outcomes are achieved. These class similarities hide the low availability of
love and marriage to black women regardless of their level of economic
advantage. For example, while some may argue that the lack of statistically
significant racial differences (that is, differences too small to be attributed to anything but chance variation in the sample) in the completed
fertility of college-educated women points to the importance of produc-

tive capacities in determining women's fertility, my research on the racial differences in the processes through which these outcomes are reached disagrees with this interpretation of the data. Instead, I argue that degreed black women's average completed fertility of 1.53 children reflects a child sacrifice in which they forgo opportunities to bear children when marital opportunities are not present. In contrast, I maintain that degreed white and Hispanic women's respective averages of 1.63 and 1.83 children ever born are achieved through decisions to postpone and limit fertility despite the opportunity or actuality of marriage.[36]

Chapters 3 through 6 are built around an analytical stance developed by demographers who study fertility differences across nations, classes, eras, and races. This theoretical framework, known as the proximate determinants framework, portends to confirm or reject hypothesized reasons for social group differences in fertility levels. Proximate determinants are like the methods of transportation we use to get to a destination. They describe the (mostly biological) means through which nations, classes, races, or eras reach the fertility outcomes that they do. Much like knowing that a group arrived at a destination in a slave ship tells us something about why they are where they are, knowing which of seven proximate determinants allows a nation to reach its low-fertility outcome tells us something about the structural and cultural context in which its citizens operate and make sexual and reproductive decisions.

Demographers using the proximate determinants framework go beyond the task of identifying an inverse relationship between fertility and education or economic class: they also tell the scientific and policy-making community how fertility inequality comes about.[37] In this case, observers find out whether poor women's earlier and higher fertility and middle- and upper-class women's fertility postponement reflect poorer women's lower access to contraception or middle- and upper-class women's decisions to delay romantic activity and limit the frequency of sexual intercourse during their youth. The former claim would support the more general academic point that women in the lower classes possess less freedom to choose the life that many women desire while the latter might suggest that poorer women both have and make the choice of love over money.

Support for various demographic theories of the relationship between fertility levels and economic conditions or individuals' productive capaci-

ties and behaviors can therefore hinge on the results of proximate determinant analyses. So too does this book rely on a series of chapters containing discussions of Wanda and the other degreed black women's choices
and constraints with respect to the proximate determinants. Using this
framework, the book shows that as a social group, these women are deprived in romantic love. Furthermore, the employment of the framework
illuminates the importance of deprivation in love and marriage to the
constitution of unequal life experiences. Deprivation in love and marriage
is shown to change the meanings and value assigned to the relations and
activities associated with reproductive labor: without love and marriage,
sex and childbearing are not necessarily valued in the same way and to the
same degree.

This book argues the point that love and marriage inequality mean
that equivalent behaviors are unequally understood and judged by self
and others—that sex for money is read and understood differently from
sex for fun, which is seen differently from sex for love, which is again seen
differently from sex for marriage. Thus Wanda's deprivation in love and
marriage develops into a deprivation in sex and childbearing as neither is
seen as a desired outcome without the benefit of love and marriage. It is
the proximate determinant analysis that tells us that Wanda's low fertility
outcome reflects marriage deprivation and a social inequality in the distribution of love rather than class advantage. It is the proximate determinant analysis that tells us that inequality is constituted not only by differences in outcomes, but also by differences in the ways those outcomes are
achieved and the ways those outcomes can be represented.

In chapter 3, I discuss the proximate determinant of marriage. This is
the most important proximate determinant in this argument about inequality in reproductive relations for two reasons. First, marriage is an
arena in which the analyses of the National Survey of Family Growth
(NSFG) data show that women's racial status is more important than the
measure of their productive capacity in determining outcomes. In marriage, degreed black women look most unlike other college-educated
women and look most like black women in the lower classes. Second, inequality in marriage emerges in the context of this study as a foundational
inequality. Much like the research focused on economic productivity that
shows that economic inequality spawns other types of inequalities (for example, in health and crime), degreed black women's marital constraints

reassert themselves in black women's interactions with other proximate determinants (for example, sex, contraception, and abortion).

Chapter 3 uses data from the fifty-eight degreed black women on their romantic experiences in order to describe the ways they find their options in romance and marriage limited. Its discussion of research subjects' constraints or lack of choice in marital behavior forms a large part of the book's argument about the ways inequities in the distribution of love can by themselves or without connection to the women's economic behavior constitute a type of deprivation and social inequality. It is in this chapter that data on Wanda's loneliness on the predominantly white college campus is brought to bear on her love rather than money outcomes. It is in this chapter that her inability to develop her on-again, off-again relationship with Justice into a viable long-term romance and/or marriage becomes a relevant subject of analysis and inquiry rather than superfluous data in the study of inequities in productive relations.

Chapters 4, 5, and 6 respectively focus on sex, contraception, and abortion. The book confines analyses and arguments to these three proximate determinants and marriage because of an interest in linking inequities in reproductive experiences to individual choices and constraints. These are the determinants over which women are capable of exerting direct control. In other words, these are the situations where they can exercise choices. Furthermore, when women make choices about sex, contraception, abortion, and marriage, they understand that these choices can affect their romantic and reproductive lives. This contrasts with the remaining proximate determinants in the demographic model (age at which menstruation begins, incidence of miscarriage or spontaneous abortion, and age at menopause), which are areas in which women lack the same kind of awareness of their ability to effect change.

Together, these analyses of degreed black women's decision-making moments with respect to sex, contraception, and abortion, as well as the comparisons of degreed black women's decisions in these areas with that of degreed women of other races and with that of black women without degrees, paint a picture of the far-reaching effects of black women's lack of access to marriage. In these three chapters lie descriptions of the way single status frustrates coitus and contraceptive use and increases the frequency of unplanned pregnancy and induced abortion. There is also evidence that women sampled in the NSFG are like Wanda in their concerns about the negative meanings and moral values assigned to nonmarital sexual activity, pregnancy, and childbearing. Constraints in these chapters are largely cultural as those deprived in love and marriage are unable to frame their sexual, contraceptive, and childbearing practices as legitimate.

My attempts to shift the terms in which Wanda's deprivations are constituted or to change the domain in which social inequality is observed are not meant to suggest that she is not an economic actor or even that her educational credentials or low wages are irrelevant in the reproductive arena. Rather, this first argument about love mattering is meant to offer an alternative to conventional and scholarly thinking about black women's sexual and childbearing behavior. Both popular stereotype and academic analyses tend to frame African American women as having a surfeit of offspring. Beginning with the infamous Moynihan Report,[38] scholars and policymakers have painted this picture using stratification researchers' observations of the high-fertility, low-money relationship, stratification researchers' statistical documentation of the fact that family poverty is more prevalent among female-headed households and is associated with teen pregnancy, and empirical scholarship describing school and employment limitations faced by young black women who became mothers as youth and as singles.[39] If a small number of African American women who were less involved in such behaviors managed to earn higher education degrees and good jobs, what could possibly be the harm in that? If anything, Wanda and her similarly educated sisters became the proof positive that the larger and poorer group of black women had more love and family than they could handle.

In this sense, this book asks the publicly conscious and aware reader to consider the highly improbable idea that the thirty-four-year-old Wanda's virginity, singleness, and childlessness are more than they appear to be. More than good planning, "moral restraint," and the independence of a successful upwardly mobile woman, these sexual and family formation outcomes are symptoms of black women's disadvantage in romance and marriage and racial inequality in the distribution of love.[40] In this book I ask readers to question the ways in which thinking about social inequality by focusing on school credentialing and career development has desensitized sociology audiences to the problematic aspects of a social space characterized by this type of structural inequality in reproductive relations.

So what does an inequality study that allows Wanda to be both sexual actor and economic actor look like? Where does an investigation that acknowledges that a social hierarchy in orgasms and offspring exists alongside the one of credentials and careers begin? Does it look to "chick flicks" and romance novels or stratification studies and ethnographies of poor black neighborhoods and urban schools? My study began by asking women a more open-ended set of questions about their desires for their lives and about their concerns during the decision making that advanced, altered, or subverted these life goals. Their answers to these questions indicated the need for an analysis that restored and integrated those aspects of the self that inequality research often strips away or artificially compartmentalizes. Thus far, I have discussed the importance of "chick flicks" and romance novels or at least their attention to dates, sex, and the experiences of pregnancy and birth as desirable outcomes. I have shown that studying the achievement of these outcomes that are unequally distributed, that are not necessarily more available to those individuals that have greater economic resources, and that can vary in value depending on the way love and marriage resources allow them to be represented should be part of an agenda of scholarship concerned to understand how inequality comes about. Below, I explain how this book's answer to this question goes beyond the inclusion of love and sex onto a list of valued goods.

This book investigates how inequality comes about by integrating the romantic life goals and the relevant racial constraints on black women's achievement of them with Wanda's choices and constraints as an economic actor. Like a good "chick flick" not driven by Hollywood's propensity to make its sympathetic and heroic protagonist a young, white, professional, the text tries to restore Wanda's status as a black woman—one who negotiates multiple contexts (that is, both market and non-market) with each decision she makes, and one who works toward multiple goals (that is, both economic and non-economic). In this textbook, Wanda and others like her want the multi-layered good life of a good "chick flick," which includes satisfying the desire for some things that money can buy and some things that money cannot. The discussion in this book is about

more than adding love goals to money goals and about more than adding "what Wanda must do for love" to our current list of structural constraints on her economic activities. It is about her integrated personhood.
If the effect of inequality research has been to strip Wanda down to her
economic essence and to accede to other aspects of her identity and interests only insofar as they have pertained to the economic sector, this text
builds her back up, appreciates a broader spectrum of her desires, and
thereby more effectively describes the fullness of the cultural and structural space in which she operates. The following chapter creates ideal
types of degreed black women out of the data that subjects provided on
their decision making across their life trajectories. It is one of the ways I
have attempted to build analyses of individuals' multiple wants and the
multiple types of constraints faced in the achievement of these wants into
the book's description of social inequality.

Simultaneous Desires, Intersecting Structures, and Multiple Selves

Maya, Imani, and Renae each had a single child (a daughter) when I interviewed them. Maya, at the age of twenty-seven, found this state of affairs
surprising since she never imagined she would have any children at all.
At the age of thirty-two, Imani, who had anxiously awaited the moment
when she felt financially ready to have this one, had feelings of impatience and anticipation since she was planning to have four or five more.
And Renae, at the age of forty-two, was disappointed: after years of helping her economically disadvantaged relatives raise their own children, she
found it difficult to accept that her series of miscarriages was the signal
indicating that she herself would have no more. Notwithstanding their
varied feelings about the present and their differing expectations for their
futures, Maya, Imani, and Renae would each be represented by a simple
numeral one in the "children ever born" column of a demographer's data
table. Furthermore, as I show in chapter 2, using national survey data,
this numeral one does not appear remarkable to the typical inequality
scholar. Once we adopt one of the conventions of inequality scholarship
and divide the sample of women up by education level, Maya's surprise,
Imani's anticipation, and Renae's disappointment come off sounding
naïve, for according to the NSFG, college-educated women in the United

States tend to complete their fertility at an average figure between one and two children.

In conventional inequality study, Maya's, Imani's, and Renae's numeral one in the "children ever born" column may reflect the importance of education level in determining the quality and outcome of a myriad of life experiences. But it is perhaps more appropriate in the context of this work to think of it as the symbol for the women's current dissatisfaction with the state of their childbearing situations. This numeral one that is in one case too much, in another case too late, and in still another case not enough, essentially means that the women have not interacted with the proximate determinants in ways that would produce the reproductive outcomes that they desired. Although Maya used contraception consistently, she did not do so successfully and was unable to go through with a planned abortion. Imani, in contrast, had an early abortion and continued to use contraception well into her marriage despite plans for a large family. And Renae found few opportunities for romance and sexual activity early in the life course when they might have led to more successful pregnancies.

This book's claims with respect to how and why three elite women can't seem to do what they want to do when they want to do it where sex and childbearing are concerned offer a different perspective on the methods and meaning of class advantage to that of conventional inequality scholarship. Where conventional scholarship focuses on the ways the limitations and possibilities associated with Maya's, Imani's, and Renae's economic roles influence their sexual and reproductive behavior and make it highly likely that they will only have just one or two children each, this text considers women's romantic life trajectories and the relations, resources, capacities, and motivations that support or challenge their achievement of desired family formation goals. Where conventional inequality research takes much of human action and deals with the economic implications of that action, this argument places women's economic action in the context of their multifaceted lives—lives in which their embodied selves and their abilities to give birth to and nurture the bodies of others take on multiple meanings depending on the interpersonal relationships, the institutional contexts, and the personal goals at play. Where conventional inequality scholarship says that Maya, Imani, and Renae are likely to have arrived at their one-child family status by weighing the educational and financial costs and benefits of having more children at earlier points in their lives, this book asks what relationships, roles, motivations, and opportunities (economic or otherwise) made it possible for them to have sex, get pregnant, and follow through with a birth at precisely the moments that they did. The book's proposition—that the road that leads to these college-educated professionals' single-daughter families may not be paved entirely by the decisions the women made about their educational and professional lives—calls into question long held assumptions about a type of rational calculation, planning, and strategic decision making that is supposedly associated with middle-class family formation. In this sense, the text asks readers to put aside centuries-old academic thinking on class differences in family formation behavior as well as the pop-sociological answers to queries about why poor people have so many kids.

Much criticism of the poor is based on the notion that their poverty is somehow related to their lack of ability to limit or control fertility.[41] Some look at large, low-income families and see poor individuals who are unable to control their sexual urges. Others compare single-mother household incomes (on average, lower) to two-parent household incomes (on average, higher) and discuss a "culture of poverty" that discourages rational decision making, future-oriented thinking, delay of gratification, and hard work.[42] In either case, high fertility, nonmarital childbearing, unplanned pregnancy, and teen parenting have intermittently been folded into these critiques of persons with inferior educations, jobs, and incomes. Both before and since the advent of modern contraception in the West, those who bear children in poverty have been vilified for their lack of forethought (for example, What made you think you could afford to take care of all of these children?), for their disinterest in planning (How do you plan to take care of this baby?), and for their inability to see the likely and problematic outcomes associated with their sexual and reproductive activity (Are you clueless about the problems that your having this baby creates for everyone else?). Such criticism implies that those who are not poor and who have smaller families are involved in all the admirable types of decision making that the poor are not—that their family formation decisions conform to the plan they have made for their financial futures, that they delay sexual and romantic gratification for future economic well-being, and that they choose hard work over hanging out at home or "screwing around" with loved ones.

This book disagrees with this description of a family formation road that supposedly ends in financial security. Instead it studies Maya's surprise, Imani's impatience, and Renae's disappointment and asks whether these women's feelings result from their experience of the consequences associated with their well-thought-out plans. After study, the book concludes that although it is possible for financially secure parents to represent their decision to have the one child that they do as part of a rational economic strategy, most of the degreed black women sampled here do not discuss decisions about romance, sex, and the use of contraception and abortion (that is, all the things that lead to and/or control childbearing) as aspects of or related to their long-term educational and career plans.

This book changes thinking about individuals' control and manipulation of reproductive relations and outcomes in a number of ways. Its discussion of degreed black women's challenges finding romance and marriage suggests that marriage and marital childbearing are not necessarily available for the planning. (See chapter 3.) The book's description of subjects' restricted access to contraceptive information and products and to moral justification for the use of contraception serves as evidence for the point that single women may be more manipulated in their sexual and contraceptive decision making than they are manipulating their fertility. (See chapter 5.) Even the narratives on their attempts to plan sexual activity with the use of contraception seem to make them morally suspect rather than free to choose, sexually speaking. (See chapter 4.) Finally, the text offers analyses of women's decisions to terminate unplanned pregnancies that demonstrate that such decisions are more often related to women's interest in maintaining status identities and avoiding stigmatized ones than they are to maintaining plans and delaying gratification. (See chapter 6.) In short, this book argues that scholarly work on and policy type analyses of class differences in family formation may exaggerate the level of rational economic planning that goes into sexual and romantic decision making and may misrepresent the motivations that middle-class women have for making the sexual and reproductive choices that they do. By allowing elite women to be sexual (as well as economic) actors, this study finds that their decisions to limit, delay, or postpone romantic relationships, marriage, and childbearing may often be coincidental with rather than strategically related to their educational and economic goals and activities.

Gender, Class, Race, and Imani's Large Family Formation Desires

In focusing its analyses on the romantic and family formation experiences of well-educated elites, this book takes a lesson from inequality scholars who have paid close attention to women's childbearing and child-rearing activities. These are the scholars who endeavor to describe how gender inequality comes about. What they tell us is that the type of control and compartmentalization of human sexual and reproductive capacities that is supposed to accompany economic mobility and/or middle-class professional development has always been more circumscribed for women than for men. Indeed such scholars have made the case that male control over reproductive and sexual processes and over emotional and physical care-giving responsibilities is only accomplished at the expense (or exploitation) of mostly female others who are left to manage and deal with the messiness and lack of predictability of this women's work.[43] Women's lower status across social institutions is in part due to their consignment to this lower status, unpaid, reproductive labor.[44] Furthermore social institutions are organized around dichotomous, hierarchical categories of male and female;[45] they are thereby set up in ways that both depend upon and devalue this lower-status "women's work" even when that work is being performed by poor men and men of color.[46] With these propositions, gender scholars make the point that male workers, the jobs that they do, and the life approaches that control, manipulate, and make feminized reproductive labor invisible are all privileged in the interactions in the formal labor market in which class inequality is generated and maintained.

The typical gender analysis of Imani's single-daughter family consequently considers her career success, particularly her recent promotion as the first female manager of her division in a finance company. And it likely links this formal labor market success to Imani's "male" control over and compartmentalization of feminized reproductive labors.[47] Evidence of such control could be found in Imani's decisions to abandon a college relationship with a non-college man who did not share her intellectual interests and to hire an in-home nanny to care for her daughter. Such evidence could also be culled from data on her interaction with the proximate determinants, including an abortion during high school and her use of birth control pills throughout a year-long unpaid internship and five years of career building. In the end, in this tradition of gender scholarship, Imani's career success gets connected to her ability to avoid or postpone involvement in the reproductive labor that typically compromises women's careers. It gets brought to bear on claims about a gendered labor market and Imani's adaptation to it as well as on arguments about the way in which she "does gender" by separating her public "male" work roles from and prioritizing her male work activities over and before her "female" family formation and care tasks.

These conclusions about Imani's family formation decision making—that are part of scholarly descriptions of women's low institutional status and that constitute examples in intellectual explanations of the impact of gendered labor markets and families on women's lives—hinge on the gender inequality analyst's propensity to frame romance, marriage, sex, and childbearing as burdensome, unpaid, reproductive labor. This framing is foundational to scholarly understanding of how gender ascriptive processes create unequal lives. But it nevertheless fails to acknowledge women's family formation desires. In addition, it deals rather clumsily with situations where women's improved economic outcomes are based in their family formation rather than their education or work activities.[48] It is precisely with regard to this framing of reproductive behaviors that the arguments in this book distinguish themselves from the type of gender analysis of Imani's decision making discussed above.

In the first place, this text's appreciation of the full spectrum of degreed black women's desires means that the analyses deal with the very real fact that Imani wants a large family. While adoption and moving in with extended kin might similarly fulfill that goal, Imani's preference is to take a journey through romance, marriage, sex, and childbearing to achieve this end. Participation in romantic relationships and her marriage, sexual, and childbearing behavior in the context of one such relationship do more than detract from her career as much gender inequality scholarship suggests; they also allow her to experience something she wants—that is, a family of her own creation.

In the second place, this text also deals with the rather complicated and controversial point that an individual's class status is not entirely achieved through his or her performance of activities in the productive sector: individuals also acquire class status through established familial connections. Many children who have never worked a day in their lives get to attend expensive colleges and universities precisely because they have access to the resources associated with the incomes and work lives of their parents. Similarly a musician and part-time substitute teacher with a volatile income tells the bank's loan officer that his wife is a pediatrician because he and the banker recognize that he can temporarily and even permanently depend upon his partner's more stable earnings and associate himself with the trappings of his spouse's occupational status. Here, Imani's romantic and reproductive activity create her class and the class status of those who are voluntarily (spousal partner) and involuntarily (children) connected to her. In addition to their function as distracting unpaid labor, then, family formation activities like romance, marriage, sex, and childbearing are desired ends for the utility that they generate in and of themselves[49] and for the fact that they build social relationships that are determinative of class status.[50]

When this book considers Imani's desire for a large family and when it asks whether her dependent child or spousal relationship can support or have a positive impact on her class achievement, romance, marriage, sex, and childbearing become important "goods." Furthermore, the book's description of degreed black women's greater vulnerability to short- and long-term periods of celibacy than that of less-educated black women and of white and Hispanic women (see chapter 4) provides relevant details about a type of social context in which Imani cannot take these particular family-related "goods" for granted. The book's qualitative analyses of the sum total of sampled degreed black women's romantic relationships find that their access to romance, marriage, sex, and childbearing is challenged. It is challenged by a normative culture in which men have a greater ability to determine who is eligible for heterosexual monogamous partnership than women. And it is challenged by a normative culture in which women's attractiveness is often determined by personal characteristics over which they have little control like their age, their race, or the educational and professional achievements of a potential partner (see chapter 3). Where marital commitment and marital childbearing can thusly be described as precarious goals, abortion, breakup, and long-term use of birth control pills take on new meanings as well. Formerly known as the tasks that disassociate women from traditional connections to reproductive labor and support successful negotiation of gender barriers to class achievement, they are here, in the context of black women's disadvantage in negotiating for romantic commitments and monogamous love, also read as roadblocks to the achievement of family formation goals.

Explaining Imani's dissatisfaction with her single-daughter family requires consideration of the ways her gender status intersects with her class aspirations. Hence, I have endeavored to look at the ways the gendered and gendering separation of work and family activities directs the career-minded woman to pursue education before and over love and a large family. But the explanation also requires attention to the ways Imani's racial status exacerbates the negative family formation consequences associated with her gendered achievement of middle-class status. To the extent that race prevents Imani from taking the opportunity to love, marry, and have multiple children with her husband for granted, abortions, breakups, and birth control pills become more than the aspiring professional's manipulation of her romantic and reproductive desires around her more highly valued career ends. Abortions, breakups, and birth control pills are also culprits contributing to Imani's unfulfilled love life. Thus, the analyses in this book locate Imani's single-daughter family in the gendered structure of the formal labor market where her middle-class aspirations are realized and in the limited availability of marital motherhood to women of her racial status.[51] And it is in places such as these, where racial difference in romance meets gender and class difference in the labor market, that the text locates itself in the intersectionality tradition of inequality scholarship.[52]

This book asks readers to appreciate the simultaneity of Imani's experiences and negotiations in the achievement of each of her life "careers"— that of finance manager as well as that of wife and mother. It asks readers to consider whether it is truly possible for her to make decisions about one without simultaneously even if unwittingly making decisions about the other. It then asks that readers look at Imani's own statement about her decision to take birth control pills for one additional year so that she and her husband would have time to put money in a trust that would go to their first child once that child was born. In this text, such a statement becomes data that is used to answer a question about whether she and the other subjects can experience class privilege, romantic misfortune, and childlessness distinctly and separately. The text answers the question in the negative, maintaining that Imani herself has collapsed her desires in love and her desires in money into the same goal. Moreover, this negative answer goes along with the book's broader argument—that inequality is observable in configurations of outcomes as opposed to single outcomes and that it cannot be constituted solely in terms of individuals' experiences in family (love) or work (money).

Gender scholars tell the field of inequality academics that workplaces and families are both institutions that depend upon and devalue "women's work"; as such they demonstrate the ways women's association with reproductive labor compromises their activities and achievements in the productive sphere.[53] This book tells inequality scholarship that love matters, that it is apparently in limited supply and distributed unequally, and that Imani's gendered negotiation of the class hierarchy happens simultaneously with a series of gendered negotiations for love and family. If gender scholarship educates women who are aspiring professionals that they must often choose between career and family formation, this book educates degreed black women that the choice for love may appear less frequently than they expect. The reproductive labor that appears and stars in the stories that gender scholars tell is in abundance: women are perpetually free to choose it; the difficulty is finding a way out of it and of managing relations with colleagues, family, and community members that would compel them to take responsibility for it even when it is not their choice. This text tells the stories about romance, marriage, sex, and childbearing that are scarce. It describes the terms under which love and family are awarded to some and denied to others, and it shows how the *negotiation of gender barriers to middle-class achievement and racial barriers to the roles of wife and mother come together to shape degreed black women's simultaneous experience of deprivation and privilege.*

Race, Gender, Class, and the Stories Maya Tells about Not Wanting Children

As was the case with all of my informants, Maya engaged in a kind of conversational multi-tasking during our interview. In addition to answering my questions with her relevant and descriptive narratives, she would sporadically add and intersperse the plot lines, thematic points, and characters from other stories. Thus, in answer to my questions about the events and actions leading up to the birth of her single daughter, Maya told a tale that began with a blind date and a new but lackluster relationship with a man to whom she was less attracted than her prior boy-friend. The tale continued on to include chapters covering Maya's lack of interest in ever having a child and her faithful and consistent pattern of contraceptive use. And then this tale that provided a relevant answer to my question culminated in high drama in the abortion clinic, where Maya changed her mind and decided to become a mother after all. But it was through the footnotes, digressions, and back stories of this interview-relevant tale that Maya was able to spin another yarn—a story that she has apparently been living and spinning for the bulk of her life.

Maya's secondary tale was clearly the longer-term and more life-encompassing of the two. It included a villain—an abusive father—who observed Maya years before she ever had a boyfriend or sex and pro-claimed that she was the one of his two daughters who would most cer-tainly become a "slut." And it included a supporting actress—a younger sister—whom her father labeled the "good girl" and whose life is offered up as material for comparison with Maya's own life. The interweaving of this secondary story with the story that answered my question enabled Maya to communicate her small amount of pride in the fact that her younger sister was the one who ended up leading the more morally sus-pect life. She was able to point out that her sister has not made it to college while Maya, by the time she was talking to me, had already completed her bachelor's degree. The secondary yarn also showed the listener that the sister got pregnant for the first time during high school and became the single mother of two children well before the point at which Maya first formed her single-daughter family.

The all-encompassing "secondary" tale that Maya tells allows the com-parison between her sister's life trajectory and her own life trajectory to function in much the same manner as the repeated claims about having used a condom every single time she had sex with her daughter's father and the declaration that she "took it as a sign from God that [she] got pregnant." All three verbalizations support Maya's effort to represent herself, her nonmarital sexual activity and pregnancy, and her status as a single parent as "moral," "just," and "deserving." They make the claim that her behavior is more moral than that that of her sister and than that of the imaginary that produced her father's predictions and pronouncements so many years before. This book's analyses suggest that this tale telling that Maya does as well as her actions around the proximate determinants are related to her worry over the "slut" representation. It is this worry that informs her rejection-turned-acceptance of motherhood—her consistent contraception followed by the hemming and hawing over abortion today or baby tomorrow.

Maya worries about the "slut" representation: she worries, she represents, and she acts so that she might represent. "The slut" organized the patriarchal distribution of privilege (freedom to make decisions about the way to spend free time, the benefit of the doubt where compromising situations make one's behavior appear problematic) and pain (beatings designed to contain, control, or punish suspected and actual behavior) in Maya's family while she was growing up. Therefore, Maya's own accomplishments and the ways in which they can be represented become her challenge to and negotiation of the barriers to all those freedoms that her sister and brother were able to take for granted. Thus, representation limits her actions in three ways. First, the "slut" representation limits by justifying her father's discriminatory exercise of his power to restrict her comings and goings. Representation also limits by shaping Maya's more or less voluntary behavior around the representations that she anticipates that her father and others in power might use to limit her action. And third, representation limits by inspiring Maya's presentation of alternative representations—assertions made that might ultimately have to be backed up with corresponding action. Here, the example is Maya's organization of her life around the image of a woman who rejects motherhood. The test of whether these assertions were about more than representation comes when Maya has the opportunity to reject motherhood and fails by departing the abortion clinic prior to the procedure.

Concern with representation and the conversational multi-tasking it inspired was common across the sample of degreed black women and across discussions of their interactions with the proximate determinants. This book argues that racial status heightens concern over being represented as sexually immoral and excessively fertile among degreed black women. This heightened concern is related to the extended duration of time that black women are likely to spend single in a social context where marriage and at the very least committed partnership increase the morality and legitimacy associated with intercourse and childbearing and change the meanings and evaluations attached to these behaviors. These women's need to create alternate representations—to be different from the ways others would represent them—is also related to the fact that black women confront a symbolic structure in which the stories that are told about them connect their "notorious" sexual immorality and "excessive" fertility to their inferior outcomes in other areas of life (for example poverty, poor sexual and reproductive health). Consequently, the data finds these women enmeshed in a kind of double talk—speech meant to defend and distance themselves from imagery associated with a racist symbolic structure. Such imagery usually brings together action and identity in ways that normalize and justify black women's exclusion and deprivation in love and money. And, as Maya's relationship with her father has shown us, such representation can and does limit.

This text's race analyses borrow from and are in dialogue with several sectors of racial inequality scholarship. These would include, first and foremost, work in the intersectionality tradition, for theory and study in this area point to the connection between the representation of Maya as sexually wanton and the treatment of her sons (or actually, her daughter) as cheap labor. Intersectionality scholarship has typically made much of representation (that is, depictions, interpretations, and narratives of reality). Such scholars have maintained that race-gender inequality depends upon the language and imagery that communicate race and gender meanings—that representation and the symbolic realm work alongside an unequal distribution of resources, power, and privileges along race-gender lines to facilitate the micro-level interactions and the macro-structural organization that shape unequal lives.[54]

Typically, intersectionality scholars have dissected and discussed images and symbolic constructs like the "welfare queen," "free labor," and "Uncle Tom," and described how these images help to create and sustain categories of persons with and without particular entitlements with respect to work, family, and citizenship. The image of the "welfare queen," for example, creates a category of women of color (usually black women) who have neither the rights to nor the resources for full-time motherhood. It also creates a category of presumably white worker-taxpayers: they pay more than their fair share of taxes because the aforementioned women reject low-status work and instead use excessive sexuality and childbearing to cheat the state out of funds for luxury goods. Just as the "slut" implies that Maya must have her independent excursions from her parents' home limited, curtailed, and punished and that her sister and brother are self-disciplined enough (or observant enough of their sister's interactions with their father) to limit themselves, the "welfare queen" articulates the need for a punitive and time- and funds-delimited welfare system—one that compels immoral and out of control women of color to work for the below minimum wage public assistance that they receive and punishes them for making the decision to become mothers.[55]

What this book shares with intersectionality scholarship are arguments about the importance of a "meaning-driven" discriminatory action to the creation and maintenance of racially unequal lives and race, sex, and class inequality. In both, there is the point that societies move and individuals act based on "mere" meaning and "insignificant" representation. After all, the imaginary that motivated Maya's father's repressive exercise of patriarchal privilege and economic control in such a way as to limit the movements and decision-making power of the darkest and shortest of his African American daughters is about the meaning and/or the signifiers of the "slut" label and not the demonstration of "slut"-like behavior. So too are Maya's assertions regarding her resistance to childbearing, her consistent contraception, and her intent to get an abortion about representation.

This book argues that degreed black women's movements and actions around the proximate determinants are often based on their fears about what intercourse (for example, "We are in a relationship"), contraception ("I am not sexually naïve"), or childbearing ("I am an irresponsible sexual actor") may correctly or incorrectly signify to others, rather than on the desirability of the fertility outcomes that are normatively associated with these movements and actions. In other words, these women make sexual and reproductive choices that simultaneously consider the literal outcomes to their actions (for example, kids, sexual satisfaction), as well as the significations that these actions and literal outcomes might make to others. They may not want pregnancy but fail to use contraception because they believe that planning and preparing for intercourse make them appear immoral or sexually promiscuous. (See chapter 5.) Or they may be interested in having a child but abort an unplanned pregnancy because they fear that nonmarital pregnancy and parenting will compromise the "middle-class" or "chaste Christian" identity that they are striving to build. (See chapter 6.) The low availability of marriage to those black women concerned with representing themselves as chaste, or merely responsible, makes this apparently "illogical" or "inconsistent" action around the remaining proximate determinants that much more likely among African Americans.

This book's race analyses also share characteristics with race scholarship on the existence and prevalence of racially discriminatory acts and on the effects of racial discrimination on life outcomes. Whereas intersectionality scholarship relies on historical data and examples of extraordinary events and individuals, students of micro-level racial discrimination focus on the things that happen to ordinary women like Maya because of their status as black females.[56] These studies tell us why Maya and her degreed and non-degreed African American sisters and brothers are so concerned about representations of blackness—why they take steps to avoid any suggestion of problematic race-gender representations in consequential social interactions. It is this work that indicates that black individuals are more likely to be stopped by police officers, turned away by landlords when they are in search of housing, sold improper or substandard consumer products, offered inadequate health services, and rejected by employers than are whites with equivalent credentials and characteristics. It is this type of race analysis that tells us how persons in positions of authority are concerned that the black individuals that they encounter are thieves, associated with criminals, lazy, or otherwise immoral; they tell us that the narratives about and representations of black people loom large in the decision-making process when powerful social actors are in a position to extend or withhold opportunities.[57] The research associated with this book develops this micro-level discrimination scholarship that explores and documents the ways the ordinary Maya is treated based on her race. It does so by making an argument about how Maya behaves because of this discriminatory environment.

This book does not prove that limiting race and gender imagery and language corresponding to prevailing race and gender resource inequities exists in the way that intersectionality scholarship typically does. Nor does this book prove that relatively powerful social actors' discrimination produces statistically significant differences between racial groups' outcomes in the ways that stratification scholars testing for hypothesized discrimination or inequality scholars describing individuals' perceptions of discrimination do. However, this text does argue that scholars aren't the only people who know about limiting race and gender representations and the existence of discrimination; it does argue that degreed black women are also aware and that they are not necessarily sitting idly by during consequential social interactions while they are being represented and dismissed. Rather, they are attempting to frame and represent their own behaviors in ways that challenge the association of problematic activities with black female identity; they are trying to behave in ways that place their own bodies outside of the categories associated with this symbolism.

Maya's storytelling shows anybody willing to pay attention that her nonmarital childbearing should not be interpreted as the irresponsible and excessive fertility of the animalistic and hypersexual black woman—a stylized stereotypical female whose lower-class status is usually framed as either cause or consequence of her superfluous fertility. By comparing her consistent contraceptive use to her sister's earlier and more prolific childbearing, Maya puts distance between herself and the imaginary that produces the "slut" representation. Likewise, discussions of her educational achievements and her initial resistance to childbearing allow Maya to make a claim on both professional work and motherhood. This semantic move defies and denies both the "welfare queen" representation and the "mammy"—a historical image of a black woman possessing neither sexual desire nor attractiveness, whose passive submission to the racial order involves the self-sacrificial decision to mother and care for other women and their children and families, as if she has none of her own. According to the arguments in this book, talk and action are undertaken as a kind of peremptory strike against discriminatory treatment. Since the degreed black women sampled in this study anticipate having to represent what they do to the people they encounter on their life journeys, they must also choose to do the things that will be consistent with the representations that they are trying to make and the identities that they are trying to build. Faced with racial challenges to marriage that make it difficult to build chaste sexual identities or middle-class, two-parent, nuclear families, single degreed black women make decisions about sexual activity, contraception, and abortion or at least talk about their sexual, contraceptive, and abortion decision making in ways that are meant to distinguish themselves from the imagery that links nonmarital sexual activity and childbearing with black women's demise in economic and familial arenas. Talk and behavior, as well as talk about behavior, are designed to prevent the discrimination these women expect to receive as they pursue, achieve, and fail to acquire money and love.

Recent work on racial discrimination in the post–civil rights era indicates that white individuals are likely to claim that their behavior and actions are not racially motivated or, in other words, that they are "colorblind."[58] Discrimination occurs with the use of subtle and apparently "colorblind" action. It might take the form of local movements to eliminate busing that are supposedly motivated by support for localized community schools rather than rejection of race and class integration in educational institutions.[59] It might look like the preference for institutional legacies in higher educational institutions despite the restriction against and low representation of racial minorities in such institutions in past generations. And it might even appear in the excessive help offered by store salespersons to black individuals whom they fear will shoplift. In any event, the fact that even the most racist of whites are unlikely to admit open racial bias means that opportunities to openly challenge racism remain few and far between. Maya's storytelling keeps explicit mention of racism at the periphery while allowing her rejection of the applicability of limiting race and gender imagery to her life situation to remain a central component of the narrative. This book's race analyses indicate that degreed black women's proximate determinant decision making supports their maneuvering within the discriminatory environment by walking that same fine line. Discussions in chapters 3 through 6 indicate that *signification and representation in this discriminatory environment motivate proximate determinant decision making* such that the decisions made may conflict with women's childbearing goals. In extreme cases like Maya's, they may even obscure, suppress, or create a convenient but insincere sense of one's own childbearing interests. The decisions may allow single-daughter families to emerge even when they are (or only appear to be) too much, too little, or too late.

The Inadequacy of Class Explanations
for Renae's Single-daughter Family

So can a story about an unequal distribution of love really exist as a part of the body of scientific scholarship on social inequality, or do we only see that select group of "impersonable" and "unattractive" women getting left out of love in the movies? Can it truly be the case that equivalent fertility signals intersecting race, class, and gender inequities and the barriers to black women's achievement of desired ends in money and love, or must there be some normative middle-class logic to childbearing and profes-sional achievement that defies racial constraints and looks like what we see on the modern sit-com where a new multicultural generation of star-lets all struggle to manage careers, families, and their Hollywood figures? This book's main arguments ask readers to contemplate an inequality that is complex—one that is not so straightforward or simple in its origins or sources as to be constituted by the distribution of a single form of cur-rency or explainable with a single stratifying process. In the face of gender scholarship that suggests that women's familial and reproductive labor generates inequality insofar as it limits women's class achievements in the formal labor market, it suggests that the lack of opportunity to love and to participate in marriage and marital childbearing is in and of itself inequality producing. In contrast to the race scholarship that has studied middle-class black individuals in order to determine whether education or class background and achievement have supplanted race as the more influential determinant of individuals' life outcomes, this book points to the importance of racial stratification in marital opportunity to the deter-mination of an apparent class equality in fertility outcomes; it argues that specific race and gender imagery informs and organizes the proximate determinant decision making that leads to class equivalency in fertility levels.

When I spoke with Renae about the end of her childbearing attempts, it was obvious that she felt betrayed by the delays and compromises she had made in her family formation trajectory. According to her thinking, the way that she had done things, the decisions that she had made about edu-cation, career, and family were the morally correct things to do. And yet she had not ended up with the family she desired. The fact that her cousins had not done "what they were supposed to do" and had nevertheless had more children made her relegation to the single-daughter family that much more nonsensical and frustrating. At the age of forty-two, Renae remained dumbfounded. Unwilling to regret the "right" choices she had made in waiting for education, career, and marriage to have children, and in providing emotional and financial support to her cousins when they had kids without financial means and with limited partner support, she longed for answers, meaning, some clue that would make the compari-sons between her "wayward" cousins' outcomes and her own make sense.

I write this book as much for Renae as I do for inequality scholars.

Her confusion, frustration, feelings of betrayal, and sentiment that others have what she has not and that this situation is unfair display the heart and drama of inequality scholarship to such an extent that it could sell to stage and screen. Moreover, Renae, with her college degree and penchant for analysis, does what inequality scholars do. She simplifies. She looks at one dependent variable at a time. And she uses her life outcomes to test a hypothesis. The problem is that the hypothesis, although verifiable around isolated data points in her life trajectory, seems inadequate to explaining her current dissatisfaction with the family status that she has achieved. This book argues that explaining this dissatisfaction is far from simple—that the creation of unequal lives is complex.

Renae is confused about the way things have turned out because while class achievement may explain why she owns a home while her cousins rent, it does not, by itself, account for or create their differential experiences with love and family formation. Renae is slowly accepting the fact that her behaviors around the proximate determinants—behaviors that apparently represent "right" choices—have landed her in a place that feels wrong. By listening to her very own feelings, she is learning what I have learned and what I am trying to disclose in this text. And that is that the degreed black women discussed here are more than and want more than their class achievements. Moreover, the things that these women want for their lives cannot be accomplished without attention to goals and constraints in love and without dealing with discriminatory representations and the barriers to both love and money that those representations create. It is therefore only fitting that the research presentation in this text should begin with a discussion of the motivations and limitations that structure subjects' degree-seeking behaviors. By adding complexity to what has been seen by Renae and career inequality scholars as straightforward, class-based decision making, chapter 1 provides a context for the book's argument about the role of choice and constraint in the achievement of unequal outcomes in money and love.

ONE

School

Makin' It

WHEN I INTERVIEWED Jacqueline (age thirty) about her degree attainment and family formation processes, she had some friends staying with her in the house where she, her husband, and her young son lived. The friends were also a young, black, married couple that had recently started a family (only in this case, the mother had had a girl). The foursome had been brought together by the two husbands, who pledged the same chapter of one of the historically black fraternities while they were in college; my subject subsequently became fast friends with the wife of her husband's fraternity brother. But Jacqueline did not feel particularly close to the fraternity brother and had not shared many of the details of her childhood with him. And so it was only after about an hour into the interview, when this man and her husband left the room next to the one in which we were seated in order to take the children to the park, that she abruptly interrupted our conversation to return to an earlier question. She now had a more forthright and detailed response to my query about when she first became aware of the fact that she was going to go to college. It went like this:

My father was definitely an alcoholic. And it was really tough. I mean—
And the home life could get really hectic. He drank a lot, and my
mom—. . . It's true that my parents did spend a lot of time dealing with
my sister, um, and helping her get through school. But my mother had
to deal with her and whatever issues my father brought up. So one of
the questions that you asked earlier about how did I know that I was
gonna go to college? When I was in sixth grade I had made up my mind
I was getting out of that house, one way or another. I think due to my
sixth grade teacher, I think because of the AP classes where everybody was tellin' me, you know, get ready for your SATs and so on and
so forth, I made a conscious choice that how I was gonna get out was
through college. And I'm really thankful for that because kids decide
to get out in a lot of different ways: you know kids say, "I'm gonna get
pregnant; I'm gonna do drugs," you know, whatever. But that was very
important to me: I knew I had to get out. So, I mean, that's . . . That is
a bad way, I think . . . for a kid to have to go through that, but it got me
to college.

Since Jacqueline's interview happened when I was approximately two-
thirds of the way into my sample, I was not surprised that she had this
sordid story underneath the more conventional one about advanced or
honors classes and parents who kept a strict eye on their children's educational processes. By this point I had run into others whose upbringings
had included fairy-tale-like horrors and who had quite deftly linked them
to their college-matriculation-based escape from these all too problematic home lives. I had already run into Jamie, a victim of sexual abuse, and
talked with Claire about how her father's series of extramarital affairs led
to her mother's ongoing resentment and pattern of ignoring Claire and
her younger siblings. These women were plentiful enough to constitute a
category of experience—or what I saw as an unconventional category of
experience—that motivated and led to degree attainment. What remained
for me at that point was to determine why such a thing should matter to
inequality study. Why should a route to degree attainment spurred on by
familial neglect or abuse change what I, or any other inequality scholar for
that matter, believed about processes of class differentiation and middle-
class family formation behavior?

The discovery that the experiences and values that lead to degree at-

tainment in a sample of fifty-eight college-educated women are varied
is thus an argument about the multiple ways educated elites can be in
the world—about the myriad reasons they have for seeking the degree
and the varied outcomes that they hope to attain. This discovery indicates
that there are multiple selves that seek the degree and multiple behavioral performances associated with this middle-class professional status.
Jacqueline experienced discomfort in her family of upbringing and came
to value the attainment of a degree as a promise of escape. But others
had different experiences and different values (for example, family loy-
alty, commitment to education, fear of ridicule or being ostracized) and
attained their degrees and achieved middle-class status for quite different reasons. My story about who these educational haves are is thus also
a claim about how unequal lives are constituted—about the multiple
means by which middle-class outcomes are generated. In the description of multiple selves below, I argue that Jacqueline's need to return to a
question about college and to answer it by disclosing her painful upbringing shows the connection between some sampled women's experiences
in their familial contexts and the motivations and values that surrounded
their degree-attainment behavior. This conceptualization of status attainment articulates with aspects of Pierre Bourdieu's theory of class formation and class relations (Bourdieu 1977a, 1977b, 1984; Bourdieu and Passeron 1977/1990).[1]

Below I report that Jacqueline is one of nine subjects with horrific
family lives during childhood; I say that these nine women's interest in
degree attainment is linked to these family experiences; and I label the
nine subjects whose degree attainment process can be described in this
way as "conforming escape artists." In other words, below I engage in an
analytical technique known as typology creation. This chapter presents
a list and descriptions of the "types" of degreed black women I encountered during the interview portion of my study. It says that there are multiple—or at least seven—logics of degree attainment in this sample and
evidences this by illuminating the different sets of motivations and constraints that surrounded these women's educational achievements. It also
suggests that one of the more famous typologies (Merton 1957)—one that
classifies individuals' values and the means taken to attain those things
that they value—can and should be developed beyond the focus on economic motivations and productive sector behaviors.

Merton (1957) was concerned with describing the range of individual responses to life in an economic system where high social rewards are promised but limitations exist on the number of people who are able to achieve these rewards. In his understanding, an unequal social system with existing but limited opportunities for upward mobility creates both conformists (individuals with conventional social values who take the socially acceptable routes to attaining those things that they value) and innovators (individuals with conventional social values who use socially unacceptable means like criminal activity to attain those ends). In such a system, according to Merton, we can also observe the ritualists who go through conventional motions even though they have lost sight of the values to which these conventional modes of behavior are attached (like the always-on-time, punch-the-clock worker who can barely afford new clothes and never takes a sick day or vacation) and the retreatists who have withdrawn from society and rejected both conventional social values and means (like religious cult leaders and their followers). Merton's rebels reject society's dominant values and means to attaining those ends, but rather than retreat they remain with the goal of restructuring the society. My introduction of the "conforming escape artist," as well as the six other types of degreed black women whom I uncovered, both adds to and alters the picture that Merton (1957) creates. It adds the dimension of experience; it elaborates upon and perhaps diversifies the list of valued ends to which highly rewarded individuals aspire; and it complicates individuals' lives by allowing them to emerge from and pursue lives beyond the labor market.

My scientific "discovery" of the conforming escape artist began during the interview stage of my research, when the strange tale of one woman's degree attainment despite her abusive family background became several women's sensible sounding stories of a slow, steady, and sure route out of a bad situation. It continued with an analysis of transcribed interview data that collected and categorized all the decisions respondents made that established the four-year college degree as a goal, maintained that goal, or advanced them toward that goal. Looking at the similarities in women's experiences and motivations around decision-making junctures produced a description of seven types—or seven combinations of "experiences" and "valued ends"—that led this sample of degreed black women to college matriculation. The "types" discovered thusly represent types of conditions and motivations from which women's decisions emerge. Consequently, women's life trajectories often reflect several of the seven "types" of decisions, and some of the women carry more than one label.[2]

It remains questionable whether these combinations of experiences and valued ends are generalizable beyond the sample of women whom I interviewed—whether a broader group of degreed black women or a racially diverse sample of college-educated men and women would demonstrate the same experiences and values around their decision making with the same frequencies I observed. After all, my sample was a sample of convenience—men and women whom I knew referred me to women whom they knew fit the study criteria (black, college educated, under the age of fifty), and these women referred me to women whom they knew, and so on. Furthermore, I collected this "snowball sample" of interviewees from just two urban areas—both in the northeastern United States. These cities are different enough from one another: one of them ranks among the largest in the United States (that is, it had over one million residents in 2000) and has a relatively high proportion of African Americans (that is, over 40 percent in 2000) while the other is considerably smaller (that is, under 200,000 people) with roughly half the percentage of black residents. But they both share heavy industrial pasts and experienced late twentieth-century declines in manufacturing that severely affected the working-class black residents of these and other northeastern and midwestern cities. Degreed black women and other college-educated individuals who currently reside in the newer service-economy-oriented cities of the south and west or in rural areas may prove to be more or less motivated by the economic factors highlighted by Merton in their college decision making than the women discussed here. They may experience greater or fewer of the types of experiences that are associated with Jacqueline's conforming escape artist behavior. Nonetheless, the importance of discussing the ways these women's experiences, values, and degreed outcomes are connected lies in the degree to which this discussion complicates our sense of who Jacqueline is and, by extension, our understanding of what sort of stuff middle-class status attainment and middle-class women's family achievements are made of.

Decisions about Love

Individuals either have or don't have a conventional love of money and the things that money can buy. Their social locations either do or do not afford them the opportunity to be trained and hired for highly rewarding jobs. Or at least so says Merton's typology of economic values and means. In such a typology (see table 1), one cannot help but call Jacqueline a conformist: her career outcome of pharmacist and her educational outcome of college and pharmacology degrees indicate that she is one of those types of people who values money (for example, she makes a relatively high salary) and who has been afforded the opportunity to achieve the things that money can buy through socially acceptable means (for example, she was admitted to college and professional school, passed a licensing examination, and was hired by a firm). But in this book's typology, which includes experiences and results from an analysis of qualitative data on how degreed individuals did what they did and understood their actions, Jacqueline is framed a bit differently.

Focusing only on the apparent conformists (that is, Merton's conformists) enables us to look at whether these college-educated women's degree-attainment decisions truly emerged from their desire for the things that money can buy and their recognition and use of opportunities to acquire these high social rewards legally. Such a focus and a look at her words that open the chapter tell us that Jacqueline does not so much value high social rewards as she wants to "[get] out of that house." And as we will see below, she does not so much choose socially acceptable education as a means to achieving valued ends as she is forced into higher education by the particular boundaries and features of her childhood in "that house." Achievement that in Merton's framework seems to be based in normative economic motivation, the "pull" of high social rewards, and the more or less exclusive structural opportunity to achieve these rewards through normative engagement with the formal labor market is here shown to be linked to reproductive relations more so than productive ones. In other words, Jacqueline's claims about her desires and the conditions under which she makes degree-supporting decisions indicate that such decisions can be about love (albeit a non-romantic and more familial dimension of love) as well as money.

Table 1. Merton's life outcome types emerging from an economic system with limited opportunity

TYPES	VALUES	MEANS OF VALUE ATTAINMENT
Conformist	Conventional values (e.g., money and the things that money can buy)	Conventional means (e.g., specialized training and high-wage job)
Innovator	Conventional values (e.g., money and the things that money can buy)	Unconventional means (e.g., crime, hustling)
Ritualist	Lost sight of values	Conventional means (e.g., ordinary education and ordinary job)
Retreatist	Unconventional values (e.g., inner peace, community solidarity, harmony with natural environment, but not money)	Unconventional means (e.g., commune residence with system of barter)
Rebel	Unconventional values (e.g., social equality, alternative community and system of governance)	Unconventional means (e.g., low-wage activist job)

Source: This table was created using Merton's (1957) description of "types" of individuals that emerge in an economic system with limited opportunity.

When Love Hurts

My conforming escape artists are so typed by an experience dimension—for example, the inhospitable circumstances in the homes of their upbringing—and a value dimension—for example, a motivation to achieve and maintain households and/or families that are independent from those of their parents. (See table 2) As Jacqueline's words above maintain, these women's degree-attainment decisions are most clearly linked to the painful experiences that permeate their familial relations. Their discussions of college aspirations and applications and of homework and work toward careers are explicitly and specifically tied to this pain.

Table 2. Decision types leading to college degree attainment among African American women

TYPES	PERCENT (# OF TIMES LABEL USED)	EXPERIENCES	MOTIVATIONS/ VALUES	MEANS OF VALUE ATTAINMENT
Conforming escape artist	10.3 (9)	Push factor Abusive or dysfunctional family of origin	Economic self-sufficiency and lifestyle removed from abuse and family dysfunction	College degree
Prominent person pleaser	26.4 (23)	Push factor Nurturing family of origin with status attainment goals	Satisfying relationship w/ prominent person or persons	College degree
Recruit	10.3 (9)	Pull factor Involvement in social engineering programs	Varying rewards associated with status seeking, profiling, and insurgent behaviors	College degree
Stigma avoider	8.0 (7)	Push factor Isolation due to stigmatized characteristic and/or upbringing in stigmatized population	Invisibility in the confines of mediocrity; physical and psychological distance from negative status	College degree

Status seeker	29.9 (26)	<u>Pull factor</u> Media and popular cultural images; conventional social mobility ideology like meritocracy	Educated professional status group membership and associated rewards	College degree
Profiler	9.2 (8)	<u>Pull factor</u> Media and popular cultural images	Rewards and reputations associated with professional and popular faddish group membership	College degree
Insurgent	5.7 (5)	<u>Pull and push factors</u> Isolation in context of upbringing; discomfort in socially-generated hierarchies	Dismantle or expose conventional systems of sanction and reward	College degree
Total	100 (87)			

Conforming escape artists are victims of physical, sexual, and/or emotional abuse; they live with the dysfunctional behavior of an alcoholic, gambling, or philandering parent; they are raised by parents who tend to remain married despite severe marital problems and who neglect their daughters because they are preoccupied with their own mental health issues or involved in codependent relationships with spouses who engage in one of the addictive behaviors discussed above. And they provide all of these details about the painful experiences of their childhood home lives in the context of interview answers that are ostensibly about the whys and hows of their engagement with degree-supporting activities. The pain of life in these families is such a salient aspect of the conforming escape artist's motivation to attend college that Jacqueline needed to return to my question about college (and not about her family life while growing up) an hour after she had supposedly answered it: she stopped and reversed herself in order to make an all-important connection between higher education and this painful experience.

While the experience dimension of the conforming escape artist—familial pain—is salient and specific, the value dimension remains vague and diffuse. Jacqueline talked about "getting out of that house"; another interviewee, Tracey, maintained that she wished to "get married and get away from her father and stepmother"; and Jamie, whose story is told below, says she wanted to "go away and never come back." That these women wanted to escape is clear. And so too are the painful experiences from which they sought escape. But just what these women wished to escape to—the ends that they value—usually remains poorly defined. What I have surmised from their collective words and actions around the specific escapes that they have crafted is that they sought independence (financial and emotional) from those situations of their childhoods as well as an ability to create less painful household and familial relationships of their choosing. They want to end up in geographic and social spaces that are distinct from the places in which they were reared. For conforming escape artists, the painful experiences in their childhood homes determines what they value in the sense that it sets up a model of all the things they do not want. But the lack of specificity around their valued ends suggests that economic factors do not "pull," direct, or motivate them toward degree attainment in the way that Merton's theoretical understanding of his conformists suggests. Instead, these women are "pushed" into degree attainment by familial pain.

When one considers breaking curfew to hang out with friends, drinking, partying, getting high, or just plain running away, those activities that eventually add up to four-year-degree attainment (for example, working hard in school, spending extra time with teachers, and thinking in sixth grade about applying to college six years later) hardly seem like the fastest, easiest, or most direct way for youth to get away from problematic home lives. Nevertheless, we should refrain from praising escape artists for their ability to see, value, and craft a conformist future. Rather, connecting their experiences and valued ends to the attainment of a degree (or degrees) and professional careers is about appreciating the way in which their problematic familial relations limited the terms under which escape would be permitted. Below I describe how their gendered positioning in their families as surrogate caretakers and domestic servants[3] constrained them to an escape route characterized by schooling and professional development.

Escape artists would have run away if they could have. They did not do so because they had non-permissive parents with long lists of rules and regulations that were not to be transgressed. Jamie (age thirty-two) was sexually abused by her father, a well-respected bank executive and board member of multiple community organizations. In her one-bedroom apartment more than a thousand miles away from the middle-class suburban home in which she grew up and to which she has never returned, she described the strict environment of her childhood home. It was this environment that limited her strategy of escape to "keeping [her] grades up" and "getting accepted to any school [she] wanted to get into, preferably the farthest one away." She stated, "My mother would lock us up in the room and leave us all day or lock us outside of the house and leave us all day. She wouldn't cook. You know, she would lock up the food, you know, and put chains and locks on the freezer . . . A lot of the time, we didn't eat. You know . . . it was a punishment, if we did something wrong, and somebody was always doing something wrong, you go to bed and you didn't eat."

Rules, intolerance of rule transgression, and the harsh punishments work alongside an assignment of excessive responsibility to prevent an escape artist's forays out of windows after curfew or her ventures out of doors during unsupervised moments. Typically, a dysfunctional or co-dependent parent wants to maintain an orderly household and decides that it will be this child's (usually, the eldest daughter's) responsibility to do the work that is associated with that order, since the parent is occu-pied in his or her dysfunctional or codependent behavior. Thus, the escape artists in these households are peculiarly poised to take on large respon-sibilities and to fulfill them to perfectionist standards at a very early age. At the age of twenty-five, Claire spoke about the way her mother (who worked in janitorial services at a local hospital) needed her to pitch in for her father (a shoe shiner at the train station) whose series of sexual affairs caused him to drop in and out of their home:

> In fourth grade, I started taking—I took over, like, following the edu-cation of all of my brothers. I signed papers; I moved them out—like taking [my younger brother] out of special ed was my thing. You know, signing all the papers, going to parent-teacher's nights. So I would go in there for myself, and then I would pick up my brothers' report cards and then talk to the teachers . . . [My mother] stopped seeing my report card maybe, like, sixth grade. She never asked for it because, like, she generally knew that I was doing well . . . I think she was just more inter-ested in me keeping the house clean than doing my academic work be-cause I think she just took it as a given that I would do my homework and that I could do it all and keep the house clean and start cooking and do all that stuff and watch the kids . . . If [my brothers] were doing something, she would, like, say "Oh, go make them stop. . . ." Or some-times [one of my brothers] would do something and she would say, "I'm going to tell Claire. You better cut it out." So it got to that point . . . And I really never pushed for them to do chores because you know it would just be a hassle for me to watch them do chores, so I just did everything, and made sure that their clothes were ready and they ate, and I did the dishes. So like I was her assistant, and I had to help with her kids.

Escape artists' escapes from their problematic home lives were typically aided by the success that they experienced early on in school. Perhaps this is because living within very strict rules and regulations and being forced to take on and fulfill household responsibilities creates youth with enough attention span, attentiveness to detail, and practice remembering and following long lists of rules to do well at memorizing spelling words and writing and rewriting lists of arithmetic problems. But more importantly, school became a place where they were rewarded for their good behavior, and they were motivated to make a habit of the kinds of conformist behaviors we associate with school success. At the age of thirty-six, Shanequa maintained that despite her parents' strictness, rewards for obeying the rules and structure came not from home, but from school. She explained that school "was one of [her] saving graces"—"one of the things that . . . held [her] together" when she "didn't think things were . . . going well." She compared the "alcohol in the equation" of her household, which made her home life "chaotic," to a "school" she described as "structured" and asserted that there was "a place to go . . . where she had definite things expected of [her]." "Definite things that [she] could achieve and feel good about [her]self" motivated an investment in school.

Jacqueline, Jamie, Claire, and Shanequa bring familial relationships to the forefront of discussions of middle-class attainment. These women made decisions to study, to spend extra time with teachers, to keep up their grades, and to attend college not because of the pull of money, fame, and the high social rewards associated with the labor market privilege of educated elites, but because of the inadequate nature of their home lives. It is because they found their primary relationships to be emotionally unsatisfying, and painful even, that they made most of their degree-supporting decisions.[4] The pattern formed by the coding and categorization of data on their decisions indicates that this experience of deprivation with respect to familial love pushes these women into degree attainment. Familial experience of neglect, an overwhelming level of familial responsibility gone unrewarded, and the excessive limitation that parents place on these daughters' freedom of movement and independent decision making all structure the desire to escape to a different set of primary relations and limit women to the decidedly conformist escape route of higher education.[5]

My decision to discuss this type of college-educated woman before any of the others has nothing to do with her numerical significance in my snowball sample (for example, at a usage rate of 10 percent this label is neither the least nor the most frequently used in the typology). Rather, I have placed my conforming escape artist in the forefront because she shifts the terms by which we discuss degree attainment and careerism from economic to familial. She forces observers to think less about values and "pull" factors that motivate individuals to do more or to behave better and to think more about the social experiences and "push" factors that shape or constrain behavior (whether those constraints emerge in a lower-class school system or a middle-class suburban home). Finally, this Cinderella of degree attainers deemphasizes inequities in quantitatively measured economic precursors to adult poverty or wealth (variables like parental career status, income, and education) while at the same time emphasizing inequities in more qualitatively measured reproductive relations (variables like content of mother-daughter, father-daughter, and sibling interactions, configuration of familial rules and punishments, distribution of household labor) and the ways such relations inspire and constrain negotiations for money and love outcomes. I turn now to a second type that similarly highlights the quality of love relationships and connects these qualities to degree attainment. In many ways, she—the "prominent person pleaser"—is the conforming escape artist's logical opposite.

When Love Helps

As indicated above (see table 2), I used the escape artist label nine times. Since I labeled my entire sample using a total of eighty-seven labels (since some women required more than one label), this represents a usage rate of about 10 percent. I used the pleaser label almost three times as much—26 percent of the time. Representing the second largest group in my sample, these women worked to please those authority figures in their immediate purview. Usually their parents set the standards that they were to meet, but other relatives or fictive kin might have served the same purpose. The key factors in these women's degree-attainment decision making are the relationship they establish with a prominent person or persons in their lives, the standards for behavior that are set by these prominent persons, and the support these prominent persons provide for them as they endeavor to please.

In the first place, pleasers are dependent upon a relationship of trust that has been nurtured by some prominent person in their lives. The reason that they work as hard as they end up doing is to please that person or because they trust that person's word about what is good for their future, without seeing it for themselves. Failing sometimes to see the long-term benefits of school and a college education, pleasers walk by faith and love as it were. They believe that the prominent person knows best, and they know that their obedience and efforts will strengthen and nurture the bonds between them and the prominent person.

Morgan was her mother's only child: their two-person family resided in the same housing project from the time Morgan was in elementary school and throughout the years that she commuted to a local college. Sometimes Morgan's mother worked and "sometimes she collected" (as in the collection of welfare), but she always relied on Morgan to obey her rules for keeping young children away from potentially harmful distractions in their rough neighborhood. Although she was not really involved in Morgan's decision to go to college, she was the prominent person who set the guidelines that kept her out of the kinds of trouble that might have interfered with school. Morgan explains this aspect of her relationship with her mother below:

> My mother was pretty much comfortable with me being myself. She knew that I wasn't gonna go off and do something that I didn't think that I should do. Basically, to me, [my mother's] word was Bible. If she said, don't do it, I didn't do it. And it wasn't so much that she would threaten like "I'm gon' beat you" or "I'm gon' do this to you." It was just that my mother had been through enough experiences in life to know what she was talkin' about.

In the second place, the prominent people whom pleasers seek to please have to have lofty goals of their own. Since the logical motivation for the pleaser's behavior does not reside in the mind of the pleaser herself, it must come from the authority figure. Thus the prominent person may be highly motivated to achieve a career or professional status and may feel strongly that the pleaser's status achievement or lack of achievement reflects on the prominent person him- or herself. Whatever the case, the prominent person's vision for the pleaser's life is necessarily bigger and better articulated than the pleaser's own goals. This was certainly the situation Sparkle faced during the years she spent in the home of her happily married parents—parents who, according to Sparkle, mutually and lovingly balanced child care and housework duties with their respective careers in secretarial work and grounds keeping for local educational institutions. During our interview, Sparkle made glowing reports on her parents' gender neutrality in the home and discussed her gratitude to her father for getting her through the first day of her menstrual cycle. Below, she expresses similar gratitude for the fact that her non-degreed parents made her own mediocre goals secondary to the ones that they had set for her. "Now keep in mind, I never wanted to go to college . . . I was so tired of school, but my parents—it wasn't a choice. It was not a choice. I am so glad it was not a choice. I would not have traded it for anything in the world. I'm so glad I went."

And third, it is of critical importance that the relationship provides more than lofty expectations. The authority figure is trusted by the pleaser and is the focus of the pleaser's efforts because such figures extend re-sources, strategies, and coping skills in addition to the expectations. The authority figure shows the pleaser how to please, provides her with tools, consoles her when she fails, and shows her how to start over. In a sense, each expectation is also an occasion to show the pleaser that she is sup-ported by the authority figure and to strengthen the bond for further ex-pectations. Deanna (who was twenty-nine when I interviewed her) be-came a nurse because her mother "kept drilling" the need for a nursing license "into [her]." She returned to school for an extra year after gradua-tion to take the additional courses that she needed for nursing in order to appease a mother who "continued to press and press and press and press." Insight into the way in which Deanna can expect support, in addition to guidance, from her parents can be garnered from her description of her mother's reaction to bad news below:

DEANNA: And then I ended up getting pregnant when I was twenty-three. Talkin' 'bout the scariest thing to have to tell your parents. I was petrified. I was "Oh my God, they're gon' kill me!" You know, "I am dead." You know, my mom . . . We told her first because as I grew up, we began to get much more closer . . . And I'm tellin' her, she was like, "Oh!" And I had already graduated from school. I was finished with college and everything, so she goes, "Oh, that's fine. You know you can get through this. We'll be here to sup-port you. Just don't get married."

AVERIL: Really?

DEANNA: That's what she said. I don't think she really cared for him.

> You know, she would never, like, she was like, "I'm not get-
> ting in your business. I don't want you to think I'm try-
> ing to tell you what to do." She goes, "Right now, don't get
> married because of a child." You know. "If you do, then you
> make sure it's the right thing. Don't just all of a sudden be-
> cause you know you gonna be shamed or it's not accepted
> by society." She said, "Right now, don't mess up your life.
> That's what's more important. Just don't get married."

Deanna grew up as one of four girls in a close-knit family. Although
her parents would eventually separate and divorce during her adult years,
they were romantic and business partners (selling cleaning products and
cosmetics) during her youth, and Deanna described them as extremely
supportive of her and her younger sisters. In the situation above, Deanna's
mother used her supportive stance to coax Deanna into taking her advice. She ended up quitting the job she had recently procured in order to
start an in-home day care center so that she could provide day care for
Deanna's child. She worked at this business for just the four years that it
took Deanna's son to make it to kindergarten.

As was the case with my conforming escape artists, prominent person pleasers do not necessarily value money or the status attributes that
money can buy. They are actively trying to nurture and maintain (usually
familial) relationships, and it is perhaps their parents' love of money
and status and their desire to please these parents that involves them in
degree-supporting behaviors and interactions. In terms of the experience
dimension that likely generates the pleaser's version of family values, the
women recall nurturing interactions with family members who virtually
celebrated opportunities to spend time with them, act in ways to protect
and secure their emotional well-being, and teach them about life. Thus,
their decisions to apply themselves when schoolwork seemed difficult, to
attend college-preparatory programming, and ultimately to complete the
college application and matriculation processes are based in these positive experiences in their families of upbringing and the value that they
place on maintaining these relationships.

Like escape artists, pleasers are all about love and family, and their
degree-seeking behaviors are generated out of the specific configuration
of circumstances in the women's families of origin. But while pleasing is

generated out of positive experiences and the desire to maintain ties with the family, escaping is generated out of negative experiences and a desire to distance oneself from these primary relations. Neither type of degreed woman pursues the degree because she values money and wants to take advantage of opportunities to earn money legally. Rather, push factors are salient in decisions to engage in degree-supporting behaviors, and all of these push factors have to do with an inequality of reproductive relations.

Escape artists and pleasers say to inequality scholars that configurations of opportunity in love and money (rather than plain old economic opportunity) create the conventional value seeker's conventional route to value achievement. They say that *family, the reproductive relations that family represents, and the love or lack of love and attention that is the currency transferred in families matter in the creation and maintenance of social hierarchies.* Jacqueline and Jamie, on the one hand, and Sparkle and Deanna, on the other hand, maintain that even class inequality—the one that is determined and defined based on differences in economic resources and interests—reflects values that do not appear economic (for example, severing or nurturing and maintaining familial relations) and experiences of deprivation and advantage that are about love rather than money.

A mostly female group of inequality scholars (for example, Higginbotham, Weber, Lareau) have in prior studies given attention to this question of whether and how love and familial relations affect or do not affect individuals' class uplift or middle-class maintenance projects. In doing so, they have focused on identifying and measuring the extent to which love and obligation, and attention to family and romance detracts from degree-supporting activity.[6] In this book about degreed black women's strivings in love and family as well as whether and how such strivings are related to their expanding educational and economic advantages, data from escape artists and pleasers show that the overlap between love and economic inequality, such as it is, is neither so obvious nor straightforward as such studies might imply: it is probably most accurate to say that different kinds of reproductive relations can and do produce similar educational outcomes and that making this admission has all to do with accepting the point that love (much like class or economic resources) matters but is unequally distributed. Because people will act in certain ways in order get the love that they want, to maintain the love that they have, or to escape a love that hurts, there are moments and lifetimes where love can motivate economic (or in this case, educational) action.[7] Escape artists and pleasers are presented here because they are women whose educational decision-making trajectories represent these moments and lifetimes—because they represent a connection between degree attainment and quantitatively and qualitatively unequal experiences with familial love.

The Decisions That Race Made

When I say that Jacqueline is a woman running from love, I say that deprivation in love might constrain young women into degree attainment. When I say that for love Deanna spends an extra year in school and forgoes marriage while pregnant, I say that abundant love can simultaneously motivate career credentialing and single parenting. When I describe who escape artists and pleasers are, I am describing situations in which negotiations around and for love may produce apparently economic outcomes—processes in which family actors maneuver with, without, and for currencies of love and where their maneuvering and negotiations spill over into or imply a certain variance in economic action. In much the same manner as my escape artists and pleasers testify to a love logic of degree attainment, my "recruits" and "stigma avoiders" suggest that there is also such a thing as a racial logic to degree attainment (see table 2). Typing the values and experiences surrounding their degree-supporting decisions demonstrates that actions to improve, avoid, and challenge racial hierarchy can also intentionally and unintentionally shape educational and economic outcomes.

Racial inequality scholars have discussed the effect of race on education and work outcomes using tests for hypothesized racial discrimination. Locating race effects in powerful white social actors' manipulation of the economic system in ways that exclude or marginalize people of color, they have sought to account for African Americans' relatively deprived educational experiences and lower level of educational achievement,[8] as well as their depressed wages and heightened unemployment rates,[9] by observing and describing differences in the ways individuals of different races are treated by the educational system and the labor market. In addition, race scholars have endeavored to describe the psychological and cultural adaptations made by individuals and communities of color to racist practice—adaptations that are expected to negatively affect black educational and employment outcomes. For example, Steele has argued that racism means that African Americans' performance on tasks and examinations is negatively affected by knowledge that their work will be used to evaluate or represent African American group fitness (Steele 1997). Similarly Ogbu and others (Fordham and Ogbu 1986; Ogbu 1990, 1992, 2003; Ogbu and Simons 1998) expect African Americans, Latinos, and Native Americans to eschew good grades and school success in order to avoid being accused of "acting white" and adopting the culture of their oppressors. What this book's description of the experiences and values that lead to recruits' and stigma avoiders' degree attainment offers is an explanation of how adaptation to racism or individuals' racial action results in (rather than detracts from) educational achievement and movement up the labor hierarchy.

An Affirmative and Collective Racial Response

First, consider thirty-two-year-old Morgan. In response to my query, "At what point did you first decide that you were supposed to go to college," she responded, "I would say I was fourteen—no—thirteen! I was thirteen. I was in the HSC program, which was basically for, um, students interested in being doctors or the health fields. My science instructor got me involved in it. And we would visit the colleges that had health or pre-med type programs, and got introduced to different types of health careers, but I knew then that I wanted to go to college to do physical therapy." Here, a program designed to introduce underrepresented minorities to the possibility of pursuing health careers provides Morgan with both professional vision and a specific strategy for attaining that vision. The data support Morgan's classification as both "pleaser" and "recruit": in the section above, she pleased her welfare-dependent mother by following all of her rules and regulations, which were designed to keep young women out of trouble in the projects; but here she is "recruited" for and engages with a program that directs all the discipline and good works that her mother inspired toward class achievement.

Next, give some attention to my interview with Mina, which occurred when she was twenty-one years old and graduated from college just six months earlier. She explained her college application process to me:

> Well what happened was . . . I went into a program when I was fifteen. It was called CEOP . . . It was at the college I went to, and it's for students who aren't yet seniors, but they . . . introduce you to college: it's got like college prep. And my brother went into the one that if you passed it you would get into college . . . He didn't wanna stay in the college, but he was in that program while I was in the program for the younger ones.

Participating in this program and achieving passing grades in the program's college preparatory courses during the remainder of her high school years constituted Mina's only application to college. She and her brother were among the many students of color from their city who experienced this specific university's use of affirmative action funding in a program designed to recruit them aggressively. The program facilitates both college preparedness and interest and eases the college and financial aid application processes for students willing to attend this university. Although Mina had envisioned attending college and pursuing a career as a lawyer before she got involved with CEOP, thus far, the bulk of her specific plans and activities associated with college matriculation or middle-class status attainment came as a result of her recruitment into this program. Hence, like Morgan, one of the labels that she carries is that of recruit.

Finally, look at the way Niani describes her degree-attainment process. She began with the job that she started a few months after graduating from high school:

> That January I got a job at a computer company as an assembler and worked my way up from there. Every two years I was being promoted, and the interesting thing was that particular company was put in this city to promote African American and, uh, Latino people within the corporate structure. So that they were getting tax breaks and things like that. And a lotta companies were doing this—getting good tax breaks for opening what's called inner city plants . . . I worked there for about fourteen years, and during my time there, um, went through a lot of management training. I came to Johnson College for a couple years doing an executive management program, which the company paid for. And then the company moved. They closed the plant here . . . When I made my decision . . . to take the management buyout that the company was offering . . . I was pregnant . . . I took a management buyout

and processed out of the company while I was in the hospital having my second child . . . I stayed home for a couple of years, um, collecting unemployment, living off the money that they gave me at the management buyout, and then I decided to reenter the workforce. Now at that time, the economy was devastated . . . It was 1992. It was horrible. There were, like, no jobs out there, particularly not in the . . . salary level that I was at—I was at $55,000 when I left. And when I went back into the workforce, I entered at $30,000 . . . But I entered into the nonprofit field, a nonprofit organization, and did some public relations and fundraising for [them] . . . I found a degree program at, um, Victory Valley College where I could go to school full-time on weekends, and so that's what I did to finish my undergraduate degree.

Here, affirmative action programming has a hand in stalling, starting, stopping, and resuming degree attainment. It similarly has a hand in jump-starting and reversing middle-class income and status achievements. Niani's diverse set of values means that she shares the label of recruit with one other label.

Recruits experience recruitment. Furthermore, in this sample, the experience of recruitment for activities supporting degree attainment was frequently sponsored by race-based affirmative action programs that targeted these girls and young women because of their minority racial status. Thus, recruitment was in these cases a racializing experience (that is, one that reinforced these women's sense of racial distinction and difference, one that required that they adopt a racial understanding of their opportunities and actions within and through these settings, and one that pulled them into activities and spaces with persons who would be seen as either racial compatriots or racial others).

In much the same way as escape artists' and pleasers' degree attainment is defined by their experiences with familial or parental love, so too are recruits' educational achievements bound up with their experiences of the racial structure. Where post–civil rights affirmative action programs were present and active, a disciplined student from the projects (like Morgan) could come to understand herself as someone who could live the life of a highly educated professional. Where such programs were in place at state-funded universities, a student with a vision, little money, and no obvious educational plan (like Mina) had an appropriate college to attend that was both affordable and accessible from her home. And where such programs were temporary and emphasized corporate placement and training over education, a willing young worker (like Niani) might postpone serious attention to college, make a decent salary without earning a degree, and revert to a degree-attainment strategy of class maintenance only when the political climate and affirmative action funding levels changed. These recruits were "pushed" into degree attainment by the structure of race relations at federal, state, and local institutional levels and by the resulting recruitment experiences that came to be associated with black racial identity in the post–civil rights era.

Recruits might also experience formal or informal recruitment by school-based academic recruitment programs. Consider Eartha's claims about her life being shaped by academic recruitment experiences:

> My life history seems to go with schooling. Like, um, when I was young—When I was in third grade, I started testing out into, um, gifted classes, and then in fourth grade, I had to go to a different school all together. So I started commuting to school when I was in fourth grade . . . In seventh grade, I ended up in Bayside Middle School for gifted children[, which] was connected to the local public university, but that was just before we moved to Texas, and then I ended up in a school, Andrews High School . . . It was quite different and I skipped two years of school. The first year I went to that school and the last year—I skipped both of those. So I started college when I was sixteen.

Several sampled women were recruited into the college preparatory track in the way that Eartha describes. Meeting some requirement in a competitive academic process (for example, testing or transcript evaluation) allowed them to attend a specialized college preparatory school or program or even to move ahead in school at a faster than normal rate. These academic recruitment experiences were significant but not as frequent as the affirmative action recruitment. More importantly, they offered such women a different sense of their short-term educational and long-term professional activities than they got from recruitment into affirmative action activities. Academic recruitment socialized the women into a much more individualized or personal sense of their own accomplishments: the women came to understand themselves as "selected" for their particular brand and level of studiousness or smarts (or even athletic talent) rather than "recruited" for their racial status.

As Bourdieu (Bourdieu 1977a, 1977b; Bourdieu and Passeron 1977/1990) has suggested, academic recruitment takes a process in which arbitrary but elite or middle-class cultural traits become standards for the movement of certain students to college preparatory tracks, setting them aside for future professional work; it then makes this process appear to be meritocratic selection. Thus, students with class privileges (or at least those who carry the language and cultural markers of the upper classes) understand a system designed around the preferential treatment of elites and their children to be confirmation of their giftedness, merit, or particular suitability for elite social roles.

In contrast, recruitment based on minority racial status socializes degreed black women to a racially divided world and to the tenuousness and time-dependent nature of their inclusion in elite class privileges.[10] Since most of the women in my sample experienced some form of affirmative action recruitment prior to college and since those women carrying the recruit label also found their degree-supporting behaviors to be inextricably tied to experiences of affirmative action recruitment, the degreed women whom I sampled tended to carry this sense of a racial structure that would and often does exclude them right alongside whatever amount of academic self-esteem or belief in their own artistic, athletic, or academic talent they might also maintain. Even when their educational and professional achievements were framed as entitlements associated with their investment of skills, hard work, and time, they were not without the understanding that such accomplishments also represent the tenuous spoils of a racial war—that their progress in these educational and professional spaces always had the potential to be understood and often needed to be negotiated in these racial terms.

Recruits share with pleasers the experience of being pushed into degree attainment by persons with loftier visions and greater identification with the value of education for future economic roles than they themselves have. But they differ from pleasers in two important ways. First, where pleasers are guided to and through higher education and high-status professions by loving family members, recruits depend on persons who are, by and large, strangers. They join those programs that sound attractive, that promise a pleasing or satisfying experience, or that assure access to the achievement of a previously established goal; and the programs' authors design, lobby for, and implement the programs with a generalized sense rather than specific knowledge of who program participants might turn out to be. Recruitment represents the collective action of many people—from those who struggled and fought to enact and amend legislative and public policies that would alter public opinion about the appropriate treatment of racial minorities and pave the way for funded programming, to those who design and propose specific programming, to those who staff and directly interact with potential and actual program participants. It thus emerges from social relationships characterized by greater conflict and much less intimacy, mutual knowledge, and personal accountability than pleasing.

Recruits also differ from pleasers with respect to the cumulative and/or long-term effect of recruitment. Pleasers rely on prominent persons with a master plan: one activity that the prominent person encourages pleasers to get involved in is likely to be connected to a second activity and a third activity; the activities string together to result in degree attainment and/or other long-term goals. In contrast, recruits' involvement in programs is less logically connected; not all the programs for which they are recruited are about college attendance, and routes to and through college are likely to be more circuitous than are those of pleasers. Furthermore, many individuals who experience recruitment may never make it to or through college: this absence of a master plan or consistency across recruitment settings as well as the lack of intimacy and mutuality in the relations that give rise to degree-supporting behaviors are likely related to recruits' low representation in a sample of women who actually go on to earn degrees. Although I used the recruit label 10 percent of the time (see table 2 above), only one woman in my sample (Wanda, from the book's introduction) was solely classified using this label.

As is the case with the escape artist, the value dimension of the recruit type remains imprecisely defined. Recruits tend to share the recruit label with at least one other label, and thus often take on the more specific values associated with that other label. Mina and Niani take on the values associated with labels that I discuss below (that is, status seeking and profiling, respectively), and I discussed Morgan's second label—that of pleaser—earlier. But more importantly, recruitment settings may have little in common with one another with respect to the values that they inculcate. Special programs for gifted and talented children in the school system, community athletic teams with coaches playing important mentoring roles, housing projects' life skills classes, and religious outreach programs focused on developing the spirituality of kids in the neighborhood may all push children into educational and career development activities and connect these activities with racial advancement while at the same time maintaining that these activities are associated with quite the varied list of valued ends (for example, elite professional status versus physical fitness, learning to play and work with others versus self-reliance, and thriftiness versus love of God and neighbor).

The elite status achievements of recruits like Morgan, Mina, and Niani have emerged and continue to emerge from the processes and products of racial struggle. Stratification scholars studying racial inequality focus on the outcomes of this racial struggle—making and testing hypotheses for the educational and income losses associated with all manner of racial deprivations and stressors. But here, discovery of the recruit type creates a racial actor—one with an awareness of the racial status requirements associated with particular educational and professional opportunities as well as the generalized race relations and racial ideology from which these opportunities emerge. Actions in these recruitment sites become part of emergent race relations and remain subject at any given time to racial interpretations. Recruits may acknowledge, ignore, remain oblivious to, or challenge these racial interpretations, but they nevertheless shape the ongoing availability of opportunities and outcomes for their racial selves and for other members of their racial group. In the discussion of "stigma avoidance" below, racial actors run from racial interpretations that justify black individuals' experiences of class deprivation rather than privilege.

A Negative and Individual Racial Reaction

In a society where black people form the stigmatized bottom rung of the racial hierarchy (that is, where negative behaviors and positions are often racialized and associated with blackness) black individuals will often feel the need to avoid stigma. In other words, they will feel the need to distance themselves and their behaviors from negative black stereotypes for fear of being barred from attractive social opportunities, social interactions with high-status group members, and/or social spaces that are of personal interest to them.

And so it was that months after her college graduation, Sparkle found herself in the middle of a job interview performing a make-believe telephone conversation for her potential employer. The woman had framed her request for this impromptu enactment of how Sparkle would handle phone calls as if it were something in which she had only a mild curiosity. But experience told Sparkle that this would be her only opportunity to prove to the interviewer that she would not slip into a speech pattern matching the local black vernacular. Her use of clear diction and standard English terms became in this moment her way of avoiding the woman's efforts to stigmatize her. Sparkle believed that failing what she read as this most obvious of speech tests would mean certain exclusion from employment. She imagined that the interviewer would base her rejection of an applicant who had otherwise seemed to have excellent qualifications on some imaginary of black workers whose style of speech is one among many of the cultural characteristics that supposedly makes them unsuitable for employment in corporate America.

Erving Goffman (1963) argues that membership in low-status racial groups constitutes a "tribal" form of stigma. Physical and cultural characteristics that constitute racial identifiers justify exclusion of individuals and groups from mainstream activities and normative social interaction. The stigma is both the mark that renders the individual abnormal and the reason that normative interaction is impossible and certain to be rejected by non-stigmatized others. Most of the sampled women were like Sparkle in that they experienced the tribal stigma of racism as a series of incidents that shared a theme but that nevertheless differed in degree. Variance occurred in the degree to which racial status was a standard for inclusion or exclusion, such that sometimes their racial status was—or could at least be imagined as—less relevant to the persons with whom they interacted or the goals that they were trying to accomplish. Variance also occurred in the degree to which their racial assignment in a given interaction was negotiable such that sometimes they were in a better position from which to manage their racial stigma—to behave or act in ways that would enable others to ignore it and to find it less off-putting.

Sparkle's deliberate and exaggerated use of standard English during the mock telephone call of her job interview is an example of an attempt to manage racial stigma in a situation where race was judged to be highly relevant. In other words, blackness was a standard for exclusion from employment with this corporation, but she was able to negotiate herself out of the "undesirably black" or "too black" racial category. However, racism—or tribal stigma—is not always experienced in this intermittent and variant manner. Furthermore, "stigma avoidance" can—in situations where the experience of racial and other stigmas encompasses more of the whole of life—become a more permanent preoccupation and an offensive rather than defensive life tactic.

Descriptions of incidents of stigma avoidance were fairly common across the sample of degreed black women. Theory and writing on the negative racial and gendered images of black women (for example, "welfare queens" who rely on sex and prolific baby making to ensure steady paychecks from government assistance programs or "matriarchs" who dominate and dismiss black men from their homes and proper masculine roles)[11] indicate that African American women are continually forced to sidestep stereotypes that degrade and control.[12] However, those women in my sample who are labeled stigma avoiders go beyond the use of stigma avoidance in interactions laden with images of stigmatized black personas. They worry about standing out in any way. While most of the women in the sample avoid stigma because they fear that incorrect assessments will be made about them by persons with the power to exclude and control, stigma avoiders fear that they will be singled out, teased, and scorned by most people with whom they have contact. They don't want to be stigmatized for being a "bum," for example, but they also worry that someone they think is a "bum" will accuse them of being too high on themselves or tease them about their success.

Stigma avoiders avoid the pointing finger no matter where it comes from. They value the anonymity that comes with what they envision as "normal" or "regular." They hope to blend into the crowd and strive for mediocrity. As table 2 indicates, I used the "avoider" label seven times, but Summer was the only person whose sole classification was that of an avoider. This is what she told me when I asked her about how she decided to go to college.

> SUMMER: I wasn't really like gung ho about college and all that. I wasn't really sure at that point what I wanted to do.
>
> AVERIL: Well, what made you decide to go then?
>
> SUMMER: The thing to do. I didn't wanna be a bum on the streets.

I wanted to make money, somewhere down the line. And I had to get out of Newark. I was just tired of the whole Newark scene. I didn't go to school—to college—just because I wanted to be somebody big. It's just I wanted to—I wanted to have a job where I would not have to live in that area—the projects. That was it. I didn't have to be big. I just had to make some money. Figured, you know, either you be a mathematician or you be a doctor or somethin', somethin' that's gonna bring you some money so that you don't have to live in Newark, in the projects. And that was my focus.

Note then how Summer's decision to attend college is based in what she seems to think are relatively low or mediocre career goals—in aims that are expressly defined as antithetical to "big." Stigma avoidance is about not standing out or being noticed. This is true whether the notice emerges from one's placement on a pedestal, one's abandonment in a ditch, or one's relegation to a cage.

Stigma avoiders lived in circumstances and underwent experiences that allowed them to become so obsessed with stigma avoidance so as to make it a way of life. Forced to wear the marks of stigma almost constantly or to continually occupy spaces reserved for the stigmatized, forgotten, and socially abhorred and excluded, their valuation of mediocrity emerges from experiences that cause them to fear the pointing finger no matter where it comes from. The experiences of stigma avoiders in this sample included childhood teasing linked to overweight status, visibly slow progress in school, recent immigrant status and perceived or actual ethnic difference, racial or other marked social isolation in residence and/or schooling, and hyper-segregation in public housing and poor black residential areas. Summer described herself as overweight during much of her youth. Furthermore, she lived among poor and black single parent families in a large public housing project—among people whom she saw as "the stigmatized." She feared being mistaken for one of them and left behind in the poverty, the inadequate housing, the limited access to jobs, and the societal scorn that all of these things imply. This is why she said the following to me: "When I was in Catholic school I remember look[ing] down on women just havin' babies. My mom had drilled into my head the idea that I should '[refuse] to walk down the street with slippers on my feet, scarf on my head, and a stroller.'" Knowing the highest costs associated with the stigma of racism and feeling that they were different from the stigmatized, both mother and daughter sought to escape (or at least to ensure that Summer would one day escape). Thus Summer's stigma avoidant behavior began at an early age under conditions of unmanageable and costly racial stigma.

Although the intermittent use of stigma avoidance in which Sparkle engaged was described by most of the degreed black women whom I interviewed, stigma avoiders (persons whose decisions were so often about stigma avoidance that they carried this label) like Summer were not common in my sample. A likely reason for this is that they strive for mediocrity. And mediocrity does not seem to be highly associated with degree attainment for African American women.[13] Summer is probably somewhat unusual in her understanding that the only alternatives to being a "bum on the streets" are the careers of doctor or mathematician, both careers requiring not only four-year degrees, but also extensive postgraduate work. Stigma avoiders experience the institutional treatment of African Americans as the symbol of a life in which criticism and stigmatization threaten from many directions, and they cope with this fear by hiding in mediocrity, or looking like "regular people." African American women who made it into my sample, selected by their degree attainment, were, for the most part, striving to be more than mediocre.[14]

My discussion of racial logics of degree attainment is meant to point out the ways in which experiences of racial inequality can structure individual decision making toward and for achievement in higher education. On the one hand, there are "recruits," whose degree-attainment decisions are largely structured by opportunities that emerged from racial struggle. They experience a myriad of program sponsors pulling them into activities that are meant to alter their lives and to re-envision the opportunities typically associated with black racial status. On the other hand, there are the "stigma avoiders," who experience the sting of exclusion for racial and other reasons and whose degree-seeking behavior promises to put them into those highly valued spaces where they can feel like one of the "normal" (as opposed to morally unworthy) crowd. The claim that racial experiences dominate these women's degree-supporting decisions suggests that *the degreed category in general and the black middle-class in particu-*

lar are peopled only with significant attention to racial matters, with significant striving toward racial uplift in the one case and racial escape in the other. Black college achievement implies moments of collective confrontation of and individual adaptation to a racially discriminating social landscape. Race forms more than a caveat, exception, footnote, or extenuating circumstance of class-specific behavior and the struggle and competition for economic resources. With respect to individuals, it organizes a way of being in the world—structuring self-conception as well as the way degree attainment and labor market opportunities are understood and experienced.[15]

Decisions about Money

Thus far, this chapter's description of the experiences and values leading to black women's degree attainment contrasts with inequality study that frames individuals as rational economic actors working to maximize personal monetary profit. It is different from scholarship that conceives of love and race as phenomena that corrupt and/or complicate what would (and some would say "should") be a more pure relationship between an individual and her labor market. Instead, in this analysis, the "impurities" of love and race stand for the social relationships and interactions out of which productive capacities and choices emerge. More than influencing the outcome of economically motivated actions, they define the boundaries and expected outcomes associated with these actions. Here, processes of middle-class achievement are about more than individuals who prioritize their educational credentialing over families and family formation; they are about an economy that relies on the actions of families and on the decisions that individuals make for love. And here, peopling the black middle class is about more than an economy with greater or lesser likelihood of doing more or less racial discrimination; it is about action that racializes—about individuals who rely on racial strategies of action and collective action that maintains racial identities.

The "status-seeking" type that I discuss below may seem more familiar to degreed and degree-seeking readers than escape artists, pleasers, recruits, and avoiders because of the way in which these women's decision making evidences an intentional connection between the pursuit of higher education and money. But its presence alongside these other types is actually a petition for an expansion of the way the scholarly community understands the contribution of individual decision making to the maintenance of class inequality from one generation to the next. My "status seekers" support Weber's class theory arguing that classes are peopled and class boundaries are maintained by the competition for entry into educationally credentialed status groups (R. Collins 1986; Grusky 1994). But they do so without admitting that this economic competition dominates the concerns of all educated elites or that individuals' differential efforts and opportunities in the economic competition are all that is required for the observed class distribution to continue. Rather, this contextualized description of "status seeking" says that there is a layered, intersecting, overlapping set of motivations involved in the creation of the category of college-educated black women.

Weberian elites (R. Collins 1986; Grusky 1994) are members of professional organizations (for example, state bar associations, the American Federation of Teachers, the American Medical Association, the National Association of Realtors, or the American Society of Mechanical Engineers). They use their professional status and educational credentials and training to monopolize the positions of privilege in the labor hierarchy. In other words, they enact policies that compel their members to fulfill certain minimal training requirements at accredited institutions and to pay licensing fees that allow them to sell the skills that they acquire. But Weber says that despite their distinctively economic actions and the wealth of economic resources that their skills' monopolies allow them to control, status elites are usually known by their lifestyles and their tastes. Pastimes (for example, golf), dress (business suits), food (sit-down versus take-out), and radio station preferences (NPR), rather than resumés tacked to their foreheads, mark them in such a way as to assure that they receive the benefits and penalties of their professional status during even those social interactions that occur in arenas outside of the labor market.

My status seekers underscore the way in which labor market constraints, the pull of economic reward, and economic competition create these class groupings of individuals marked by their educational and professional training and their lifestyles. But these women exist alongside others whose degree attainment and lifestyle standards might not be explained with such reference to the organization and culture of economic classes. Furthermore, as Merton (1957) has suggested, reference to economic classes need not mean complete acceptance of the economic order or the rules for status attainment in that economic order. As we shall see below, "status seekers" are joined by other types of women whose degree-attainment decision making does occur around economic values and means but who nevertheless fail to conform to the expected pattern (that is, individuals striving for conventional things in conventional ways).

Money Is as Money Does

Reward, challenge, competition: like a spoken racquetball competition, Imani's descriptive and verbose answers to my interview questions bounced through these three themes in a way that would have been predictable had I recognized the pattern sometime before the interview ended—had I not been so distracted by the specificity of the details of each story she told. This rhythm of payoff or reward, followed by explanation of the difficult challenge that leads to this payoff, followed by intense competition with others or self to meet these challenges, is the very rhythm of "status seeking." Listen.

> One of the big reasons that I really wanted to go to Baldwin [High School] was that I really wanted to be on their IAO team. IAO was the . . . state-wide academic competition in which students—high school students—compete in ten different areas . . . They test your knowledge of social studies and math and . . . basically all different areas. And so I was like—oh—Baldwin was known to be a powerhouse . . . they had won all the championships . . . People were always so surprised: "How did this quote-unquote inner city school [do] so well up against Claymont High and up against all the Uni—you know, University High, all the quote-unquote white schools?" That was basically the gist of it. "How could these kids do so well?"
>
> So I knew about this, and before I even came to Baldwin . . . I said, "I'm gonna get my mother to let me come to Baldwin. I'm comin' and I'm gonna be the captain of the team." . . . So anyway, yeah, I finally convinced my mother to let me go. She did let me go. I did go, and I did become the captain of their IAO team . . . I could remember one of my friends—a black guy who I had known ever since, like, elementary school. He . . . was on the Uni team, and he jumped the fence at [my] high school because we were in there studying. It was, like, 11:30

at night. And Lavinsky [the coach] had a rule: we would study until midnight every single night, and it was in the newspapers. And Josh jumped this fence . . . and he came and he saw the light on in Lavinsky's class. And he came—and I said "Josh!" . . . He said, "Oh my God! I can't believe it." He said, "They said that in the papers. I just had to see it for myself—to see if you guys really studied 'til midnight every night." He was like, "Yeah, we gon' be in trouble."

Like the racquet-propelled bouncing ball, Imani's story moves from the glorious reputation of the academic team, hits on the challenging activities associated with team membership, bangs against the competitive speeches and fence-climbing foes that team membership involved her in, and returns once again to the newsworthy reputation of the team. Her description of how she came to attend the high school that she did and its intense and recognizable rhythm shows hers to be a status seeker. Representing almost 30 percent of the labels used (as per table 2 above) and almost 39 percent of the women whom I was able to classify using a single label, Imani expresses desires that reflect all the values of status seekers—(1) group membership, (2) lifestyles, practices, and behaviors of group members, and (3) material and nonmaterial rewards associated with group membership.

Inasmuch as conforming escape artists and prominent person pleasers force us to think about women's desires and constraints in love or reproductive relations and how these inequities in familial experience can push women into degree attainment, status seekers confirm that degree attainment does have an economic rationale. Status seekers like Imani are "pulled" into degree attainment by the possibility of achieving membership in one or more elite status groups. They place value on the employment skills, the educational achievements, and the jobs that membership in these status groups implies. They therefore explain their motivations to achieve the college degree and to make particular degree-supporting decisions by their desire to be a part of a particular professional group, to be allowed entry into a group of elite educational achievers at one or more levels of schooling, or to reside among and socialize with a set of people who have or will soon have particularly specialized or rarified careers. Seekers see their membership in these elite groups as a value in and of itself—understanding these groups to represent a certain superiority that is distinct from the superior monetary rewards associated with the status. For Imani, this meant that being a Baldwin High IAO team member was a recognizable reward before she had entered and won the competitions and long before these educational achievements would lead her to the cash associated with her career in finance.

Seekers' first value listed above, that of group membership, necessitates the second value, that of lifestyles, practices, and values of the group members. As Randall Collins (1986) reminds us, Weberian status groups are exclusive groups whose members distinguish themselves by their lifestyle. Their behaviors mark them, setting them apart and deeming them worthy of esteem. Status seekers in this sample monitor the behaviors and strategies of elite professionals. Their choices reflect the need they have to conform to certain behaviors for fear of being shunned or excluded, not by persons intimate with them, but by anyone who has the desired status. Below, Ashley (age thirty-six) describes the way she developed the strength to let go of the emotional bond with her first boyfriend. Note the way her "status-seeking" posture causes her to monitor the lifestyles of members of the black elite. Also note how she is only able to change her behavior once she realizes that failing to do so could mean exclusion from membership in a group of urban black professionals.

I just knew this relationship wasn't going anywhere. But actually, I knew it before, but it was more like an emotional bond. Ah, in terms of sex, he was the first . . . you know, my virginity stopped there, and it was more like an emotional thing even with trying to get out of the relationship. We broke up every other weekend, and I just felt like, like he had started to see other women, which had probably been going on anyway . . . It was a terrible situation . . . So once I went away, it was so funny. I moved to Atlanta; it was my first time just really being exposed to a lot of professional black people. I remember just calling home and saying, "Mother, there are just so many professional blacks here, carrying briefcases." I was just like, "Where have you been all your life? Just in the little town of Hardeeville." So I was there, you know, I was embarrassed to say that I had this ex-boyfriend, and you know, well, women would talk about, "Oh I have this boyfriend, and he's in college, and da da da da da. He decided to go to medical school." And what was I gonna say? He worked for this factory or something, you know. So it was like almost embarrassment when I moved there to even talk about that situation. So I felt like I had to really erase this situation from my life, basically, and kind of start afresh. So, I really did.

It is not enough that Ashley is in summer school working toward a career in engineering. Like all true status seekers, she wants more than entry into the engineering field: she also wants to dress like these people, carry her belongings in the same kinds of vessels, live in the same metropolitan environment, and date the same kind of men. In short, she values both their professional status and their lifestyles and practices.[16]

The third value, that of the rewards of status, both explains and bolsters the first and second values mentioned above. It stands to reason that persons would come to value group membership and the lifestyles of the members when members are the recipients of substantial rewards because of their membership and the lifestyles to which they adhere. In the modern capitalist era, Weber argues that professional status groups control disproportionate amounts of social wealth by monopolizing highly valued positions in the labor market (R. Collins 1986). Because their skills' monopolies are supposed to be reflected in their higher salaries, status seekers like the twenty-eight-year-old Andrea become frustrated when the coveted rewards for status group membership do not follow inclusion. In her statement below, she expresses this frustration with respect to her current job at a local utilities company.

I think, ah, race has been—it can work for you or against you. As far as I can tell, people have always had fairly low expectations for me in this particular organization, and so I do average stuff, and they think it's great because they weren't expecting that I could do average stuff. At the same time, I'm not given the opportunity to do some of the things that my counterparts that are white and male, particularly white and male, are given the opportunity to do . . . I should say [the organization] is white male dominated of course at the executive level. Uh, and . . . I wouldn't hesitate to say that the majority of the lower level employees are African American. And as a result, I think African Americans tend to be viewed as lower level employees regardless of their position in the company . . . While I like the work that I'm doing, I continue to be very cynical about corporate America . . . If I had an opportunity to advance in the line of work that I'm in, I probably would like to stay there, but I don't see an opportunity for me there. My boss is a white male, and while I very much like him . . . he is the golden child and there isn't going to be too much opportunity to shine because . . . whatever work comes out of our department is going to be credited to him . . . I really see wanting to run a business for myself . . . I call the shots, or well, the economy calls the shots. The quality of my product or the quality of my service and the work that I put in determines how well I succeed. It's not determined by who likes me . . . and not what somebody thinks of my personality who's interacted with me. It's not some executive who says, "Oh yeah, she's got on open-toed shoes again, she'll never be an executive. And it's not based on, "Well, yeah, but I'm sure her supervisor played a hand in that . . ." It's my work. It's my responsibility.

Andrea's statement is about her dissatisfaction with the relatively low level of rewards that she is receiving. She argues that the credentials and work activities that granted her entry into her information science career (in other words, group membership) should translate into the opportunity to be rewarded with career advancement and increased income. In addition, she makes the point that in her work environment, lifestyle evaluation (for example, a judgment about the shoes one wears) is a legitimate (if unofficial) basis upon which to exclude people from these rewards. Her statement thereby shows an understanding of how each of the seeker values are connected, one to another, even as it asserts that race and gender negatively affect black and/or female seekers' attempts to achieve these three tiers of valued ends

Although the reverse is true with escape artists and recruits, status seekers' experiences are less salient and more diffuse than their values. These women have become acquainted with the career status groups and with the associated lifestyles and rewards by a number of methods, including parental guidance, media observation, school or other academic program guidance, and other social interactions in which members of elite groups can "advertise" their status, lifestyles, and rewards and can convince the subjects that these things are possible for them as well. Sampled women were typed as status seekers because they have taken the sum total of these experiences and internalized the desire for high-status group membership as well as the valuation of the lifestyle demands and rewards. They therefore articulated their youthful desires for the college degree more clearly than the other types of women I encountered, and they behaved as if the economy ruled. These are the girls who became degreed black women because their experiences in the context of socializing institutions (for example, families, schools, and mass media) served to make present training opportunities and future economic roles both attractive and salient to their long- and short-term interests. Furthermore, they are by and large convinced, in much the same way as Bourdieu (Bourdieu 1977a, 1977b, 1984; Bourdieu and Passeron 1977/1990) has described, that the training, culture, and work activities of educated elites are more valuable, more esteem-worthy, and more important than those of individuals who end up at the lower end of labor hierarchies.

This convincing, and the consequent valuation of elite professional status groups, happens by both demonstration and invitation; for Imani, Ashley, and Andrea are not simply dazzled by the lights of medical pathologists, lawyers, and journalists "as seen on TV." Instead, it is as if they come to value the economic roles and rewards even as they understand these statuses, lifestyle demands, and incomes to be within their grasp. Thus Imani speaks about being a part of the academic elite of what was understood to be a "ghetto" school—a place where black people like her are included in the group that excels in academics. Ashley too is convinced of the value of emulating the lifestyle of the briefcase-carrying urbanites only after being afforded the opportunity to leave her small-town home and exist among black people, in particular, engaging in these behaviors. And Andrea's thinly veiled cynicism about the importance of close-toed shoes at her corporate headquarters exists within a confession that she is actually marginalized or not fully included in this status career—that her race and gender actually constrain her opportunities to strive for full membership and appropriate rewards at this company. In this description of the how and why of the emergence of elite status seeking, Andrea's complaints thus form a negative case. Without experiences indicating that the potential exists for genuine inclusion, individuals like Imani, Ashley, and Andrea would have likely developed a disdain for rather than an investment in seeker values.[17]

It is the status seeker's salient and specific values and the more diffuse experiences structuring these values that are reflected in the dominant concerns of inequality scholarship. Insofar as stratification scholars and inequality ethnographers worry about whether poor individuals are people who "value" the wrong things and make poor choices or people who are restricted from opportunities by a closed labor market that discriminates, so too do Imani, Ashley, and Andrea show themselves to be the actors depicted in these economic, education, and work-related models of inequality. They value the money and the high moneymakers that drive this cash economy; these values remain at least in part dependent on the perception that opportunities for inclusion in the status group competition are available; and educational and economic action appears to emerge from and be directed toward choices and constraints in this economic status competition. As indicated above, however, this straightforward class-based decision making—this striving for rewards determined by positioning in the relations of economic production—is far from universal. Rather, it describes who some elite black women are and how such economic rationales came to dominate their strategies of action. Below, I describe two other types of women whose degree attainment similarly references economic values and constraints, but who nevertheless emerge from different formative experiences and are guided by different values.

Money Is as Money Appears to Do

As table 2 indicates, I used the "profiler" label eight times. Just two of the fifty-eight women in my interview sample were classified solely with this label. One such woman was Aleah, who was twenty-nine years old when I interviewed her. Her descriptions of her decision making around degree-supporting activities had a certain rhythm, but it was more halting and irregular than Imani's. She would express interest in an activity, attempt to do what was required in order to be allowed to participate in that activity, and then, once involved, stop or change directions, expressing interest in something else. I identified this persistent fluctuation in motivation around education and career development activities as a shallow version of the status-seeking type.

I listened as Aleah discussed the abrupt end to her career as a sales manager despite finding her first job in that field fun and financially rewarding. Beginning as "a manager in training," she had only "one month to get all of this information that [she] needed to have" to take over as manager. She worried that it was too much responsibility too early in her career but pressed on because she believed the district manager, who said that "[she] could do it." She eventually became confident in her ability to do the job, maintaining, "Once I became the manager, I kinda got the hang of it." But then she decided to quit when a disgruntled employee whom she had had to fire "threatened to kill [her]." Notice the back-and-forth, stop-go-then-veer-to-the-left rhythm of her story? Talking to "profilers" or reading their statements in a data file is a bit more difficult than conversation with traditional status seekers. The latter exhibit clear direction and consistency across activities. The former read as lukewarm in their intentions and aims and are more likely to second-guess and/or reverse directions in the narrative. It is more difficult to make an assessment of where profiler plots might be leading or whether and for what reason their details are significant.

Recognizing that the situation with the disgruntled employee was an isolated incident but feeling unsupported by her district manager, Aleah does not just leave her particular job. She goes further—forgoing opportunities to apply for other available jobs in the same field and opting instead to take off time from work and change careers. Initial hesitancy about the opportunity for advancement to the manager position and an abrupt abandonment of the whole enterprise indicate that she was "profiling" rather than intensely interested in such a careerist path through life.

Profilers can fail at being true status seekers in three ways: first, they might possess the conventional status-seeker values but lack the deep attachment to the lifestyles and behaviors associated with those values; second, they could possess the conventional status-seeker values but only briefly or temporarily such that they are only present situationally and not across the long-term life trajectory of decisions and behaviors; and third, profilers might possess some conventional elite status-seeker values but these might exist alongside their value of the status and rewards associated with non-elite groups that they might perceive as faddish. Aleah represents an example of the first and second kind of failures. She has an interest in an elite and financially lucrative career that is unattached to valuation of the high-stress lifestyle demands of that career and that is only of temporary interest to her. At the age of thirty-eight, Niani represents a case of the third. Carrying the label of profiler along with that of the recruit (see above), she does not particularly value the college degree. Instead, she values the high income that is sometimes tied to the college degree and, at the same time, adult status. Below she explains how a desire to be "grown" and to make money led her to a rejection of college attendance after high school. "I graduated—When I graduated from high school, I had this thing that I wanted to be an adult. I wanted to go to work every day and make money and come home with money like grown people do. And I just didn't—I didn't have anybody pushing me to say go to school. My mom really wasn't saying, 'You gotta go to school; you gotta do this.' Um, and so I just didn't go." While Aleah has a commitment to some of the status-seeking values that is short-term and not very deep, Niani, does not, upon graduation from high school, have the values of conventional status seekers. The persons she profiled at this time were independent, working adults. College matriculation would have meant that she would have to postpone this association with adulthood.

Profilers' more superficial version of status-seeker values appears to be generated overwhelmingly in families and households where parents or primary caregivers were not members of the educated elite. Their preferences and aspirations seemed to emerge in experiences and settings that convey more information and appeal about the rewards than about the lifestyles, behaviors, and requirements associated with the status groups of educated elites. Thus despite being "pulled" by the bright lights and big dollars often associated with educated professionals, profilers appear both uninformed about and in many cases disinterested in many of the things traditionally associated with elite group status seeking.[18]

Love of Money Is the Root of All Evil

Status seekers and profilers both appear to love money and the esteem that high incomes buy. Profilers might love some of the associated lifestyle demands less than the status seekers do, and status seekers may be more exclusively focused on the educationally credentialed professional status group than are profilers, but they share an interest in money and esteem. While my "insurgents" are like status seekers and profilers in terms of their acknowledgment of and willingness to play at least some of the rules of the status-seeking game, the "pull" of economic reward does not loom as largely for them as it does for profilers and status seekers. Rather, they want to tear down and rebuild the traditional system of status attainment and reward. They want to be members of a different group in a different system whose precise characteristics are not yet realized.

Appearing just five times on my list of labels (see table 2), insurgents are women in a state of rebellion against the values, lifestyles, and even the associated rewards of the people who surround them. Some discuss never feeling at home in their families, not in the same way as escape artists who point to the negative treatment that they received, but with a focus on their desire for completely different ends and ways of being than their parents wanted for them or than their siblings desired for themselves. Others discussed disappointment with the type of education that they were receiving and maintained that they believed other things than the things that were being taught were what were important and necessary. All of them have general problems with the way in which the society as a whole is set up and/or the way individuals engage with social institutions. Their degree-attainment activities are motivated by their explicit valuation of social systems that would ensure more egalitarian relations between individuals, a more equitable distribution of social wealth and well-being, and less individual preoccupation with work roles, earning money, and consumption.

Like Merton's rebels, insurgents behave in ways that reflect their desire to be both included in and in the process of changing status groups: they wish to rebel against and at times restructure social institutions. It is not simply that they often disobey their parents, but the point of their activity is to disobey their parents, not to have fun or to take an easier route to some other end. Furthermore, unlike escape artists who desire to be far away from the people or situations that they find problematic, insurgents maintain engagement with the sources of offense, sometimes because they believe they can effect change and sometimes to make their voices of discontent heard, but it is essentially this engagement that indicates that rebelling rather than running away like an escape artist is their goal.

At the age of thirty-seven, Randi described an engagement with school that was clearly linked to a palpable resistance to the dominant culture in her elementary and higher educational settings:

And when I was six, my parents got divorced, and I moved with my mother and my sister back to Evanston. And, um, my mother decided that she wanted to live in a white neighborhood, so I grew up in a white neighborhood . . . Probably at the time, we were one of three black families in my neighborhood . . . And, um, I had, um—I think one thing that's very important about my childhood is that . . . my early childhood coincided with the civil rights movement and the black power

movement, and those were things that had an incredible effect on me
. . . I mean somehow it's very related to the fact that I wound up as neglected by my parents and had sort of issues about my own self-esteem
. . . So when I was a little girl, I was really into the Black Panther Party,
and I had a junior "Black Panther" party in my basement and a lot of
those junior "Black Panthers" were white. [Laughter] But anyway, and
I was very, very political. I didn't say the Pledge of Allegiance, and, um,
that was very controversial in my school—but not so [controversial],
because of all those liberal white folks, and they were like "Okay. She's
cool."

By college, Randi's unwillingness to say the Pledge of Allegiance had
turned into an interaction with school that was almost entirely predicated on political resistance in whatever form it might take. She does not
desire to be elsewhere and is in fact happy to be in a setting where her
role is to be against the majority culture and to tell "the system" what
it is doing wrong. She continues describing her educational experiences
below, saying,

Anyway, so, I get accepted to these colleges, I go to Harvard . . . So I go
to Harvard, and, um, and I immediately got into politics, and I became
a socialist and I was coordinator of the Anti-Apartheid Coalition, and
I was all over the Feminist Alliance and, um, I had founded this organization—Students in Community—so we could advocate and organize
the homeless—I haven't thought of that in a long time, had a ball, so
much so that I didn't go to class much, but I was havin' a good time . . .

Randi's insurgence reflects both a rejection of and dissatisfaction with the
system of status and reward and an engagement within and around that
system to try to restructure it from within. This peculiar type of status
seeking—one that submits to the requirements and lifestyle demands of
elite group membership on the one hand and that questions the very system to which they have submitted on the other hand—is what I call "insurgence." Since their longings and desires are as deep as those of seekers
but the object of their desires opposes those of status seekers, they are
essentially inverted status seekers.

The experiences that inform insurgent values all have to do with the
possession of minority status and viewpoints within social arenas. As

Randi's discussion of life in a white neighborhood and a white school makes clear, elite parents and school officials, as well as the gatekeepers of the most exclusive social spaces, seem to create insurgents out of some of their least accommodating citizens. By creating conditions for the inclusion of minority viewpoints—conditions that require that complaints, exceptions, and reorganizations be filed in certain ways and lodged by persons with appropriate credentials and experience, they encourage individuals who might otherwise abandon the whole project of capitalist striving to find some of their interests met in these spaces. Thus, while Randi wanted to live in a black neighborhood and act out her understanding of a more radical black politic, as a child in the home of her "bourgeois integrationist" mother she had to settle for peopling her junior "Black Panther" party with young white "Black Panthers." Her mother gave her the space to act out her opposing viewpoint in the basement of their integrationist home, and so too did her white liberal elementary school allow her to bow out on the Pledge of Allegiance. She was not the only sampled woman to learn, accept, and utilize the lesson that her very inclusion might form the foundation of defiance and revolution.[19]

Where escaping and pleasing revolve around inequality in reproductive relations, *seeking, profiling, and insurgence revolve around women's engagement with inequities in the productive sector.* As Merton's (1957) discussion of the conformist suggests, these women use their relatively high levels of economic opportunity to pursue ends in and around the economic arena. In what appears to be the most common instance this amounts to a kind of class striving—a recognition of the rules of the existing economic hierarchy, a valuation of the rewards promised to the economic winners and losers, and a decision to work within the rules to pursue these most highly valued rewards. But in other instances individuals may not recognize or accept all the rules associated with the competitive game; they may buy into some but not all the social values that accompany elite status seeking, or they may respect the rules only insofar as they create the opportunity to challenge and change the logic and result of the economic hierarchy. Insofar as inequality theory suggests that individuals are people making constrained choices around the economic arena, degreed black women of these three types fit the bill. And yet, their choices remain difficult to predict as their interpretation of their rights to and the ultimate importance of high levels of economic opportunity remain varied.

At the beginning of this chapter, I shared the question that guided my analyses of black women's degree-supporting behavior. I asked why variance in the values and experiences out of which degree-supporting decisions emerge would matter to inequality scholars or to my study of degreed black women's experience with reproductive inequality. And now, having spent this chapter's pages cataloguing these differences, I feel compelled to argue that this variety in motivated action is exactly the point. How do individuals get sorted into their relatively high and low positions in educational and educationally related labor hierarchies? They make decisions to attend or not attend certain types of schools; they decide to heed or not heed the advice of certain teachers; they make up their minds to involve or not involve themselves in para-educational programming that facilitates educational achievement; they attempt or do not attempt to focus their training on credentials toward an attractive career and/or a high-income job; and they do or do not manage to postpone, forgo, or circumvent romantic, racial, or other entanglements that might hinder progress toward educational and professional goals. But how do these decisions get made? On this question, inequality scholarship has largely focused on assessing the degree to which the opportunity to make or not make these kinds of choices is constrained by membership in particular social groups, or by particular social interactions and experiences. But here, attention is given to the neglected question of individuals' motivation to make such choices in the first place. It is these motivations—for example, the values and sets of social relations and experiences from which they emerge—that are varied.

At this point in the history of the sociological investigation of inequality, it seems clear that unequal educational and employment outcomes emerge from situations where individuals with relatively equivalent interest in high-income careers and the associated degree-supporting activities face different sets of structural constraints on their efforts to realize those aims in school and in the labor market. This chapter's analysis adds to this discussion by making another truth apparent: its data show that it is also true that there are differences in individuals' interests in, reasons for, and definitions of degree-supporting activities that lead to high-income careers. Sampled women's decisions indicate that *privilege and deprivation across multiple sets of social relations and inequities in these relations create variance in the types and levels of interest in focusing on degree-supporting and employment activity.* While some degree-supporting activity reflects high labor market aspirations and the relative absence of structural constraints on education and training (that is, status seeking), other instances imply an absence or relative abundance of familial love (escaping and pleasing) and the corporate challenge or individual negotiation of racial stigma (being recruited or avoiding). This variance occurs both across and within individuals as there are seekers and pleasers who make stigma-avoiding decisions as well as profilers who benefit from recruitment, recruits who seek status, and insurgents who feel the need to escape and must do so under strict household guidelines.

This chapter's descriptive work is about giving a name to status seeking and generating the list of precise characteristics that would allow scholars to identify status seekers. It amends prior inequality studies by its actual investigation of the specific experiences, decisions, and actions that create the class categories above those of poor black people or of the black "underclass." It is this analysis that supports this text's examination of whether black, Hispanic, and white women have similar childbearing outcomes to one another and different outcomes from less educated women because of the values that pull individual status-seeking women into making those choices that support career and education. If this hypothesis turns out to be true, such a conclusion would confirm or elaborate upon an already existent trend in inequality research in which school and employment behaviors and outcomes form the center from which unequal experiences in life's multiplicity of arenas emerge.

But this chapter has also been about describing status seeking alongside other combinations of experiences and values. Here its descriptive conclusions suggest that while an in-depth analysis of status seeking may be warranted, the central and at times exclusive role that inequality scholarship gives to money logic and to school and work decision making is unwarranted as even educational and career achievement and inequality emerge from activity around non-economic logics and domains. As is the case with status seeking and other decisions about money, descriptions of decision making that are associated with love and race are also used in this text's arguments about degreed black women's experiences with reproductive inequality. It is an argument that says that inequalities of love emerge from an individual's choices and constraints in multiple sets of institutional relations; it is an argument that illuminates the ways in which inequities across different sets of institutions act in concert or at cross-purposes with one another to create the quantified inequities in outcomes that are typically observed by inequality scholars. The following chapter gives a broad quantitative description of reproductive inequality, including the ways degreed black women's family formation outcomes compare to those of less educated black women and of college-educated white and Hispanic women. It sets the stage for the analyses of the remaining chapters: these discussions make conclusions about whether the varying decision-making logics developed above are relevant in explaining how love inequalities come about.

TWO

Family
Unequal Roads to It

IN THE INTRODUCTION to this book, I called Imani (a thirty-two-year-old financial analyst), Maya (a twenty-seven-year-old social worker), and Renae (a forty-two-year-old dietician) naïve. Or actually, I stated that inequality scholars might find Imani's expectation that she would have many more children to add to her single-daughter family, Maya's surprise that she didn't make it to old age as a childless woman, and Renae's confusion about her daughter's only child status to be naïve. For training as inequality scholars tells us that these women's early life-course beliefs that they would somehow distinguish themselves from other similarly educated women with respect to their life experiences must reflect a certain naïveté.

As discussed across the inequality literature, educational attainment remains one of the more important variables, determining or accounting for differences in occupational status and earnings,[1] and a myriad of other life experiences and outcomes (for example, health and life expectancy,[2] likelihoods of experiencing divorce or incarceration[3]). Indeed, the last twenty-five years has seen a virtual cacophony of noise from racial inequality scholars who argue that, in the post–civil rights climate, race remains an important distinguishing variable for some of these very same life outcomes, since race has been so overshadowed by the importance of education and its associated class status variables.[4] Why would Imani (except for a lack of familiarity with social inequality study) expect a family of five children when most of the other women at her education level and occupational status have one or two? Why should Maya (except for minimal or inadequate sociological training) think that she would be in the very small group of women who complete their reproductive period childless? And why is Renae (unless she missed all of the media's quotable quotes from feminist scholars and journalists on gender in corporate America) so surprised that her decision making around education and career might have implied limits on the eventual size of her family?

Outcome Differences: Class or Race

In this chapter, I have taken the time (and the data from the National Survey of Family Growth [NCHS 1995]) to show how the single-daughter families of Imani, Maya, and Renae have come to be heralded as evidence of a certain racial "equality" across middle-class individuals, regardless of their respectively impatient, surprised, or disappointed feelings about this small family size. I also join the cacophony of race scholars who scream about racial inequality still mattering, as I discuss findings of analyses that show differences in the underlying family formation patterns that lead to this racial "equality" in childbearing. Together these statistical descriptions of college-educated women's similarity in outcomes but difference in processes that lead to these outcomes argue against the idea that the childbearing decisions of college-educated women are based solely or mostly in their choices and constraints around degree attainment or professional status seeking. Educational aspirations, professional encumbrances, and a gendered relationship between work and family do not motivate or enforce a choice to limit family size in the straightforward manner suggested by the apparent prevalence of single-daughter (and single-son) families across the category of black, Hispanic, and white women with college degrees. Rather, the class and non-class variance in degreed women's discrete actions around marriage and marital and nonmarital childbearing points toward both racial inequalities in romantic

love relationships and an intersection between racial and class-based experiences as causal factors in the varied decisions that degreed women
make that lead to these similar fertility outcomes.[5]

Classy Fertility

In the world of instructional resources for demography, "classy fertility" might work as a kind of catchall phrase, or shorthand, for the explanation of differences between high- and low-status women's family size
in economic terms. The strategy of "classy fertility" would describe the
way middle- and upper-class women, as well as upwardly mobile women,
delay or forgo having children as they pursue educational and work-
related goals.[6] Then again, demography textbooks might note that families from poorer, less industrialized nations did not participate in "classy
fertility" since they needed many children to work on family farms or to
act as caretakers for elderly parents in their mostly agricultural economies and in their nations without social security programs.[7] Furthermore,
there are a plethora of scholarly arguments about the limited educational
and income achievements of poor women who have multiple children
in their teens and early twenties—arguments that explicitly claim or implicitly suggest that if such women's fertility pattern was "classier," then
they might improve their chances of completing high school and living
above the poverty line.[8] In sum, "classy fertility" can effectively serve as an
appropriate label for all those instructional moments when demographers
share and explain why they consistently find that high-status women have
fewer children than low-status women. For this discussion of the economic reasons for this finding emerges across studies that discuss the relationship between national fertility levels and the relative prosperity of
nations[9] and those that compare individual women or groups of women
within a single nation across educational or socioeconomic status hierarchies.[10]

This book has some use for the concept of "classy fertility" since its
analyses do contain evidence that the decision making of degreed women
around childbearing is based on class. For example, table 3, which is based
on the National Survey of Family Growth (NSFG [NCHS 1995]) data, shows
that women with higher education levels have fewer children on average
than women who did not complete high school or even than those who
have high-school diplomas or GED certificates. The table further under-

Table 3. Mean parity (number of live births) of women by age and education level

AGE OF WOMEN	NON-HISPANIC BLACK			NON-HISPANIC WHITE			HISPANIC		
	LESS THAN HIGH SCHOOL	HIGH SCHOOL DIPLOMA	COLLEGE DEGREE	LESS THAN HIGH SCHOOL	HIGH SCHOOL DIPLOMA	COLLEGE DEGREE	LESS THAN HIGH SCHOOL	HIGH SCHOOL DIPLOMA	COLLEGE DEGREE
Under 20	.23‡	.39‡	n/a	.06**	.09**	n/a	.20	.11*	n/a
20 to 24	1.92	.80‡	.08	1.61	.41**	.06	1.62	.71†	.44
25 to 29	2.83‡	1.54‡	.55	2.11**	1.16**	.33	2.59	1.35	.78†
30 to 34	2.74†	1.77	.95	2.17*	1.67	.99	3.00‡	2.06‡	1.36
35 to 39	2.69	2.12†	1.43	2.43	1.90*	1.49	3.15‡	2.20‡	1.57
40 to 44	2.88	2.20†	1.53	2.56	1.94*	1.63	3.37†	2.14	1.83

Source: Data for the above calculations are taken from reproductive histories of women sampled by the NSFG (NCHS 1995).

Notes: * T-test on the difference between the average number of live births in this race-education group and the average number of live births among non-Hispanic black women at this education level indicates that the difference is statistically significant at the .05 level.
** T-test on the difference between the average number of live births in this race-education group and the average number of live births among non-Hispanic black women at this education level indicates that the difference is statistically significant at the .01 level.
† T-test on the difference between the mean parity in this race-education group and that of non-Hispanic white women at this education level indicates that this difference is statistically significant at the .05 level.
‡ T-test on the difference between the mean parity in this race-education group and that of non-Hispanic white women at this education level indicates that this difference is statistically significant at the .01 level.

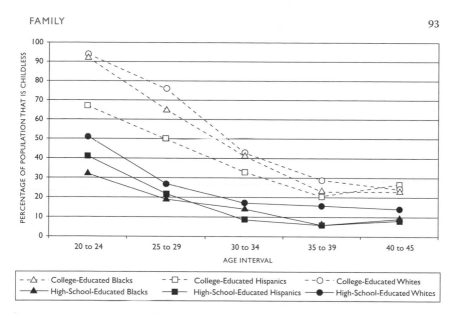

1 Percentage of the population that is childless among college-educated and high-school-educated (no college) black, Hispanic, and white women. Cross-sectional data are taken from the NSFG (NCHS 1995). Calculations from data are listed in table A1.

scores this point by showing that these class differences in average fertility are larger than the differences in average fertility across racial groups. In table 3 the differences between degreed black, Hispanic, and white women's completed fertility (fertility in the forty to forty-five age group) are small (less than 0.33 of a birth) and statistically insignificant. At the same time, college-educated white women have 0.9 fewer children than whites with no diploma; and degreed black and Hispanic women differ from the women with no diplomas in their respective groups by at least 1 birth, on average.

Evidence for the "classy fertility" story can also be found in this book's investigation of the incidence of childlessness. Trends in childlessness show that in each racial group, women with college degrees are more likely to have postponed (or completely forgone) children than those who stopped schooling or educational training with the high-school diploma or GED. As indicated in figure 1, fewer than 20 percent of the group of high-school-educated women aged thirty to thirty-four remain childless, while more than 30 percent of degreed Hispanic women and more than 40 percent of degreed white and black women have yet to have a single child. Although degreed women's rates of childlessness fall during their late thirties—during a time when the logic of "classy fertility" indicates that even the most high-achieving women have completed their education and early professional development activities—roughly 25 percent of the degreed women in each of the three racial groups remain childless at the end of the reproductive period (compared with approximately 15 percent of high-school-educated white women and fewer than 10 percent of high-school-educated black and Hispanic women).[11]

Finally, the appropriateness of the "classy fertility" label to the findings of this book's study is underscored in discussions of the types of decisions that black women made with respect to the achievement of the college degree. In the last chapter, I showed that a significant portion of women (some 30 percent of my convenience sample of college-educated black women in which Imani, Maya, and Renae are all included) made particular degree-attainment decisions because they were impressed by and wanted to attain or retain the status and rewards of college-educated professionals. These "status-seeking" decisions covered a varied set of situations and opportunities, including where one should attend high school, whether one should get rid of a factory-worker boyfriend, and how appropriate open-toed shoes are at work. I argued, more specifically, that these women's "status-seeking" activities signaled women's experience of opportunities for middle-class attainment and their valuation of the incomes and lifestyles of educated elites. As such, their similarly low childbearing outcomes (as well as their fertility similarity with other groups of educated elites) might also be governed by an interest in emulating the family formation behaviors of educated elites.

But despite this book's claims about a racial equivalence in middle-class childbearing levels, despite its evidence of similarities across race in middle-class women's likelihood of postponing childbearing, and despite its report on the status-seeking motivations that surround many of degreed black women's decision-making moments, I stop short of locating this book completely in the "classy fertility" tradition. Rather, I argue that using the "classy fertility" logic to understand degreed black women's low fertility or even the apparent racial "equality" in childbearing when it comes to middle-class women would be a mistake.[12] This book contains both quantitative and qualitative analyses in which class and class-based decision making fail to explain women's experiences and outcomes. The remainder of this chapter discusses quantitative evidence from the NSFG (NCHS 1995), which is inconsistent with the "classy fertility" story.

Races to the Altar

Scholars have frequently called attention to the low incidence of marriage in the black community[13] and argued about whether this too is a class problem—that is, about whether the trend is created by the large number of poor black people who may be unable to marry for reasons related to their poverty.[14] But here, in this book, my focus on middle-class black women's experiences illuminates the point that marital opportunities and choices are highly related to African Americans' racial status rather than their class status. It is with the NSFG (NCHS 1995) data on marriage that I challenge the "classy fertility" logic discussed above—a logic that suggests that opportunities and choices in love correspond to opportunities and choices in money. The same NSFG (NCHS 1995) data that indicate that Imani's, Maya's, and Renae's single-daughter families are just classy enough (or small enough) to make them appropriate representatives of the American middle class, regardless of their black racial status, also show us that when it comes to marriage behavior, degreed black women represent their racial rather than class group. In addition to demonstrating that these women's marriage behavior is more related to racial than class variables, the data likewise suggest that there is no such thing as "classy marriage" (or that few marital experience differences between groups appear to be based in differences in economic or education levels).

Below, figure 2 describes racial differences in the proportions of "currently unmarried" and "never married" women during six age intervals. It shows that black women are considerably less likely to be married than either Hispanic or white women: at no point during the reproductive years are fewer than 50 percent of black women unmarried; more than 60 percent of black women in all but the final age interval are unmarried. This is in stark contrast to Hispanic and white women, who spend all but the teenaged and early twenties age intervals with fewer than 50 percent of their populations unmarried.

This large percentage of black women who are unmarried at particular ages is related both to the high number of women who have never mar-

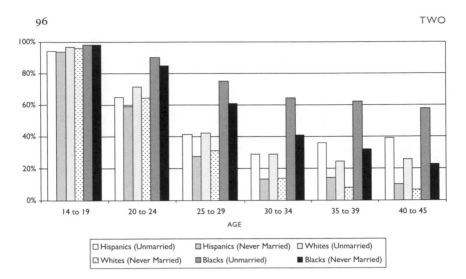

2   Percentage of unmarried and never married Hispanic, white, and black women. Cross-sectional data are taken from the NSFG (NCHS 1995). Calculations from data and significance tests on racial differences are listed in table A2.

ried (notice in figure 2 the slow decline in the height of the black bars, representing never married black women) and to the high rates of marital dissolution that is not followed by remarriage during later age intervals (represented by the increasing distance between the bars representing the "currently unmarried" and the "never married" categories of black women).[15] Black women are isolated in their experience of a relatively slow pace to first marriage, but their high rates of separation without remarriage resemble a trend observed among Hispanic women in the NSFG (NCHS 1995).[16]

Figure 3 compares marital experience by race and education level. It demonstrates that white women, regardless of educational level, spend the greatest part of the reproductive period married (the picture suggests at or about 40 percent), while Hispanic women spend at least 30 percent of the reproductive period married and black women at all but the lowest education level spend just 25 percent of the reproductive period married.[17]

It is upon examination of figures 2 and 3 that it becomes clear that there is no such thing as "classy marriage." While some class differences in marriage exist, they pale in comparison to racial differences. Figures 2 and 3 demonstrate that the general marriage picture for white women is one of advantage: they have the greatest likelihood of being married and

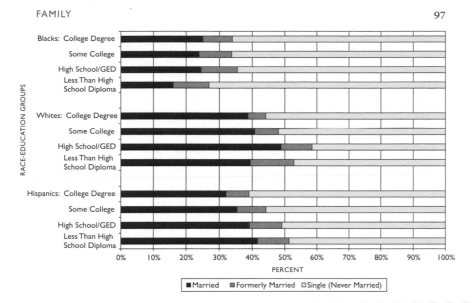

3   Percentage of race-education groups' reproductive years lived at married, formerly married
     (separated, divorced, widowed), and single (never married) statuses. Life-course data are taken
     from the NSFG (NCHS 1995). Calculations from data used to produce this graph are listed in
     table A3.

spend the greatest portion of the reproductive period married; in this regard, the only apparent class difference is that white women who earn
just the high-school diploma and have no post-high-school training or
college seem to be more advantaged than other white women. For black
women, in contrast, the pictures indicate marital disadvantage: they have
the lowest likelihood of ever marrying and spend the lowest portion of
their reproductive years married; in this regard, the single class difference
is that black women without high-school diplomas are at a greater disadvantage than other black women. And Hispanic women fall in the middle:
they appear almost as likely to marry as white women, but because of
marital dissolution that is not followed by remarriage, they spend a lower
portion of the reproductive period married than white women; class differences among Hispanics show slight declines in the time spent married
as education level increases.[18]

    Despite the small but observable class differences, the above analyses
tell a race-based rather than class-based story of marriage. They argue
against the use of money to explain love outcomes, and instead maintain
that understanding reproductive inequalities requires that more atten-

SOCIAL VARIABLES	PROXIMATE DETERMINANTS	FAMILY FORMATION VARIABLES
School Class Work Race Power Age Marriage	Marriage Sex Contraception Abortion	Nonmarital Childbearing Marriage Marital Childbearing

4   Influence of social variables on fertility through proximate determinants.

tion be given to race-based experiences. The data on racial differences in marriage challenge the "classy fertility" logic of love outcomes in two ways. First, they point to the fact that women's productive capacities and behaviors are not in all cases easily connected to family formation outcomes: education or gross national product per capita may appear to explain why some women have fewer children than others but give us little information on why some women are highly likely to marry or to divorce and remarry while others spend large portions of their reproductive years as singles. Second, the data on the large racial differences among middle-class women in the chances of marrying and in the average time spent married suggest that the racial similarity in college-educated women's achieved fertility (one means of family formation) is disconnected from their marriage experiences (another means of family formation).

In this book's introduction, marriage was included in a list of proximate determinants to fertility, or a list of the routes women take to achieve their fertility outcomes. Thus marriage is both a means to and an end of family formation. Figure 4 above provides a visual depiction of the relationship of proximate determinant means to family formation ends.[19] *Given marriage's status as a proximate determinant, the racial inequality in degreed women's experience with it suggests that white, Hispanic, and black women are taking different routes to their small families.* White and Hispanic women may use or count on marriage to achieve these families while black women attain small families despite their lack of marital experience. Differences across race in the ways low fertility is achieved suggest that there are racial differences in decision making in the reproductive arena. These differences therefore conflict with an understanding of middle-class black, Hispanic, and white women as participants in some singular logic that we might in turn name "classy fertility," and they conflict with a logic that says that opportunities in the arena of money directly translate into opportunities in the arena of love. Below, analyses of race and class differences in the relationship between marriage experience and childbearing continue to challenge the idea that this singular logic (rather than varied constraints and choices in the reproductive arena) creates the apparent racial "equality" in middle-class childbearing observed above.

Process Differences: Decisions about Marriage and/or Childbearing

Nonmarital childbearing is not typically understood to be "classy fertility." And this observation exists on two levels. First, in the scholarly community, having a child out of wedlock as well as single parenting (more broadly speaking) have been identified as activities that lead to a whole host of problematic outcomes, including premature exit from schooling, unemployment, welfare dependence, and depressed wages and income.[20] Some studies go so far as to conclude that nonmarital fertility does serious harm to young women's lives, as it—in and of itself—compromises their ability to mitigate or escape the materially disadvantaged circumstances of their childhoods.[21] In this sense, the empirical evidence and theoretical claims made in the academic literature make the point that women in the higher and lower classes may be differentiated from one another with respect both to the type of childbearing that they do and to the number of children that they have. Whether having children out of wedlock is a cause or consequence of lower-class status, the fact that nonmarital childbearing and single parenting are empirically and theoretically associated with lower-class outcomes in much of the academic literature makes it impossible to place these behaviors in the category of "classy fertility."

Second, the association between single parenting and low status in both class and racial hierarchies also exists beyond the bounds of academia, in forums as diverse as policymakers' chambers and think tanks, television sitcoms and talk shows, and everyday conversations in college classrooms, at church board meetings, and around family dinner tables. In these circles (as well as, to be honest, in some academic books and articles), the discussion of nonmarital fertility and the associated socioeconomic consequences has taken on a more moral tone. Women who "choose" to get pregnant and to have and raise children out of wedlock are here framed as people who either knowingly or unknowingly (and therefore unthinkingly) get into situations that they cannot handle without financial or in-kind support from parents and extended kin, charitable organizations, or the state. Whether they were conscious or unconscious of their likely or eventual dependence, their decisions and behaviors are thusly called irresponsible, selfish, and immoral. It would be inappropriate to label behavior so morally denigrated as "classy" as such labeling ignores the positive evaluation of elite styles and behaviors that the word "classy" carries.

Now despite its rather notorious reputation, nonmarital fertility (like marital fertility) is simply a method or a strategy of achieving the childbearing outcomes observed above. And substantial research exists that maintains that it is not a strategy that middle-class women (or at least those who aspire to the middle class) use with great frequency. If the racial equality in college-educated women's childbearing outcomes can be explained by a "classy fertility" logic or—put another way—if it can be explained by some class-based decision-making process that operates across races, we would expect that rates of nonmarital childbearing would also be low across the three racial categories of degreed women. And indeed, the nonmarital childbearing rates of college-educated Hispanic and white women are low relative to women with less education, but this class difference does not exist to the same degree among black women.

The Only Game in Town

Given the data on marriage in the black community specified in this text and elsewhere, nonmarital fertility might more appropriately be called "the only game in town fertility." For in any setting where marriage rates are low and babies are still desired, nonmarital childbearing becomes the only game in town. Similarly, restricting the pregnancy and birth experience to only those black women who marry would mean that fertility in the black community would drop precipitously. This is shown most clearly in demographic investigations that find that recent increases in the fraction of births to unmarried black women are mostly due to increases in the fraction of women who are single throughout their late teens, twenties, and thirties rather than to significant increases in the percentage of single black women who choose to have a baby.[22] Although some church pastors and political commentators are astonished that a clear majority of black children (roughly two-thirds) are now born to unmarried women,[23] demographers who monitor these trends have surely recognized that it is unlikely that African Americans would have continued to replace their population from one generation to the next had this era's declines in marriage been accompanied by no change in the average black woman's willingness to have a child while unmarried.[24]

To the extent that nonmarital fertility is "the only game in town fertility" for relatively high fractions of women in the African American community and for periods that occupy long durations of their reproductive years, their response to this state of affairs will heavily influence both the number of children born to black women and the fraction of these births that are nonmarital. Women who respond by waiting indefinitely for marriage in order to have children (that is, those who depend on the proximate determinant of marriage to reach their family formation goals) will decrease the number of black births and, at the same time, help to keep the fraction of nonmarital births in the black population low. In contrast, women who respond to late marriage and few reproductive years spent married by having children out of wedlock will increase black births even as they also raise the fraction of nonmarital births among African Americans.

The correspondence between the following figure on percentages of births to married, formerly married (that is, separated, divorced, or widowed), and single (never married) women (figure 5) and the earlier figure on percentages of women's reproductive years spent married, formerly married, and single (figure 3) suggests that at least some of the black women respond to marriage challenge by having children out of wedlock and that at least some of the nonmarital fertility that we observe among African Americans is the "only game in town fertility." Or, in other words, the African American response to being the group that has the least experience with the proximate determinant of marriage has been to become the group most likely to experience an out-of-wedlock birth. Figure 5 demonstrates that a clear majority of Hispanic and white births occurred within marriage, while black nonmarital births are more common than births within marriage in every education level category but the college-educated one. Unmarried black women have not allowed Hispanic and white dominance in the marital arena to sideline them in the pregnancy and childbearing game. Insofar as nonmarital fertility has become

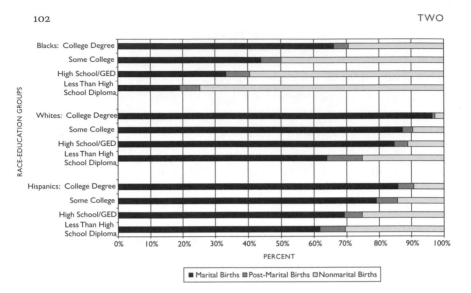

5   Percentage of race-education groups' total births that are marital, post-marital (separated, divorced, or widowed women), and nonmarital (never-married single women) births. Reproductive history data are taken from the NSFG (NCHS 1995). Calculations from data used to produce this graph are listed in table A4.

the only game in town, a significant portion of single black women have depended upon this out-of-wedlock childbearing to form families and to reach the fertility levels identified in this chapter's table 3. Although degreed black women have a lower fraction of nonmarital births than other African Americans, they appear significantly more dependent on nonmarital childbearing (almost 30 percent of their births) than degreed Hispanic and white women (almost 10 percent and under 2 percent, respectively) in the achievement of their "classy fertility" outcomes.

Thus, examination of figure 5 alongside figure 3 illustrates three things. First, in demonstrating that African Americans are most often single and have the highest percentages of nonmarital births, these analyses provide some clue about the way low marriage rates limit group reproductive options and, concomitantly, point out the significance of time spent single for out-of-wedlock childbearing. Second, figure 5's illustration of how much more dependent degreed black women are on nonmarital child-bearing than degreed Hispanic and white women for the achievement of their "classy fertility" outcomes acts as further evidence against the idea that these similar fertility levels reflect a racial "equality" in degreed women's family formation experiences, choices, and constraints. But the comparison of figure 5 and figure 3 permits a third observation as well. This observation makes room for a class argument alongside the racial arguments made above.

A class story about nonmarital fertility also emerges from comparisons of the graphical depictions of groups' marriage (figure 3) and nonmarital childbearing experiences (figure 5). This class story begins with the transformation of equivalent percentages of reproductive years spent single by all but the lowest education level group among black women in figure 3 into quite different percentages of nonmarital births in figure 5 (almost 30 percent for degreed black women, about 50 percent for black women with some college but no degree, and almost 60 percent for black women with high-school diplomas and no post-graduate training). Why, the pictures ask, do the different education groups have such different fertility responses to the same low marriage rate challenge?

The class story ends with the observation that the percentage of births to single women goes down as education level increases in each of the three racial groups depicted in figure 5. Since these class trends were not so evident in the graphical representations of the time spent married, separated or divorced, and single (see figure 3, one more time, and note that in no racial group case do the black marriage lines get steadily shorter as one reads down from college degree, to some college, to high school diploma, to no high school diploma in the way that they do in Figure 5), it is unlikely that the percentage of nonmarital births can be understood as some straightforward reflection of the amount of time women in a group spend single. Instead, there appear to be class differences in single women's decision making about childbearing. Thus *racial status seems to have an effect on the degree to which nonmarital fertility can be described as "the only game in town," but single women's sexual and reproductive decision making with respect to nonmarital fertility is also somehow tied to educational achievement and/or class-based experiences* in each of these racial groups.

It might be helpful at this point to shift attention from Imani, Maya, and Renae and their dissatisfaction with their single-daughter families back to Wanda (the thirty-four-year-old underpaid Christian elementary school teacher who was also discussed in the introduction). It was Wanda's virginal, never married, and childless status that I used to illuminate the importance of studying inequality in the reproductive arena as opposed to the productive arena. And it is the connections between her virginal, never married, and childless statuses that I exploit here in order to explain the significance of different experiences with the proximate determinant of marriage and different reproductive responses to these experiences in the creation of childbearing outcomes.

Wanda's lackluster experience with the proximate determinant of marriage means that, for her, nonmarital fertility is "the only game in town fertility." Her virginal response to her lackluster experience with this proximate determinant of marriage (or, in another formulation, the influence of the marital status social variable on her experience with the proximate determinant of sex) ultimately means that her childbearing outcome is nil. While work in chapters 4, 5, and 6 more fully explores the reasons why women like Wanda end up sitting on the sidelines during the only game in town, below I present NSFG (NCHS 1995) analyses that point to important connections between race, class, and women's nonmarital fertility behavior. I do this to provide further evidence of the point that nonmarital fertility is a site of difference implicated in degreed black, Hispanic, and white women's achievement of their apparently similar "classy fertility" outcomes.

Sitting on the Sidelines

I maintained in the introduction that Wanda's inability to turn her educational credentials into a husband changed the meaning of sexual activity and childbearing for her: outside of the marriage context, these became sins to be resisted rather than reproductive arena goods to be enjoyed. At the age of thirty-four, Wanda is involved in making decisions about whether to have sex outside of marriage, whether to try to adopt a child, and whether to work harder on developing Justice, her sometimes friend, sometimes romantic date, into a more committed relationship. These are necessarily different from the decisions being made by a married thirty-four-year-old woman, even if she too has earned her bachelor's degree and the two women work at the same office, in the same job. While the women's educational achievements and current earnings may have important effects on the shape and size of unfolding families in each case, marital status fundamentally shapes the nature of the sexual and reproductive decisions that each woman must make. Even in cases where these women are making a similar decision, like whether to become a mother, marital status shapes the list of strategic options available for achieving that particular goal. Analyses presented below demonstrate how degreed women in the different racial groups make different decisions and choose from different strategic options even as they distinguish their fertility from that of less educated women in their respective racial groups—or even as they accomplish their relatively low, "classy fertility."

The decomposition analyses below look at whether differences between group fertility rates can be attributed to high-school- and college-educated women's decision making on marriage or their decision making on childbearing. More specifically, they ask whether high-school-educated women end up with more children because they are more likely to get married (and consequently to begin childbearing at the higher rates that married women, regardless of race or class status, tend to do) than college-educated women or because they were more likely to make the decision to have a child (regardless of whether they were single or married) than college-educated women.

For the analysis depicted in figure 6, I have first separated out the difference between degreed black women's low (or "classy") fertility outcomes and high-school educated black women's high fertility outcomes into differences between fertility rates (or births per woman) at each of six age intervals. This difference, represented by the dark gray bar over or under each of the age groups on the horizontal axis, is largest during the first two age intervals. And these large and negative differences during the early intervals indicate that degreed black women have "classier" fertility than their less educated sisters because their fertility rates are much lower than those of less-educated black women during their teens and early twenties. Furthermore, degreed black women's modestly higher fertility rates at older ages apparently never make up for high-school educated black women's earlier and higher fertility performance.

The second step in the creation of figure 6 was to use decomposition techniques to separate women's marital decisions from their childbearing decisions in the accomplishment of these class differences in fertility. The small size of the white bars that represent differences in marital decision making indicates that degreed black women are not making different decisions about marriage (or getting the opportunity to make different decisions about marriage) than high-school educated black women are.

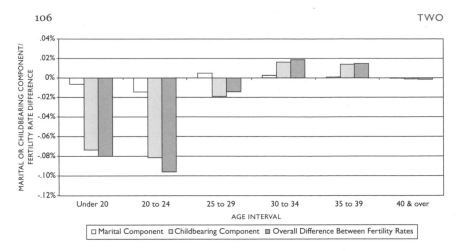

6   Marital and childbearing components of fertility rate differences between college-educated
    black women and black women with only a high-school diploma or GED. Results of
    decomposition analysis based on reproductive history data from the NSFG (NCHS 1995)
    are found in table A5.

Instead, degreed black women achieve their "classy fertility" outcomes
by "sitting on the sidelines" at ages when most black women are still unmarried (see, for example, figure 2) and during a time when a greater fraction of high-school educated black women are deciding to participate in
"the only game in town" (or nonmarital) fertility. And this is why the light
gray bars (representing differences in decisions about childbearing) extend downward and are virtually equivalent to the dark gray fertility difference bars. Black women, regardless of education level, are the most
likely to be single during each of the reproductive age intervals; they are
therefore more likely than Hispanic and white women to be in the position to decide on a nonmarital birth or not. But in addition, figure 6 demonstrates that the decision Wanda makes to sit on the sidelines during
the only game in town is a decision that is more prevalent among degreed
than less educated black women.

    I completed similar decomposition analyses for Hispanic and white
women (see figure 7 below and table A6 and figure A1 in the appendix). Unlike degreed black women, who achieve low fertility by deciding
against nonmarital childbearing during their young adult years, degreed
Hispanic and white women accomplish their "classy fertility" outcomes
and respectively distinguish themselves from less-educated Hispanic and
white women with the decisions that they make about both marriage and

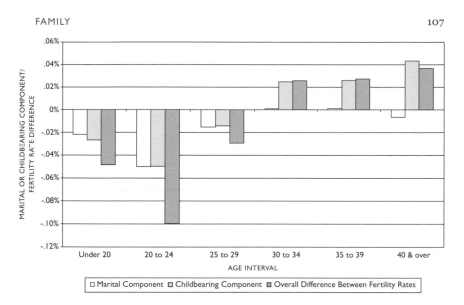

7   Marital and childbearing components of fertility rate differences between college-educated
    Hispanic women and Hispanic women with only a high-school diploma or GED. Results of
    decomposition analysis based on reproductive history data from the NSFG (NCHS 1995) are
    found in table A6.

childbearing. Given Hispanic and white women's higher involvement with
marriage discussed above, it makes sense that marital decision making is
more consequential in the creation of the class differences in fertility that
emerge in these groups than it is with respect to class differences in fertility among black women.

The information in figure 7 is in some ways similar to the results of analyses of class differences among African Americans depicted in figure 6.
In both figures, class differences during the early half of the reproductive period (when the dark gray bars are extending downward) favor the
high-school educated women; and then during the later age intervals, the
college-educated women achieve higher fertility rates. However, the story
that I told about education level differences in the black community needs
to be adjusted in order to fit the Hispanic case. Among Hispanic women,
differences in decision making about marriage (measured here by group
differences in the proportion married) do support high-school educated
women's achievement of higher fertility during their teens and twenties.
College-educated Hispanic women's decisions to postpone marriage during schooling and early work years (that is, under the age of thirty) appar-

ently account for about half of the large differences in fertility rates. This
is why the first two boxes in the series are about the same size and about
half the length of the third box (the one that is dark gray in color and represents the total difference between the two age-specific fertility rates).

The role of marriage in the creation of class differences in fertility
among white women is similar to the role it plays among Hispanic women:
for both groups marriage acts as a resource for forming families and for
having children. The graph of the decomposition of differences between
college- and high-school-educated white women (found in figure A1 in
the appendix) and the story it reveals differs from the Hispanic case only
in degree. Class differences in white fertility rates are slightly larger both
before and after the point at which high-school educated women's rates
cease surpassing degreed women's. And differences in marital decision
making contribute slightly less to these differences than they do among
Hispanic women (about 42 percent and 45 percent in each of the lowest
age intervals). But the overall point remains the same: white and Hispanic women achieve "classy fertility" by more frequent decisions to postpone marriage during their teens and early twenties, and by decisions to
postpone having babies whether single or married during this same time
period.

Those loyal to the "classy fertility" story and to a larger inequality study
tradition in which education, work, and productive arena behavior drives
much of life (including that which happens in the love and family arena)
might look at the decomposition analyses here and conclude that degreed
black women are making the same decisions as degreed white and Hispanic women. After all, degreed black women are also predominantly an
unmarried group of women during the younger age intervals, and they
too resist having children during these younger years to a greater degree
than the less-educated black women to whom they are compared. These
same analysts might conclude that the racial differences in behavior only
exist in the lower classes, and that it is these lower- or working-class black
women who are making the decisions to have children without marrying
who are behaving "differently." However, I believe that the context described by the data on marriage challenges this interpretation.

The NSFG (NCHS 1995) data on marriage mean that the similarities
in the latter halves of figures 6, 7, and A1—where the degreed women
achieve higher fertility rates than their high-school-educated counter-

parts through differences in childbearing rather than marital decision making—cannot be taken as a similarity across race in degreed women's behaviors. When degreed black women are similar to high-school educated black women with respect to marital behavior, it means that they are highly likely to be unmarried—to have never married even—during their thirties. And it means that childbearing differences are achieved in no small part through decisions to participate in "the only game in town fertility." At the same time, when Hispanic and white women are similar to their less-educated counterparts, it is highly likely that they are married. Their achievement of higher fertility rates during these later age intervals tends therefore to be decision making about marital rather than nonmarital childbearing. The similarities in the latter halves of the decomposition graphs (figures 6, 7, and A1 and table A7) are, like the degreed women's similarity in completed fertility levels in table 3, ultimately quite deceptive. For these similarities can only be accomplished if degreed women in each of the three racial groups have marriage behavior that is similar to that of the less-educated women in their racial groups and different marriage behavior from one another. And the similarities can only be accomplished if single degreed black women make different decisions about having a child out of wedlock than single white and Hispanic women with degrees.

Figure 8 underscores the points being made above—points about race and education level differences in decision making on nonmarital childbearing and about racial inequality in the experiences and achievement of "classy fertility." The picture graphs the fraction of black and white women's overall fertility rates that is attributable to nonmarital fertility. It thereby shows how relevant differences in decision making with respect to marriage and nonmarital childbearing are in the achievement of fertility outcomes. In the picture, degreed black women fall in the middle of two distinct patterns of fertility achievement. The one—belonging to high-school educated black women—is characterized by the relative importance of nonmarital childbearing to the achievement of observed fertility levels. In this pattern, virtually all the childbearing that is happening at the beginning of the reproductive period is out-of-wedlock childbearing. The fraction of nonmarital childbearing drops over the course of the reproductive period but remains high—at or near 40 percent in the late twenties and early thirties, and still more than 20 percent of all childbearing in

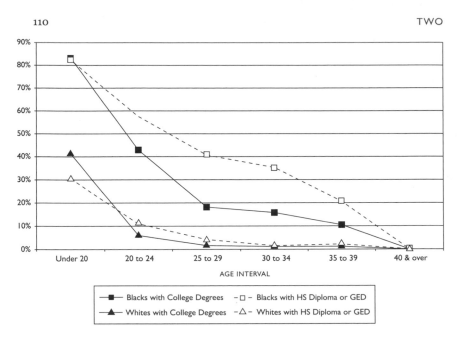

8   Percentage of college- and high school-educated black and white women's fertility rates
     that is attributable to nonmarital fertility. Fertility rates and nonmarital fertility percentages
     are calculated using reproductive history data from the NSFG (NCHS 1995) and are found in
     table A7.

the late thirties. The second pattern—belonging to white women with low
and high educational achievement—is characterized by the relative unim-
portance of nonmarital childbearing. During the teen years, when almost
no one is married, nonmarital childbearing still amounts to less than half
of overall fertility rates for white women, and it plummets to about 10 percent in the early twenties and then to a trivial fraction (under 5 percent)
by the late twenties. *In the midst of these two patterns fall degreed black
women, whose fertility outcomes clearly rely more on women's decisions to
have children while unmarried than white fertility outcomes (regardless
of education level) rely on such decisions, but who nevertheless are less dependent on nonmarital childbearing than are high-school-educated black
women.*

   Unfortunately no neat and tidy answer exists to the question of why
black women's shared experience of marriage (for example, their similarly low marriage rates and their similarly low number of years spent

married) fails to translate into a shared approach to nonmarital child-bearing. The suggestion of the data presented here would be that both race and class matter. On the one hand, racial status appears to structure decision making on marriage such that black women, regardless of education level, spend more of their reproductive years single than Hispanic and white women. On the other hand, education level, or class, is clearly somehow connected to single black, white, and Hispanic women's use of nonmarital childbearing as a resource for family formation; it is most relevant to the least educated women in each of these groups and grows less relevant as education increases. Where African Americans are concerned, this relationship between class and nonmarital childbearing stands for degreed black women's seats on the sidelines while black women without college degrees are deciding, to a greater extent, to have children without marrying.

Where degreed women and their "classy fertility" are concerned, this relationship between class and nonmarital childbearing intersects with a relationship between race and marriage, allowing a somewhat deceptive similarity in degreed women's fertility outcomes to emerge. In reality degreed black, Hispanic, and white women face an unequal set of circumstances and make different decisions in the achievement of these fertility outcomes.

Who Sits, Who Plays, and Other Questions about Difference

In the beginning, this chapter was about Imani's, Maya's, and Renae's naïveté—how they believed that their childbearing outcomes would conform more to their varied youthful expectations than to their similar college-educated status. But it quickly developed into a story about the racial inequalities in degreed women's family formation processes: it became a story about black women's deprivation in marriage, about race and education level differences in nonmarital childbearing, and about degreed black women's lower likelihood of resorting to nonmarital childbearing even in the face of extensive time lived as single women. Thus, in the end, the chapter challenges the notion of Imani's, Maya's, and Renae's naïveté: it suggests that their respective feelings of impatience, surprise, and disappointment with regard to their single-daughter families may be connected to inequities in the way that they experience family formation—to differences in the decisions that they get to make and in the strategic options from which they are allowed to choose—rather than to differences in parity.

This chapter is also about the best way to observe these inequities. For these inequalities of love are not made intelligible by observation of the similarities in Imani's, Maya's, and Renae's single-daughter families or by identification of the fact that their small family size mimics the low fertility of degreed black, Hispanic, and white women in the NSFG (NCHS 1995). (Indeed, studying these similarities leads to "classy fertility" conclusions, including points about single-daughter and single-son families that reflect the privileges and choices of class elites, including theoretical claims about women's postponement of family formation and limitation of family size in order to dedicate time and financial resources to the achievement of middle-class status, and including descriptions of an elite cultural milieu that values small family size.) Instead, these love inequalities become knowable by observing the non-class-based variance in women's family formation processes. These would include the racial differences in marriage, the race- and class-based differences in reliance on nonmarital childbearing, the different sets of decisions and strategic options considered by women of different marital statuses, and even the variance that exists in the decision making of Imani, Maya, Renae, and, of course, Wanda.

The remaining chapters use data on decision making on the proximate determinants of marriage, sex, contraception, and abortion in order to describe and account for the differences in the means by which degreed women achieve their similarly "classy fertility." They use that data to answer some of the more obvious questions raised by the inconsistencies between demographers' "classy fertility logic," inequality scholars' myopic focus on the productive sector, and degreed women's actual decision making on sex, love, and family. Such questions include the question of how the limitations on family size associated with completion of a college degree come to mean postponement of marriage and marital childbearing for white and Hispanic women on the one hand, and a seat on the sidelines of love and family for a disproportionately high share of degreed black women on the other. They also include the question of whether it is okay to interpret Imani's delayed but impatient marital childbearing, Maya's earlier, but unplanned nonmarital childbearing, and Renae's late

but too abruptly ended marital childbearing as variants on the single activity of "status seeking"—that is, as the consequences of decisions they
made about money—or whether one or more of these women's actions
might instead represent decisions they made about something else, like
love or racial constraints. And they include the question of what African
American racial status might have to do with Wanda's virginal, childless,
and single statuses.[25] The task of answering these and other questions begins in the next chapter with a description and analysis of degreed black
women's decisions and experiences in romantic love and the ways their
romantic relationships do and do not culminate in marriage.

THREE

Marriage
"I Do" It When and If I Can

AS WE SAT together on the plush living room couch of her two-bedroom townhouse, Shawn, a thirty-two-year-old speech therapist, gave me the quick and dirty version of the relationship that led up to her marriage. "Make a long story short," she began, "my girlfriend worked with him. She said, 'I want you to meet my girlfriend.' We exchanged phone numbers through her. We called each other in April of 2000. We spoke for three hours. We didn't meet face to face until July of 2000. And we met and haven't been apart since. And we've been married fourteen months, and some days." In this abbreviated reckoning, the journey from singlehood to marriage seems relatively straightforward—direct and painless, even. The opportunity for conversation, fulfilling romance, and eventual marriage present themselves without direct effort from Shawn. She seems to like what is being offered and only has to claim it and make it her own.

However, when Shawn speaks about the beginnings of her relationship with her husband at greater length, the marital outcome does not seem so preordained. At one point she describes her discovery of the mismatch in their feelings:

I did tell him . . . I loved him, even though he didn't tell me until eleven months later, and even though it hurt, I appreciated it . . . I felt as though we shoulda been moving together, and here I am saying, you know, "I love you," and he didn't say anything back, and I'm like, "Huh," you know like, "Hello. Did you just hear what I said?" And he said, "You know that's very nice," or something—I'm like, "What do you mean that's"—You know, I'm not saying this to him, but "What do you mean that's very nice?" But he just wasn't at that point in our relationship. We had been dating what a month—a month and a half. He wasn't at that point to say that very thing . . .

Shawn's words here are a sure sign that what she describes as her "Cinderella wedding" was neither inevitable nor predictable.

This chapter uses degreed black women's descriptions of the ways they have entered, maintained, and exited romantic relationships in order to add the specificity of romantic relationship negotiation to scholarly discussions of black women's race- and class-based disadvantages in marriage. In the analysis of the 202 romantic relationships experienced by the degreed black women whom I interviewed, Shawn's relationship with David was classified as a "dating and rating" relationship—a type of relationship that seems to have a low likelihood of resulting in marriage. I created a typology that describes two basic dimensions of degreed black women's experiences in these relationships. In this typology, "dating and rating" relationships are characterized first by their relatively slow progression to the point of serious commitment and second by the existence of no other goals outside of the romantic ones for the relationship. The first of these characteristics makes these relationships particularly vulnerable to ending without marriage. These dating and rating relationships comprise the largest plurality (40 percent) of relationships experienced by the sampled women.

In theory and in quantitative work on marriage, the details about romantic relationships like Shawn's are never discussed:[1] they are the taken-for-granted means to the marriage or non-marriage end. What we see when we look at this marriage literature are studies that tell us about men who are "unmarriageable" because of their low educational credentials, unstable employment, and histories of or present-day incarceration;[2] we see scholarship that concludes that women choose male spouses for their economic characteristics (for example, educational credentials and incomes) while men focus on women's social characteristics (like religion or race) when making marital decisions;[3] and we see research that argues that individuals who marry have higher health, wealth, and happiness than those who do not.[4] The large majority of this marriage knowledge is based on outcome data—on the demographic characteristics of individuals who are or are not married. Matches between marriageable men and women with the right racial traits or religious beliefs in populations of healthy, wealthy, and happy individuals just seem to happen. Moreover, there is little, if any, explanation of how the individuals find their partners and manage to exclude people who are poor, black, and unhappy from marriage-based partnership.

But in this book, romantic relationships form the "process" or "experience" data that tell us how unequal love outcomes come about. I use data from the beginnings, journeys, and endings of degreed black women's romantic relationships to explain the process through which individuals' romantic experiences lead to marriage or long-term singleness. Thus, the chapter describes degreed black women's romantic journeys: the romantic relationship typology characterizes two basic dimensions of these relationships, including, first, the pace of progression to serious commitment and, second, the presence or absence of non-romantic interactions. In addition, it shows how degreed black women's circumstances and choices influence the experiences and outcomes of these romantic relationships.

The sum total of this chapter's arguments indicates that degreed black women's experience of deprivation in romantic partnership and marriage develops and intensifies over time. I begin by arguing against the construction of a false dichotomy between studious girls who become career women and precocious young women who become involved in romance and family formation at an early age.[5] In this regard, I maintain that degreed black women demonstrate an interest in satisfying romantic relations early in the life course and that educational settings facilitate rather than block young women's romantic activity—two points that contrast with the ways in which women's educational success and school settings are conventionally discussed in inequality literature. Thus, you will not find the conventional gender argument about resistance to romance facilitating black women's career development here.[6] Instead, I illustrate how women's marriage delays are the outcomes associated with an education credentialing process that directs women with a variety of different attitudes about schooling and careers toward similarly "weak" structures of romance, despite interest in marriage.

Next, I focus on describing degreed black women's involvement in "stronger" romances that tend to occur later in life and that do lead to marriage. For reasons that I explain in the chapter, these stronger relationships appear less available to degreed black women than the "weak" romances of their school and early career days. Finally, the chapter focuses on the weak romantic journeys during degreed black women's later reproductive years that once again fail to develop to the point of marriage. Later in the life course, weak romance is structured by an awareness of the scarcity of opportunities for love rather than women's belief in or focus on their expanding futures. In short, data on relationship processes offer a glimpse of the experiences—the choices, the limitations, and the contradictions inherent in the simultaneous pursuit of love and money—that constitute degreed black women's deprivation in marriage.

Where Dating and Status Seeking Meet

Although one woman I interviewed indicated that she had never dated or had a boyfriend by the time of the interview when she was thirty-two years old and another woman reported at the age of thirty-five that she had experienced 8 significant romantic relationships, on average, sampled women reported on 3.8 relationships each. The five types of relationships in the typology that describes these degreed black women's romantic journeys are associated with different rates of progression to marriage and different levels of prevalence in the sample. The exact rates at which I observed the dating and rating relationship and the other four relationship types progressing to marriage are presented in table 4 below.

Brenda's dating and rating relationship with Joey began when the two met through mutual friends in college. Although they did not attend the same school, when friends of hers who knew friends of his took a road trip to his campus for a party, Brenda went along. She ended up exchanging telephone numbers with Joey before the evening was over. And thus began these romantic partners' use of "dates"—or romantic interactions with one another—as tests—or opportunities to "rate" one another as well as the potential of the relationship. This step-by-step decision-making

Table 4. Distribution of relationships and rate of progression to marriage by type

RELATIONSHIP TYPES	% OF MARITAL RELATIONSHIPS (#)	% OF ALL RELATIONSHIPS (#)	RATE OF PROGRESSION TO MARRIAGE
Dating and rating	30.77 (12)	40.36 (90)	13.3
Speedy climax	30.77 (12)	14.35 (32)	37.5
Delayed entry	30.77 (12)	16.14 (36)	33.3
In and out	0 (0)	11.21 (25)	0
Sleeper	7.33 (3)	16.59 (37)	8.1
Unclassified	0 (0)	1.35 (3)	0
Total	99.64 (39)	100 (223)*	17.5

Note: * Although this table classifies the 202 relationships discussed by the qualitative sample of African American interviewees, a few of the relationships in the sample technically fit into more than one of the above categories. This total of 223 reflects the total number of labels used to classify the sample.

process, in which investments in the relationship escalate only after positive "rates" of earlier "dates" and consideration of other options for how one might spend dating time, structures the slow progression to serious commitment in dating and rating relationships and their low likelihood of ending with marriage. In the case of Brenda and Joey, it took Brenda seven months to decide that the "long distance" between their two campuses and her close friend's dislike of Joey outweighed the "fun" they had at "retro clubs" with their group of road-tripping friends. At this point, she ended the relationship.

During our talk in the food court of a suburban mall where we both liked to shop and which was close to where Brenda grew up, this still single twenty-five-year-old would ultimately describe five romantic relationship casualties—all dating and rating relationships. Based on the romances in my sample, dating and rating relationships are highly associated with schooling and other professional development opportunities. This type of relationship predominates early in degreed black women's life trajectories while they are still in school and involved in early career activities. Indeed, many of these relationships begin because women attended the same schools as their future boyfriends or because, as is the case with both Shawn and Brenda above, they were introduced to these men within and through members of their school-based networks.

The lengthy time periods associated with diploma and degree completion in high school and college translate into relatively low pressure on relationships to develop quickly: the sampled women can and do therefore take the time to get to know men in whom they find an initial interest, investing slowly and thinking about the desirability of and potential problems accompanying each romance-intensifying step prior to taking it. Insofar as the continuous attendance at high school and college facilitates these long and precarious journeys to serious romantic commitment, the structuring of romance around dating and rating relationships is intimately bound up with educational credentialing and elite status attainment. This relationship type, its high prevalence within my sample of interviewees, and its weak structure that rarely leads to marriage are products of environments and interactions that support educated elites' status attainment. As the second part of Shawn's opening narrative makes clear, the slow tempo of this type of relationship characterizes romance during degreed black women's early reproductive years even in situations where the women themselves would be inclined to throw caution to the wind for love, lust, and a quick trip down the aisle.

When School Reigns

Dating and rating highlights the errors in magnifying the importance of an inverse relationship between education and family formation. Some authors talk about this inverse relationship by saying that poor and/or working-class women's lack of access to or problems attaining adequate educational training directs them into adult activities at younger ages. These scholars are usually talking about teen childbearing and to a lesser extent, low-wage work.[7] Others discuss this inverse relationship by saying that early family formation activity lowers women's educational achieve-

ments, employment probabilities, occupational statuses, and, consequently, the household incomes in the families that they form.[8] But in
this book, I want to argue against or at least minimize the importance of
this inverse relationship between education and family formation—this
apparent opposition between the achievement of money and the achievement of love—that is present in the scholarly literature. I want to do so
regardless of whether that inverse relationship is discussed as poor young
women's lack of access to and engagement with schooling and their consequent choice to pursue motherhood, or depicted as lower-class black
or Hispanic women's descent into school failure and poverty as a result of
early childbearing. Instead I want to use dating and rating relationships
to make the point that there isn't such a discontinuity between education
and romance as some quantitative analyses of class differences in romantic outcomes (for example, fertility) and some qualitative investigations
of lower-class women's romantic outcomes (for example, fertility) might
indicate. Educational settings come with their own set of romantic relations. And degree-seeking individuals are not completely barred from the
fulfillment of romantic and sexual desires.

It is true that schools facilitate Shawn's and Brenda's achievement of
credentials and training for high-status employment. But it is also true
that schooling indirectly facilitates the early romantic interactions of
these and most other women who were sampled. Schools support romance by collecting and assembling ready supplies of single, same-age,
romantic partners. They do so by removing the potential interference of
parents and other older generation authority figures who may be present
in some student-dominated spaces but whose numbers are too small to
watch and/or intervene in the myriad of student activities that are periph-
eral to the manifest purposes of schools. They do so by providing what
are apparently free or low-cost spaces of romantic assembly, including
student centers, athletic fields and facilities, dining halls and snack bars,
student lounges and libraries, campus area cafes and nightclubs, as well
as semi-private or completely private dormitory bedrooms. And they do
so by providing sites for low-cost or free dates, including parties or more
formal dances, concerts, lectures and readings, sporting events, plays,
and exhibits. Although much of this facilitation is not technically free
and is rather funded by organizational budgets through tuition, taxes, and
charitable donations, the persons involved in the romantic interactions

in these settings bear a disproportionately low share of the costs associated with their dating and sexual experiences. An inverse relationship between family formation and education hardly captures this aspect of educational settings. Insofar as lower-class youth are denied access to particular kinds of educational settings, they are also denied access to these relatively "easy" and "cheap" romantic interactions, even as lower-class women may marry and/or have children at younger ages than women who spend more extensive time in schools and activities involving their school-based networks.

But if Shawn's and Brenda's educational involvement and class mobility privilege them in romance, they also privilege them in a type of romance that is subject to the institutional environment that facilitates its existence. Dating and rating relationships are—by the standards of marriage specifically and family formation generally—relatively "weak" relationships. They come to women and men in spaces and times of their life trajectories when they are forced to compete with a seeming spate of opportunities to combine adult sexual behavior, adult work roles, and adult family formation in one's youth. Faced with such heavy competition, relationships and partners fail to survive the cost-benefit calculations that characterize these types of romantic relationships. This is particularly true when "status-seeking" women (and, I suppose, men) are involved in making the cost-benefit calculations.

Because "status seekers" were the women in chapter 1's discussion of degree-attainment processes who valued the educational, income, and lifestyle achievements associated with schools and whose experiences told them that their chances for inclusion in elite professional status groups remained viable, they are the women here who routinely disinvest in their dating and rating relationships when such relations come into conflict with economic or career goals. Consider, for example, one status seeker's explanation for her breakup with a high-school boyfriend to whom she felt quite attached. At twenty-three, Danielle (currently a married boarding school teacher and residential counselor) told me that her "boyfriend in, um, twelfth grade . . . was one of the closest friends that gave [her] the most support [she] needed [her] senior year." Nonetheless, the couple broke up during the second semester of her first year in college. As she explained, "We broke up, I think it was, ah, February or March of my first year in college, and we just basically grew apart 'cause he was still in high school and I was in New York, at, you know, school. And I just had too many different experiences, and he was still in the high-school experience, so we just didn't connect anymore." Like many status seekers, Danielle is matter-of-fact and unapologetic about the distance (in this case, one thousand miles) that she put between her and her boyfriend in order to attend the college of her choice; she believes that her decision makes obvious sense even as she acknowledges that it is a contributing factor in the relationship's demise.

Similarly, Nadine's description of the end of her relationship with Chris points to the way in which status seekers normalize this valuation and consequent prioritization of schooling and professional credentialing over and before development of romances to the point of marriage. This customer service manager at a local insurance firm was thirty years old and single, but cohabiting, when I interviewed her. She told me, "Someone [Chris] proposed to me when I was a sophomore in college, but I was too young; I wanted to finish school." Nadine's relationship with Chris ultimately ended because of her refusal to marry at this time. In these cases, status seekers' educational opportunities and endeavors facilitated the beginnings of dating and rating relationships, but the relationships were doomed by the values that motivated the education credentialing and career building in the first place.

Status seekers' values motivate disinvestment in early romance, generally speaking, but they also support disinvestment in romances with specific men. Above, Danielle and Nadine choose between schooling and romance in general, but, below, women's valuation of elite jobs, pastimes, and financial rewards diminishes their evaluation of particular men and, consequently, ongoing involvement with them. When Sharon, a twenty-five-year-old temp living with her parents and trying to figure out what to do with her business major, told me that she broke up with her last boyfriend despite being "in love with" him because "he couldn't balance a checkbook" and she "didn't wanna be bankrupt and homeless," she was engaging with her status-seeking values to make a decision about whether a relationship with a particular man might compromise her class achievement goals. Similarly, when Sierra (age twenty-eight) explained that her relationship with Reese suffered because she "pushed him" to "get back on the right track," she too relied on status-seeker values to decide that she could not sit idly by in a partnership with a man who had settled for work in a "car park" after his business venture failed. And even as Nancy, a thirty-one-year-old attorney, listed the qualities she wanted in a romantic partner prior to marrying (for example, "If he wasn't in school, I wanted him working . . . That . . . to me was more indicative of just, you know, having some ambition . . . No kept men . . ."), it became clear that status seekers' values inform these women's "rates" of both potential and actual "dates," helping them to decide with whom to begin, continue, and mostly exit dating and rating relationships.

Status seekers' romances in these early years may be the victims of their own status seeking. But the ability of schools and related institutions to facilitate romance characterized by the dating and rating structure in- dicates that these relationships would hardly have fared better if status seekers' own values had not come into conflict with them. For school— and especially college—environments are organized around status seek- ing. This is why the dating and rating romance is so well suited to and tol- erated by this environment. Thus, women in educational settings, whether they are motivated by status-seeking values or not, swim against the tide if they try to replace dating and rating with other relationship structures that might be more closely linked to a marital outcome. They fight against status-seeking partners (who might end or decline the opportunity to begin relationships for the very same reasons as the status-seeking women discussed above). They must also fight against friends, family members, school counselors, and teachers who say in subtle and not so subtle ways that these relationships are not supposed to be "serious," that other and perhaps better possibilities for romance are present and available in one's own immediate environment, and that one should make decisions about intensifying commitments to romance based on cost-benefit analyses that consider romance alongside other options about the way to spend schooling and early professional years. Thus, Aleah and Diane, who were typed respectively as "profiler" and "pleaser" in the analyses completed for chapter 1, found themselves in beleaguered dating and rating relation- ships that faced the possibility of demise from multiple directions even though their decisions in neither education nor romance were informed by status-seeking values.

Aleah was called a "profiler" in chapter 1 because her commitment to elite status-seeking values was neither as deep nor as long lasting as that of the traditional status seeker. Her words below demonstrate the ways in

which her educational activities supported her youthful romantic involvements, but they also indicate how educational settings are more specifically tied to involvement in dating and rating—or, as far as development
to the point of marriage is concerned, "weak"—relationship structures.
Aleah and I discussed the romances that occurred at the end of high
school and during summer college preparatory programs:

> ALEAH: Then I went out with someone else, and I think I may of had
> sex with him maybe, like, five times. But he cheated on me
> so I had to leave him alone. I mean he went to Central to
> this . . . program, during the summer, right after we gradu-
> ated. I went to Bennett; he went to Central. He was hanging
> around this little girlfriend. And one of the girls who was
> in the summer program lived down the street from North
> Carolina Central. And on one of the weekends we went to
> her house, and I said . . . , "My boyfriend's right up the street.
> Let's go up there," you know, and caught him in a lotta non-
> sense, and that's another story in itself. But I caught him in
> a whole lotta nonsense, and we broke up. But, you know, he
> was like, "Okay, I want you back." So I went back with him
> for a little while, but then because he was still up at Central
> and I had come back to Bennett, it was like I don't know
> what he's doin' up there, and so we just kinda broke it off . . .
>
> AVERIL: How come you broke up with the first guy? Do you
> remember?
>
> ALEAH: Because I think I just liked this other guy better.

Schools show Aleah and other coeds a horizon of possibilities—romantic and otherwise. They make opportunities to do the type of cheating she
describes or at least to compare a current romantic partner to potential
others easily available. And they embed romantic choices in a set of educational and/or professional opportunities that are set up for single, un-
encumbered individuals as opposed to couples trying to build partnerships. The creation and advertisement of life's numerous possibilities that
goes on in and around educational settings both facilitate romantic interactions and diminish the stability of specific romantic relationships.

Related institutions (like the family) likewise support the schools' structuring of the highly vulnerable romance: Diane, an interviewee whose des-

ignation as a "pleaser" indicates that she is guided to college by a desire
to please family members, is also pushed, encouraged, and manipulated
to organize romance around the dating and rating structure. Never mind
the relatively low value she places on elite status and lifestyles: parental
ascription to the normative patterns of degree attainment slowed the development of her relationship with the man she ultimately married:

> We talked about it [marriage] during college. Why did we wait so long?
> Because of me and my family's expectations . . . They expected all of us
> [Diane and her three brothers] to wait until after graduation for mar-
> riage, and we got married one year after my graduation . . . My parents
> pressured me to move away for college; they wanted me to date other
> people and they tried to break us [Diane and her husband] up . . . As far
> as education was concerned, they were lovingly manipulative . . . My
> dad's side of the family came from a certain class and they felt they had
> to keep that up . . . What the kids and grandkids were gonna do was
> always important . . . College wasn't a choice.

Whether the norms are communicated by parents who fund degree
attainment, peers who act simultaneously as comrades in degree-seeking
activities and advice givers in romance, or individuals and organizations
that extend education and career opportunities to single girls but not married women, status-seeking and non-status-seeking women journeying
toward degree attainment are sanctioned in ways that support their use of
the dating and rating relationship in romantic interactions. Powerful social actors like Diane's parents teach, encourage, manipulate, and at times
do their very best to compel would-be degree attainers to involve themselves in dating and rating relationship structures—or, in other words—to
proceed slowly toward serious commitment, using cost-benefit analyses
each step of the way in order to consider the potential drawbacks of romance in general and of particular romantic partners.[9]

Dating and rating relationships are many things. They are relationships that proceed slowly to the point of marital commitment owing to
the step-by-step rational calculation that characterizes partner decision
making; and they are relationships that include no other interactions outside of the romantic ones. They are also relationships that are facilitated
and structured by the cultural logic of middle-class professionals' credentialing processes: women who seek degrees because of values consis-

tent with this logic routinely use such values to postpone or forgo serious romantic commitment as well as to exit dating and rating relationships entirely; women who may be less motivated to keep their romances on chopping blocks for the sake of school and career find themselves normatively constrained into this means of organizing romantic relations by role players in educational and education-related institutions. Finally, dating and rating relationships are currencies through which privilege and deprivation in a romantic economy are distributed. Inasmuch as they are the peculiar province of those who are extended opportunities for sustained educational development well into their young adult years, they are not equally available to all, despite what outcome data on poor women's early sexual activity, childbearing, or marriage might suggest. Furthermore, inasmuch as they are structured by the culture and logic of elite educational systems, they are also limited in their scope and breadth by the inequality-making characteristics of educational systems. This means that relationships are less "serious" than they would be if they did not reflect the privileging of elite cultural strategies and values around balancing education, work, and romance. It also means that black women's romantic relationship opportunities might be limited by the race-gender makeup of schools and racialized aesthetic hierarchies on high-school and college campuses. Even as class advantages appear to increase women's involvement in these dating and rating relationship structures, degreed black women may find their access to such relationships limited by the race-gender characteristics and cultures of their school settings. I return to a more thorough discussion of the race and gender constraints on women's involvement in romance and marriage at the end of the chapter.

The claims in my argument above challenge strict ideas about an inverse relationship between reproductive and productive labor—ideas that indicate that those involved in dating and sexual activity as youth risk exclusion from professional development activities. Furthermore, the connection being drawn between education and romance also contrasts with work on gender that visualizes romance as a distraction imposed upon female students, slowing and eliminating their pursuit of credentials and careers typically associated with the highest-earning males.[10] In this sense, data on the progress of women's school-era romances move the scholarly literature away from a conception of young women deciding between (or having the opportunity to decide between) education and profession on the one hand and romance and family formation on the other. Instead, such data use the prevalence of the dating and rating relationships in a sample of degreed black women to argue that elites' pursuit of career credentials happens alongside and simultaneously with their youthful participation in romance and sexual activity.

And if this description of the forms and limitations of romance hatched within or through the spaces of elite professional socialization constitutes the direct evidence for an association between elite training and involvement in "weak" romantic structures, then descriptions of women's romantic behaviors outside of the moments and spaces of elite status seeking form the indirect evidence for the same. Below, degreed black women find themselves involved in wholly different structures of romance—in "speedy climax" and "delayed entry" relationships. Both relationship types underscore degreed black women's desires for romance and their pursuit of love and marriage; and both relationship types also illustrate the ways in which black women's engagement with higher education and high-status career opportunities facilitate "weak" structures of romance and not "strong" ones.

When Love Reigns

In the list of types in table 4 above, "speedy climax" relationships are almost three times more likely than dating and rating relationships to culminate in marriage. Recall that dating and rating relationships proceed slowly toward commitment and consist of solely romantic interactions. While speedy climax relationships also consist of only romantic interactions, they differ from dating and rating relationships in that the individuals involved proceed quickly to the point of serious commitment. Thus women in speedy climax relationships do not engage in cost-benefit analyses before intensifying commitments or even deciding to marry. Instead they take "leaps of faith," "follow their hearts," or act based on "feelings" such as "love at first sight." This difference in the structure of romantic relations accounts for the fast rather than slow pace to serious commitment and for the high rather than low likelihood that the relationship will result in marriage.

Speedy climax relationships are, according to the data in table 4 on rates of progression to marriage, a good deal "stronger" than dating and rating relationships. And an argument that degreed black women's limited experience with these "stronger" romantic structures is determined by the constraints of their professional credentialing processes rather than by the women's individual proclivities and preferences further supports the point that degreed black women pursue rather than reject love and family—that they are deprived of marital opportunity rather than simply focused on careers. My evidence for such an argument follows: it includes the point that degreed black women like Danielle, Ashley, and Tracey appear perfectly willing to and capable of involving themselves in speedy climax relationships after they have completed degree attainment and professional development activities or to the extent that their romantic relations exist outside of the spaces, places, or normative structures associated with elite credentialing and professional status attainment.

One way to think about the high prevalence of "weak" dating and rating relationships and the low prevalence of "strong" speedy climax ones in a sample of college-educated women would be to consider the possibility that these different structures of romantic relations reflect two different kinds of women. In this scenario, dating and rating relationships would be the province of the rational economic calculators and speedy climax relationships would belong to the emotionally or hormonally propelled sexual actors. The degrees and the professional occupational statuses attained across this exclusive sample would explain the prevalence difference since women whose primary interests are dating, falling in love, marrying, and having children and who consequently find themselves in speedy climax relationships can hardly be expected to appear very frequently in a sample of highly educated professionals.

Although this scenario may in part be true (see my discussion of the little truths that may be found in this scenario with respect to Tracey below), and although there are mainstream gender and class inequality scholars and demographers who use outcome data to say that this scenario explains race and class differences in marital and fertility behavior,[11] the romantic life trajectories of women like Danielle and Ashley indicate something different. Instead, examination of their experiences suggests that women who "think" about romance in a way that protects their individual economic interests (in other words, as status seekers and some of the parents of pleasers do) are not so distinct from the women who "rush" into serious romance, sexual activity, and childbearing before or instead of adequately securing their financial futures. Thus, this study finds evidence that women's organization of early romances around the dating and rating structure does not preclude later involvement in a less "rational" or "calculating" type of romance.

What the data actually say is that degreed black women want romantic relationships, and that they act according to their opportunities and limitations in order to get them. For degreed professionals, these opportunities and limitations often mean dating and rating relationships available in their schooling and professional development spaces. But school ends, careers become more secure, and when the supply of easy and cheap romances associated with school and school-based networks begins to abate, other opportunities for a girl to keep warm on a lonely Saturday night may present themselves. Then, suddenly, the same status-seeking Danielle, who earlier thought it was reasonable to travel one thousand miles away from a boyfriend who "gave [her] the most support," morphs into a type of romantic decision making that relies on minimal information about who her partner is and that jettisons consideration of relationship costs and benefits in the name of following something that "feels right."

Status seekers unconstrained by the limitations and sanctions of their degree-seeking activities do throw caution to the wind in the face of the opportunity to satisfy romantic desires gone unfulfilled. Note the absence of cost-benefit calculations in status-seeking Danielle's discussion of the beginnings of her speedy climax relationship with Norris and their decision to marry:

> . . . So I give him my email address. Five minutes later, he emails me . . . I'm thinking I gave him my email address at seven. He emails me at 7:05. Is this like psycho? What's going on? So [we] emailed and figured out we . . . had all these connections. Started dating back in October. End of October, we started dating. And then we started talking about getting married in December. Proposed to me in March. Married in August . . . I think, um, from about, after about two weeks of dating, we sort of knew, we knew that we were just meant to be together. You know, I mean we started talking about having kids and getting married and how we were gonna fix our house. I remember the first time—I

think he said it the first time. Um, I was like, are we seriously talking about this? We've only been dating for, like, three weeks. Then it was like . . . if it feels right . . .

Similarly, Ashley (a thirty-six-year-old status seeker and recruit who left her career as a chemical engineer in order to raise two small children) came to the end of a long search for a lifetime romantic partner when she became involved in the speedy climax version of romance with her future husband. Their relationship began with a meeting at church, an invitation to a second event in the same church, and then a single date—after which she called her mother and said, "I met the man I'm gonna marry." Ashley herself claimed to be surprised at the absence of rational calculation in her and her partner's romantic decision making: when Carl approached her father to ask for permission to marry her, Ashley's reaction was, "Huh? We just met!" Even then, in the midst of it, she recognized that this romantic relationship was significantly different in terms of pacing and partner decision making than the five ones she had had previously. She nonetheless pursued it to the marital end, and had, at the time of the interview, pursued it through six years of marriage.

It is true that speedy climax relationships are a relatively small minority of the romantic relationships experienced by degreed black women. In Danielle's case, they represent one of the three relationships that she discussed during the interview; in Ashley's case, they represent one of the six; and they amount to only 14 percent of the relationships observed in the total sample. But it is not true that the prevalence of these speedy climax relationships in my sample is low because Danielle and Ashley are rational and calculating economic actors whose success in school and career can be attributed to these behaviors and whose romantic interests assume a low priority for them. Indeed, the scholars who make these arguments about different women and their different attitudes toward sex and school or love and money are conventionally writing about women who "fall prey" to the speedy climax relationships and the pregnancy and marriage outcomes of these relationships during their youth.[12] In contrast, women like Danielle and Ashley mature into rather than out of speedy climax relationships. This trajectory of romantic relationships makes it difficult to dismiss the speedy climax relationship structure as the folly of youth who are immature and, we assume, unable to calculate the long-

term economic costs and benefits of their unrestrained youthful involvement in sex, love, and family formation.

The existence and timing of the speedy climax relationships in this
sample suggest that these relationships rather reflect the high desirability
of romantic experiences and individuals' general (rather than particularized, personality-dependent) interest in pursuing romantic opportunities and outcomes. Accepting this point makes it easier to see the links
between the romantic limitations endemic to sites of elite professional
training and credentialing and the low prevalence of the speedy climax
relationships. The sample of degreed black women's romantic relationships is characterized by a low portion of speedy climax relationships for
the same reasons that it contains a high fraction of dating and rating ones:
that is, *involvement in higher education and early career development activities both facilitates romantic interactions and shapes them in ways that
depress the likelihood that they will result in marriage.* Relationships that
have their roots in and develop from those spaces and places outside the
schools and workplaces of young professionals (for example, churches,
neighborhoods, and extended family gatherings)—relationships like the
ones Danielle and Ashley had with their husbands—are free to assume a
rather different and, in some cases, "stronger" form.

In a minority of cases, speedy climax relationships comprise a more
significant portion of degreed black women's romantic experiences. These
women were more likely to marry and spent more time married than
those degreed black women who were more typical of the sample because degree attainment and professional development were made subject to and organized around their romantic goals. Herein lies the element
of truth to the scenario discussed above in which different women—or
less educationally and economically successful women—are the ones who
end up in speedy climax relationships. For Tracey is different from the
"status-seeking" Danielle and the "status-seeking" and "recruited" Ashley.
But the difference here does not lie solely in the one's interest in love
and the other two's interest in money. Nor does it lie in the educational
and economic failure of the one and the schooling and career success of
the other two. The difference between the Traceys and the Danielles and
Ashleys in the sample lies in the ways in which love and money—and the
pursuit of love and money—can come together in these women's lives.

Tracey's involvement in speedy climax relationships from the beginning
of her romantic life trajectory up until the present is not a story about the
ways women's adoption of nurturing and reproductive care roles restricts
educational and professional achievements. Instead, her exclusive organization of romance around the speedy climax structure reflects a struggle
to achieve a love and a family that require rather than replace educational
and professional achievement.

When I spoke with Tracey, she was thirty-four and married to the man
who represented the fourth of her four speedy climax relationships. Two
of these relationships had ended in marriage, and one had included an engagement to be married but ended before the wedding could take place.
Unlike Danielle and Ashley, whose degree attainment was based in status
seeking, the activities that led to Tracey's undergraduate business degree and her career in the insurance industry were based on a need to
escape an abusive situation in her family of origin: she therefore carries
the "conforming escape artist" designation in chapter 1's list of degree-
attainment types. Like most "escape artists," Tracey was concerned from
an early age with forming a more hospitable family of her own, and her
focus on marrying and having a baby led to her repeated involvement in
speedy climax relationships. Below she explains how degree attainment
and career development activities were designed around these love and
marriage goals:

> TRACEY: I didn't know exactly what I would do with my math degree.
> So, you know, at first I was thinking I would work for [a]
> big computer company or some major place or something
> or go to an education school and get my teaching creden-
> tial. And then I struggled so much. I knew that there was no
> way I would get a job. Do you know what I mean? I'd have
> to go to school for my education master's. And as sorry as
> it sounds, even when I went to college, I almost went to be-
> come a teacher's aid or something that took two years so
> I could get out and get married quicker. And thank God I
> didn't. But halfway through my math major, I went, "What
> am I gonna do with this?" And then someone said some-
> thing to me about business and the insurance companies
> recruiting there, and I immediately switched to the busi-

ness program. That's why I went to school five years instead
of four . . .

AVERIL: Was this part of your personal plan or was this the only circumstances under which your parents would agree or he
[your fiancé] would agree?

TRACEY: I didn't care what my parents said. But I thought it was just
what you do. I first—When we were first together, I was
gonna get married and . . . commute to school and be a
married little college student. But then when all that didn't
work and we got back together, then it was like, okay when
I graduate, I'll just get married.

When Tracey follows her feelings into romantic relationships, rushed
engagements, and minimally considered marriages, she is looking for a
commitment to interpersonal, emotional exchanges, to shared resources
and decision making, to marriage and having and parenting children.
Furthermore, she is looking for and trying to achieve this same list of
goods when she picks a college major and applies for a job. Her understanding is—and her understanding was, at quite a young age—that educational or career opportunities are attractive insofar as they demonstrate
their ability to support her valued romantic ends of love, marriage, and
family. Thus, Tracey's leaps of faith into serious romantic commitments
and marriage not only involve proceeding in ignorance of the type of information that would allow for calculation of the costs and benefits of
entering marriage with a particular partner; they also involve delaying,
taking detours from, altering, or jettisoning educational and career development plans that may conflict with the progression of this relationship
toward the marital end.

Tracey illustrates how progress in speedy climax relationships, whether
the marital end is eventually realized or not, involves the rearrangement of
other aspects of one's life (including education and career building) so that
they are supportive of or at least do not conflict with the quick resolution
of the relationship in marriage. She also illustrates a situation in which the
values and opportunities that motivate and support degree attainment are
out of synch with the dominant cultural logic of college-prep programs
and higher educational settings. Tracey—with her love logic rather than
money logic of degree attainment, with her boyfriends from the neighbor-

hood rather than the campus, and with her discordant relationship with the parents who fund and encourage degree attainment—finds opportunity and support for the pursuit of her romantic endeavors outside of the physical spaces and cultural logic of elite credentialing that she occupies. In this way, she is able to organize such romantic interactions in ways that are typically precluded by elites' educational and training activities, or, in other words, in speedy climax as opposed to dating and rating structures.

The romantic life trajectories of degreed black women like Danielle and Ashley tell us that dating and rating relationships are prevalent in the sample because love matters to these women—because *women engage with and try to participate in both the romantic and the economic opportunities associated with degreed professionals' credentialing processes.* Key to understanding their low marriage rates is understanding that the best versions of romantic opportunity in these settings are constituted by a series of weak relationships that are unlikely to lead to marriage. But once women leave educational settings and/or can act more independently of parental, school, workplace, or even peer guidelines for economic achievement, they can and obviously do follow their feelings, fate, or faith into very different romantic regimes. Tracey's story about her efforts to escape from the relative impoverishment of love that she experienced in her parents' household to the caring relations she imagines to be present in romantic partnership, childbearing, and childrearing uses different words and images to communicate a similar message. She too is interested in combining economic and romantic success, but her different experiences, motivations, and romantic opportunities mean that she is less reliant on the "weak" dating and rating relationship structures born of engagement with elite schooling culture and career activities than are most of the women sampled.

A formative experience of deprivation in love orients Tracey's economic activities around the protection and conservation of and the risky investment in her romantic opportunities; and this, in turn, makes the nature of the observed relationship between love and money in her life quite different from that of the status-seeking and prominent-person-pleasing women who share her status. The rare occurrence of a reproductive lifetime of speedy climax relationships culminating in marriages like Tracey's and the relative scarcity of speedy climax relationships across the lifetimes of women like Danielle and Ashley speak to the ways in which elite status attainment opportunities and strategies are encoded with specific kinds of romantic and sexual opportunities. These data also speak to the ways these elite processes encroach upon and shape the organization of love and romance at the individual and institutional levels. Below, the discussion of "delayed entry" relationships picks up where this discussion leaves off. It explains how a very different version of "strong" romance is in conflict with the life experiences of and consequently remains largely unavailable to the degreed black women whom I interviewed.

When Stability Triumphs Over Mobility

The data that inform my description of black women's delayed entry relationships indicates that delays are far more complicated than the literature about delaying love for school and career suggests. At the foundation of work in this area are Malthus's (1798/1965) ideas about the relationship between poverty and fertility control. Like Malthus,[13] contemporary academic theory, policy recommendations, and editorial opinions expect that young girls who are willing to delay pursuit of their romantic goals will ultimately achieve the love that they want. More importantly, they predict that the long-term outcome of these delays will be higher educational achievement, improved occupational statuses, greater incomes, and a more financially secure family and household—or a more "moneyed love"—than women have when they begin childbearing as teens.[14]

This Malthusian reasoning has been challenged by Kathryn Edin and Maria Kefalas (2005): in their work, *Promises I Can Keep*, they question low-income mothers about their fertility timing, asking them whether they thought that they should have waited until they were older, married, and more financially secure to have their children. And in large part, the women express little regret: they cite the presence of their children, the positive experience of parenting, and the inability to imagine what would have become of their lives had they not risen to the responsibility of loving and being there for their children. Similarly, Arline Geronimus (1986, 1987) also challenges Malthus: her "weathering hypothesis" explains the teen childbearing activity of poor, urban women of color by suggesting that such women desire motherhood under social conditions that make beginning their families at an early age a logical and less costly choice. She cites the women's family history of poverty, their high likelihood of youthful unemployment, their probable occupation in jobs with no maternity leave in the latter part of their reproductive years, and the early morbidity and mortality of parents, grandparents, and other potential childcare providers as plausible reasons that poor women choose to have children while young. In both of these scholarly examples, Malthus's causal logic is refuted by claims that delaying romance does not necessarily make for a healthier and wealthier life.

This book's analysis of degreed black women's romantic relationships joins Edin and Kefalas's study and Geronimus's hypothesis in questioning Malthusian reasoning, especially its lack of attention to the romantic costs that may accompany the delay of marriage. And at first glance, the column of table 4 describing rates of progression to marriage and indicating that delayed entry relationships are almost twice as likely to result in marriage as the average romance suggests that there are romantic benefits rather than costs to delaying one's romantic pursuits. (See the last column of table 4 which indicates that only 17.5 percent of the total sample of relationships progressed to marriage while 33 percent of delayed entry relationships did.) That is until you consider who and what these delays are all about. In actuality, the delays in delayed entry relationships lower women's accessibility to this structure of romance even as they increase the "strength" of or likelihood that these relations will result in marriage.

When I spoke with Nancy about how she met her partner in the second of her three romantic relationships, she gave me a sheepish look as if she did not really want to say and then continued:

> We went to high school together, and I had no interest in him in high school at all. None whatsoever. We were friends, but that was about it. And then we met again, um, the year I started law school. And it was kinda cute because he was like, "Oh, I used to like you in high school, and you didn't pay me any attention." I was like, "Oh, you silly guy." And the thing about it that was bad was I remembered him from high school as this really sweet nice guy . . . So I'm like, "He can do no wrong. He's too good to do anything wrong. He's a really nice guy" . . . And so I kinda went down that path and um—and it was good for a while.

Nancy's words describe the classic delayed entry relationship, one in which the slow pace of progression to serious commitment is caused by the existence of both non-romantic and romantic interactions. These relationships do not begin with romantic interactions. In some cases, the woman and man first develop and maintain a platonic friendship, and in others they initially know one another as informal acquaintances who meet up with one another intermittently while pursuing their own individual lives. In either case, romance is something that they decide to pursue in what is best described as a second stage of their relationship.

Data indicate that there were two ways in which the delay in romantic involvement progressed. In one situation both relationship participants fail to consider romance, are disinterested in romance, or find it impossible to pursue romance at their initial meeting and during their initial interactions. The romantic relationship either begins when they make a formal decision to change directions and try out a romantic relationship or else it develops gradually with the interactions and efforts slowly changing directions to include romance. In the alternative scenario of delayed entry relationship, one party is interested while the other is not. In this case, the first stage of the relationship, whether it be friendship or not, is characterized by some level of pursuit: the interested party makes efforts to make him- or herself available for a future romantic relationship or to directly or indirectly persuade the other person to consider such a relationship. The romantic stage (that is, the second stage) begins when the formerly disinterested person develops a romantic interest, assuming the earlier interest of the person in pursuit has not waned or that his or her availability status for a romantic relationship has not changed. Such was the case with Nancy above, who ignored Cyrus's flirtations during high school and succumbed to them once they met again during her matriculation at law school.

Although Nancy describes a romance that ended without marriage above, delayed entry relationships are like speedy climax relationships in that they have a relatively high rate of conversion to marriage. A third of these relationships progressed to the point of marriage, which is slightly lower than the marriage rate for speedy climax relationships, but still more than twice that of the dating and rating type. What is interesting about the fact that delayed entry and speedy climax relationships share high rates of conversion to marriage is that they are dissimilar on both dimensions of the typology. In table 5 below, I show how each of the five romantic relationship types is classified with respect to the pace of progression to serious commitment and the existence or nonexistence of non-romantic

Table 5. Dimensions of degreed black women's relationship structures

PACE (AND DIRECTION) OF PROGRESSION TO COMMITMENT	TYPES OF INTERACTIONS		
	Romance and acquaintance/ friendship	*Romance only*	*Total (%)*
Fast (→)		Speedy climax 14%	14
Slow (→)	Delayed entry 16%	Dating and rating 40%	56
Slow (↔)	In and out 11%		11
Not applicable (∅)	Sleeper 16%		16
Total	43%	54%	97

interactions. It is clear from this table that these two types are structural opposites: where the one moves quickly, the other is arrested in its development; where the one is focused solely on romance, the other is complicated by its platonic beginnings.

Table 5 indicates that the quality that appears to account for speedy climax relationships' high rate of marriage that I identified above (that is, the fast progression to serious commitment or the forgoing of large amounts of information gathering and rational calculation) is a sufficient but unnecessary cause in the achievement of high rates of marriage. What then accounts for the success of delayed entry relationships with respect to the marital outcome? Analyses suggest that the delay facilitates women's choice of compatible and attractive romantic partners using the same rational calculation of those in dating and rating relationships but without incurring as many relationship casualties.

Women in delayed entry relationships use information about potential partners in order to select an individual who has qualities they would find attractive in a spouse and with whom they can expect to get along. This is similar to what happens in dating and rating relationships except that in delayed entry relationships this information gathering precedes romance. Note Jan's description of the beginning of her relationship with her husband:

> Damon and I . . . majored in the same thing. So basically what happened was . . . we started having a platonic relationship. We were really good friends. We majored in the same thing so we had the same interests, and we talked about shop, I guess, a lot . . . I didn't see him like a boyfriend or anything like that at first . . . And then his senior year . . . I started looking at him differently, like, he's kinda cute . . . But let me back track a little bit . . . I knew, like, Damon was like a really cool person. He would do stuff 'cause he knew my boyfriend was jealous, and, um, I would—like we would walk on campus and I was like, "Can you walk like five steps ahead of me so he can't see us together" 'cause he was really crazy, 'cause he was very abusive as well . . . Um, so after I broke up with him, Damon and I just started hanging out together even more, and that's when I felt like I started looking at him like, you know, he's kinda cute and everything . . . And, ah, basically [my girlfriend and I] planned this trip to Memphis . . . So I said . . . "Me and my girlfriend are going, and we would love for you to come hang out with us and stuff." And he was like, "Yeah." He was like, "I have family there . . . So we ended up going to Memphis and stuff for the weekend, and the next thing I knew, we were together. And from that point, we've been together ever since. We were married—it'll be twelve years this October.

Jan explains how her non-romantic interactions with Damon showed her what kind of person he was, let her know what he was willing to do to accommodate their friendship, and perhaps even indicated to her that he would make a good marriage partner. With her previous boyfriend, she dated him in a dating and rating relationship in order to discover that he was jealous, abusive, and would probably be a bad marriage partner.

Because partners already know each other before they choose to enter the romantic relationship, fewer poor choices are made and fewer relationships dissolve over issues of incompatibility or the discovery of negative or problematic characteristics. When non-romantic interactions show these women that a potential partner tends to cheat on his girlfriends or is bossier than they would like, then their relationships with these men never become romances. What is a failed romance among dating and rating relationships never makes it into the delayed entry relationship category. Fewer relationship failures exist among the delayed entry relationship group because many of those predestined to failure never make it to the status of romances.

The delay in delayed entry relationships also supports involvement in relationships that are more likely to lead to marriage by allowing individuals to collect information about potential partners over longer periods of time than dating and rating relationships. This means that involved individuals are in a better position to act on information that dating and rating relationships may miss entirely, including and especially status changes over time and the effect of those status changes on the readiness of individuals for serious romantic commitment. Marie's delayed entry relationship that led to marriage began in her hometown, to which she returned after college. She kept in contact with her husband for over four years as a friend before the two decided to pursue a romantic relationship:

> I met my husband while I was working on my teaching credentials. I was teaching without my credentials at a parochial school . . . [where he was also] working . . . We didn't really date seriously then . . . We met in 1984 but didn't marry until 1992 . . . I remember telling him that high-school educations come a dime a dozen. He had been in the service [military], and I told him to go back to school and get his degree, especially if Uncle Sam is paying . . . First he went to a two year college . . . and I went to his graduation. Then he went to a four-year college, and I attended that graduation too . . . Later on we started really dating.

Had Marie entered a cross-class, dating and rating relationship with Bobby at their initial meeting, she may have, within a couple of months, come to judge him to be an unsuitable man for marriage and discarded him, the romance, and any other significant interaction with him. However, Bobby changed over the extensive course of their friendship, and he came to more closely approximate a partner whom she felt had the human capital resources to withstand the vicissitudes of the modern economy and labor market. And since he was a friend and not an ex-boyfriend with whom she was no longer speaking or to whom she was wary of extending her trust, she was comfortable with pursuing a more serious romantic relationship with him once he had achieved his new college-educated status.

The structure of the delayed entry relationship that allows for long-term information gathering before romance is what makes the outcome so different from instances where rational calculation is used in the context of dating and rating relationships. However, this same two-stage structure explains in some measure why such relationships constitute such a low fraction (just 16 percent) of degreed black women's romances. Delayed entry relationships are most likely to be found in situations in which women maintain social network and geographic stability over time. Since women must meet someone for a second time or change the terms of a relationship after some initial phase in order to have a delayed entry relationship, women who have them tend to be socially positioned to run into the same men again and again over a longer duration of time. Stability means that the men whom women meet and get to know remain in rather than disappear from their social networks. When women are interested in serious and committed relationships, these men may or may not be romantically available, but they are present. In contrast, women who are not geographically stable and who are changing geographic locations and networks of interaction over time may have no idea where to find most of the men whom they have met and gotten to know over their history of moves and changes. Thus it appears that it is a special set of degreed black women who find themselves in the type of position that affords them the opportunity to enter delayed entry relationships: those who change schools, employment, and geography in their journey to professional status are less likely to enter these relationships. Furthermore, even within this special set of stable degreed black women, only those whose youth-era male friends and acquaintances have also managed to stay in the same geographic areas and maintain the stability of their social networks have the opportunity to try out romance in a new relationship phase.

This book's analyses of degreed black women's educational, career, and romantic life trajectories indicate that degreed black women are quite mobile during their late teens and twenties. Most move from the metropolitan area in which they were raised at least once in order to attend college. And on average, women in this sample moved 1.8 times—or almost twice—after the point at which they became single adults but while they still remained single. For some, like Marie, these two moves meant that they simply moved back to their hometowns after college, but for the large majority, these two moves meant that they began and ended their lives as twenty-something singles in areas where they were strangers and where they had to establish new networks of sociability. Since much of this movement was about college or graduate program matriculation or beginning careers and service opportunities, the moves constitute both a change in social and romantic networks and labor migration in support of elite status attainment. Malthusian academic theorists, politicians, and journalists would therefore take comfort in this movement to the extent that delays mean greater economic achievement and financial security for women's future households. But such movement does frustrate the achievement of marriage and family by disrupting the stability of women's networks and frustrating repeat meetings with suitors, some of whom may have matured from immature schoolboys with little sexual, educational, or career sophistication into attractive potential marriage partners. As is the case with speedy climax relationships above, schooling and career development frustrate women's involvement in these "stronger" delayed entry relationships.

Much of the literature on class differences in family formation focuses on the relationship that has been summarized thus far across this chapter's description of dating and rating, speedy climax, and delayed entry types of romance. This relationship says in a myriad of ways that women's economic success is tied to delays in their family formation activity. Past scholarly research tells us that these delays allow women who prioritize careers or women who are extended opportunities for high-status careers to train for and secure high-status occupations before or even instead of adopting reproductive care roles.[15] In describing the processes that lead to degreed black women's deprivation in marriage, I have tried to illustrate the ways in which these delays in childbearing and marriage actually come about. I have therefore argued that these delays do not reflect degreed black women's lack of interest or participation in romantic relationships and that they are not necessarily completely of these women's choosing. Instead, I have talked about the structure and availability of romance or the forms or shapes of relationships that constitute college-educated black women's romantic opportunities and means of fulfilling romantic, sexual, and family formation aims. I have concluded that these opportunities are most consistently available during the women's schooling and early career years and that limitations exist in settings of elite socialization and training that constrain the organization of most romantic interactions around the dating and rating structure. The romantic journeys most likely to result in marriage are less available to degreed black women precisely because of the time and activities associated with their pursuit of these educational and economic opportunities. However, black women's participation in these and other types of relationships outside of the credentialing context demonstrates the degree to which they value family formation.

Obstacles to degreed black women's fulfillment of romantic, sexual, and family formation goals are often present during the early reproductive period when dating and rating relations predominate. During that time, however, these women tend to perceive that opportunities in general and that their romantic opportunities in particular are vast and expanding. Some of this thinking is conditioned by institutional settings in which educational and professional opportunities are extended: such opportunities are presented to young black women in ways that imply that future professional occupational roles are the truly scarce opportunities and that there is an oversupply of the men, sex, and babies that can cut off women's access to these more precious employment roles. And at other times, these women's thinking may just reflect the folly of youth who incorrectly assume that a myriad of choices in play and work will be ever present as their futures unfold.[16] In either case, degreed black women take more notice of existing obstacles to their goals in love later in the reproductive period. Their sense of limitations develops as a direct result of the decline in access to dating and rating relations (for example, as they get further away from large coeducational settings replete with single men and low-cost dating destinations) and of the failure of their dating and rating relationships with respect to the achievement of family formation goals. The sense of limitations and the ongoing wish to form families give rise to the yet to be discussed "in and out" and "sleeper" types of romantic relationships. These types are significant in the sense that they reveal the racial and gendered limitations on my subjects' involvement in heterosexual relationships and elucidate the sadness and lack of control women feel in their approach to marital goals.

Where Desire Meets Undesirability

Above I contrasted Danielle's and Ashley's speedy climax relationships at the end of the observed portion of their romantic life trajectories with the dating and rating structures they had experienced during their schooling and early work years. I showed how the move from education, career building, and intense status-seeking activity allowed for a change in the structure of romantic decision making from slow and calculating to faster, emotionally responsive action. The move allowed the love logic of decision making present in speedy climax relationships to replace the earlier money logic that prevailed in those environments that facilitated women's involvement in dating and rating relations. Furthermore, I argued that the switch in romantic relationship type reflected degreed black women's romantic desires unrestrained by the logic and limitations of their degree-seeking environments.

This narrative of degreed black women's romantic experiences seems thusly driven by their unfulfilled romantic desires and the opportunities and constraints they face in meeting them. The dominance of the "weaker" dating and rating relationship type represents a class-based constraint on marriage, but these women experience other constraints on their romantic goals, like the race- and gender-based constraints on marriage discussed below. Experience with romantic constraints—with the lack of progression of existing romantic relationships as well as with the lack of opportunity to enter romantic relationships at all—leaves women both unfulfilled and available, setting the stage for their pursuit of romance outside of relations that take on the dating and rating form. Just as the repeated failures of Danielle's and Ashley's dating and rating relationships leave them available for experimentation with a different type of romance, so too do delayed entry relationships reflect availability to partners previously rejected—or else not considered—during a prior period. In the discussion above, availability supported involvement in "stronger" relationships, or relationships more likely to result in marriage, but, as indicated below, this is not always the case. The *"in and out" and "sleeper" relationships reflect excessive availability and desires gone unfulfilled*. These final two relationships are even "weaker" with respect to marriage likelihood than the dating and rating situations described above.

When Availability Prevails Over Rationality

I remember listening with eager interest as Karie, at the age of twenty-six, listed the complaints she had about her ex-boyfriend: "He was a smoker. That was the main issue. Major problem. He wasn't a Christian. He didn't profess to be . . . This is gonna sound silly: He didn't have any hobbies. He has nothing to do with his time. You know what I mean? Just nothin'. I was like, 'Lord, I never thought that was important,' but it is. I need you to have something to do with your time. I don't need to be your hobby. You know what I'm sayin'?" This list, according to Karie, was problematic enough to support a recent decision to break up with Sheldon "for real." She repeated the "for real" a couple of times and went on to explain that she needed me to understand this meant she would never get back together with him. Almost two years before our interview, Karie had returned from out of state to live with her parents and start a new job as an attorney. And as I sat at her mother's dining table, I went along with her. I mean, I continued giving my verbal and non-verbal cues of agreement, even though, having gone through more than two-thirds of my fifty-eight interviews, having listened to friends' lists of complaints, and having offered up lists of my own at times, I wondered whether Karie's "for real" could truly be trusted.

It wasn't that the complaints that she offered seemed weak or petty. Nor was it the case that she exhibited delusions of grandeur during other segments of her interview. But Karie's relationship with Sheldon was an "in and out" relationship, and this means that she had likely given this list of complaints to others—maybe not interviewing researchers, but probably friends or a sibling—before and had nevertheless managed to return to Sheldon. The women sampled described their in and out relationships as ones in which they were moving "in and out" of a romantic relationship with the same man. While delayed entry relationships have two basic stages, in and out relationships potentially have an infinite number. When the couple meets, they usually pursue a romantic relationship, but their goals change and they typically move into a second stage characterized by platonic friendship, limited informal contact, or no contact or interaction at all. At some point, goals change again, and they resume romantic involvement. The romance is inevitably followed by another breakup, which is potentially followed by another period of romance, and so on, and so on.

Karie maintained during the interview that she met Sheldon when she was fourteen and he was seventeen and that the couple had "dated on and off for truly eleven years." Her return to the area in which she had grown up had prompted another romantic phase in this ongoing saga. It was therefore difficult for me to say whether "for real" was just another moment in the continuing cycle or an actual exit from the relationship.

In and out relationships are characterized by a slow, back-and-forth structure that apparently never progresses to marriage and the existence of other phases of relationship besides the romantic ones. While they reflect high levels of network stability in much the same way as delayed entry relationships, they do not share their high marriage rate—the rate of progression of the former is zero while that of the latter is 33 percent. This is most likely due to the fact that they also seem to reflect incompatibility, a characteristic that would seem to lead to lower rates of marriage. Karie's list is an example of this kind of incompatibility. As she clearly maintained, it is impossible to imagine living with someone who has a list of characteristics or a way of interacting with you that you find problematic:

> I really felt strongly that after a certain age you don't date for fun. You do date for fun, but you're not dating just to have a good time. I'm dating 'cause I wanna spend time with you seriously. And I also don't spend my time with someone I couldn't live with. That's a waste a' my time. That's a waste of my dating time. You know what I mean? It is. If it don't work out that's fine. That's another issue . . . But it needs to be somebody I know that I could at least, up front, I feel like I could go somewhere with this. I knew I wasn't gonna marry him . . . And I think because I had all these opinions about the relationship, I wasn't good for him either. You know, he didn't need to be with me, and I didn't need to be with him. 'Cause I don't think I could be a supportive half to him.

As Karie articulates it, "rational" women who are interested in marrying do not "waste . . . dating time" in relationships with partners whom they know they cannot live with and they know they cannot marry. And yet Karie herself claims to have returned to Sheldon every couple of years for eleven years, Deanna did the same thing for ten years with her son's father, and Kim, whom I discuss further below, spends much of her time in college leaving and returning to the same guy. The big question, then, when discussing in and out relationships, is not the question about why these relationships fail to progress to marriage, but instead the question about why supposed relationship exits are followed by returns to romantic relations with the same incompatible and problematic partners.

The degreed black women who moved in and out of romance in 11 percent of the 202 sampled relationships might also be described as moving in and out of "rationality" and in and out of "reality." For women like Karie sound quite rational and calculating about their romantic decisions when they start listing the problematic characteristics of partners or the untenable scenarios in relationships and subsequently linking these lists to relationship exits. But they are either silent or return to a less rational discussion of feelings when the subject moves to their returns to previously rejected partners. In other words, they repeatedly switch between the type of decision making that accompanies dating and rating relationships and the type of decision making that accompanies speedy climax relationships—between money logic and love logic. For Deanna, this meant that at times she decided simply to "[be] there" for the father of her son whom she knew to be a "nice guy" and a "nice person" and at other moments she decided "to do [her] own thing" because he was "not responsible" and her need for "stability" and "structure" could not be met by a man who chose to have "jobs here and there, not real consistent, career-oriented jobs."

Furthermore, my statement about moves in and out of reality reflects the way in which these women alternatively do and don't engage with the reality of their unfulfilled romantic desire and the limited options they have for addressing this desire. Logical or rational exits from romance with incompatible partners presuppose that romantic goals can be achieved elsewhere. As women leave in and out relationships, their lists of rational reasons focus on the negative aspects of their current solutions to the problem of unfulfilled romantic desire, and they give little attention to the reality that their desire might remain unfulfilled outside of these relationships. At the same time, excessive availability to the imagined better relationship that never comes or to equally or more problematic partners facilitates the women's engagement with their real romantic options, with the possibility of long-term singleness and living with the chronically unfulfilled desire for romantic love that such singleness entails. Here, the women become open to romantic opportunities that may be less than adequate, and in and out partners are often waiting just around the corner. Kim's discussion of her in and out relationship with Earl is illustrative of this kind of shifting back and forth.

Kim was one of the few subjects whom I interviewed in my own apartment. She had a busy schedule, working in her first career as a social worker in several health facilities, where she advocated for nursing home patients and their families, and training in a master's program to become a nurse practitioner. She believed it would be easier to drop by my place after her last health facility of the day than it would be to schedule an appointment with me that she might miss. That evening, she told me about her in and out relationship with Earl during college and explained how he would "drive [her] crazy" with his lack of emotional availability and his habit of standing her up for important dates like meeting her parents. Despite these rational reasons for their frequent breakups, she was still, more than five years later, shifting in and out of this rationality, maintaining, "I wish it could have worked out," and exclaiming, "Like I really, really did like him as a person . . . I really enjoyed his personhood so much."

But unlike some of the other women sampled who have spent large fractions of their reproductive lives in an in and out relationship, Kim seemed to understand that these relationships are structured by excessive availability, since her words clearly link the shifts in and out of rationality to shifts in and out of the reality of her unfulfilled romantic desire. As she explains below, her romantic interactions with Earl ended "for real" because her romantic desire was filled and her availability had declined:

And so then he called me. Like we hadn't talked for like a year, maybe two years, and he calls me Thanksgiving, you know. And I was really happy to hear from him, whatever, and he was like, "Um, you know, I got this great job in Houston, and I'm doing some positive stuff with my life whatever whatever whatever, and I wanna know would you marry me?" And I was like, "I'm getting married in July. So I can't really marry you." You know, but that was like his image that he always just thought that I would just be there . . . for him . . . But I mean the strange thing I—I don't know—I really think had I not been already in a relationship that felt good . . . Had I not had another person I felt like that about, I probably would have waited around for him or just dropped whatever else I had. And that's why I think I was just dating people kind of indiscriminately 'cause it was like, well that's who I love, but I can't really have him right now, so I could spend time with other people.

If unfulfilled desire drives degreed black women's pursuit of romantic opportunities, then excessive availability can make a mockery of their attempts to use rationality in pursuit of their romantic aims. Rationality is of little use when weighing the costs and benefits of the various ways of remaining unfulfilled. This is why Kim's decisions between "dating people kind of indiscriminately," "wait[ing] around" for an unsatisfying relationship with Earl, and "dropp[ing] whatever else [she] had" are all framed above as equivalently fruitless options. Like the hungry person who uses a cost-benefit calculation to decide between chewing on Styrofoam or plastic pills, Kim, Karie, and the other women who return to in and out relationships that they have already calculated as pointless do so because they are hoping that those calculations are wrong, and they leave those relations because they calculate that their dreams of more promising opportunities beyond this particular partner must be about to come true. In each recurring romantic scenario, they see only a facsimile of the love relationship that they want but they are responding to real feelings of desire. During each recurring breakup, they see no promising romantic opportunities, but struggle against real feelings of undesirability.

When Undesirability Is Known

Watching from the upstairs balcony of a party she is not permitted to attend, a girl like Jennifer learns of her undesirability. It is an undesirability that belongs to girls like her, to women like her mother, and to women who desire to love and be loved by men whose desires can be met elsewhere. And this fact of understanding one's own undesirability—the fact of believing she will not be loved—enables Jennifer's construction of noncommittal, but emotionally protective relationships with men:

> I had problems with my initial relationships with men. I think for one, with my mom, I had the idea that men wanted one thing: they get between your legs and then just, "See ya." You know what I mean? So I was really serious about that. I mean I kinda imagine my mother having all of those kids and not one man, you know what I mean? I mean it turns out we had all different fathers, so there's five kids, five men. She tried some kinda logic to lumpin' some of us together. Some of us, you

know, took last names of the guys, and some of us took maiden names and weird stuff like that, but, ah, she's never been able to inform us of who's who. She don't know. Um, so um, from that picture even though she didn't say it to me, just from that picture, I just envisioned that men don't hang around much.

What Jennifer described as "problems in [her] initial relationships with men," I call "sleeper" relationships. They are "sleeper" because despite their lack of progression to serious romantic commitment, and the fact that not all of the relationship's interactions are necessarily romantic, a few (8 percent according to table 4) manage to sneak up on women and develop to the point of marriage. They are "sleeper" because most of the romantic interactions happen in and around the bedroom. And they are "sleeper" because whatever desires for love and the building of family relations that Jennifer has are "put to bed" by the routinization of romantic relations focused almost exclusively on sexual activity.

Guttentag and Secord (1983) suggest that black women learn undesirability in racially defined marriage contexts. For them, a low sex ratio (in other words, a ratio of males to females that is less than one) in the black community means that African American women are choosing their partners in a social context where women are in relative abundance. They are consequently valued less than women in racial communities where the sex ratio is high and women are more rare. The lesser "value" placed on them means that men will not need to make the level of commitment required by marriage in order to have female companionship and sexual availability. Relationships or sexual liaisons will be short-lived and families will educate daughters in ways that allow them to live in economic independence from men. For them, women like Jennifer's mother are impregnated and abandoned by a lifetime of male partners not because they are black per se, but because their blackness means that they live in a marriage community of "too many women." For them, undesirability is a price point—a community's adjustment to the laws of supply and demand. And Jennifer learns her price point in the familial context, by observing her mother's romantic experiences and actions.

Sierra and Sparkle learn their lessons about undesirability in the racially integrated contexts of their college campuses—in dating scenes that suggest that the racial definitions of Guttentag and Secord's (1983) marriage contexts are constructed and reconstructed by actors on both sides of racial lines. On Sierra's small liberal arts college campus, black women were restricted to the black male partners who form their ostensibly low sex ratio context by white men who feared the consequences of acting on their romantic desires when black women were the objects of those desires:

> There was this [white] guy there [at my college]. He was like a member of the football team . . . I didn't know that until later: my friend said that he was interested in me. She told me this later, after he had graduated. But that the only reason he didn't ask me was that he knew we would have gotten hassled by the guys on the team . . . And, um, actually we had had, um—There was another—There was another couple on campus—a mixed couple, and, um, I heard they usually—they used to write stuff on the bathroom—the male bathroom—to the guy about dating a black girl and stuff.

In contrast, Sparkle cites the actions of black men, pointing to their ability to cross racial dating lines and to penalize black women who do the same. Her passionate complaint indicates that African American men, by expanding their dating pool to include white women (or other non-black women), alter sex ratios—creating or exaggerating the "oversupply" of women that Guttentag and Secord (1983) argue is driving black women's low "value" in sexual and dating arenas:

SPARKLE: And one of the biggest things that my brother, my husband, my mother, my father, [and I had a fight about] . . . and I told them as long as we're black, we're never gonna have that discussion again: I'm totally against black men dating white women, but I am not against black women dating white men.

AVERIL: How come?

SPARKLE: When I was away at State, I saw those black athletes. They always had white women on their arms. They always drove those white women's cars. When those white women's parents would come to visit them, all their pictures were taken down off the wall 'cause their parents could never know that their boyfriend was black. However, the two times that a black girl dated a white guy on that campus, she was shunned by the black community . . . I was the only girl spoke to her . . . And she finally left. She felt no warmth, no friendliness from the blacks. And I said, "But we're accepting this from these athletes—these basketball players, these football players. Yeah, they come to our parties—they come to the black parties—the black fraternity and sorority parties, but at the same time, they still hung out with their other white friends and datin' all these white girls. But it's not accepted vice versa. Why? Why do black men look at black women differently if they date a white guy, however, you can have your cake and eat it too?" . . . My parents said, "Sparkle, we'll never agree on it." They tell me that's a double standard. Call it what you want. I can only go based on what I witnessed, what I saw, what made my stomach turn. That made my stomach turn. Watching these black men marry these white women, and—and I—I wasn't shy to have discussions with them on it.

Sparkle indicates that black men are in a position to exploit the dating scene, having the power in the dating and relationship arena to call the shots and get white women to go against parental and majority group wishes. In her description black women are not understood to have such advantages, as gendered dating customs dictate that they must wait until one of the few non-black men who are interested pursues them, and they suffer recriminations from black community members when they choose to respond affirmatively to these non-black men's flirtations.[17] The undesirability that Sparkle and Sierra learn in racially integrated higher education settings is a racial boundary maintained and policed by individuals' "personal sexual acts" and their responses to the "personal sexual acts" of others.

Sparkle shares Joane Nagel's (2003) argument about the way in which personal sexual acts and informal or institutionalized responses to the personal sexual acts of others help to maintain or strengthen ethnic and racial boundaries. Both women—the research subject and researcher—argue that an individual's race-gender status is a critical variable when determining the significance of sex acts for the maintenance or violation of boundaries between groups, with black women's romantic options being more restricted than black men's because of their differing race-gender statuses. Both women also use data from the mass media as well as summary statistics on interracial relationships to make the point that sex ratios, black male gender advantages in so-called marriage markets, and, ultimately, even black women's apparent undesirability are generated and maintained by a certain gender inequality in the policing of sexual behavior at the boundaries between racial groups.[18] Thus Sierra and Sparkle learn about their own and other black women's undesirability in experiences at the intersection of race and gender inequality-making systems. Where black males' greater power to invite white women into an ostensibly racially bounded dating market meets dominant white communities' greater efficacy in enforcing racial dating boundaries in such a way as to exclude black women, there black women like Sparkle struggle against the creation of their own undesirability by supporting black women's "privilege" in race-sex boundary crossing (or, in other words, black women's permission to date non-black men even as black men are restricted from dating non-black women).

As my discussion of the tandem arguments of Nagel (2003) and "Sparkle (2000)" indicates, this book is not the first work to discuss the race-gender dynamics and representations that inform and constitute black women's low social status. Indeed, intersectionality scholars have repeatedly linked such representations to deprivation and privilege. Where black women are concerned, work in the intersectionality tradition has tended to focus on the ways in which depictions of black women facilitate their exploitation as low-status laborers, support their restriction from access to full social and political citizenship, and devalue their roles in reproductive labor.[19] For example, Patricia Hill Collins (1991, 2004) has described the images that cast lower-class black women as hypersexualized and sexually immoral welfare cheats and maintained that such images support political agendas that force young black mothers to work for welfare benefits. Collins (2004) has also described the images of bitches and mammies (who, in the contemporary era, are the black women who are likely middle class) that appropriately subjugate their own and their families' needs to the priorities of modern employers. Similarly Brodkin (1999) maintains that the privileges of whiteness were extended to European males in processes that simultaneously framed white females as their dependent wives with a special and important role as nurturing mothers of the next generation of white citizenry. At the same time, Euro-ethnic cultures were framed as superior to the "deficit" culture of African Americans, and African American women's culturally inadequate motherhood legitimated the political and economic processes that herded them into low status and dirty labor roles alongside black males in a seemingly "ungendered" way. In these works, black women are made undesirable in the media, in the world of exploited labor, and in the political arena as the competition for scarce resources and the maintenance of white privilege require actions and representations in which black bodies are exploited and black people are excluded from free market competition and full rights and protections.[20]

Whether in the gender dynamics in families of upbringing, on the heterosexual dating scene of college campuses, in welfare legislation and its enforcement, or even in iconic media representations of hypersexualized or bitchy black women who can take care of themselves, this book links the ongoing construction of black women's undesirability to their involvement in *"sleeper" relationships. Such relationships emerge from women's acknowledgment of their relatively low power with particular partners as well as with a community of potential partners.* Women learn about their low power from witnessing and participating in the romantic relations in which their romantic undesirability is continually being reconstituted. The sleeper relationship is a strategic response to known undesirability and low power in heterosexual dating dynamics. It is a response organized to address unfulfilled romantic and family formation desires that matter but a strategy predicated on the fact that power to address these desires within racist and sexist arenas is limited.

Below, Danielle discusses dating experiences in college. In much the same way as Jennifer's above narrative winds its way from her mother's checkered sexual and family formation experiences to her own, Danielle's words diagram a trajectory moving from undesirability construction, through women's apprehension and acknowledgment of a certain powerlessness in undesirability, and on to their strategic response in the form of sleeper relationships:

DANIELLE: The seniors at Columbia tried to play a lot of the freshmen. So after just that whole experience, Lisa and my other girlfriend, Leticia and Ingrid and that little group, they were just like, "Look, we can have just as much fun as you guys [are] trying to have." So they would party, they'd, you know, go on dates with guys. They would have 'em pay for dinner, and "The thing is I'm not in any type of commitment situation. No. Yeah, I went out with Paul last weekend; I'll go out with David this weekend; Okay I'm going out with Michael on Saturday; I'm free on Sunday night. You know, we just—We want to see everyone have fun, you know" . . .

AVERIL: So you would say the environment was one that didn't really connote serious relationships . . . And, ah, did you, um, think that you're not being seriously involved had anything to do at all . . . with your education and goals or did you just—Or was it just sort of you got turned off and it was like, "Well, I don't really wanna be bothered with this"?

DANIELLE: I just got turned off.

Finding themselves unable to command high levels of romantic attention and care, degreed black women enter sleeper relationships that provide them with access to sex, and, at times, very minimal levels of romantic companionship in the form of sporadic dates. These ambivalent benefits are claimed even as women hold onto a higher ideal of romantic care that as yet remains unavailable to them. By not asking for the romantic commitment or love that normative romantic relations in their families, dating communities, and college campuses (or, for that matter, the race-gender dynamics at work in historical and contemporary political processes and media representation of black individuals) repeatedly tell them is unavailable to them, they benefit from but avoid committing to situations in which they assent to their undesirability and consent to the romantic exploitation or maltreatment that is its companion.[21]

Sleeper relationships are like in and out relationships in that they represent a controlled response to frustrated desires and excessive availability. Observing and participating within the spaces of our basic social institutions (for example, families, schools, work, politics, mass media) that reflect intersecting inequality systems of race, class, and gender, degreed black women struggle to achieve a love that matters. Media representations that support black women's genderless exploitation as low-status labor make their way into human resources offices and employment centers as well as into college campuses and dating destinations and interactions because the women and men involved and potentially involved in every date or budding romance are simultaneously workers (or potential workers), media consumers, and sexual actors. Similarly, mothers' troubles with men easily find their way into daughters' early sexual experiences because such daughters are both the abandoned daughters of a series of their mother's male partners and the women who both protect themselves from abandonment and prepare for life on their own. As long as love matters, and *as long as individuals live lives of simultaneity in which they are both potential laborers and lovers or in which they are both the products of and producers of families, it is possible for an undesirability constituted across a myriad of social institutions to limit access to love.*

Inequality scholarship has all too often located the consequences of a socially constituted undesirability in black individuals' underachievement in school, work, criminal justice, or politics. At times these "primary" inequalities are fed back into inequalities of family formation as when black males' high incarceration or high unemployment lowers their marriage rates or when black women's poor educational performance and school dropout accelerate their involvement in precocious fertility. But here, in this book, where unequal social relations can be organized around a scarce love that matters, "sleeper" and "in and out" relationships reflect the race-gender constraints on black women's access to high-quality romantic care—constraints that they alternatively try to resist and to overcome.

At the beginning of the chapter, I argued that romantic "process" data would support the reader's understanding of how unequal love outcomes come about. And I was concerned to represent degreed black women's desire to be involved in romantic love and marriage lest quantitative data on their relatively low marital outcomes and on the inverse relationship between women's education and their fertility be interpreted to mean that love, romance, and marriage were low priorities for or were appropriately placed on the back burner by those who would be class elites. I have endeavored instead to demonstrate that black women's low likelihood of marriage is conditioned by the low value of their romantic options rather than the low prioritization that they give to romance. Those relationships least likely to develop into marriage fail in this regard because of their lack of viability as options for marriage. In the one instance, actors on both sides of the color line as well as historical and contemporary inequality-making processes across multiple social institutions repeatedly construct black women as undesirable romantic partners. The in and out and sleeper relationships that emerge from this state of affairs reflect race-gender constraints and black women's limited options to negotiate for a better deal with a more attractive and compatible partner or for relationships with greater and more long-term commitment and care. In the other instance, dating and rating relations reflect class-based constraints associated with the organization of romance around education and professional development opportunities. Although black women may have the greatest opportunity to act on romances that occur during the early reproductive years—when they are in school—the rules and cultural codes for romance within educational and professional settings lead to a weak romantic structure as well. In the next chapter's discussion of sex and the ways unequal sex makes for unequal family formation experiences, the link between degreed black women's participation in romantic relationships and their race-class-gender status is further underscored by direct comparisons of their sexual experiences with those of women in other race-education groups.

FOUR

Sex

Is Everybody Doing It?

O N E D A Y Janet decided it was time to lose her virginity. How did she know? She spoke with some friends and realized that she was falling behind. What did she do about it? She found herself a man. Did she do it with him? Yes. What happened when it was over? Nothing.

Because the loss of virginity is supposed to be such a cataclysmic event—the culprit that is often blamed for leading young girls into motherhood before they are ready—the answer to the last of my four questions might turn out to be the greatest source of contention.[1] Nevertheless, neither qualitative nor quantitative data indicate that college-educated black women turn the loss of virginity into an opportunity for nonmarital childbearing. Instead, the words of Janet and others like her tell listeners that sexual initiation is a rite of passage—a symbol of adulthood and independence in which virgin girls approaching their late teens feel compelled to partake. The compulsion or sense of readiness for sexual activity comes from interactions with same-sex peers more so than pressure from a boy in the context of a particular relationship. And the opportunity to have this first sex is not necessarily easy to come by, so it is often distinct from long-term romantic relationships.

This chapter describes the social influences on degreed black women's nonmarital sexual activity, including their decisions to have their first sex and the reasons for their experiences of nonmarital celibacy after the point of sexual initiation. The chapter also compares their sexual behavior to that of similarly educated white and Hispanic women and to less educated black women using the National Survey of Family Growth (NSFG [NCHS 1995]). I use these race and class comparisons of women's answers to sex survey questions in combination with degreed black women's sexual narratives to begin explaining why black women with college degrees are less likely to respond to marriage deprivation with nonmarital fertility than their less educated black counterparts, who are similarly deprived in marriage. In this regard, the conclusions of this chapter focus on the point that degreed black women's opportunities to have nonmarital sex are limited—more limited than the opportunities of less educated black women and more limited than those of white women with college degrees. And in much the same way as infrequent marriage constrains these women's involvement in marital childbearing, lower intercourse frequency presages their lower rates of nonmarital childbearing.

Janet's description of her first sex and her discussion of her attempts to involve herself in subsequent nonmarital sexual activity loom large in this chapter's argument. From her description of the feelings that precipitated her first sex to her explanation of what her decision to lose her virginity meant to her mother, the story that she tells exemplifies degreed black women's struggles to have heterosexual intercourse and the ways that those struggles distinguish them from similarly educated white and Hispanic women and from less educated black women. For Janet and most of the other degreed black women in my sample, the initiation of sex in the second half of their teen years appears to be normative. The same is true of their inclusion of sex in nonmarital romantic relationships. However, despite their apparently normative sexual desires, these women appear to have a relatively difficult time making sex a normal part of their lives. This relative lack of sexual activity seems to lower their rate of nonmarital childbearing when compared to black women who do not attain college degrees.

The evidence of degreed black women's limited opportunity for non-marital sex and the nonmarital childbearing losses that result from this situation comes from my data on women's sexual initiation experiences, on the frequency of their subsequent nonmarital sexual experiences, and on the timing of women's first sex, first marriage, and first birth experiences. Analyses of these data reveal that degreed black women have less sex than they believe is appropriate, that they have less sex and fewer non-marital births than less educated black women, and that they have less sex than similarly educated Hispanic and white women.

Time to Do It

This section of the chapter introduces readers to Janet—an absolutely effervescent twenty-two-year-old medical student whom I interviewed outside on a warm summer day. Using her sexual initiation experience, I show readers the meanings that are attached to sexual initiation among the respondents in my sample—meanings that associate loss of virginity with adulthood, independence, and emancipation from parents. Here, I argue that these meanings emerge from the specific activities and relations that bring about sexual initiation and move it from possibility to reality in college-educated black women's lives. The degree to which sexual initiation comes to signify an emancipatory rite of passage for the young women has to do with the fact that same-sex, same-race peers provide socialization around the loss of virginity and with the fact that ongoing relationships with steady boyfriends were less critical to the process.

For women like Janet, the struggle to turn their understanding of appropriate nonmarital sexual activity into a lived sexually active reality begins with sexual initiation. In these cases, the loss of virginity is a developmental challenge. It is a journey that starts with a teen girl becoming convinced that she is ready to have sex—with her getting the distinct sense that she is falling behind other young women in this arena of social development. And it is a trek that ends when that teen girl finds and has sex with an attractive and willing partner.

Degreed black women's limited opportunities for nonmarital sexual activity reveal themselves in protracted searches for attractive and willing partners with whom these women can have their first sexual experiences.

Thus, it is only fitting that Janet opened discussion of her first sexual experience with a description of the guy who turned out to be that partner for her. I include this description below along with her answers to my probes for more detail, as the more extended dialogue demonstrates the ways the opportunity to be "normally" sexually active is intertwined with the where and how of finding sexual partners.

Discussing Walter, the man with whom she first had sex, Janet began,

> There was this guy I met at a party when I was sixteen; he was twenty; he went to Hampton. I was very impressed by that. And when I was seventeen, he was twenty-one, he was a senior, he was pre-med, and I was so crazy about him, so I lost my virginity to him. He wasn't my boyfriend. I didn't want him to be, but all the girls at school were like talking about having sex, and I had—was curious. I wanted to get it over with the first time, so then I could move onto times that I would enjoy 'cause everybody said it was gonna be—it was gonna hurt, so I wanted to lose it to him—I did. And then I didn't talk to him anymore after that. I wasn't interested.

When I prompted her to talk about how she met Walter, Janet went on to say the following.

> My cousin had a friend who was, um, a frat boy and she took us to his house for, like, a get-together. It was just, like, her and him and me and my friend and this other guy—these two guys. We talked to the guys, and this guy, he thought I was older than I was. I didn't bother to tell him 'til like the next year that I was younger. I mean . . . I liked him. I did like him, but I didn't like him like I wanted to be with him. I liked him like I wanted to lose my virginity to him. [Laughter] And I did use a condom. Yeah, so I was safe . . .

In response to my queries about whether and how they had come to the decision to have sex, Janet said emphatically,

> I had been thinking about it. And you know all the girls in—on the—in the dorm—we'd sit around. We'd have, like, these little chats, you know, we'd sit at—Late at night, we'd sit outside our doors, and we'd talk about stuff, and we'd talk about sex and boys, and I didn't have anybody that was like a steady. I didn't, you know, I didn't have anybody that I

could lose my virginity to 'cause I didn't have a boyfriend, so I thought well, hmm, I know him. And . . . [Laughter] So then the next year when I wasn't afraid to do it anymore, I did it.

Janet's story wound down with her discussion of the "after-party" of interactions that she had with Walter and with her mother:

I worked in a Dairy Queen, and he came to visit me after that, and I was like, "[sigh] What do you want?" And he was like, "Oh, you know, I wanna talk to you." I was like, "Please, you—now, don't get mushy on me, all right? Let's not do this." And I was—I really wasn't interested. I know my mom was like, "What the hell's wrong with this girl?!?" You know. I told her like a week later that I did it. She cried . . . She was like, "You had sex, and you didn't—you know I didn't give you permission," and I was like, "I don't need your permission" . . . I think that was when she realized that . . . she didn't have any control over what I did anymore.

Janet's comments above represent only the very small beginnings of my conversation with an interviewee who ultimately required little prompting to expound on her oft foiled and frustrated sexual attempts. Without jettisoning the biological analyses that claim that the timing of first sex is related to a physical maturity evident in the early beginning of menses and an increased presence of testosterone (Udry 1988), I focus here on Janet's characterization of sexual initiation as social and personal. For hormonal cues may support an adolescent's burgeoning sexual interest, but Janet relies on social interactions with peers to determine when (for example, around the age of sixteen) and with whom (for example "a steady" would be the most obvious choice, but an impressive older pre-med student who isn't a boyfriend will do) she should act on these cues. She also relies on social interactions with peers for clues about how she should experience her loss of virginity (for example, painful and unpleasant, but an important step in her own personal pursuit of enjoyment in later sexual encounters). Finally, Janet demonstrates the importance of social meaning in her decision to initiate sexual activity when she uses her loss of virginity as a symbol communicating emancipation from her mother's control. Here, she reminds her mother of the independence-signifying and adult-like character of her actions: she thereby shows how first sex became a tenable action for her in an evolving set of social interactions that revealed its character as a thing about which a girl who is no longer "afraid" and a girl who might be mistaken for "older than [she is]" can strategize, plan, and execute.

In addition to illustrating how interactions with peers and parents shape both sexual initiation and what sexual initiation comes to mean, this look at the social side of Janet's experience of first sex points to the ways race and education (or schooling) intersect in degreed black women's lives both to facilitate and constrain their nonmarital sexual activity. By ensuring involvement in a sexual initiation experience that is preceded by a long search for a suitable partner, racial status and schooling intersect in Janet's life to raise her age at first sex and to isolate that experience from longer term romantic relations.

It is the school that provides the space and the social setting that maintained Janet's multiracial but mostly black group of peers. These peers' chatter and laughter late into the night included juicy details about painful virginity loss followed by subsequent enjoyable sexual encounters— details that jump-started Janet's long journey to the loss of her virginity, a journey that began at the age of sixteen. At the same time, attendance at the predominantly white boarding school on an affirmative action scholarship meant sharing classrooms, meals, and recreational activities with a largely white crowd of boys, none of whom Janet could call a "steady." From her black peers in the racially isolated setting, Janet learned that she was on her way to becoming a late sexual initiator. And in the race-sex dating dynamic of her racially isolated school setting, Janet learned that the achievement of "normal" virginity loss would require that she work to locate a partner and that she accept the fact that he might not be someone who shared her day-to-day existence. Thus, race and the school setting that facilitates college attendance and degree attainment intersect in social experiences that tell Janet that it is "time to do it" all the while that she is learning that "it" might be a single emancipatory act with a well-chosen but impermanent man in her life.

Black girls who find themselves in whiter school settings (as well as in single sex school settings) because of their own and/or their parents' desires to support their eventual college matriculation are complicit in the delay of their sexual initiation. They are complicit because the simultaneity and the intersecting quality of the unfolding of individuals' economic and family formation trajectories mean that they cannot make decisions that address the race- and class-based exclusionary processes that limit the educational mobility of lower-class and/or racially disadvantaged youth without simultaneously making decisions that affect the racial distribution of partners in their school-based dating pools. This racial isolation associated with the schooling of future black elites then constitutes one of the mechanisms raising degreed black women's average age at sexual initiation and lowering their levels of nonmarital sexual activity and child-bearing relative to black women who achieve fewer educational credentials. By whitening dating pools and lengthening the search for partners, certain schooling experiences associated with the attainment of a college degree delay young women's sexual initiation and isolate it from ongoing romantic relationships. While this may please (and may have even been consciously desired by) their parents, it seems to frustrate young black women for whom love and the inclusion of romantic and sexual experiences in their young lives matter.[2]

The portion of women in the qualitative sample who discussed strategic searches for partners with whom they could lose their virginity that went on outside of their single sex or predominantly white school settings is just one example of data in support of an argument that degreed black women initiate sex later than less educated black women. Below, the tables displaying the statistically significant race (see table 6, below) and class (see table 7, below) differences in the age at virginity loss also provide evidence in support of this point. Tables 6 and 7 respectively distinguish degreed black women's average age at virginity loss of 18.43 from that of degreed white (19.20) and Hispanic women (20.16) and from that of black women who earn no diplomas (15.15), high-school diplomas (16.57), and some college credentials (17.16).[3]

Tables 6 and 7 make two points. The first is that racial differences in the age at sexual initiation (particularly between white and black women) are smaller than class differences. That is to say that although black women, regardless of education level, begin having sex earliest and Hispanic women begin having sex latest, loss of virginity appears to be more tied to educational achievement than it is to women's racial status. The second point is that degreed black women are the latest initiators among the black women sampled in the NSFG (NCHS 1995) but the earliest initiators among women in the college-educated group. Taken alone, these

Table 6. Racial differences in mean age at first voluntary sex (between black and white women and black and Hispanic women)

	# IN SAMPLE	MEAN	DIFFERENCE FROM BLACK WOMEN	T	P<
Whites			*Black mean-White mean*		
College degree	1408	19.20	-.78**	-3.72	.000
Some college	1566	17.73	-.56**	-4.33	.000
HS diploma/GED	2246	17.12	-.54**	-5.51	.000
< HS diploma	661	15.54	-.39**	-3.23	.001
Hispanics			*Black mean-Hispanic mean*		
College degree	134	20.16	-1.73**	-4.66	.000
Some college	305	18.67	-1.50**	-6.88	.000
HS diploma/GED	465	18.20	-1.63**	-9.66	.000
< HS diploma	502	17.33	-2.19**	-12.30	.000

Source: Data for the above calculations are taken from the NSFG (NCHS 1995). Sample sizes for black women were as follows: 268 for college degree; 590 for some college; 906 for high-school diploma/GED; and 525 for less than high-school diploma. Significance tests on the differences between white and Hispanic women are found in the appendix in table A8.

Notes: "T" designates the value of the "t-statistic" in the difference of means significance test. The probability that this statistic and the listed difference result is due to sampling variation or the "luck of the draw" (rather than differences between racial groups in the actual population) is less than the figure listed in the final "$p<$" column of the table.

** Results of a t-test indicate that the difference from the mean age at first voluntary sex for black women is significant at the .01 level.

quantitative descriptions of differences between racial and education-level groups in the age at virginity loss and of how degreed black women fall between less educated black women and degreed white and Hispanic women suggest that the delay in Janet's sexual initiation is a figment of her own imagination, since she falls somewhere in the middle of the distribution. The information in the tables also suggests that her experience of delay is connected to processes that also delay the loss of virginity among similarly educated white and Hispanic women and that seem to delay the loss of virginity to an even greater degree in these groups.

Table 7. Education level differences in mean age at first voluntary sex (between women with and without degrees)

	# IN SAMPLE	MEAN	DIFFERENCE FROM WOMEN W/4-YEAR COLLEGE DEGREES	T	P<
		Some college			
Black	590	17.16	1.27**	5.75	.000
White	1566	17.73	1.48**	13.33	.000
Hispanic	305	18.67	1.26**	4.02	.000
		High school diploma or GED			
Black	906	16.57	1.86**	8.88	.000
White	2246	17.12	2.09**	21.02	.000
Hispanic	465	18.20	1.96**	5.59	.000
		Less than HS *diploma*			
Black	525	15.15	3.28**	15.45	.000
White	661	15.54	3.66**	31.80	.000
Hispanic	502	17.33	2.82**	7.99	.000

Source: Data for the above calculations are taken from the NSFG (NCHS 1995); the sample sizes for degreed women are as follows: 268 for blacks; 1,408 for whites; and 134 for Hispanics

Notes: "T" designates the value of the "t-statistic" in the difference of means significance test. The probability that this statistic and the listed difference result is due to sampling variation or the "luck of the draw" (rather than differences between education level groups in the actual population) is less than the figure listed in the final "*p*<" column of the table.

** Indicates that the difference from the mean age at first voluntary sex for women with four-year college degrees is significant at the .01 level.

At the same time, examination of tables 6 and 7 in light of the qualitative data highlights the importance of race and intersections between race and schooling in delaying degreed black women's nonmarital sexual activity and differentiating it from that of less educated black women. In combination with Janet's and other women's tales of sexual initiation, tables 6 and 7 illustrate the importance of race in individuals' experience of virginity loss. For example, I argue that the impatience that Janet and other women in the sample expressed about the pace of their virginity loss and the sense of urgency they felt about losing their virginity before getting to or upon arriving at college can only make sense if such young women are receiving their cues about "appropriate" virginity loss from their black peers, many of whom do not end up graduating from college. Feelings of impatience would hardly make sense if these women's reference group consisted of college-bound white and Hispanic teens whose pace of virginity loss (according to table 6) is even slower than that of degreed black women themselves. Instead, it appears that degreed black women respond to African American community cues about appropriate virginity loss, but, like Janet, they are more likely to be constrained from acting on those cues by the race-sex dynamics of dating in integrated school settings than less educated black women.[4]

I have advanced the argument maintaining that an apparently independent class effect in table 7 (for example, one that appears to affect the age at sexual initiation of all women with degrees, regardless of their race, in an equivalent manner) may mask and take credit for increases to degreed black women's ages at virginity loss that are actually associated with the intersection of their African American status and the race-sex dynamics of their college preparatory school and classroom environments. This argument begins with the data from degreed black women that indicate that same-race peers are instrumental in influencing the actions women take to accomplish their first sex. The argument includes an explanation of the way an experience of racial isolation in available dating pools that slows sexual initiation only affects students of color who move to whiter dating settings for schooling and does not affect students of color who do not move (and whose schooling may be arrested because they did not have the opportunity to move). Nor does it affect white students who need not move.[5] Below, the argument is developed further by a description of the ways shared meanings of virginity loss reflect degreed black women's high likelihood of experiencing it outside of romantic partnership. For even those black women who did not struggle to find their first sexual partners, as Janet did, talked about a sexual initiation that reflected their independent and grown-up decision-making behavior and that was isolated from romantic partnership.

Randi and Rose were two of the women in the interview sample who began having sex at earlier ages than Janet. Randi said that in her case "early" meant "sixteen—fifteen really" and Rose said, "fourteen or fifteen." But these women's early initiator status did not stop them from sharing Janet's understanding that first sex and sexual activity is about emancipation, independence, and showing mothers that daughters have the right to make their own decisions about sex. Randi happily told me that her mother was "scandalized" by the fact of a sexually active daughter while Rose explained in a less animated tone that her mother was "confused" and just could not understand why her daughter was having sex.

The shared understanding of early sexual activity as a series of isolated acts constituting youths' individuation and emancipation seems thematically related to the lack of connection between the loss of virginity and long-term romance—something that is also common across early and late sexual initiators in the interview sample. Despite finding first sex partners relatively easily, Randi and Rose initiated sexual activity with men who were interested in sex but not romance. This access to sex but not romantic partnership is a less extreme version of Janet's access to sexual initiation but not subsequent sex, described above. In both situations, voluntary participation in or strategic action to bring about sexual initiation implies the existence of a sexual actor who can make sense of the relationally experienced sex act as an individual achievement or accomplishment. And this is where degreed black women's shared sense of a sexual initiation as important to personal development and as a facilitator opening doors to subsequent and more sexually fulfilling relationships makes an isolated experience of virginity loss meaningful and desirable. This is where the meanings attached to the loss of virginity set the experience up to be claimed by girls or young women whose mothers might interfere, and whose available male sexual partners and potential partners may be uninterested in or unavailable for the development of long-term relationships with them. The next section of the chapter deals more explicitly with the degree to which a sexual initiation that is isolated from romance and ongoing relationships is distinctively a degreed black women's experience. For now, it is important to take notice of the way in which the meanings attached to sexual initiation support sexual initiation despite a lack of access to romantic partnerships across the sample of early and late initiators in the interview sample.

In the end, the racial isolation of elite schooling underscored a shared understanding about "normal" first sex that existed across the group of degreed black women. An understanding that first sex is about relatively isolated acts of youths' emancipation appears to come first from young women's interactions with peers and parents that seek to usher young women into the privileges and responsibilities of adulthood (peers) or to protect and restrict young women from the same (parents). Whether the fantastic tales about sex have the effect of enticing or scaring, inviting or threatening, they similarly reinforce the link in meaning between having sex and being a grown-up that appeals to girls involved in the performance of maturation on several of life's fronts. But for the young black women who experienced a race-sex isolation associated with the college preparatory tracks and schools as well as those who moved into such spaces in predominantly white universities where they were racially outnumbered and where sex ratios among black students might be as low as one male to two females,[6] the lesson about normal first sex (and likely subsequent nonmarital sex) as an entity distinct from a "steady" or one's "first love" is underscored in the search for the suitable partner who is ultimately unavailable for long-term romance.

Janet's narrative speaks alongside the race and class differences in age at first sex. Its song is the chorus of college-bound black women who become aware that "normal sex" is unavailable to them when they find that they cannot initiate sex at the times that they observe their relevant others (for example, other black female teens) doing so. Its voice is the tale telling of the black college matriculates who recognize that normal sex is unavailable to them when decisions to engage in a more strategic version of sexual initiation require the divorcing of sex from romantic relationships.

Did It

Whether degreed black women's opportunity for first sex appears after a long search for an attractive partner or presents itself "early" through more ongoing contact with peers in school and neighborhood settings, it is highly likely that it yet remains divorced from the opportunity for long-term romantic involvement. This section of the chapter argues that degreed black women's first or early sexual experiences are distinguished from that of women in other race-education groups by the degree to which they are divorced from opportunities for long-term romance. I rely on NSFG (NCHS 1995) data from women in the different race-education groups as well as qualitative data from degreed black women on their lack of success with involving themselves in sexual romantic relationships. Furthermore, the qualitative data is also used to show how low levels of sexual activity or high levels of celibacy can be constituted both by sex without romance and romance without sex. Both are conditions familiar to those black women who have difficulty entering committed romantic partnerships with males of their choosing.

The distinctiveness of degreed black women's first or early sexual experiences from opportunities for long-term romance, love, and ongoing sexual activity is not only present across early and late sexual initiators in my relatively small snowball sample of interviewees. It can also be found in the survey data from the national sample of the NSFG (NCHS 1995). Degreed black women's answers to survey questions about recent sexual activity reflect relatively high likelihoods of experiencing short- and long-term celibacy after sexual initiation. In figure 9, women in the different race-education groups are divided into virgins (represented by the black sections of long bars), sexually initiated women who have had no sex during the prior three months (represented by the dark gray sections), and women who have had at least one intercourse experience in the prior three months (represented by the light gray sections). Here, degreed black women reveal themselves as the group of women most likely to be sexually initiated and celibate. Figure 9 (and Table A9 in the appendix) indicates that almost 24 percent of degreed black women fall into the sexually initiated and celibate category. This compares with approximately 12 percent of degreed white women and 17 percent of degreed Hispanic women. The greater prevalence of this experience among degreed black women supports the point that opportunities for first sex are more likely to be discontinuous from opportunities for sex in the context of ongoing romance in this population.

Table 8's catalogue of the racial differences in the average number of celibate months women experienced during the three years prior to the interview also supports this point. It indicates that degreed black women's average of 8.1 months of celibacy was greater than that of degreed whites by almost two months. Indeed black women in all but the lowest educa-

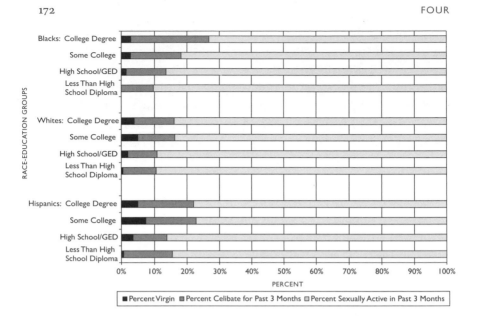

9   Percentage of respondents who are virgins, celibate non-virgins, and women reporting
    intercourse during the past three months. Calculations are based on cross-sectional data from
    NSFG (NCHS 1995) respondents over the age of nineteen. Calculations are found in table A9.

tional categories reported more celibacy than white and Hispanic women,
although, with respect to Hispanics, the differences were not statistically
significant.

In real, on the ground terms, the data on degreed black women's relatively high rates of short- and long-term celibacy after sexual initiation
are reflected in their ongoing struggles to act on sexual desires and to
make sex a normal part of their romantic lives. These women's understanding that they face difficulty achieving romantic partnerships that include normal sexual activity exists in their direct testimonies about their
negotiations for sex and romance during the course of their romantic life
trajectories as much as it exists in these survey differentials. With regard
to women in the interview sample who had experience with the sexual
drought (or celibacy after initiation) symbolized in the dark gray sections
of figure 9's bars, three experiences—life without romance, sex without
romance, and romance without sex—seemed to hang together in an instructive configuration that repeatedly highlighted the importance of
committed romantic partnerships to the experience of consistent sexual

Table 8. Racial differences in mean number of months of celibacy during three years prior to interview (between black and white women and black and Hispanic women)

	# IN SAMPLE	MEAN	DIFFERENCE FROM BLACK WOMEN	T	P<
White women			*Black mean-white mean*		
College degree	1415	6.30	1.81*	2.27	.024
Some college	1511	5.59	1.04*	2.06	.040
HS diploma/GED	2121	4.07	1.17**	3.10	.002
< HS diploma	409	3.93	.09	.15	.880
Hispanic women			*Black mean-Hispanic mean*		
College degree	134	6.63	1.47	1.24	.215
Some college	300	5.98	.66	.90	.370
HS diploma/GED	441	4.80	.43	.77	.441
< HS diploma	416	5.48	-1.46*	-2.09	.037

Source: Data for the above calculations are taken from NSFG (NCHS 1995) respondents over the age of nineteen. Sample sizes for black women were as follows: 268 for college degree; 581 for some college; 878 for high school diploma/GED; and 390 for less than high-school diploma. Significance tests on the differences between white and Hispanic women are found in the appendix in Table A10.

Notes: "T" designates the value of the "t-statistic" in the difference of means significance test. The probability that this statistic and the listed difference result is due to sampling variation or the "luck of the draw" (rather than differences between racial groups in the actual population) is less than the figure listed in the final "*p<*" column of the table.

* Indicates that the difference from black women's mean number of months of celibacy is significant at the .05 level.

** Indicates that the difference from black women's mean number of months of celibacy is significant at the .01 level.

activity. Below, the data from 58 degreed black women's 202 romantic relationships illustrate the point that limited access to romantic partnership and the resulting elevated celibacy rates are experienced in at least two ways—through episodic and repeatedly renegotiated sex without romance as well as through episodic and repeatedly renegotiated romance without sex.

Sexual Relations

In Janet's case, the origins of her life without romance lay in her race-education status, as her struggle to have what she viewed as a normal sex life continued to work itself out in racially isolating school settings even after the strategic loss of virginity episode. At the large university where she completed her bachelor of science degree in biochemistry, she remained in a predominantly white, class-privileged school setting. There, she got involved in a dating pattern that initially allowed her access to sex but not romantic relationships, as well as a "bad reputation" in the campus's relatively small black community. About her search for love while trying to live down this reputation she had developed by getting sex but not romantic relationships from guys who seemed accessible to love but weren't really, Janet would remark, "I needed to like somebody, and I needed somebody who liked me." And it was in this moment of needing that which she could not find on a myriad of isolated dates with the campus's far-too-approachable black football players that Janet happened upon Kevin, a man who was offering romance without sex.

Janet's description of her relationship with Kevin began with a very long period of getting to know each other through work at the same local movie theater and an even longer period of dating without sex. The latter longer period started when Janet—after several weeks of working up her courage—said, "I like you. I want you to be my boyfriend," and Kevin responded by being "really flattered" and the couple commenced "going out." The sexual desire embedded in Janet's need "to like somebody" and need for "somebody to like [her]" became obvious to me with her actions to bring this long latter period of dating without sex to a close. She told me, "So this went on for like two months, and I wanted to have sex, 'cause really I like it . . . I was ready." Then she explained how she had broached the subject with Kevin, asking, "You know, are we gonna have sex?" to which he responded, "Well, you know, I just don't have sex with anybody." But Janet continued, asserting that she didn't "either," and proceeding "to ask him all the questions that they ask you when you give blood" and explaining to him that she didn't "wanna get pregnant" and didn't "want to catch any disease," until he finally said, "Oh yeah, well since we've talked about it, now I think we can do it." Here, in our conversation, Janet's repetition of an inarticulate "Yay, Ooo!" was meant to recall for me her feelings of satisfaction about and anticipation of the inclusion of sex with romance.

But the relevant point for understanding degreed black women's higher celibacy rates is that Janet's narrative concludes without Kevin and Janet ever having sex. Instead, she ends the description of the relationship with two upsetting discoveries that she made after they had broken up. First, she discovered that he "was dating this Indian girl" a couple of months after he supposedly broke up with her in order to concentrate on a heavy course load and part-time work. And then, during the subsequent school year, she discovered that he was "openly gay," which "hurt" but which served as the explanation she needed for why, despite all that talking, they "didn't have sex that night" or any other night.

Because of the unarticulated desire for sex buried in her list of emotional pleas, romance without sex with Kevin failed to solve Janet's problem of needing to like somebody and needing somebody who liked her. The relationship ultimately decreased rather than increased her level of sexual activity and added to the list of specific ways in which she felt her access to love and romance was constrained. Before Kevin, she experienced difficulty achieving the sexually constituted romance. Rendered an undesirable female by her unconcealed interest in sex, she found herself increasingly less able to negotiate for romantic partnerships or even repeated sex acts in the context of the campus's community of black football players and the clique that surrounded them.[7] Subsequently, the discoveries that she made after she and Kevin broke up similarly demonstrated her limited romantic opportunity. Only this time she was reminded of her romantic constraints through her inability to achieve a romantically constituted sex. Here she imagines that Kevin's romantic partnership and the sex benefits package that typically comes with it is available to women racialized in other ways—for example "this Indian girl"—and eventually to other men, but not to her. Both the sex without romance and the romance without sex represent different stopping points on a journey Janet takes to address her challenge finding a romantic partnership and the sexual benefits package that ostensibly goes along with it. The journey itself is a message to inequality scholars who would fail to consider the ways in which outcomes in love—and not an abstract love but one that includes commitment to sexual satisfaction—matter.

Configurations linking romantic celibacy and romance-less sex to lives without romance reveal the relational constraints that are at the base of black women's high celibacy rates. Among the women in my interview sample, mutual affection and committed romantic partnerships appeared to be the surest routes to consistent sexual activity.[8] This is why the struggles that Janet had with finding attractive men who were interested in partnering with her lowered her frequency of intercourse. Andrea's and Sparkle's difficulties establishing committed relationships with men of their choosing also led to inconsistent sex and decreased levels of sexual activity.

In a slightly different journey from the one taken by Janet, Andrea moved from romance with a man made less desirable because of his suspicious interactions with other women, to sex without romance, and then to life without romance or sex. Describing the relationship and their breakup, she maintained,

> Our problems in the relationship centered around time, and ah, then, these other women, because I never met any of these other women. For one thing, you know, if you're still friendly with these people, I should be introduced to your circle of friends. If you can't introduce me to somebody, that calls into question your relationship with them. He didn't understand that. So, we had to break up. Now we continued to have a sex—We continued to have a sexual relationship, but there was no romantic relationship after about fifteen months.

Andrea would go on to say that "for almost two years after the relationship, [she] continued to have a sexual relationship with [Rodney]" and that "although [she] never gave indication to him, [she] still wanted it to be something more." Her sense of romantic relationship constraint or, as she put it, her sense that "[she] wasn't moving forward and the relationship wasn't moving forward" finally convinced her that the sex without romance "was no longer a good thing to do." And this decision brought her frequency of intercourse, which was already lowered and made more inconsistent by the loss of the committed romantic relationship, down even further to intimacy's version of absolute zero.

Sparkle presented me with still another scenario that brings the role players of romance without sex and sex without romance together in the lives of women who are challenged with respect to the achievement of romantic partnerships. Her description of the difficulties she had establishing a committed romance with the right guy (I call him Jarvis) while keeping the wrong guy (I call him Anthony) at arm's length makes it clear that both males and females might find that constraints on their ability to establish committed relationships with desired partners are the reasons for inconsistent, infrequent, or nonexistent intercourse. Sparkle told me,

> But, um, this was a guy who—he would come to my apartment and spend the night. And he would get up every morning and see me take birth control pills, and he couldn't understand why I was takin' birth control pills when we were not being intimate. And I told him I had to be on the pill to regulate my period, which was not true, which was a lie. I was on the pill because I was being intimate with Jarvis . . . Whenever we were in emotion to do that: we were not committed; we were not in a relationship, but you know you just wanna get together every now and then. It was for that reason that I was taking birth control pills . . . So I was never intimate with him. He never understood why, but he respected it, and he just liked to just lay there beside me . . . We came across as an item. Only he and I knew that we weren't being intimate . . . He just didn't understand why . . .

Here, both Sparkle and Anthony struggle in vain against unwilling partners. Without a commitment from Jarvis, Sparkle can expect no more than inconsistent, infrequent, and romance less sex, regardless of the tacit gift of sexual exclusivity that she makes to him. And despite the appearance of a commitment from Sparkle, Anthony gets no sex and consequently remains confused about the status of their relationship in the face of these sexual refusals.

Sparkle's and Andrea's narratives about inconsistent and infrequent sex without romance and romance without sex lend support to the point that Janet's romantic trajectory makes about high rates of celibacy after initiation among degreed black women. The point is that these *scenarios of romance without sex and sex without romance occur in situations where individuals have difficulty achieving committed relationships* with desired partners. In addition, *these scenarios produce periods of inconsistent, infrequent, and even nonexistent sexual activity* rather than an abundance of "free love," a lifetime of frequent and satisfying one-night stands, or even the routinized rendezvous of weekend lovers that we often imagine that youth and singleness symbolize.[9]

Outside of situations of committed romance and mutual affection, sex, if it happens, must be continually renegotiated. Avoiding celibacy requires ongoing or continuous attention to the activities of finding and attracting (what my sample of females tended to rely on) or pursuing partners and impressing and negotiating with these potential sex partners until an agreement is reached about whether, when, and where sex will take place. Each of these tasks requires an investment of time, and time may be invested in one of more of these tasks several times over before an individual is lucky enough to be rewarded with one successful experience of sexual intercourse. This time, whether one sees it as a period filled with fun and flirtatious games of chase, beckon, and bed or a moment characterized by repetition of the monotonous exercise of dressing up, waiting near the dance floor, exchanging phone numbers, and waiting by the phone, is time spent celibate.

Religious Relations

The relationship between the challenge of finding a committed partnership, romance without sex, and degreed black women's elevated celibacy is exacerbated by women's and/or their male partners' religious beliefs in maintaining pre-marital celibacy. For such individuals, the relationship standard for romantically constituted sexual activity is more stringent and the level of commitment from potential partners that is required for consistent sexual activity to occur is higher. Moreover, religious motivations to confine sex to marital relationships come into direct conflict with the delayed marriage strategies associated with romances that occur during women's schooling and early professional development years. As discussed in the last chapter, women in these early relationships delay marriage for education and professional opportunities that imply remaining a dependent of one's parents or moving to another geographic region, or they delay permanent commitment to current partners because they imagine and expect that future partners will be just as available for marriage later in the life course. But even as these educational factors may keep religious subjects from marrying early, religious insistence on pre-marital celibacy is unlikely to result in the maintenance of romantic relations without sexual intercourse. As indicated by Janet's narrative above, both normal sexual desire and the normative association of sex with romance pushes these religiously celibate dyads toward either relationship failure or the maintenance of romantic interactions that include inconsistent or sporadic sexual activity. In Francine's case, religious insistence on premarital celibacy brought about the end of a relationship; in Sierra's case, it structured a romance that involved sporadic bouts of nonmarital sex up until the relationship ended for reasons having nothing to do with religious celibacy.

After explaining that involvement in a new Christian organization on her college campus convinced her that the sex that she was having with her boyfriend was wrong, Francine discussed the end of their relationship. I asked her, "So what you are saying is that you decided that you wanted to be celibate?" and she answered, "Yes. And he wasn't interested in that." And then I confirmed what I had heard, saying, "You mean, he did not want to continue the relationship without sex?" and she assented with, "He wasn't interested in coming along with me, so we separated." In this case, religious factors lowered Francine's frequency of intercourse by ending her romantic relationship and, thereby, eliminating romantically constituted sexual activity. In Sierra's case below, religious commitment created inconsistent or sporadic sex in the context of a romantic relationship that never quite met the standards for marriage.

Sierra struggled to maintain her relationship with her first love (Reese), weathering one long period of separation when she left her hometown to attend college and another period of trying to support him in his professional endeavors once she graduated and returned to the city of their upbringing and the relationship resumed its original intensity. During this latter phase of their relationship, Sierra settled into a pattern of inconsistent sexual activity with Reese. Concerns about his educational and financial decision making made her hesitant about marrying him and ultimately led to their breakup. And without the movement into marriage that would have morally legitimated more frequent and consistent sexual activity, Sierra and Reese struggled unsuccessfully to remain completely celibate.

Although religious belief and practice make Francine's and Sierra's motivations different from Janet's, Andrea's, and Sparkle's, the point about relational sexual activity remains the same. A committed romantic part-

nership facilitates regular intercourse in ways that other romantic arrangements (including sex without romance and religious romance minus
the religiously important marital commitment) do not. The difficulty that
degreed black women have getting into these kinds of committed partnerships (be they marital or not) with men of their choosing has depressing
effects on their frequency of intercourse and, in so doing, on their childbearing achievements.

Marital or Marriage-Like Relations

The points being made above about the connection between disadvantage in achieving committed partnerships and disadvantage in levels
of sexual activity are further underscored by the degree to which rates of
celibacy after initiation are even more elevated among women who are
unmarried. Insofar as marriage stands for the achievement of one of the
more serious levels of commitment from a desired partner, celibacy after
initiation should be lowest among married persons and highest in the
category containing those persons whose difficulty achieving committed
partnerships means that they have not yet been able to marry or are unable to maintain marital commitments. And figure 10's depiction of rates
of nonmarital celibacy shows that in every race-education category such
rates are indeed higher than the celibacy rates in the general population
(including married, never married, and formerly married women) that
were displayed above in figure 9.

Given the importance of romantic partnership for the consistent
achievement of intercourse experiences, African American women's elevated rates of celibacy in figure 9 are clearly related to their low rates of
marriage. Similarly, figure 9's depiction of white women's racial advantage
in sexual activity after initiation can also be linked to their higher likelihood of being married than black or Hispanic women of reproductive age.
But figure 10 highlights the fact that degreed black women's low involvement with marriage and the marital sex benefits package remains un-
compensated for by involvement in nonmarital sex—whether we think of
that compensation occurring through the sexually constituted romance
or through romantically constituted sex. Rather, unmarried black women
with college degrees and highly educated Hispanic women maintain high
celibacy after initiation. Note, however, that these celibate Hispanics do
not have as large or as important an effect on the dark gray sections of

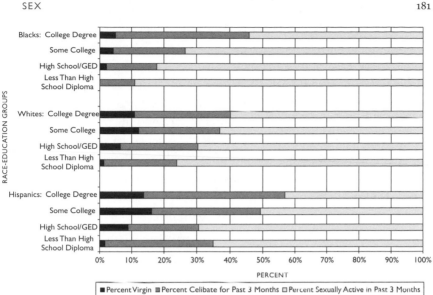

10   Percentage of unmarried respondents who are virgins, celibate non-virgins, and women
     reporting intercourse during the past three months. Calculations are based on cross-sectional
     data from NSFG (NCHS 1995) respondents over the age of nineteen. Calculations are found in
     table A11.

figure 9 because the proportion of highly educated Hispanic women who
are married and sexually active through marriage represents a greater proportion of the general Hispanic population than married women represent among black women.

   Caught in the negotiations and renegotiations for sexually constituted
romance and romantically constituted sex that those living lives without romance endure, these larger proportions of degreed black women
who are single experience short- and long-term celibacy after sexual initiation that depresses their nonmarital childbearing and overall fertility
throughout the reproductive life course. Less educated black women
who are similarly deprived in marriage appear in figure 10 to be more involved with nonmarital intercourse. To the extent that they too depend
upon committed romantic partnerships for this more consistent and frequent intercourse, they seem more likely to be involved in committed
nonmarital romantic relationships than are the degreed black women in
the interview and the NSFG (NCHS 1995) samples. Perhaps it is also the
case that their low marriage rates result from an inability to move these

relationships toward the goal of marriage rather than the limited access to partnerships that constrains degreed black women's family formation activities. In any case, non-degreed black women's lower likelihood of being celibate after initiation means that their childbearing outcomes are differentiated from those of degreed black women through the "proximate determinant" of sex. At the intersection of race and the attainment of a college degree lie different experiences with romantic partnerships, with women in the less-than-high-school-diploma, high-school-diploma, and some-college categories apparently having access to romantic partnerships (or at least to the frequency of intercourse that occurs between partners) but not marital commitment and with black women with degrees apparently having less access to romantic partnerships whether marital or not.[10]

Is That It?

At the center of the discussion of this book is the argument that although degreed black women share fertility outcomes with equally educated white and Hispanic women, they experience tremendous racial inequality in the achievement of these apparently similar outcomes. Deprivation in romantic love is just one of the unequal experiences that distinguish their family formation processes from college-educated women of other races. In the previous chapter this deprivation was discussed in terms of their challenge in finding marital partners and their process of romantic discovery in which they learned the meaning of their race-gender status for undesirability on the marriage market. Here, the discussion has been about nonmarital sexual activity and degreed black women's greater confinement to long- and short-term celibacy than both the non-degreed black women who share their challenges in marriage and who outperform them in childbearing and white and Hispanic women at all education levels who are more likely to marry and less likely to be celibate than these women, regardless of their level of fertility performance.

Below, I continue making comparisons across race and education levels, this time focusing on the family formation experiences and consequences associated with degreed black women's difficulties achieving romantic partnerships with desired partners. I find that the partnership difficulties fundamentally alter these women's family formation experiences so that these experiences differ from those of non-degreed black women: though similarly deprived in marriage, these women achieve enough romantic partnership to raise levels of nonmarital sexual activity and childbearing. I also find degreed black women's family formation processes to be different from those of college-educated white and Hispanic women, whose delayed and depressed childbearing is also achieved through the establishment of romantic partnerships, and, for whom, at least with respect to whites, the period of family formation delay includes higher levels of nonmarital sexual activity. The tables and figures below, based on NSFG (NCHS 1995) data, describe these different family formation experiences at the intersection of race and education level. These are differences that begin with different experiences of sexual initiation and are carried through in the different meanings of sexual initiation for family formation in women's lives, but they are also differences that are belied by the similarity across race in college-educated women's childbearing.

So what then is the consequence of the relatively unsuccessful search for sex partners that Janet has undertaken between the ages of sixteen and twenty-two? Does the strategic beginning of her search at the age of sixteen and the achievement of her long-awaited sexual initiation at the age of seventeen mean something for her future marriage and childbearing prospects? In table 9, I list the associations between the ages at which women lose their virginity and the ages at which they marry and have their first child. In other words, I provide a measure of the degree to which the women who start having sex early are also the ones who start forming their families earliest. For those groups that have high and positive associations (for example, closer to one), sexual initiation is a moment of great significance—marking the establishment of stable romantic partnerships and signaling the impending adoption of spousal and/or parenting roles. In contrast, groups with measures of association closer to zero are groups for whom the significance of sexual initiation for family formation is low: first sex likely remains isolated from partnering and other family formation activity.

Table 9 indicates that the association measures for each of the race-education groups below are all statistically significant. That is to say that the timing of sexual initiation is at least minimally associated with the timing of family formation events among black, Hispanic, and white

Table 9. Associations between age at first voluntary sex and first family formation events

	FIRST MARRIAGE				FIRST BIRTH			
	AGE†	# IN SAMPLE	R	P<	AGE‡	# IN SAMPLE	R	P<
Black								
College degree	24.8	174	.226**	.003	24.9	161	.353**	.000
Some college	23.4	328	.182**	.001	21.5	419	.515**	.000
HS diploma/GED	22.2	483	.161**	.000	20.2	766	.453**	.000
< HS diploma	21.6	160	.276**	.000	17.6	388	.420**	.000
White								
College degree	24.2	1084	.263**	.000	27.5	789	.241**	.000
Some college	21.9	1129	.372**	.000	23.7	954	.389**	.000
HS diploma/GED	20.6	1865	.406**	.000	22.0	1706	.422**	.000
< HS diploma	19.2	368	.440**	.000	19.1	405	.502**	.000

				Hispanic				
College degree	24.1	108	.444**	.000	25.8	91	.425**	.000
Some college	21.8	223	.482**	.000	23.0	215	.542**	.000
HS diploma/GED	21.1	351	.482**	.000	21.1	380	.624**	.000
< HS diploma	19.9	337	.627**	.000	19.8	424	.781**	.000

Source: Data for the above calculations are taken from NSFG (NCHS 1995) respondents over the age of nineteen.

Notes: "R" designates the value of the correlation coefficient, a measure of the relationship between two variables—in this case, the age at which women in specific groups first have sex and the age at which they begin forming families. The probability that this relationship and the listed value of "r" is due to sampling variation or the "luck of the draw" (rather than an actual association between these variables in the population from which the sample was drawn) is less than the figure listed in the $p<$ columns of the table.

† Indicates mean age at first marriage.

‡ Indicates mean age at first birth.

** Indicates that the association between the age at first voluntary sex and the age at first family formation event is significant at the .01 level.

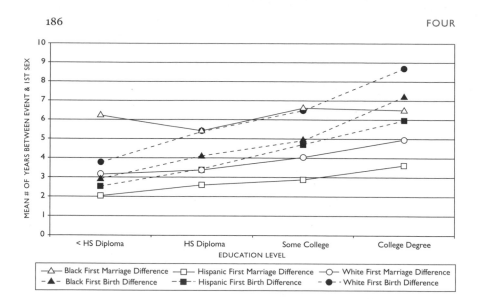

Mean of the difference between age at first marriage and age at first voluntary sex and of the difference between age at first birth and age at first voluntary sex. Calculations are based on reproductive history data from the NSFG (NCHS 1995) and are found in table A12.

women at each education level. But the table also indicates that the associations tend to be highest among Hispanic women and among women in the lowest educational categories. Among black and white women, especially college-educated black and white women like Janet, marriage and childbearing are more detached from the moment and timing of sexual initiation.

Figure 11 draws a similar picture to the one narrated by table 9. It plots the average distance (in years) between first sex and first marriage and between first sex and first birth for black, Hispanic, and white women at four different education levels. Here, too, sexual initiation shows itself to be most consequential for the family formation processes of Hispanic women: they exhibit close ties between sexual initiation and first family formation events, while the data on degreed black and white women indicate longer distances between sexual initiation and the first marriage and first birth events. Hispanic women's solid line with open square nodes falls at the bottom of the picture and indicates that the least educated Hispanics spend about 2.0 years between sexual initiation and marriage while those at the highest education level spend 3.6 years.[11] Their line contrasts with white women's higher solid line with open circular nodes: it shows a similar slope upward as education level increases but depicts the higher average distances of 3.1 years (for those with no diploma or GED) and almost five years (for those with a college degree) between first sex and first marriage. But both Hispanic and white women exhibit shorter distances between first sex and marriage than black women, whose thin solid line with the triangles is the highest (among first-marriage-first-sex difference lines) as well as the only one without a clear upward slope. Among black women, those with high-school diplomas (as opposed to those with less than a high-school diploma) have the shortest average distance between first sex and marriage (5.4 years); they are followed by those without high-school diplomas (6.2 years), then by those with college degrees (6.5 years), and then by those with some college (6.6 years). Thus, in this figure (also see calculations from data in Table A12), the cues that Janet's narrative offers about the low significance of sexual initiation for family formation in degreed black women's lives ring true: sexual initiation neither signals nor promises involvement in romance and family formation, for it might be followed as easily by inconsistent or nonexistent sexual activity as it is by marital or nonmarital sexual relationships.

Taken together, table 9 and figure 11 tell us that first sex is of highest significance for family formation among Hispanic women and of relatively low significance among black and white women. The table and graph also tell us that this significance of sexual initiation for family formation or this entanglement of sexual initiation with family formation is more critical than the timing of sexual initiation per se in the determination of family formation outcomes. For Hispanic women at each education level achieved the highest fertility (see chapter 2) despite being the latest group to initiate sex (see tables 6 and 7 above) and, consequently, the group that spends the lowest fraction of their reproductive years sexually active. The high associations between first sex, marriage, and birth and the apparent ties between opportunities for virginity loss and for romantic partnership among Hispanic women sampled by the NSFG (NCHS 1995) therefore trump black and white women's earlier entrance into sexual activity in the fertility outcome race. Furthermore, highly educated women across racial groups achieve lower fertility outcomes than their less educated counterparts by means of the long years spent between sexual initiation and first birth (ranging from an average of 6.0 years among degreed Hispanic women to 8.7 years among degreed white women) and not because they begin having sex at slightly later ages than the less educated women in their respective racial groups (table 9 indicates that college-educated women tend to start having sex less than two years after their less educated racial counterparts). Thus, the question of what causes the detachment of sexual initiation from family formation events remains a salient one in terms of the degree to which it signifies racial inequality in family formation experiences and in the degree to which it is determinative of fertility outcomes.

The overall message of this chapter and these analyses of college-educated black women's race and education level inequality in interaction with the proximate determinant of sex is that among degreed black women this detachment of sexual initiation from family formation is in some part accomplished by the constraints on their access to romantic partnership. Challenges finding romantic commitment shape the experience of virginity loss, isolating it in fact and in meaning from love, romance, and commitment. These same challenges structure high nonmarital celibacy rates after sexual initiation—rates that emerge in experiences of sex without romance and romance without sex. With respect to consequences, the isolation of first sex from committed romantic partnerships by definition isolates it from marriage, since marriage is, simply put, one form of committed partnership available to individuals. And the lack of access to romantic partnerships lowers the frequency of intercourse, producing celibacy rates that lower chances of pregnancy and nonmarital childbearing.

It is possible that white women—particularly college-educated white women—establish distance between first sex, first marriage, and first birth because of a similar restriction on their access to romantic partnership. And it is also possible that non-degreed black women have lower associations between first sex and family formation than they would have but for their lack of access to romantic partnership. Nevertheless, my argument about the data analyzed here is that degreed black women's challenges in this regard appear unique. College-educated black women's uniqueness is, first of all, evident in the data that say that college-educated white women's average distance between first sex and marriage is not so large as that of degreed black women's, and that it is still considerably larger than the group's average distance between first marriage and first birth. Marriage follows sexual initiation by about 5.0 years, on average, among degreed white women, while the figure is about 6.5 years for degreed black women. Challenges in finding romantic partnerships during degreed white women's early reproductive period, to the extent that they exist, seem to resolve themselves about 1.5 years before they do among degreed black women. The existence of such challenges also seems doubtful when one considers the greater amount of time white women spend in the marital state (see chapter 3's discussion of marriage differences across race and class) as well as the fact that their nonmarital celibacy rates after sexual initiation are among the lowest in figure 10.

Also, as indicated above, white women with college degrees postpone childbearing another three to four years after the point at which they marry. The difference between first sex and first birth in this group is 8.7 years—3.7 years longer than the difference between first sex and first marriage, and it is a signal that family formation as a whole occurs at a slower pace within this socioeconomic group. Since these women continue to postpone first births even after the point at which they are clearly involved in the highly committed romantic partnership of marriage, this slower overall family formation pace appears to emerge for reasons other than difficulties with romantic partnership. In contrast, degreed black women's unique difficulties achieving romantic partnerships are reflected in an average distance between first sex and first marriage of 6.5 years and an average distance between first sex and first birth of 7.2 years. The very short distance between first marriage and first birth or, in other words, the acceleration of the pace of family formation once marriage has occurred indicates that for these black, college-educated women the achievement of family formation dreams appears to be stalled by the reality of their limited romantic opportunity.

As for non-degreed black women, who clearly share college-educated black women's disadvantage in marriage, they have experiences and outcomes in the love arena that yet remain distinguishable from those of black women with degrees. Data depicted above indicate that non-degreed black women not only begin having voluntary sex at earlier ages but that their rates of celibacy after initiation are lower than those of black women who have graduated from college (see figures 9 and 10). It is true that sexual initiation has low significance for marriage in these groups, but their sexual relations with romantic partners support associations between first sex and first birth that are higher than those of highly educated black and white women. Alongside shorter average distances between sexual initiation and first birth (2.9 years for the least educated group, 4.1 years for those who completed high school, and 4.9 years for those who completed some college versus 7.2 years for degreed black women; see figure 11), these higher associations suggest a greater availability of sex (whether in or outside of committed romantic partnerships) during the early reproductive years than is suggested by Janet's young life and the NSFG (NCHS 1995) data on college-educated black women's sexual activity. Numerous scholarly sources suggest that the romantic partnerships that facilitate the higher nonmarital childbearing rates among lower-class black women in particular are especially fragile and that few if any survive to the point of marriage.[12] Nonetheless they do exist; they do support sexual activity, pregnancy, and childbearing in—as figure 11 indicates— roughly the same number of years after initiation as white women begin forming their families through marriage. At the same time, figure 11 also shows us that of the three race-education groups, *degreed black women are alone as they wait the longest (6.5 years) after virginity loss for the beginning of families.*

In theory, the disentanglement of sexual initiation from family formation need not signal low levels of involvement in romantic partnerships, whether those partnerships represent marriages or other kinds of romantic commitments. In other words, they need not be about black women's deprivation in love and degreed black women's particular deficits with respect to sex and romantic partnership. Indeed, the arguments of a number of demographic and inequality scholars have been that the disentanglement of sexual initiation from family formation has rather signaled women's freedom from consignment to reproductive labor.[13] Such theorists and empirical scholars have claimed that lower- and working-class individuals and families across the globe increase their educational and economic resources by delaying childbearing and/or opting to have small families. But this improvement in women's and in poorer families' economic circumstances that likewise implies lower fertility is, in the contemporary era, more often accomplished through women's differential interactions with other proximate determinants—through the magic of contraception and abortion and not marriage and sex. As data on degreed white women in this chapter hint at, contraception and abortion make it possible for women to have love, marriage, and the consistent sex that marriage and other forms of romantic partnership imply even as they minimize fertility and extensive involvement in reproductive labor and concentrate on improving their educations and access to employment in the formal sector.

Although low marriage and sex and high contraception and abortion both result in lower fertility outcomes, and although low marriage and sex and high contraception and abortion may both be the province of U.S. women with advanced educations, the experience of romantic isolation and love deprivation is quite different from the experience of a partnered exercise of family planning. In the final two chapters of this book, I turn to analyses of quantitative and qualitative data on the proximate determinants that ostensibly allow women to experience liberation and love simultaneously (for example, contraception in chapter 5 and abortion in chapter 6). These analyses suggest that even the liberation promised by the use of contraception and abortion is experienced differently and is characterized by different levels of effectiveness in the context of love deprivation.

FIVE

Contraception
To Plan It or Not to Plan It

CONSIDER NANCY, who was thirty-one years old and childless at the time of interview. She told me that she had been sexually active since college and had always used contraception to delay fertility until some unspecified point after marriage and after her career had been established. She maintained, "I was very motivated not to have kids. I was fitted for a diaphragm, but I was afraid I was gonna put it in wrong. I used condoms consistently because I was deathly afraid of sexually transmitted diseases."

Also consider Tristan's description of her experiences with birth control pills and the diaphragm (during the time that she "needed a break from the pill"). Her words support a more general claim about what contraception offers to women: she fervently believes that contraception allows women to choose how much reproductive labor they will do and to plan when they will do it. At the age of forty-two, Tristan is married and has three children whom she maintains she deliberately spaced three years apart. She explained, "I had no problem with either method because I was clear in my mind. I was clear that I know how many children I want to have.

People talk about, 'But it was in the heat of it' [as an excuse for not using contraception], but I wanted to be real clear. I was comfortable that the diaphragm would be as effective for me as the pill was."

When I started the study that has culminated in this book, this is what I expected to find—women whose consistent and successful contraceptive use matched their relatively high educational and professional achievements. The problem was that consistent and successful contraceptive planners like Nancy and Tristan weren't the only women I encountered. And the number of women I interviewed who were different from Nancy and Tristan forced me to reconsider my idea that educational motivation and achievement were the major determinants of pregnancy prevention action and of class differences in fertility outcomes.

I started with the expectation that degreed black women had lower fertility than less educated black women and equivalent fertility with degreed Hispanic and white women because of their greater involvement in contraceptive planning than the former group and their similar attachment to contraceptive planning as the latter groups. But I was forced to confront and explain data from the National Survey of Family Growth (NSFG [NCHS 1995]) that indicated substantial racial difference in contraceptive practice. Indeed, degreed black women's contraceptive use turned out to be as different from white women who shared their education level as it was from that of less educated black and Hispanic women. And alongside the racial differences in contraceptive use, I also had to confront and deal with data on inconsistent and unsuccessful contraceptive use from my sample of sexually active, college-educated, African American interviewees. Together, those reporting inconsistent use or unsuccessful use of contraceptive devices comprised a little more than half of the sample, and their behaviors needed to be somehow reconciled with the low fertility that degreed African Americans shared with other degreed women and with the higher fractions of nonmarital births that they shared with less educated black women.

My analyses of interview data from degreed black women and of survey data from the NSFG (NCHS 1995) produced an explanation that reconciles some of these apparently contradictory data. The explanation makes three claims about the contraceptive practice of women in the United States and accounts for variance in that contraceptive practice in ways that are at times only indirectly related to race and education level variables. In this regard, the chapter first argues that marriage deprivation and single status constrain family planning, planned sexual activity, and the contraceptive activity associated with such plans. They do so by way of the stigma attached to women's involvement in nonmarital sex and child-bearing. Significant portions of the population of single women distance themselves from contraceptive planning as a means of avoiding stigma for premeditated wrongdoing. Because it is related to marriage depriva-tion, this stigma-avoiding resistance to contraception is most observable among African Americans who are the most marriage deprived.

Although I argue that marriage deprivation leads to inconsistent use of contraceptives, the chapter's conclusions do not completely negate the tradition of scholarship that explains variance in contraceptive practice by class differences in the motivation and opportunity to make and fol-low through on contraceptive plans. For my data also support a second argument—that contraception remains an important player in the game in which degreed black women distinguish their nonmarital childbearing behavior from that of less educated black women. It is just that the cen-trality of this second claim is tempered to some extent by a third point: that degreed black women's mid-range rates of nonmarital childbearing reflect both the choices of contraceptive-using planners and a type of in-consistent and ineffective contraceptive use that was more typically found among less educated black women and that is apparently associated with marriage deprivation. Put another way, degreed black women have lower nonmarital childbearing rates than less educated black women and higher nonmarital childbearing rates than white and Hispanic women with de-grees. Indeed, these higher nonmarital fertility rates underlie equivalent fertility across the college-educated sample in the NSFG (NCHS 1995). Ex-plaining this cross-race similarity in degreed women's completed fertility requires attention to both degreed black women's class-based contracep-tive planning behavior and their more distinctive unplanned nonmarital fertility, accomplished through inconsistent and unsuccessful contracep-tive use.

My explanatory narrative reconciles qualitative and quantitative data trends in a way that complicates and at times challenges my earlier as-sumptions about the relationship between school, work, and women's contraceptive planning. It amends assumptions about educated elites who have fewer children than women without their higher educational credentials because of their planned approach to life and the availability of a modern contraceptive regimen. These assumptions reflect an understanding about birth control that can easily be found among family planning novices and experts alike. That is that contraception is a key—if not the key—means of planning fertility.

If you think about it, other means of fertility limitation, including marriage delay, abortion, and abstinence between births, just do not lend themselves as readily to claims about individuals' or couples' "planning" behavior. Marriage delay coupled with abstinence before marriage has historically worked to postpone the onset of childbearing rather than to manipulate it once it has begun.[1] Similarly postpartum abstinence (more common on the continent of Africa and in other non-industrialized places) has worked in the opposite way, allowing for some manipulation of fertility timing once childbearing has begun.[2] And abortion, because it happens after one has already become pregnant, may indicate the need to maintain course on a plan, but does not imply the same forethought as does the prevention of pregnancy in the first place.[3] Even in areas of communist Eastern Europe, where the lack of availability of contraception made abortion a major means of fertility limitation, the prevalence of abortion can readily be linked to poor planning at the macro-level or, in other words, the lack of governmental ability to plan for the contraceptive needs of couples in a planned economy.[4]

But more importantly, the association between contraceptive planning and the achievement or maintenance of elite status reflects long-standing intellectual traditions in demography, sociology, and social policy that link fertility planning and the availability of contraceptives to social mobility. As early as 1890, the French demographer Arsene Dumont spoke of a phenomenon he referred to as "social capillarity," which essentially argued that those wanting to get ahead socioeconomically postponed and limited childbearing as a strategy of achieving the move up the social ladder.[5] His understanding of fertility planning as a prescription for individual success is the other side of a demographic theoretical coin in which the same ideas are made into warnings to elites: here John Stuart Mill's argument that high fertility drains family resources and can cause families to be downwardly mobile in the class hierarchy is one of the obvious historical examples (see Weeks 2007). In the twentieth-century United States, Rainwater's (1969) explanation of why "the poor get children" made more explicit arguments connecting planning to contraceptive use and socioeconomic status. He maintained that members of the working class lack a belief in the predictability of the future and the sense that they can alter their own destinies. He framed high, unwanted fertility as the consequence of a laissez-faire attitude toward contraception by working-class couples who do not believe that they can manipulate or plan their own socioeconomic ends.

Furthermore, a rich empirical research tradition tests and backs up these theoretical claims about fertility differences based in elites' greater involvement in contraceptive planning. Scholars studying the adoption of contraception by women in the developing world have continually found that the most educated women are the first and most likely to use contraception.[6] Investigations of teen and/or unplanned and/or nonmarital pregnancy and childbearing in the United States repeatedly concluded that school success, educational opportunity, and high educational aspirations and achievement are all highly correlated with women's likelihood of using contraception.[7] Moreover, feminist scholars and policy analysts since Margaret Sanger have argued that class differences in knowledge of and access to family planning services have restricted lower-class women's opportunities to improve their economic circumstances and to create families around education- or employment-centered escapes from poverty.[8] And even those who have maintained that poorer women may actually be deliberately planning their earlier fertility have located these women's unwillingness to engage in the more middle-class baby-postponement agenda in their inability to plan on (or to expect) more lucrative career futures.[9]

In short, the educated elite bias with which I entered this investigation of the processes leading to degreed black women's low fertility outcomes was grounded in logic and a lively theoretical and empirical tradition. It nonetheless offered little assistance with efforts to make sense out of racial differences in degreed women's contraceptive use and the contraceptive experiences of degreed black women. So there I was, a sitting duck, puffed up with the knowledge of my demographic forebearers, well positioned to have my assumptions shattered. The discussion below recalls the journey that both shattered my assumptions and gave birth to a narrative that represents the intersection of race and class phenomena in degreed black women's contraceptive experiences and documents the contraceptive consequences of a racial deprivation in romantic love. In the following two sections, I focus on descriptions of qualitative and quantitative data demonstrating degreed black women's contraceptive inconsistency and linking such inconsistency to greater experiences of unwanted pregnancy. Having rejected pregnancy wantedness (and, by implication, planning) as a reason for black women's inconsistent contraceptive use, the remainder of the chapter presents my explanation of the process in which the marriage challenge frustrates black women's contraceptive practice and raises their levels of unwanted pregnancy.

Observing Inconsistency

All fifty-three respondents in my interview sample who had engaged in voluntary sexual intercourse at the time of interview had had some experience with contraception. Just about 72 percent of them managed to "successfully" control their fertility (meaning that they at no time had a child when they had not planned to have one), but only 43 percent managed to do so through "consistent" contraceptive behavior (meaning that during those times when they were not trying to get pregnant, either they or their partner used contraception while having intercourse). The 56.6 percent of sexually active respondents who were not like Nancy and Tristan (that is, who were not both consistent and successful in their contraceptive use) fell into one of three logical categories delineated in tables 10 and 11 below. The first of these categories is composed of women who were successful at controlling fertility despite an inconsistent pattern of usage (28.3 percent); the second category is made up of women who were unsuccessful at controlling their fertility probably because they had an inconsistent pattern of contraceptive usage (17 percent); and the third category includes women who consistently used contraception but were unsuccessful at controlling their fertility because of contraceptive failures that were resolved in births (11.3 percent).

One of the main reasons that these analyses were more complicated than I expected was that the academic discussions of class differences in fertility and of the relationship between education and contraceptive use with which I was familiar were not helpful in terms of explaining women like Mia—women who seem to demonstrate a motivation to limit or postpone childbearing that is similar to that of Nancy and Tristan and who

Table 10. Possible patterns of contraception

	CONSISTENT (C)	INCONSISTENT (I)
Successful (S)	CS	IS
Unsuccessful (U)	CU	IU

Table 11. Observed patterns of contraception in sample of degreed African Americans

	% CONSISTENT	% INCONSISTENT	TOTALS
% Successful (#)	43.4 (23)	28.3 (15)	71.7 (38)
%Unsuccessful (#)	11.3 (6)	17.0 (9)	28.3 (15)
TOTALS	54.7 (29)	45.3 (24)	100 (53)

seem to be aware of contraceptive options, but who nevertheless are in-consistent in their use. During our interview Mia explained:

> I used birth control pills for three to four years in a row in order to help me with my period, particularly the mood changes and weepiness that I used to get. But I never took them straight [regularly] because I do not trust the way doctors use medication with African Americans. With my only long-term boyfriend, I sometimes used condoms, although sex always feels nice without a condom. I told my boyfriend that if I got pregnant, I was keeping the child, so condoms always made him feel protected. I also used the day after pill four or five times.[10]

Nor do the arguments about educated women's fertility limitation assist in explanations of Maya's fertility outcomes: she too demonstrates moti-vation and knowledge of contraceptive methods, but contraception did not work for her in the same way that it apparently did for Nancy and Tristan. As indicated in the book's introduction, Maya was twenty-seven at the time of our interview. She has one child and works as a social worker. She insists that she never wanted any children and plans to have no more. She states, "Before I had my daughter, I used pills and condoms. One of the pills was making me sick, and I was in the process of changing pills when I met my new boyfriend. So I was only using condoms when I got pregnant. I used protection the whole time I was having sex with him. I didn't understand what happened. I took it as a sign from God that I got pregnant." In my analysis, I classified Mia as an "inconsistent successful" contraceptive user and Maya as a "consistent unsuccessful" one. Both women are included in the 56.6 percent of degreed women who fall outside of the "consistent successful" group, and they show us how educational goals and outcomes and the motivation to postpone or limit fertility might nonetheless result in significant incidence of inconsistent or unsuccessful contraceptive use in a population of elite professionals.

Data from the NSFG (NCHS 1995) support the idea that the Nancys and the Tristans are more typical of the educated elite and that the Mias and the Mayas are more typical of the women in lower classes. For one, a simple comparison across race and education level groups shows that "fecundable"[11] women were more likely to report that they were "not contracepting" if they were in the lower education level categories. In table 12, women in the first two categories ("not fecundable," "not sexually active") do not require contraception to avoid pregnancy, and women in the third category ("seeking pregnancy") do not wish to avoid pregnancy. Greater portions of those who remain are "not contracepting" when they are in the lower education level categories. Furthermore, as table 13 indicates, never married women who were "contracepting" were more likely to report that they had "contracepted" during their last intercourse experience if their educational achievement was high. Thus in table 13 we see that the degree to which women are consistent in the use of the methods of contraception that they have adopted also varies by class, as those in the lowest education level categories were the most likely to have forgone contraception at last intercourse.

But like Mia's inconsistent contraceptive use or Maya's consistent but unsuccessful use of condoms, the clear racial differences in contraceptive use in tables 12 and 13, despite a control for education, disturb the neat picture in which highly educated women are the planners who use contraception effectively and those without higher education credentials are the ones who fail to plan or fail to follow through on plans by not using contraceptives. In particular, table 13's figures indicate that single black and Hispanic women are more inconsistent in their contraceptive use than white women. These differences exist at each education level, including that of college degree holders.

Furthermore, figure 12 illustrates these racial differences in another way. Below, this figure shows that degreed women have higher likelihoods of using contraceptives during intercourse than non-degreed women in their own racial group, but we also see that white, Hispanic, and black women with college degrees do not share likelihoods of contraceptive use. The contraceptive behavior of degreed white women is as different from that of degreed black and Hispanic women as it is from whites at the high-school diploma level. Both race and class differences are large: regarding women who have never been married, the figure indicates that less than 20 percent of degreed white women failed to use contraception at last intercourse, but almost 40 percent of high-school educated white women and 40 percent of degreed black and Hispanic women failed to do so.[12]

In addition to the large racial differences, the neat story about class and contraceptive use is also disrupted by differences between the information presented in tables 12 and 13 and what those differences imply. Above, table 12 shows race and education level differences in the fraction of women who report that they are "not contracepting." And it also indicates that the fraction of women who report that they are "not contracepting" remains relatively small in each of the race-education groups—never more than 8 percent of the group. However, in table 13, which summarizes what women who have never been married are likely to do in a particular intercourse experience, large fractions of the race-education groups were "not contracepting" during their last intercourse experience. Furthermore, the race and education level differences in contraceptive behavior measured in this way are much larger. The fact that higher fractions of women are implicated in inconsistent use of contraception (depicted in table 13) than in the wholesale rejection of contraceptive practice (depicted in table 12) suggests that educational motivations and career plans are less relevant for explaining the type of contraceptive variance that is

Table 12. Percentage of women at each contraceptive status within each race-education group

EDUCATION LEVEL	< HS DIPLOMA	HS DIPLOMA/ GED	SOME COLLEGE	COLLEGE DEGREE
		Black women		
Not fecundable	40.7	45.4	36.9	30.6
Not sexually active	21.3	7.5	10.8	17.1
Seeking pregnancy	4.1	4.8	5.1	5.4
Contracepting	26.7	35.1	41.3	42.6
Not contracepting	7.2	7.2	5.9	4.3
TOTAL	100	100	100	100
(#)	(567)	(871)	(572)	(258)
		White women		
Not fecundable	26.9	47.9	33.9	26.7
Not sexually active	40.0	7.8	13.5	11.0
Seeking pregnancy	2.5	4.0	3.4	4.4
Contracepting	25.0	34.2	44.9	54.6
Not contracepting	5.7	6.0	4.3	3.3
TOTAL	100	100	100	100
(#)	(927)	(2167)	(1569)	(1372)

Source: Data for the above calculations are taken from NSFG (NCHS 1995) respondents.

largest and perhaps most consequential across the women sampled in the NSFG (NCHS 1995).

Educational achievements and career goals should distinguish women in terms of their motivation to prevent or postpone pregnancy and consequently in terms of their probabilities of being found in the "not contracepting" category in table 12. After all, those "fecundable" women involved in planning childbearing around education and career should either be "seeking pregnancy" or "contracepting," while those who are not making such plans should end up in the "not contracepting" category. Unless we believe that women's interest in planning childbearing around careers changes back and forth between intercourse experiences, then we should not expect educational achievement and career-oriented decision

Table 12. *Continued*

EDUCATION LEVEL	< HS DIPLOMA	HS DIPLOMA/ GED	SOME COLLEGE	COLLEGE DEGREE
		Hispanic women		
Not fecundable	39.1	42.4	30.5	27.9
Not sexually active	20.9	10.5	19.0	14.7
Seeking pregnancy	4.0	3.7	3.9	4.7
Contracepting	29.3	38	42.7	47.3
Not contracepting	6.6	5.3	3.9	5.4
TOTAL	100	100	100	100
(#)	(545)	(455)	(305)	(129)

Notes: "Not fecundable" includes sterile, sterilized, pregnant, or postpartum women. "Not sexually active" includes virgins and respondents who have not had sex during the three months prior to interview. "Seeking pregnancy" includes respondents who are not contracepting because they are seeking pregnancy. "Contracepting" includes respondents contracepting with chemical contraception (birth control pills, Norplant, Depo-Provera shot, and the morning after pill), barrier contraception (male and female condoms, diaphragm, cervical cap, IUD, sponge, foam, suppository, and jelly or cream without diaphragm), or natural contraception (natural family planning, calendar rhythm, withdrawal, and "other" forms of contraception). "Not contracepting" designates respondents who use no contraceptive method.

making to explain why some women adopt contraception and use it consistently and effectively while others adopt a method but only use it some of the time. In effect, relying on ideas about highly educated women's greater motivation to plan childbearing in order to explain degreed black women's contraceptive behavior and nonmarital childbearing outcomes might only explain why the large majority of them are not in the "not contracepting" category in table 12. It does not really explain why so many of these women (between 17 and 29 percent) in the contracepting group are not actually using contraceptives during a particular intercourse experience.

Differences between tables 12 and 13 indicate that *inconsistency in contraceptive use despite commitment to pregnancy prevention and to a particular contraceptive method is more common than a complete rejec-*

Table 13. Percentage of single (never married) women in each contraceptive status group who nevertheless report using no contraception during their last intercourse experience

RACE-EDUCATION GROUP	# IN SAMPLE SIZE	CHEMICAL CONTRA-CEPTION*	BARRIER CONTRA-CEPTION*
Black women at last intercourse			
< HS diploma	144	62.5	32.1
HS diploma/GED	220	37.7	32.4
Some college	148	25.0	22.0
College degree	49	29.2	17.6
White women at last intercourse			
< HS diploma	166	39.5	21.6
HS diploma/GED	246	21.6	19.7
Some college	283	14.8	12.8
College degree	205	9.7	14.1
Hispanic women at last intercourse			
< HS diploma	67	47.4	37.5
HS diploma/GED	62	48.3	41.2
Some college	44	37.5	7.1
College degree	9	25.0	25.0

Source: Data for the above calculations are taken from NSFG (NCHS 1995) respondents.

Notes: "# in sample" is the designation for the total number of single (never married) women of that race and education level in the NSFG who are not virgins, sterile, sterilized, pregnant, postpartum, or seeking pregnancy, and who have had sex during the three months prior to interview. "Chemical contraception" includes birth control pills, Norplant, Depo-Provera shot, and the morning after pill. "Barrier contraception" includes male and female condoms, diaphragm, cervical cap, IUD, sponge, foam, suppository, and jelly or cream without diaphragm. "Last intercourse" indicates the respondent's last sexual intercourse during the three months prior to interview.
* Indicates the current contraceptive status of or the contraceptive method generally used by the respondent.

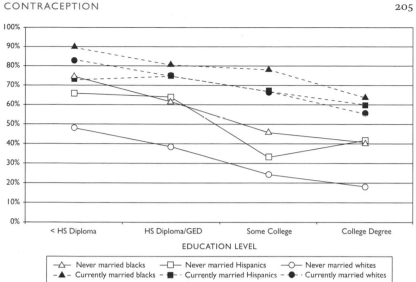

12 Percentage of respondents who did not use any contraception (including chemical, barrier, or natural methods or withdrawal) at their last intercourse during the three months prior to the interview. Calculations are based on data from the NSFG (NCHS 1995) and are found in table A13.

tion of contraception. And, unfortunately, there is much less theory that relates racial and educational status to contraceptive inconsistency or the failure to adhere to one's own contraceptive plan. What little we do know about inequality and inconsistency comes from empirical observation of women's decision making in the context of heterosexual romantic relations. It tells us that inconsistency reflects women's low negotiating power in these relationships. In addition, the empirical literature suggests that gender inequality in heterosexual romance and the resulting contraceptive inconsistency may be exaggerated among poor women and women of minority status.[13]

Locating Unwanted Pregnancy

In the introduction to this book, I gave a detailed account of Maya's life. (Yes, this is the same twenty-seven-year-old Maya who experienced the contraceptive failure above.) Offering her story as a an example of a woman dissatisfied with her fertility outcome of one child, I described the way her father's labeling of her as a "slut" motivated her ongoing efforts to represent herself as more sexually moral than the child her father labeled "the good girl." I suggested in the introduction's analysis of the disjuncture between college-educated black women's fertility wants and outcomes that Maya's inability to follow through with a planned abortion resulted from the distance between her self-presentations of sexual morality and her actual desire to have a child after all.

Below, my discussion of race and education level differences in pregnancy wantedness picks up where the introduction's description of Maya leaves off. It suggests that some of the differences in contraceptive consistency discussed above might reflect group differences in fertility wants and consequently in the level of motivation to prevent pregnancy. By looking at race and class differences in pregnancy wantedness, I leave open the possibility that women with the kind of ambivalence to childbearing that Maya displayed in her premature departure from the abortion clinic were more inconsistent about following through on their contraceptive plans precisely because they were more open to childbearing. But I only found the link between contraceptive inconsistency and pregnancy wantedness that would have supported this point some of the time.

By calculating the ratio of unwanted to total pregnancies for each woman who had ever been pregnant in the NSFG (NCHS 1995), I was able to investigate whether women in the different race-education groups averaged different or equivalent levels of pregnancy wantedness. I calculated this ratio by placing pregnancies described as "unwanted," "mistimed (too early)," or "not sure" in the numerator and the total number of pregnancies (including the above listing and those described as "on time," "overdue," or "indifferent") in the denominator.[14] I found that education level differences in pregnancy wantedness were for the most part relatively small. Among black women, differences between degreed women (whose average ratio was .5) and women with some college (average ratio of .56) and between degreed women and those with a high-school diploma or GED (.55) were too small to be considered statistically significant. Education level differences among whites were slightly larger and statistically significant but still on the low end. See table 14 below.

Table 14 implies that education level differences in contraceptive inconsistency are associated with small or negligible differences in pregnancy wantedness. This fact supports an argument that women with high-school diplomas have greater inconsistency about their contraceptive use

Table 14. Education level differences in the mean ratio of unwanted† to total pregnancies (between women with and without degrees)

	# IN SAMPLE	MEAN RATIO	DIFFERENCE FROM WOMEN W/4-YEAR COLLEGE DEGREES	T	P<
			Some college		
Black	482	.5640	−.0608	−1.80	.073
White	1102	.3871	−.0645**	−3.86	.000
Hispanic	245	.4033	−.0452	−1.01	.314
			High school diploma or GED		
Black	828	.5481	−.0449	−1.40	.161
White	1873	.3953	−.0727**	−4.89	.000
Hispanic	411	.4223	−.0642	−1.55	.124
			Less than HS diploma		
Black	437	.6478	−.1446**	−4.47	.000
White	457	.5149	−.1924**	−9.10	.000
Hispanic	451	.3910	−.0328	−.796	.427

Source: Data for the above calculations are taken from the NSFG (NCHS 1995). Sample sizes are listed in the "#" column. Sample sizes for degreed women used in the analyses were as follows: the category of degreed black women contained 188 respondents while the categories of degreed white and degreed Hispanic women contained 951 and 101 respondents, respectively.

Notes: "T" designates the value of the "t-statistic" in the difference of means significance test. The probability that this statistic and the listed difference result is due to sampling variation or the "luck of the draw" (rather than differences between education level groups in the actual population) is less than the figure listed in the final "*p*<" column of the table.

† Includes pregnancies classified as "unwanted," "mistimed (too early)," or "not sure" by NSFG respondents; other possible classifications were "on time," "overdue," or "indifferent."

** Indicates that the difference from the mean ratio of unwanted to total pregnancies for same race college-educated women is significant at the .01 level.

than those with college degrees because they have greater ambivalence about preventing childbearing than the more highly educated women do. After all, despite the fact that their contraceptive inconsistency means that they are more likely to experience a pregnancy, they end up wanting their pregnancies about as frequently as the women with more education in their respective racial groups.

But this reasoning does not work when the explanatory task is the racial differences in contraceptive use and pregnancy wantedness. African Americans sampled in the NSFG (NCHS 1995) are both the most inconsistent users of contraception and the most likely to describe their pregnancies as "unwanted," "mistimed," or "not sure." Thus their inconsistency in contraceptive usage cannot be explained by a greater ambivalence about or openness to childbearing. Table 15 indicates that this paradoxical situation of being very low on contraceptive consistency and low on pregnancy wantedness affects black women at each education level: at .5, degreed black women's average ratio of unwanted to total pregnancies is the lowest among the black women in the sample. It compares with about .33 for Hispanic and white women with college degrees.

Note that racial inequality in unwanted pregnancy should not be understood as black women's excess pregnancy, usually resolved in abortion, or a detour on the way to experiences of "wanted" pregnancies and births. Rather, the inconsistent contraceptive use and unwanted pregnancy that is its obvious result is an important component of black women's family formation experience. Thus figure 13 is constructed to illustrate the point that where white and Hispanic women accomplish their fertility outcomes mostly through the experience of "wanted" pregnancies and births, black women's achievement of the similar fertility outcomes only happens because of their experiences with carrying high fractions of their unwanted pregnancies to term. Figure 13 indicates that women of all racial groups, including black women, are very similar in terms of the average number of pregnancies that they take in order to achieve particular fertility levels. For example, according to the figure, it seems to take, on average, 1.75 pregnancies to achieve one live birth and over 3.5 pregnancies, on average, to achieve three live births. These averages are similar no matter what the racial group. However, a larger percentage of these pregnancies are unwanted among black women.

Table 15. Racial differences in the mean ratio of unwanted† to total pregnancies (between black and white women and between black and Hispanic women)

	# IN SAMPLE	MEAN RATIO	DIFFERENCE FROM BLACK WOMEN	T	P<
White women					
College degree	951	.3226	.1806**	5.73	.000
Some college	1102	.3871	.1769**	8.51	.000
HS diploma/GED	1873	.3953	.1528**	9.62	.000
< HS diploma	457	.5149	.1329**	5.46	.000
Hispanic women					
College degree	101	.3581	.1450**	3.07	.002
Some college	245	.4033	.1607**	5.32	.000
HS diploma/GED	411	.4223	.1258**	5.58	.000
< HS diploma	451	.3910	.2568**	10.46	.000

Source: Data for the above calculations are taken from NSFG (NCHS 1995) respondents.

Notes: Sample sizes are listed in the "#" column. Sample sizes for black women used in the analyses were as follows: the category of degreed black women contained 188 respondents while the categories of black women with "some college," with a high school diploma or GED, and with less than a high-school diploma contained 482, 828, and 437 respondents respectively.

"T" designates the value of the "t-statistic" in the difference of means significance test. The probability that this statistic and the listed difference result is due to sampling variation or the "luck of the draw" (rather than differences between racial groups in the actual population) is less than the figure listed in the final "$p<$" column of the table.

† Includes pregnancies classified as "unwanted," "mistimed (too early)," or "not sure" by NSFG respondents; other possible classifications were "on time," "overdue," or "indifferent."

** Indicates that the difference from the mean ratio of unwanted to total pregnancies for black women with similar education is significant at the .01 level.

Significance tests on the differences between white and Hispanic women are in table A14 in the appendix.

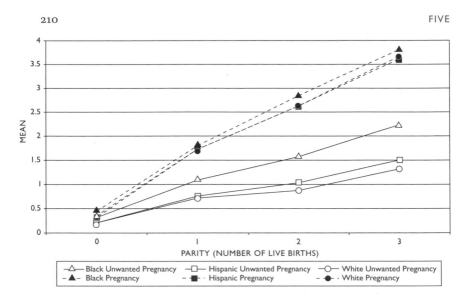

13   Mean number of pregnancies described by black, white, and Hispanic respondents as
     "unwanted," "mistimed or too early," and "unsure," and the mean number of pregnancies
     experienced by black, white, and Hispanic women of different fertility levels. Calculations are
     based on data from the NSFG (NCHS 1995) and are found in table A15.

Since black women's higher levels of unwanted pregnancy do not push
the total number of pregnancies that black women experience up and
over that of white and Hispanic women at the same fertility levels, black
women's inconsistent contraceptive use and the unwanted pregnancy
that is tied to it can be understood as part and parcel of the achievement
of similar fertility to white and Hispanic women.

Degreed black, Hispanic, and white women share low fertility, but they
do not share rates of contraceptive practice. White women are more likely
to make a contraceptive plan and to stick to it during a particular intercourse experience than are degreed black or Hispanic women. While this
elevated level of contraceptive inconsistency is not reflected in degreed
Hispanic women's likelihood of describing a pregnancy as unwanted, it
does show itself in black women's high likelihood of doing so. This means
that it is unlikely that their contraceptive inconsistency can be explained
by their greater ambivalence about having children. Moreover, the unwanted pregnancy is an important factor in black women's achievement
of parity with white and Hispanic women in fertility. Thus the data on race
and educational level differences in pregnancy wantedness make black

women at each education level appear either resistant to or constrained from achieving their fertility outcomes through contraceptive planning behavior. The narrative that explains why this is so must do so by showing us how the contraceptive planning that might bring black women closer to the levels of pregnancy wantedness experienced by white and Hispanic women is problematic for them.

Explaining Inconsistent Contraception and Unwanted Pregnancy

Most readers are not likely to be fazed by Maya's sudden departure from the abortion clinic after years of asserting that she wanted no children and practicing consistent contraceptive use. Ambivalence about abortion seems normal (and moral) enough to most of the individuals who share Maya's and my world. But my qualitative data-driven explanation for degreed black women's inconsistent and unsuccessful contraceptive use focuses on ambivalence about the use of contraceptives, a phenomenon about which the American public appears to have much less sympathy. Below, I begin with a description of Rose's problem with contraception. Her experiences illustrate the way in which the stigmatization of single women's sexual behavior supports inconsistent contraceptive use.

Late one cold, weekday evening, I had a conversation with the thirty-one-year-old interior designer and part-time rehabilitation specialist who gave herself the pseudonym Rose. When she explained her antipathy to all the brands of contraception that she had used, she gave me my first hint that degreed black women's inconsistent and ineffective contraceptive use might be causally related to the social cues they received about their "problematic" sexual activity. Rose's explanation began with the statement that she "did not have a good foundation for contraception." She then proceeded to describe the problematic interaction she had with her mother on the day they visited the doctor and she first requested birth control pills. As she spoke, she exhibited great discomfort—an agitated wringing of her hands, a repeated darting of her gaze between me and several of the corners of the empty cafe that surrounded us, and a sudden effort to rush her words and skate superficially over this section of the conversation. Looking back at her transcribed words a year later, I was struck by the way in which my request that she talk about her experience with contraception seemed to re-create some of the same discomfort that her mother's reaction had provoked in the physician's office more than fifteen years before. It suddenly seemed possible that the earliest interactions that a young woman had around her decision to use contraception could have a lasting effect, influencing sexual and reproductive decision making much later in life.

> ROSE: When I was sixteen, I went to my mom because I thought I was pregnant. I found out I wasn't pregnant, but I wanted to get birth control pills. When she found out I wanted birth control pills, she just walked out of the doctor's office.
>
> AVERIL: Why did she walk out?
>
> ROSE: She could not understand it.
>
> AVERIL: Couldn't understand what?
>
> ROSE: She couldn't understand why I was having sex much less why I wanted birth control pills.
>
> AVERIL: Did you get the pills then?
>
> ROSE: No, but when I finally did get it, I would forget to take it, and I would end up taking three or four pills at a time. Eventually, I just ran out of pills. I used the diaphragm once. I hated that. I hated all of it.

Rose links her sporadic and ineffective contraceptive practice to her mother's unwillingness to discuss contraception (or the teenaged sexual activity that made it necessary) many years earlier. Furthermore, Rose still finds discussing contraception disquieting—making it difficult to imagine how she handles procuring it from health professionals, learning to use it effectively, negotiating its use with a partner during a sexual encounter, and remembering to use it on a regular basis. Indeed, Rose prefers to distance herself from all manner of contraceptive devices, and in her conversation with me, she does so rather effectively by redirecting talk from contraceptive devices and toward descriptions of her own newfound success with attempts to be celibate.

Thus, Rose ends up rejecting contraceptive devices as part and parcel of her performance of a chaste or celibate sexual identity. As her mother did fifteen years before, she rejects contraceptive devices, denies her contraceptive needs, and distances herself from any identity she has had as a sexually active single woman all in the same moment. Her three abortions (that is, the true indicators that ambivalence about her fertility wants does not underlie her inconsistent contraceptive behavior) become in this same moment "mistakes" that allow her to "thank God for forgiveness."

Parental Rejection of Sexual Plans

The trouble with contraceptive planning and about feelings of ambivalence with regard to contraception, then, is really a trouble about sex. The highly variant outcomes in terms of both contraceptive consistency and success across my sample of college-educated black women are directly related to socialization in contexts where the main messages about how to become sexually active women are ones about not becoming sexually active women and about maintaining silence about or facing shame and stigma for becoming sexually active women. Thus Rose's testimony about the relationship between a parent's rejection of her teen daughter's early sexual activity and the adult daughter's long-term antipathy toward contraception formed a frame in my mind. The frame ended up supporting a library of stories describing the ways women's freedom to make a range of contraceptive choices is frustrated by a context that denies and/ or stigmatizes single black women for their sexual activity. One of the more prominent features of this context in which college-educated black women develop into sexual actors and contraceptive decision makers is their early interactions with parents who deny or reject their decisions to be sexually active.

Not many early interactions with parents about sex and contraception went like Rose's did—the forthright request for birth control pills followed by a mother's outright refusal to her daughter's contraceptive demand. However, even those parents who proactively approached their daughters and provided them with contraceptive information and devices tended to do so with a "forked tongue." In these cases, access to fertility control was granted, but it came with a message that said that if they were truly good girls—girls who did as they should—then they would not actually need that contraception. Alicia, who emerged as an inconsistent user of contraception and was thirty-five and a single mother at the time of our interview, described what I call the parental "forked tongue" as follows:

They told me and my sisters everything and allowed us to ask questions. They even told us that if we needed birth control or anything
like that, we should ask them. I asked my mom for birth control pills
when I was seventeen or eighteen. She asked me why I wanted them,
and I told her for the obvious reasons. She made me tell my father, and
he told me that I didn't have to get into doing all of that, but they got
me the pills. I remember that a nurse who lived next door to my family
used to bring me the pills.

Note that the superior level of access to contraception provided by Alicia's
parents (they were among the most open parents discussed by women in
the sample) is nevertheless accompanied by a negative evaluation of her
decision to have sex. Jan, who emerged as a consistent contraceptive user,
tells a similar story. She was thirty-three at the time of our interview and
was the married mother of four children.

> JAN: My mom told me not to have sex, but she took me to the
> o-b-g-y-n to get pills because she wanted me to protect my-
> self.
>
> AVERIL: When did you get them?
>
> JAN: Before I left for college. My mom said she didn't want me
> getting pregnant and messing up my education. She didn't
> say anything to me about sexually transmitted diseases
> though.

Again, Jan's mother helped her to get contraception and indicated that
she wanted her to use it, but she also communicated her desire that Jan
abstain from sexual activity.

Parents trying to decide how best to advise teenaged daughters about
sex and contraception may find it frustrating that Alicia's and Jan's outcomes are so different—that the one turned into an inconsistent user and
that the other turned into a consistent user. After all, their parents both
used the exact same strategy of education—one of inculcating daughters
with the normative understanding that young single girls should not be
having sex and then granting them access to contraceptive methods to
protect themselves in case they strayed from this normative requirement.
However, if you think about it, there is little surprise that both Alicia's
inconsistent use and Jan's consistent use arise from the similar behav-

iors of these relatively generous parents. No good daughter can obey both sides of a conflicting message. Hence, some, like Jan, focus on the need to protect themselves and use contraception consistently while others, like Alicia, focus on being the type of woman that their parents would like them to be—the type who does not need contraception because she is not planning to have intercourse.

A trio of scholars (Cooksey, Rindfuss, and Guilkey 1996) investigating national changes in contraceptive use between 1978 and 1988 came to a similar conclusion about the cultural conflict in which parents and daughters are immersed. In an explanation of white fundamentalist Christians' increases in age at first intercourse but not in contraceptive use and non-fundamentalist whites' increases in the use of birth control at first intercourse but not age at first intercourse, they made the claim that sex education can be successful at delaying adolescents' first sex or increasing their use of contraception but not both. Thus, this study is like this book in that both maintain that institutions (whether they be families, religious organizations, or schools) have difficulty communicating a message about both abstinence and consistent contraceptive use.

Silent and Ineffective Plans

Silence on things sexual and the consequent isolation in contraceptive decision making is a second feature of the environment that stigmatizes single black women's sexual activity. Parental silence, in particular, was a common way to deny daughters' nonmarital sexual activity; it constituted a passive refusal to be involved in decisions to have sex and a subtle communication to daughters that they were on their own when it came to figuring out the where and how of actually having sex. About half of the degreed black women in the interview sample (52 percent) received no information about either sex or contraception from their parents while another 21 percent reported that parents had told them what sex was and explained to them about how women became pregnant but withheld information on contraception. Thus parental silence meant that almost 75 percent of my sexually active sample relied on other social relationships or institutions for their contraceptive education. As the last column of table 16 (below) shows, some of these women did get this education from others in their social circles—from siblings or peers in their friendship

Table 16. Sources of information on contraception (percentage of interview sample of degreed African Americans reporting sources)

REPORTED SOURCES	FIRST SOURCE OF INFORMATION			ALL REPORTED SOURCES OF INFORMATION		
	% OF CONSISTENT USERS	% OF INCONSISTENT USERS	TOTALS	% OF CONSISTENT USERS	% OF INCONSISTENT USERS	TOTALS
Self-education	27.6	47.8	36.5	25.8	42.3	33.9
(#)	(8)	(11)	(19)	(8)	(11)	(19)
Parents	31.0	17.4	25.0	32.3	15.4	25.0
(#)	(9)	(4)	(13)	(10)	(4)	(14)
Siblings/peers	31.0	13.0	23.1	32.3	19.2	26.8
(#)	(9)	(3)	(12)	(10)	(5)	(15)
Institutions	10.3	21.7	15.4	9.7	19.2	14.3
(#)	(3)	(5)	(8)	(3)	(5)	(8)
Totals	100	100	100	100	100	100
(#)	(29)	(23)	(52)	(31)	(25)	(56)

groups (26.8 percent) and from health-care practitioners or the instructors of school sex education courses (14.3 percent). But 33.9 percent of the sample (the largest plurality) had to educate themselves about it.

What happened when parental silence was accompanied by sibling silence, peer silence, and the silence of health and education institutions (that is, when sampled women taught themselves about contraception and made decisions about pregnancy prevention in isolation)? Contrary to what parents may have hoped, denial of their daughters' sexual activity and silence on contraceptive matters failed to create degreed black daughters who remained abstinent until and unless they were married. Instead, sampled women's testimonies indicate that they were sexually active (see chapter 4) and that silence simply became their poor educator—producing sexual actors who were ignorant and confused about how contraception worked and who were, as a result, inconsistent and unsuccessful contraceptive users. In table 16, inconsistent contraceptive users were much more likely to be self-educated on contraception than consistent users were. (The largest pluralities of consistent users learned about contraception from ambivalent parents and siblings and peers.)

Because the numbers in table 16 come from my convenience sample of degreed black women and not from a random sample of black women in the U.S. population, the association between isolation in contraceptive education and inconsistency in contraceptive use cannot be generalized to that population. However, several quantitative studies have shown that individuals who learn about contraception in their school's classroom settings (for example, in formal sex education courses) are more likely to use contraception at first intercourse.[15] Furthermore, although the research on the effect of parental education is a bit more divided,[16] the qualitative data presented here do offer information about how the silences that surrounded degreed black women's nonmarital sexual activity and their isolated decision making creates inconsistent and unsuccessful contraceptive use. In this regard, I present a story that Eartha told me.

I interviewed Eartha, a childless, thirty-five-year-old divorcee working as a consultant. Her story began with a revelation about a small gap in her contraceptive knowledge and ended with an abortion. She connected the dots between incomplete information, inconsistent and ineffective contraceptive use, and unplanned pregnancy as follows:

EARTHA: I went to the student health center in college for birth con-
          trol pills, and they made me sick. So I tried to use con-
          doms, and the boyfriend that I had at the time, who I now
          think was impotent and gay, could not keep an erection
          with them. So I started using the diaphragm . . . I guess
          at that time I did not know that there was more than one
          kind of birth control pill. Had I known, I could have just
          gone back to the health center and asked for another pre-
          scription, but . . . This may seem stupid, but I went back to
          the health center to get fitted for a diaphragm. They gave
          me one, but they said not to use it for the first two weeks.
          Now I realize what she meant was that I should not rely on
          it as my method of birth control for two weeks, but at the
          time I took it literally and I didn't use it.

AVERIL: Why would she not want you to use it for two weeks?

EARTHA: Because it takes practice for you to learn how to use it cor-
          rectly, so she did not know if I would do it right at first.

First comes Eartha's admission that she would not have made the decisions that she did but for her bad reaction to the pill that she was pre-
scribed and her inadequate information about the range of possible pill
prescriptions. Then comes her exclamation that her interpretation of the
health-care provider's instructions regarding the diaphragm was "stupid."
Eartha's monologue paints a picture of a decision-making process that
was ill-informed and that relied on assumptions rather than informative
conversations about contraceptive devices. Self-taught on sex and contraception, she was without the interactive processes that facilitate both increases in knowledge and the development of skills or expertise. Because
she was committed to a pattern of silence on sexual and contraceptive
matters, her attempts to use the various birth control devices—pills, condoms, diaphragm—were hampered in the same way that the dishes of
a fledgling cook might suffer from the requirement that she or he work
solely from a cookbook and forgo all past and present conversations with
or observations of more experienced cooks in action. Eartha's privatized
sexual behavior and contraceptive decision making results in both inconsistent and ineffective use of the diaphragm and, ultimately, her first of
several unplanned pregnancies. Both contraceptive consistency and suc-

cess decline in an environment where silence on things sexual is the norm and when requests for assistance with or information about sexual and contraceptive practice break those norms.

One problem with silence for contraceptive consistency and success is that it forced women like Eartha into a naïve trial and error kind of contraceptive practice. They discovered important caveats and tricks of the trade surrounding use effectiveness[17] by engaging in isolated fact-finding missions and guesswork and by learning from mistakes. Jacqueline was one of the seventeen women in my sample who experienced twenty-two contraceptive failures despite descriptions of their high motivation to prevent pregnancy and their consistent contraceptive use. Like Eartha, she learned more about the birth control pills she used because of a mistake she made and not because she was in the habit of chatting with others about the decisions she was making and about the contingent situations in which pill use might be less effective. She was married with a young son when I interviewed her, and she described her significant efforts at maintaining a consistent pattern of contraceptive usage during college when she was sexually active and single. Nevertheless, as we sat in her kitchen, she confessed to a contraceptive failure and a consequent abortion during her college years. I asked whether she was on the pill at the time she had gotten pregnant.

> JACQUELINE: I was on the pill, but I had had the flu for two weeks.
> AVERIL: You were taking antibiotics and the pill at the same time?
> JACQUELINE: No, but I did not take into account that I was taking the pill every morning and throwing it up also.

In this case, it is not clear whether someone in Jacqueline's social network would have informed her about this potential problem with the pill if she had been more chatty during sexual and contraceptive decision-making moments. What is perhaps more clear is that isolated decision making and the privatized aspects of contraceptive practice limit the opportunities that women have to hear and share the kind of information and assistance that would maximize success with contraception. Unlike the new mother learning how to take care of an infant's fever or the cancer victim's efforts to manage the effects of chemotherapy, young women learning to be sexual actors forgo the conversations with more experienced relatives and friends and the advice of support group members who know better than they do.

Degreed black women's efforts to maintain the normative silence on sexual and contraceptive matters often implied that they would choose to use the least effective contraceptive methods and to use contraception less consistently. For example, Terri was involved in a lesbian relationship when I interviewed her, but during her twenties, when she was still having sex with men, she gave greater priority to keeping her nonmarital sexual activity a secret than she did to finding and using the best methods of pregnancy prevention. Ashamed of her behavior and expecting to be judged harshly by persons who would hear about it and her contraceptive needs, Terri was attracted to those contraceptive methods that required fewer interactions with persons in what she saw as an unsupportive environment. Such methods tended to be less effective than those requiring contact with health-care providers.[18] Terri explained,

> At first, I used no contraception at all, but I was paranoid about getting pregnant, so I used the pullout [withdrawal] method. The first time I got contraception was at Occidental during a summer program for minorities. I was using the pill at that point because I was in a relationship. After that I used the diaphragm, and I sometimes used no contraception at all. I was afraid of being pregnant because I wasn't doing the right thing, but I didn't want to get caught doing the wrong thing. I was lucky I didn't get pregnant. The last time I had unprotected sex with a guy was when I was twenty-four or twenty-five, and I used the morning after pill . . . I did not talk with any of my friends about it because my best friend was very religious, and she did not have sex until she got married five years ago.

Terri's contraceptive strategies—focused as they were on fear of discovery and a determination to maintain silence with respect to her sexual and contraceptive behavior—created the conditions for both inconsistent and unsuccessful contraceptive use. Fear directed her away from the places where she would have to talk about her sexual needs or to ask and re-ask professionals for pills or a diaphragm; and fear directed her toward the withdrawal method or no contraception at all. She feared getting "caught" in sexual activity, and since nonmarital pregnancy and the planning behavior that would prevent nonmarital pregnancy were both means of getting "caught," Terri's use of less effective contraceptive methods in an inconsistent manner was her way of avoiding discovery via pregnancy or visible planning behavior. On a related note, one clinic-based medical study of social influences on adolescents' contraceptive choices reported that African American females preferred injectable to oral contraceptives and concluded that this preference was related to subjects' requests for a method of contraception that would not be detectable by anyone else.[19] While their desire to keep silent about their contraceptive use may rival Terri's own, the clinic's injectable solution to their problem is less "silent" than Terri's withdrawal, as it still requires the "noise" of repeat visits to the clinic and ongoing interaction with health-care providers who deliver injections.

Rejection of the Planned Sexual Self

Terri behaves the way she does because of the way in which contraceptive planning outs the unchaste woman. It makes the intentionality behind a woman's sexual activity a known fact to those who would reject her for that sexual activity, including parents, friends, and strangers, and the woman herself. Indeed, a third aspect of the environment in which degreed black women make their sexual and reproductive decisions is that it socializes them to view their own nonmarital sexual activity negatively. Contraceptive inconsistency and the use of less effective pregnancy prevention methods become the strategies of practice for those degreed black women who reject their own nonmarital sexual behavior—for those who wish to deny (to themselves and to others) that such behavior is premeditated and to distance themselves from the stigmatized women who plan their sexual activity and prepare for it with contraception.

Marie was one of the women in my sample who was socialized to reject her own premarital sexual behavior. Furthermore, her words connect this third relevant feature of the environment to the two discussed earlier. For one, her description of her mother's "thorough" sex education course indicates that she experienced a parent's rejection of her sexual activity: when I asked her whether her mother told her about contraceptives, she said, "Her policy was abstinence . . . Mom really discussed abstinence." Then, when I pursued the matter to ascertain whether she talked with others about contraceptives, she discussed her efforts to maintain silence on sexual and contraceptive matters, saying, "I researched my own information on contraception. I always had a physician, but I did not feel comfortable talking with the physician about contraception until I was in my late twenties." Finally, her description of her decisions to use or not use contraception during specific intercourse experiences connects those decisions to her distaste for her own sexually active self.

MARIE: Initially, I wasn't for contraception, but as you become older, there are more concerns. I hated the IUD because I did not like the process. Eventually I settled into using condoms.

AVERIL: How did you feel about them?

MARIE: Well, I felt much more comfortable because up until that time, I was not using anything. I was thinking, "I should be waiting 'til I get married." . . . I thought that what I was doing wasn't right, so that's why I wasn't talking to my friends about contraception methods. With my husband, prior to marriage, I was using the rhythm method . . . When I started having sex a couple of years into college, it was a conflict because I felt that I shouldn't be doing it anyway, partly because of my Christian beliefs.

AVERIL: Do you think that it's harder to think about contraception as a Christian?

MARIE: I feel it's harder to think about contraception if there is a moral issue around having sex in the first place.

Marie's life as a sexually active single and her performance of the chaste sexual identity both come to an end with failure on the rhythm method, unplanned pregnancy, and the movement of her wedding day to a date four months earlier—all of which occurred when she was thirty-four years old. By then, she had returned to school and earned a master's degree, purchased her own home, and achieved significant advancement in her job in education administration. And yet it is doubtful that she did any of these other things under the same conditions as she made decisions to have intercourse and to use or not use contraception—for example, enduring isolated silence, forgoing the advice and support of relatives and friends, fearing penalty of stigma, and managing feelings of shame. These conditions give rise to the contraceptive practice that Marie describes— one that amounts to neither outright rejection nor routinized commitment. Rather it is a hybrid dance with halting, stop and go movements that exist between no contraception, inconsistent use of the least effective means of pregnancy prevention, and lack of success with contraceptive efforts.[20]

Thus, those degreed black women seeking to please ambivalent parents, those women working to maintain the normative silence on sexual and contraceptive matters, and those women feeling shame and denial with respect to their own sexual feelings all have reasons to resist planning intercourse. In this latter case, planning means forgoing deniability: one cannot maintain that one's engagement in an activity one believes to be wrong (for example, murder or premarital sex) is a mistake or an unforeseen consequence if one has taken active steps to prepare for that activity (for example, bought a gun or taken birth control pills). At the same time, the rejection of contraceptive planning is used as a method of resisting the impulse to do what one believes is wrong: it will be easier to forgo wrongdoing (for example, murder or premarital sex) if one does not have the tools associated with that activity close at hand (for example, a gun or condoms).

Tamika, a married, twenty-five-year-old mother of two, told me that her mother's messages about the problems with premarital sexual activity made her feel that "sex was dirty." As a result, she recalled, "I spent my teenage years feeling badly about everything that I did." She went on to explain how she resisted using contraceptives in order to forestall her own involvement in "dirty" sex. I asked her if she had used contraception during those times that she had actually had premarital sex.

TAMIKA: I can't say that. We did, but not on a—on a regular basis. Like I wouldn't—I didn't take the um—I started takin' the pill when I got married. But I just would feel so guilty, if I, at that time [before marrying], you know, if I took the pill, because I was like, "Well that means you gonna have sex. If you're trying not to have sex, then you shouldn't take the pill," you know . . . My girlfriends . . . too . . . Yep. We would not do it. We would not get on the pill.

AVERIL: So just because you felt like at that point that would take a whole lot of advanced planning to actually be in the doctor's office saying this is what you wanted and—

TAMIKA: But once you made that—that—that you were saying that you were gonna have sex basically. That, you know, that's not what you were supposed to be doing, and that's not what you felt you should be doing, so don't plan for it, 'cause you not gon' do it. If you plan, then that gives you an excuse to do it.

Here, inconsistent and unsuccessful contraceptive use amounts to more than forgetting to take one or two pills or abandoning an erection-frustrating condom for withdrawal. It also functions as a means to an end.[21] Tamika and her friends believed that using contraception facilitated nonmarital sex while not using it strengthened their resolve in situations where they were tempted to have sex. Because it was understood as something that helped them to behave in ways that they thought they should and to be the type of women that they believed themselves to be, resistance to involvement with contraceptive planning was a strategic move designed to support these women's self-actualization.[22]

It is true that the degreed black women sampled here used contraception to limit, postpone, and plan childbearing around education and careers, but it is also true that in order to do so, they had to negotiate around the meaning of contraceptive planning. Contraceptive technology gave them the opportunity to plan how many children they would have and when they would have them. But actually using contraception implied certain constraints on the way their decisions would be understood by themselves and by others in their social circles. These women found that they could not manipulate the interpretive link between a decision to use contraception and the status of the decision maker as a sexually active individual. To the extent that they saw that status as a stigmatized one, their efforts to avoid stigma (that is, to resist being placed into a negative category of persons) frustrated both consistency and success with contraception. Women's strategies for negotiating these constraints included hiding the evidence of contraceptive use, avoiding potentially informative conversations about sex and contraception, using those less effective means of contraception that implied fewer interactions with others, and completely forgoing contraception during some intercourse experiences.

The explanations of sampled black women's resistance to contraception offered here echo some of Kristin Luker's (1996) claims about the gender bind within which teenage women are caught as they try to negotiate between a responsibility for birth control that has been thrust almost exclusively upon young women and the low status, respect, and romantic negotiating power that is accorded to females who appear prepared for sex rather than swept up in the emotion of it all. Indeed, the introduction to Luker's book argues that our knowledge about teenage pregnancy and childbearing might well benefit from some consideration of the continuities across the experiences of early (teens) and late (women in their late thirties and early forties) participants in nonmarital childbearing. This gendered contraceptive bind within which the sexually active women (and not just those who experience nonmarital births) in my sample sat appears to represent one such continuity.

One of the more important discontinuities between the argument in this book and Luker's work (1996) is the latter's emphasis on a class divide in women's family formation solutions to large scale social and economic changes—changes that have made it difficult for most Americans to match or exceed the economic achievements of their parents. While it is no doubt true that degreed black women's postponement of family formation is linked to what has become the middle-class strategy for improving their future economic prospects in the face of these changes, this book argues that race and marriage are also quite central to the creation of patterns of contraceptive inconsistency. I turn to a discussion of the importance of race and marriage to the creation of contraceptive inconsistency below.

Race, Marriage, and Degreed Black Women's Reluctant Contraception

On the one hand, this chapter's explanations for patterns of contraceptive use have thus far included the expected class-based motivations to plan and manipulate childbearing around educational achievements and career building—the motivations with which women like Nancy and Tristan have clearly become engaged. Decisions to adopt and follow through with contraceptive plans may, in these instances, be understood as "status-seeking" decisions in the sense that they are aligned with the status-seeking decisions made in chapter 1's description of degree-supporting activities. They emerge from status-seeking women's engagement with the opportunities for educational credentialing, their desires to achieve elite careers, lifestyles, and rewards, and their motivations and abilities to adopt that which has been effectively framed as an elite strategy of family formation.

On the other hand, the chapter's explanatory narrative has also included women's reluctance to involve themselves in contraceptive use that is symbolically linked to planning sexual activity. Decisions to forgo, sporadically "flake on," and fail in the execution of contraceptive plans are here associated with "stigma avoidance"—a kind of decision making that certainly supported women's degree-attainment activities in chapter 1, but one that did so in a more indirect manner than status seeking. In these cases, women sought to avoid the racial restrictions they faced by behaving in ways that symbolically distanced them from an "undesirably" black category and the culturally black attributes that typically legitimate race-based exclusion. Below, the conclusion of my explanatory narrative introduces the race-based aspects of this stigma-avoiding reluctance to engage consistently in contraceptive planning behavior.

First, African American racial status is implicated in the development of patterns of inconsistent contraceptive use because such status is also linked to marriage deprivation. Women like Marie and Tamika not only explain how inconsistent contraceptive use emerges from women's desire to avoid stigmatization for premeditated premarital sexual activity; they also make the point that marriage minimizes one's likelihood of becoming a target of such stigma. After all, the sexual activity that these women do not want exposed, the sexual activity that they do not want to get caught planning or executing is premarital sexual activity. Isn't this why Marie moves her wedding date—in order to avoid the stigma of nonmarital pregnancy, also known as the visible evidence of her premarital sexual activity? Furthermore, both Marie and Tamika indicated that they were much more comfortable about adopting and sticking to contraceptive plans once they were married. Tamika even makes the statement that she "started takin' the pill once [she] got married" as if neither the inconsistent pill use she told me about during her single years nor her single sexually active self counts. To the extent that marriage deprivation in the black community means that women who would like to confine sexual activity to marriage but lack the opportunity to marry make up a greater portion of the single black population than they do among Hispanic and white women, we would expect the higher inconsistency of contraceptive use among black women that we observe in table 13 above. For those unable to use marriage to avoid stigma are that much more likely to rely on unplanned sexual intercourse and inconsistent contraceptive use to do so.

Second, degreed black women's racial status is also linked to contraceptive inconsistency because their limited access to committed nonmarital romantic partnerships is likely to discourage contraceptive planning during specific sexual encounters. Here, the last chapter's argument that degreed black women's high celibacy rates are linked to their high degree of confinement to situations of sex without romance and romance without sex becomes relevant. There I pointed out that sex without romance does not result in the orgy of excessive intercourse experiences that popular culture suggests it does, since the who, where, and when of each successive sexual encounter must be strategically negotiated, and—dare I say—planned. When low access to romantic relationships relegates black women to situations in which they must negotiate each successive sexual encounter, these negotiations for sex and for encounters that could potentially lead to sex throw the planned aspects of their behavior into relief. Forgoing, flaking, or failing at contraception may become the only means of suppressing or denying premeditation and planning. Research showing that contraceptive use develops as the relationship becomes more serious and that involvement in non-monogamous or casual sexual relationships reduces women's use of contraception[23] further supports the point that those deprived of serious romantic relationships are less likely to use contraception consistently and effectively. So too does research arguing that women living in environments that are unpredictable are less likely to be consistent in their contraceptive use.[24] Lack of access to committed romantic partnerships and the limited access to the regular sex that that implies suppresses the threat of pregnancy and the felt need for contraceptives. And here again, *race shapes women's contraceptive inconsistency through degreed black women's decreased access to committed romantic partnerships and romantically constituted sex.*

Third, consideration of the relationship between race and romance resolves a third paradox in the data on contraceptive use—the fact that black women's relatively inconsistent patterns of contraceptive use are tied to low, rather than high, levels of pregnancy wantedness. No illogical causal relationship between highly inconsistent contraceptive use and low levels of pregnancy wantedness in the black community is necessary if both variables are causally related to marriage. In my undergraduate survey research methods course, I talk with my students about hidden or third variables that obscure or manufacture relationships between the two variables of actual interest. I warn them that women may appear to have a lower admission rate to graduate school than men if you do not consider the specific departments to which men and women apply. If women tend to apply to departments in which admissions are more competitive, women's lower admissions rates may be an artifact of the lower admissions rates of the particularly competitive departments where they applied.[25] In such a situation, understanding gender inequality in graduate admissions would require an explanatory narrative of gender inequities at an earlier life stage—college or elementary education even—when interests or competencies in particular subject areas are being developed.

In this book's analyses of contraceptive use, the "hidden" or third variable creating associations between race and unwanted pregnancy is marriage. For example, women are, regardless of racial category, more likely to describe pregnancies as unwanted if they are single. Considering only never married singles, degreed white women's ratio of unwanted to total pregnancies is .9; this compares with a ratio of .32 for the total NSFG sample of degreed white women. The same trend is observable among black and Hispanic women, with ratios respectively moving from .5 to .8 and from .36 to .64 as the analysis moves from the total sample to never married singles in the respective racial groups. Because black women spend so much more time as never married singles than white and Hispanic women, data from single women push the overall ratio up in the black population generally and among degreed black women in particular. Thus, the experience of *unwanted pregnancy in the face of inconsistent contraceptive use is a black experience* not because the two are causally related in the black community but because marriage deprivation leads to the latter and single status (which is highly likely in light of marriage deprivation) leads to the former.

The notion that marriage deprivation causes unwanted pregnancy among black women and that single status leads to unwanted pregnancy among women in general might not seem like a particularly radical notion, but it nevertheless is a departure from the way in which associations between lack of contraceptive practice and high unwanted fertility are conventionally understood. Demographers and policymakers in the arena of reproductive freedom tend to discuss the concept of "unmet need," in which they argue that unwanted pregnancy is a sign that women's need for contraception is not being met. Fertility in these interpretations of women's social context is elevated and excessive in the sense that if women had physical access to the contraceptive services that they wanted and they were not bound by normative constraints, significant portions of their pregnancies and births would never come to be.

In contrast, *viewing pregnancy wantedness as a signal of racial deprivation in marriage suggests that the wantedness of pregnancies is out of women's contraceptive control*—that pregnancies are shaped less by women's specific childbearing wants and their varying levels of ability to access contraceptive services in line with those wants than by women's lack of control over their options to marry and their inability to plan family formation around marriage. While the fertility that results from this type of unwanted pregnancy might be described as excess among non-degreed African Americans in the sense that such women's fertility remains higher than that of similarly educated white women, data from Edin and Kefalas's (2005) work seem to argue against this idea.[26] Furthermore, with respect to college-educated black women, their fertility is at parity with (or possibly less than) that of degreed Hispanic and white women only because of this "excess" fertility and "unwanted" pregnancy. Meeting women's unmet contraceptive needs would, in this latter case, depress their fertility below the already low level achieved by highly educated black, Hispanic, and white women and thereby eliminate the observed class similarity in fertility outcomes. Focusing on this aspect of unwanted pregnancy forces us to consider whether creating the stigma-free access to contraceptive services that might remove all unwanted pregnancy from black women's family formation experience would truly result in a situation that reflected their actual fertility wants. Here it might be useful to think about Maya, who ran from stigmatizing nonmarital pregnancy right up until she ran out of the abortion clinic.

Maya ran from the abortion clinic because, despite years of contraceptive plans and public declarations about not wanting children, she decided that she could tolerate or make room for a child in her life after all. In this chapter, I have used her story to show that contraceptive failures like hers as well as inconsistent contraceptive use like Mia's are necessary to create the observed racial "equality" in fertility outcomes among degreed women. Furthermore, they are the product of racial inequality in marriage, opportunities for romantic relationships, and the experience of unwanted pregnancy. Thus, the conclusions of this chapter illustrate the more general intersectionality lesson taught by this book. This is a lesson about how racial inequality (as in differential access to romance and marriage) and gender control and domination (as in women's opportunities in work and play being linked to their ability to present chaste sexual selves) might be the bricks out of which an apparent class equality in love outcomes is built.

The next and final chapter on abortion makes a similar point as it describes a similar racial inequality in abortion that is linked to black women's marriage deprivation. And here again, a story stressing degreed women's similarly high motivation to use contraception and abortion across racial groups would capture appropriate connections between women's fertility postponement and their degreed educational outcomes but nonetheless miss a big part of the point. That is that these decisions to use contraception and abortion are often led by the meanings attached to these behaviors and what they represent—by what they say about whether someone can be called a "good girl" or a "career woman"—rather than strategic action to achieve particular fertility desires, per se.

SIX

Abortion

The Usefulness of It

THIS CHAPTER OPENS with descriptions of decisions made by Tracey, a thirty-four-year-old, college-educated, African American woman in my interview sample. Tracey was labeled a "conforming escape artist" in the analysis completed for chapter 1's discussion of degree attainment. She was so labeled because the activities that supported her achievement of the degree were based in the perceived absence of love in her family of upbringing and her desire to "escape" to a more secure love relationship and family of her own. I have chosen to open with this woman's abortion not because her decision-making pattern occurs frequently enough to be called typical or because it is isolated enough to be framed as peculiar. Rather, I believe that doing so will help to demonstrate the point that a decision to abort can be all about love.

Tracey was thirty-one when she terminated the second of her three pregnancies. She offered the imminent demise of her marriage as the reason that she decided to abort, maintaining that she made the decisions to get an abortion and to separate permanently from her husband at the same time. She explained the dual decision as follows.

When me and Jay were getting divorced, I was pregnant. It was right at the time I kicked him out, and I was either gonna have it or [pause] or not have it. And I thought about it for four weeks . . . And I wasn't even divorced; I was just separated . . . And I wasn't sure I even wanted to have it. So it's not like I was dying to have an abortion. I wasn't even sure I was dying to get rid of him. I had just kicked him out . . . I had just found out I was pregnant . . . and we were just getting ready to separate. And actually, when I decided to have the abortion, that's when I decided I wasn't takin' him back. I was like look, "If I'm not gonna have the baby everything's—um—this is it." That was like really the window. Like if I had kept the baby, I'd a kept him, but when I decided not to have the baby, I said, well if the baby goes, I can get rid of him with a good conscience, and this is it. I'm startin' anew. And that was it.

In chapter 1, conforming escape artists like Tracey were motivated to attend college because of deprivations and desires in love. In chapter 3's discussion of romantic relationships, Tracey was the escape artist who searched for boyfriends outside of degree-attainment settings and disregarded conventional strategies for degree attainment when such strategies jeopardized romance. And here, Tracey's "maybe-maybe-not-abortion-and-maybe-maybe-not-divorce" speech means that this conforming escape artist's decision making on her unplanned pregnancy is more of the same. For the decision that she makes to terminate her pregnancy is explicitly linked to her interest in performing a romantic version of motherhood—a motherhood that stands for a stable romantic partnership or is constitutive of success in the context of romantic relations. Tracey finds abortion to be useful in this moment because of her inability to conceive of and embrace a motherhood that occurs in the context of and despite love's demise.

This decision to terminate pregnancy that is about love was neither common nor peculiar in my interview sample. But it does articulate with both the broad conclusions of this book and the specific arguments of this chapter. Central among these broader conclusions is the point that desires and deprivations in love are at the base of degreed black women's low fertility outcomes and constitute present but hidden racial inequalities in degreed women's experiences. The evidence from this chapter that speaks to this broad point demonstrates that degreed black women's involvement with abortion is distinguished from that of degreed whites and Hispanics by racial group differences in access to romantic love. I find that degreed black women terminate a greater fraction of their pregnancies than degreed Hispanic and white women and than non-degreed black women because of their experiences at the intersection of low racial and high educational status: race-based disadvantages in marriage combined with class-based rejection of nonmarital childbearing mean elevated levels of abortion for elite black women. And as Tracey's story makes evident, elevated levels of abortion can easily be associated with failure at the achievement of romantic love.

With respect to those conclusions more specific to this chapter, Tracey's abortion is both typical and atypical. What is typical is the degree to which abortion constitutes a resource and the strategic "backstage work" that allows women to manage their identities: it allows them to assent to or reject the specific tasks that define motherhood in the context of salient sets of relations (including economic, romantic, and familial relations). But there was variance across the sample with respect to which sets of relations were salient when women's unplanned pregnancies occurred. Tracey's use of abortion to communicate about love and to signify the end of romantic relations and the rejection of a particular romantic partner was not so typical. Similarly, the degree to which she understood motherhood as a romantic outcome—as both evidence and mission of romantic life partnership—was not so common across this sample's decision making on unplanned pregnancy.

Instead, the chapter continues below with its analyses of the way in which elite signification and the performance of elite identities depend upon particular love outcomes. It argues that the love outcome of an elite motherhood—defined in the context of economic class relations—relies on elite status and status-seeking women's use of abortion to distance their family formation behavior from that of low-income black women. Low-income black women's behavior includes but is not limited to nonmarital childbearing, and in this sample, decisions to terminate pregnancies were more commonly linked to elite status signification in economic class relations than they were to love and romance.

An explanation of degreed black women's elevated levels of nonmarital childbearing when compared with other elite women is also included in the chapter, and it too is focused on degreed black women's performance of identity. However, here the point is that the diversity of experiences, values, and sets of relations that lead to degree attainment means that abortion for the sake of an elite-defined motherhood is not always the likeliest outcome in cases of degreed black women's unplanned nonmarital pregnancies. While decisions to terminate pregnancies might be linked to elite status signification—or even to romantic relationship signification like Tracey's, decisions to follow through with nonmarital pregnancies tend to be tied to signification in the context of familial relations. During salient interactions in families of upbringing, motherhood often—although not always—gets defined in ways that are consistent with decisions to carry nonmarital pregnancies to term.

Distinctions in Money, Distinctions in Love

The analyses that follow argue that women's participation in elite cultures supports their use of abortion to shape families in ways that mark them as "elite" or "worthy" of elite status rewards. The research I present augments scholarship that offers explanations of elites' greater propensity to terminate pregnancies based on rational choice theory—explanations that tend to focus on poorer women's greater valuation of children and family and such women's limited prospects for and resources to achieve high educational credentials and incomes.[1] Rather than claiming that poor women forgo abortion because they value the love they think they can have more than the money they think they cannot have, the argument in this book maintains that motherhood is valued across all class groups. For elite and elite status-seeking women, this value of motherhood supports pregnancy termination when the activities and identity markers that define and make elite motherhood recognizable cannot be achieved. Thus, motherhood and children remain important and valued outcomes of elite status achievement; they remain valued outcomes that express and communicate an elite feminine status.[2] Black women have not historically or typically been allowed access to this elite femininity and its associated privilege of a socially esteemed motherhood. For such has been the province (or prison, depending on how you look at it) of elite white women.[3]

In the data on degreed black women's experiences with abortion, pregnancy termination emerged as critical to processes of elite status seeking insofar as it facilitated women's achievement of elite versions of motherhood and enabled their rejection of non-elite versions of motherhood. It accomplished this in the following ways: it prevented childbearing from happening during and potentially interrupting schooling; it allowed women to rely on class achievements or professional work (as opposed to welfare) for financial support for childbearing and childrearing; and it enabled women to resist nonmarital childbearing. In women's discussions of each of these three uses for abortion, there is evidence that black women seeking to establish or maintain membership in educationally credentialed status groups (that is, black women involved in chapter 1's "status seeking") are responding to a cultural rejection of the family formation behavior of lower-status women and are consequently invested in distinguishing their reproductive style from the patterns of women who are poor and black (that is, chapter 1's "stigma avoidance"). Thus, these women's involvement in this type of distinction making reflects both class- and race-based processes.

While we often think of culture in terms of values, this chapter's argument emphasizes the symbolic dimension of culture. It says that abortion is the strategy that makes the "signal" of married, educated mother possible. It says this because abortion helps women to shape motherhood in ways that distinguish it from that of lower-status women, because abortion supports women's compliance with normative strategies for achievement in higher educational and professional settings, and because abortion allows women to demonstrate their acceptance of and facility with elite ways of combining love and money. Abortion is here understood in terms of a culture that provides individuals with the signs, symbols, language, and meanings to communicate to others about who they are, what they are about, and what class they are in. It is a culture that enables them to give their audiences some indication of the ways they should respond to and treat them.

The culture to which I refer in this chapter is therefore an "interactionist" and performance-based culture, like the one Erving Goffman (1963) describes. Just as this culture informs professors that dress in bathrobes and slippers is an incorrect signal for their performance in classroom settings, so too do status-seeking women come to understand that teen pregnancy constitutes an incorrect symbol for use in the presentation of an elite identity.[4] Furthermore, abortion is here understood in terms of a culture that supports the type of class "distinction-making" Pierre Bourdieu (1984) has identified—one in which class differences in access to re-productive technologies and fertility control and manipulation quickly become a "taste" for the particular style or brand of family formation that signifies and represents status. For it is Bourdieu's theoretical claims that would tie elites' access to expensive fertility enhancement technologies during their latter reproductive years and after they have had time to build successful, high-income careers to their preference for a motherhood that includes jogging strollers, Baby Einstein videos, "mommy and me" classes, and elaborate nurseries filled with infant appropriate stimuli.

Don't Be a Fool . . . (Abort and) Stay in School!

Over the course of my interviews with the fifty-eight college-educated black women in my sample, I spoke with thirty-five women (or 60 per-cent) who had experienced at least one pregnancy and eighteen women (or 32 percent of the entire sample) who had experienced at least one abortion. These eighteen women had a total of twenty-nine abortions. One elite cultural belief that led to these abortions was the principle that a young woman cannot both have a baby and continue schooling. This belief was based in "common sense," the knowledge products of scientific and policy-making communities, as well as the heavy social sanctioning of teen pregnancy and childbearing.[5] It supported abortion through its insistence that the pursuit of elite educational credentials is an individual enterprise that happens during the last years of a person's maturation and development process and prior to the assumption of adult roles such as full-time work and parenthood. The belief and its connection to a norma-tive strategy of elite status attainment in which degrees precede babies was so much a part of degreed black women's strategic pursuit of goals in the work and family formation arenas that discussions blaming educa-tional goals and activities for the termination of pregnancies offered little elaboration on or explanation for abortions beyond a simple statement about having been in school at the time that pregnancy occurred. Such was the case in my conversations with both Aleah and Jessica.

Aleah (aged twenty-nine) was separated from her husband and living in an apartment with her daughter and son from the marriage when I interviewed her, but the abortion she discussed had occurred more than a decade before. Back then, her decision to terminate the pregnancy had seemed automatic, as if the situation had presented no alternatives for action but abortion. She tried to tell me how she felt, maintaining that she "wasn't ready" and recalling her reaction to the pregnancy, with the words, "I mean, I'm like, 'I'm pregnant; what am I gonna do? I'm a sophomore in college. What am I gonna do?'" Jessica, a single, forty-three-year-old drug rehabilitation counselor, responded to a pregnancy during her freshman year of college as if she too believed that abortion was the obvious choice in her situation. She explained her abortion with a single sentence: "I knew I wasn't comin' home with no baby." The assumptions underlying the statements in both of these examples speak more loudly than anything that is stated explicitly, and in each case, underlying assumptions point to an apparent incompatibility between childbearing and a young woman's youthful age and student status. What this incompatibility seems to mean is that childbearing at this moment will require leaving school and thereby threaten the individual woman's completion of the specific schooling tasks associated with elite status seeking.

The timing of abortions and the situations of those who carried unplanned pregnancies to term in the interview sample also indicated that the understanding that school and childbearing are incompatible and the obedience to the rule of degrees before babies is widespread among those with student status and professional aspirations and with those who support them in their educational endeavors. Thus eighteen (or 62 percent) of the abortions in my sample occurred while the woman was under the age of twenty-one, and sixteen (or 55 percent) of them were given to women who were actually enrolled in high school or college at the time that they became pregnant. Furthermore, just four of the women in the sample carried unplanned pregnancies to term during their teens and early twenties, and only one of these four women was enrolled in school at the time that she did so. This was Aleah, whose reasoning for terminating her first pregnancy is discussed above. As an eighteen-year-old sophomore, she terminated the pregnancy and remained in school; as a nineteen-year-old junior, she chose to carry the pregnancy to term, but she took a couple of years off of school in order to do so. With regard to the remaining three, Maya had left school for financial reasons and was working when she became pregnant. Jane had dropped out of school two years before carrying her pregnancy to term. And Niani originally rejected college after high school: she decided to go through with an unintended pregnancy from her position as a full-time worker with no particular aspirations for college. Thus, even the women who carried unplanned pregnancies to term during their youth support the point that the schooling aspect of status seeking is seen as particularly problematic for childbearing and childrearing and that women enrolled in school seek abortions as part of their participation in a normative strategy associated with the culture of elite status seeking.

In the sociological literature on teen pregnancy and childbearing, dropping out is consistently associated with the childbearing behavior of young women whose past performance in school and/or whose poor status indicates that their future job prospects and earnings look relatively bleak. Young women are presumed to take note of the experiences of those in their immediate surroundings and of their own likelihood of succeeding in school and the workplace; then they supposedly make a cost-benefit analysis to determine what they will lose by carrying early pregnancies to term.[6] The higher likelihood that the women in my sample had of deciding on abortion rather than leaving school would be understood by scholars of this literature as predictable given these women's early school success and their aspirations for and expectations of high-status employment in their future.

But this book doesn't read sampled women's beliefs in the incompatibility between school and childbearing in precisely this manner. Rather than supporting the taken-for-granted fact of an incompatibility between school and childbearing[7] or women's rational cost-benefit analyses in light of that fact, this book highlights an elite class cultural system in which women's love relations and the outcomes of those relations matter. It suggests that there are decidedly elite versions of childbearing, motherhood, and parenting (and not just of education and work).

In any "version of motherhood," beliefs about motherhood are connected to norms or guidelines about how motherhood should occur and are made intelligible by a language system and a set of symbols that allow individuals to recognize and place themselves in activities, interactions, and/or tasks that would be recognized or understood as motherhood in those cultural terms. Abortion may or may not make it possible for a woman to achieve a college degree, as some of the scholars analyzing relationships between educational achievement and childbearing suggest.[8] But it certainly preserves or makes a course correction on a journey toward a version of motherhood that is decidedly elite in that it implies the completion of higher educational and professional training prior to and not instead of or during childbearing and childrearing. Aleah's and Jessica's reasonings around their abortions are not articulations of desires for school or particular school-related career outcomes. They are not even articulations of what they want to do. Instead, they are utterances of that which they cannot imagine or conceive of doing. Their abortions (and even Aleah's later decision to carry the second pregnancy to term) reflect the ineffability of an alternative to abortion that would include the maintenance of student status.

Abortion supports the performance of motherhood, but it is an elite version of motherhood—and it is *one that constitutes a valued end associated with women's elite status-seeking activity.* This version of motherhood is known by and valued because of the ways in which it facilitates elite women's performance of femininity and the way it is class distinguished from versions of motherhood that might more comfortably begin with dropping out of high school or even with continued attendance at college courses with a pregnant belly. To embark upon elite motherhood without completing school becomes a concession to one's own inadequacy with regard to one of the very behaviors that defines and distinguishes it from low-status motherhood.

Ain't Nothin' Goin' on but the Rent: You Got to Have a J-O-B, If You Wanna Keep the Baby

If "schooling first, then baby" is a rule for achieving elite professional status and motherhood (and not instead of motherhood), then childbearing and childrearing using income from personal employment and personal wealth is an elite-sanctioned strategy of family formation.[9] Degreed black women's efforts to conform to this elite strategy of "personal employment-funded" parenting led to abortion also, although this reasoning was not as common as the need to complete school. For example, Cheryl's abortion right after graduating from college was explained with her assertion, "I got an abortion because I did not have a job. If I had had a job, I would have done otherwise." Here Cheryl, currently a married caterer with two children, is actually concerned with the legitimacy of the source of her family funds. For her claim that preventing her abortion would have required "a job" actually bypasses the list of baby supplies she could not afford to purchase and focuses on a discussion of the strategy for acquiring those supplies that would have made sense for and been acceptable to her.

At the time of her abortion, Cheryl was involved in a job search connected to her recent college degree. Given the male-gendered orientation of most professional worksites, a pregnant belly would likely have complicated and compromised the level of success achievable in that search.[10] But what is important to note is that Cheryl did not even consider the strategies for funding parenting that the works of Anderson (1989), Edin and Kefalas (2005), Geronimus (1987, 1997), Luker (1996), and Stack (1974) indicate are acceptable strategies to poor (and oftentimes black) women—strategies like receiving support through longer-term residence with her parents or extended kin, applying for Medicaid, and accessing food stamps and cash assistance through the state welfare program if she hasn't found "a job" by the time of the baby's birth. Instead, Cheryl's decision making on abortion focuses on whether she can approach the reproductive task in a culturally appropriate manner, where cultural appropriateness is evaluated based on educated elites' normative strategies for financing family formation. And Cheryl's abortion is here revealed as a component of elite status seeking, as it demonstrates her aspiration to a higher-class version of working and "self-sufficient" motherhood—one in which a professional job attainable because of her recently earned college degree plays a prominent role.

In her writing about teen pregnancy, Kristin Luker (1996) has argued that poor women's sexual and reproductive decision making needs to be understood in the context of the last half-century's large scale social and economic changes. They include advances in contraceptive technology, rising economic inequality and the declining fortunes of the working and middle classes, and a women's movement that precipitated rising divorce rates and families headed by male and/or female parents who can both be workers in the formal sector. An elite self-sufficient motherhood is thus a relatively new cultural concept—one that requires feminist language about what women are able to do and not do (for example, have professional careers in the productive sector and parent at the same time) and symbols that make it possible for claims to legitimate motherhood to be based in women's financial means rather than their marriage to a man. The elite self-sufficient motherhood to which Cheryl's abortion rationale alludes is also reliant on evaluative and symbolic structures associated

with the relatively recent mass production of contraceptive technology
and the imposition of family planning culture around the globe. Here,
health and governmental and nongovernmental advocacy institutions
make it possible for individual women to imagine a most convenient economic time to dedicate to childbearing and to act as if the decision to
plan reproductive activity so that it happens then and only then is theirs
to make.

Critical to the argument in this book, then, is the point that Cheryl's
claim that a job would have changed her course of action with respect to
her pregnancy should not paint a picture in readers' minds of rational
choice theory's degreed black women—women who terminate pregnancies after emptying piggy banks, counting pennies, figuring out how many
of those pennies are needed to parent, and coming up short. For women
have had babies and engaged in tasks that constituted motherhood for
centuries before there were "things" called "pennies" to count. Instead,
Cheryl should be understood as a woman whose engagement with elite
status seeking has thus far been reasonably successful and who draws on
the relatively new language of the recent women's and family planning or
reproductive rights' movements in order to describe the tasks that constitute a particular version of motherhood and to articulate the terms under
which a woman like her participates in motherhood. Sure, she could have
had the baby without the job, but that might not be defined or understood
as motherhood by her and certain relevant others in and around her life.
And it certainly would not be read as a legitimate performance of elite
motherhood.[11]

Andrea was twenty-four and an information technology specialist involved in a management training program for a utilities company when
she aborted her first pregnancy. Although her words maintain that she
terminated the pregnancy because she lacked the money to parent, she is
like Cheryl in that she is also not talking about economic survival of her
family, per se. Instead, she too remains focused on the source of finances
and what that source indicates about the version of motherhood and
childrearing in which she will partake. She began answering my queries
about how she decided on an abortion.

ANDREA: Well, even though my boyfriend at the time wasn't physi-
          cally abusive, there were—I was beginning to have con-

cerns at the time about his personality. And I also didn't feel like I was ready to raise a child. And I certainly didn't think he was ready to raise a child even though he had a child from another relationship. Um, he didn't have much interaction with that child, and I saw those things as clues.

AVERIL: And how come—you said you didn't think you were ready to raise a child? What were you looking for? What would have made you ready?

ANDREA: For the most part, finances even though I was, you know— I think—finances. And now [can] I afford this thing. [*Here Andrea is gesturing toward a beautiful exotic bird sitting in an elaborate cage behind us as we spoke.*]

AVERIL: Basically you were thinkin' that—you thought you needed to have more money put away? Or more money in terms of salary? Regularly?

ANDREA: I thought I should have more money in terms of both. I thought I should have more money put away, which I didn't at the time, and in terms of the salary. And my boyfriend made very little money in comparison to what I was making, and that's another subject entirely, . . . 'cause I didn't think he could afford to handle it either.

Andrea's reasoning references a slightly more complex picture of elites' "self-sufficient" motherhood than Cheryl's does, for the latter suggests that a job alone would have sufficed to create a version of motherhood in which she would have willingly participated. In contrast, Andrea required more than "a job": she also wanted to have a relatively high income and to have created a "nest egg" of savings. Furthermore, she considered the financial resources that she had at her own personal disposal alongside those that were available to her boyfriend, which were, in turn, considered alongside his personality, their relationship, and the parenting skills (or lack thereof) that he demonstrated in interactions with his child from a previous relationship. But the thirty-year-old Andrea, who still works for the same utilities company, is actually doing more than providing a longer list of acceptable sources for family funds. She is also showing me how information about possible funding sources translates into a decision about unplanned pregnancy, and how that translation process is dependent upon the versions of motherhood available in the cultural system of the elite class.

Andrea's words ultimately communicate that she was unable to prove—using income achievements, past parenting behavior, and former savings and investment action—that she and her partner were worthy of and ready to perform an elite status seeker's version of appropriate parenting. Abortion does not here represent the prioritization of an individual woman's money and earning power over her desire to love and care for a child. Instead it concedes her inadequacy to the task of elite parenting and preserves and shows her interest in achieving an elite class distinction-making version of motherhood. If individual women adhere to a requirement that says that their class achievements and/or the working out of love relationships with partners who have attained certain elite class achievements make them worthy of motherhood, then motherhood becomes an expression of rather than a detractor from elite status.

The reliance on employment income and savings is a key characteristic that sets professional elite versions of motherhood apart from motherhood in the lower class. In her volume describing middle-class women who choose to parent while single, Rosanna Hertz (2006) indicates that the possibility of using high professional statuses and incomes to set single-parenting behavior apart from oft-maligned welfare-dependent parenting was an important precursor to the expansion of middle-class women's involvement in nonmarital parenting.[12] And here, the use of abortion because of the inadequacy of one's own or one's partner's class achievements shows how children are valued as part of women's performance of an elite status identity. Children should therefore be thought of as desirable outcomes, in and of themselves, and desirable as vehicles of elite signification, insofar as they allow for the performance of a recognizably elite femininity.[13]

It Beats a Shotgun Wedding

A third elite norm around family formation—the understanding that elites eschew nonmarital childbearing—also led to abortion among women in the interview sample. Degreed black women took great pains to distinguish themselves from single parenting, and abortion was useful in supporting their efforts to do so. Even women who had already attained their college degrees and who had incomes and health insurance from professional employment might nonetheless distance themselves from nonmarital childbearing because of what they believed that it signified. The fact that abortion was chosen despite an interest in children and motherhood and despite claims that motherhood was not likely to interfere with educational credentialing or the achievement of the career and income outcomes associated with elite status-seeking decisions suggests that elite rejection of nonmarital childbearing is not so much a practical action as it is a signifying one. Below Karie articulates a distaste for nonmarital childbearing that suggests she has problems with its likely effect on her status identity.

Although Karie, a twenty-six-year-old attorney, described her abortion to me as a "sacrifice" she had made to attend law school and pursue her long-term dream of a career in law, as she went on this seemed to be less relevant than her desire to avoid nonmarital childbearing. For Karie struggled with her unwillingness to marry her boyfriend or even to include him in the decision about the pregnancy. Given the couple's high level of incompatibility and pattern of frequent breakups (see chapter 3 for details), she believed that her decision came down to whether she was interested in being a single parent or not. And in this regard, she concluded, "No way could I be a single mother. And I didn't want to marry the father. Same guy I just broke up with. Same guy. But I knew he would want to [keep the child], so I didn't let him know [about the abortion] either, 'til after."

For the purposes of this argument about abortion's role in defining and shaping elite motherhood, it is important to note that Karie's abortion did show itself to be an individual's rejection of a version of motherhood inconsistent with elite class culture, rather than an individual's skills- or resource-based inadequacy to the job of single parenthood. It did so in the list of possibilities for continuing with the pregnancy that she presented and dismissed. Besides the possibility of marrying the father, mentioned in the quote above, Karie also told me that delaying law school (since the pregnancy occurred during the summer between college graduation and the beginning of law school) or "leaving the baby with [her] parents" while she pursued law school were options she considered that would have allowed her to go through with the pregnancy. Her sense that these were doable options but unattractive ones underscores the point that her decision reflects symbolic acceptance of an elite cultural aesthetic around childbearing (for example, "I find nonmarital childbearing distasteful") as much as or more than it amounts to strategic adherence to required norms for degree attainment or the achievement of a particular professional status (for example, "I have neither time nor money to attend school and parent at the same time"). Karie's unwillingness to take advantage of her resources for single parenting indicate that she was ultimately aborting to resist communicating the meanings or significations associated with single parenting more so than she was resolving her inability to ensure that her baby would have had his or her physical and emotional needs met.

When I say that Karie's rejection of single parenting constitutes acceptance of the elite cultural aesthetic around childbearing, I mean that adhering to elite cultural norms around family formation is not just about maintaining time or money to pursue money-related goals: it is also about signifying elite status, resisting marginalization in elite settings, and claiming the identity of and superior treatment accorded to an elite professional. Abortion consequently remained useful to degreed black women who believed that nonmarital childbearing and single parenting would communicate low or negative status and trigger the substandard evaluation and treatment typically directed at lower-status versions of motherhood. As indicated above, this is a cultural argument as opposed to an economic rational choice argument: it questions whether young women enrolled in school and degreed women without jobs or "nest eggs" of savings really believe that they are without the physical and emotional resources for parenting while attending school or developing careers; it concomitantly questions whether disaffected students and lower-class women can be thinking about the same list of possible resources and yet coming to the conclusion that motherhood "makes more sense" than abortion.

Instead, the argument in this book suggests that descriptions of poor women's choice of motherhood over marriage and furthering their educations should rely more on the meaning resources that allow women to define motherhood as economic "struggle" and "sacrifice" than on the higher valuation of motherhood by low-achieving students and women in the lower class.[14] The argument in this book maintains that women involved in elite status-seeking activities like Karie are thinking and communicating to audiences in a language that cannot read elite motherhood from a canvas that depicts nonmarital childbearing. In this situation abortion is also desirable because of what nonmarital childbearing communicates or even tells a woman about herself (for example, "I am, or others may see me, as a sexually irresponsible woman rather than as a professional mother").

Further evidence that elites use abortion to eschew a nonmarital childbearing that is more typical of lower-class women can be found in the examination of race-education group differences in the response to nonmarital pregnancy. Figure 14 below depicts (using data from the National Survey of Family Growth [NSFG] [NCHS 1995]) never married women's likelihoods of terminating (black portion of the lines), losing (grey portion), and carrying pregnancies to term (light grey portion). Generally speaking, abortion seems to be much more likely among the highly educated. Single black and Hispanic women who have some college or college degrees have terminated between 30 and 45 percent of their pregnancies. In contrast, single black and Hispanic women who end their educations before or with the high-school diploma tend to abort fewer than 20 percent of their pregnancies. Furthermore, single white women exhibit similar class differences, with those at the some college and college degree levels respectively terminating 55 and 78 percent of their pregnancies and those at the less than high-school and high-school diploma levels respectively terminating just under 25 and just over 35 percent of their pregnancies. Such class differences in the resolution of nonmarital pregnancies support the point that Karie's and other degreed women's distaste for nonmarital childbearing is tied to their relatively high educational achievements. They indicate that degreed black women are neither isolated in nor the most extreme with respect to the use of abortion to reject nonmarital childbearing and thereby perform a more elite distinguished version of motherhood.[15] They also underscore the point that performances of elite motherhood are likely to be compromised by the resolution of nonmarital pregnancies in nonmarital births.

Elite Signification in Black and White

Thus far this chapter on abortion has suggested that degreed black women's involvement with abortion is based in their interest in performing an elite version of motherhood. I have maintained that rationales for abortion that focus on the need to complete school, secure a professional

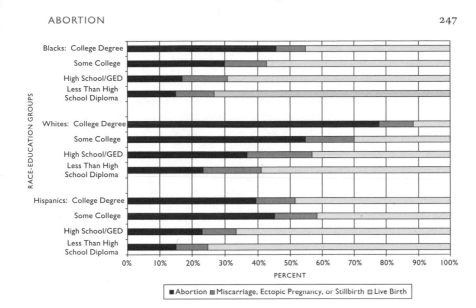

14 Percentage of pregnancies to single (never married) women ending in abortion, in miscarriage, ectopic pregnancy, or stillbirth, and in live birth. Calculations are based on reproductive history data from the NSFG (NCHS 1995) and are found in table A16.

job, or marry prior to childbearing reflect women's identification with an elite definition of motherhood—with a motherhood defined around economic class relations and understood as both reward and role associated with the achievement of an elite feminine status. Although I have focused on the class-based aspects of the processes in which elite definitions of motherhood emerge and become reasons for pregnancy terminations, as the obvious racial differences in figure 14 above suggested, these *abortions for the sake of an elite defined motherhood are the product of unequal race relations as well.*

The section below describes the race-based processes involved in and the intersectional aspects of this argument. I explain how racialized bodies have come to exist at the center of that which elite motherhood is defined against. I maintain that degreed black women find themselves vulnerable to exclusion from the performance of an elite-defined motherhood because of the pathologized sexual and reproductive behaviors that their black and female bodies represent. Subsequently I discuss analyses of NSFG (NCHS 1995) data that underscore degreed black women's heightened vulnerability to and involvement in abortion. Here, they find themselves most implicated in abortion because of their position at the intersection of race-based romantic disadvantage and class-based rejection of nonmarital childbearing and motherhood. Finally, this section closes with my negative case evidence of race- and race-class-based constraints on degreed black women's achievement of goals in love and money. In this instance, I bring elite black women's racial connection to symbols of low-status motherhood together with their experience of marriage challenge and with their class-based proximity to settings and interactions where individuals speak and understand through elite-defined signs and symbols. The combination of these three factors means that degreed black women carry the burden of managing race-sex stigma beyond the moment of deciding for or against stigma-avoiding abortion.

Equality Means Never Having to Run from a Racial Symbol

Above, I discussed Andrea's decision to have an abortion when neither she nor her boyfriend's salaries were judged adequate to the task of parenting and because "concerns . . . about his personality" indicated that romantic relationship difficulties were on the horizon. Below, her reasoning around pregnancy termination continues. It illustrates how the issue of salaried parenting becomes tied up with romantic relationship problems and the desire to resist nonmarital childbearing. It illustrates how racial symbols confuse, blur, and tie all of these issues together:

> Although my parents have been extremely supportive [of my brother and his children who were born out of wedlock], I have always tried to do right in their eyes . . . At the time, my older brother had had two children, and I don't think that it changed the way they looked at him, but I don't feel that that was—that that was good enough for me at that point. I think, you know, I didn't want to be a statistic . . . being a young, unwed, black mother. I—you know—the—it's—that situation is perpetuated in the media, you know how sad it is, and et cetera and et cetera. And while there are plenty of good, young, unwed black mothers out here, it's never been portrayed in a very positive—in a positive light. And I don't want to be portrayed in that way. I didn't want to be lumped in that category.

In her statement about the problematic identity of the young, black, unwed mother, Andrea highlights the decision for elite motherhood and abortion in support of it as the rejection of a symbol rather than the systematic evaluation of financial resources available for childcare and diapers. She shows how elites' financially "self-sufficient" motherhood is defined not so much for child's flute lessons and private schooling as against racialized symbols of low-status motherhood. Andrea's, Karie's, and the NSFG elites' resistance to nonmarital childbearing is thus based in the power that it has to communicate low status. And the power of nonmarital childbearing to communicate low sexual morals, low economic status, and a low rather than elite version of motherhood is in part due to the way in which dominant institutions (for example, science, politics, media, health) have framed the high prevalence of nonmarital childbearing among African Americans.

Inasmuch as the relatively new cultural concept of a woman who professionally trains, climbs the career ladder, and mothers relies on the language of women's equal rights and reproductive rights movements, so too is such a concept defined against at least two other versions of motherhood. First, it is defined against a traditional marriage-based motherhood that was critiqued by the equal rights and reproductive rights movements for saying that a woman's motherhood was only legitimate when paired with her husband's breadwinning. And second, elite "self-sufficient" motherhood and abortion for the sake of it are also in dialogue with a state- or welfare-dependent motherhood that has developed in a parallel manner to elite motherhood, but that has typically been maligned in scientific policy reports and the mass media. Luker (1996) argues that this state- or welfare-dependent motherhood that begins earlier in the life course has essentially been poorer women's alternative response to some of the large scale social changes discussed above. It is this second, negatively cast motherhood that has been racialized as a symbol of black motherhood.

Images of welfare-dependent single mothers who apparently began childbearing at early ages and whose poverty and welfare dependence are the result of early school-leaving associated with pregnancy and parenting are decidedly black images.[16] They have been so since the so-called Moynihan Report (Office of Policy Planning and Research 1965) linked African Americans' high rate of poverty to a description of the black community's disproportionately high share of female-headed families and since advocacy groups and politicians came to narrow the policy-making focus on teenagers and their pregnancy and childbearing. For five decades of policy debates, media reporting, and advocacy group slogan development, nonmarital childbearing, teen pregnancy, welfare dependency, and black women have effectively functioned as symbols for one another. Indeed Luker (1996) is not the only scholar to suggest that speaking about teen pregnancy (or welfare-dependent parenting) was a way to talk about strategies to address decidedly black persons' behavior and dependency on the state without announcing the racial motivations of ideas and initiatives.[17]

Nonmarital pregnancy communicates to mainstream elite and/or professional audiences that black women's bodies—college educated or not and professionally employed, insured, and salaried or not—are culpable in the creation and maintenance of a social problem that begins with their precocious and irresponsible sexual activity, makes its way through poverty and state-supported families, and ends in their offsprings' school failure, delinquency, and future criminal activity.[18] In chapter 1's description of black women's degree-attainment processes, I maintained that although few women "stigma-avoid" their way to college degrees, most black women with college degrees and professional jobs have at one time or another been required to give some attention to the task of stigma avoidance (that is, to distance themselves from stereotypical characteristics that justify African American exclusion from higher educational opportunities or high-status professional work and leisure). Here, I am saying that abortion to avoid nonmarital childbearing constitutes both elite status seeking and racial stigma avoidance insofar as black women like Andrea are focused on performing an elite version of motherhood and insofar as black women's pregnant bodies are all too often read as the problematic lower-class black statistic that elite women are striving not to be and claiming that they are not.

The science, policy, and media activities that denigrated black women's high rates of nonmarital childbearing created the symbolic links between these "black" sexual and reproductive behaviors and poverty as well as other social ills by comparing black women's nonmarital, state-dependent motherhood to white women's traditional motherhood based in marriage. This placing of blackness, poverty, nonmarital childbearing, and single parenting on the one side and whiteness, economic self-sufficiency, marriage, and marital childbearing on the other is a "race-making" or "race-

maintaining" process. Race-making processes establish or maintain hierarchical divisions and relations between interacting groups of individuals
sharing heritable physical traits that are theoretically linked to moral,
emotional, intellectual, and psychological traits. They run the gamut from
labor market segregation processes that channel ethnic immigrants into
devalued, low-income, dirty work to high-profile policy reports and scientific studies that identify and make causal statements about group cultural differences leading to socially unequal outcomes.[19]

It is this latter racial inequality making via symbol construction that
leads to the situation wherein Andrea must worry about the way nonmarital childbearing constructs black women as non-elite regardless of
their education, salary, and training. Indeed, it is this racial inequality-
making process—one that produces symbols of sexual immorality, irre-
sponsibility, and a socially legitimated poverty and exclusion out of black
women's bodies—that pulls elite status and status-seeking black women
into stigma-avoiding activity around their family formation behavior regardless of the specifics of and the normative or non-normative status
of their sexual and reproductive decisions. Below, NSFG (NCHS 1995)
data on abortion and Deanna's, Sparkle's, and Ashley's experiences show
how racial disadvantages in marriage and a symbol of low-status single
motherhood that shares degreed black women's bodies burdens black
women with the management of racial stigma and thereby alters their experiences and outcomes in love.

Inequality Means Managing Racial
Stigma for Nonmarital Childbearing

In chapter 2, college-educated women's similarly low fertility was dependent on racial group differences in family formation processes. More
specifically, the description of data from the NSFG (NCHS 1995) demonstrated that black women across education levels married later, were less
likely to ever marry, and spent less time married during the reproductive period than Hispanic and white women. These racial disadvantages in
marriage and, consequently, the extensive amount of time black women
spent single were, in turn, associated with black women's high fractions
of nonmarital births. In this chapter, chapter 2's analyses are relevant in
the argument about black women's vulnerability to race-based exclusion
from elite motherhood. The analyses act as evidence for the point that

race-based disadvantages in marriage create racially unequal experiences with abortion in support of the performance of an elite maternal identity.

Figure 14 above indicated that all highly educated women resist nonmarital childbearing to a greater degree than less educated women in their own racial groups. It also showed that highly educated black and Hispanic women were actually less likely to terminate nonmarital pregnancies than were highly educated white women. However, black women's extensive time spent single and their higher vulnerability to nonmarital pregnancy means that figure 14's depiction of never married women's pregnancy outcomes is more typical of the experiences of degreed black women than those of degreed Hispanic and white women. Thus disadvantage in marriage leads to higher overall fractions of terminated pregnancies among black women in the college-educated category, despite the fact that the never married black women in that category are less likely to abort pregnancies than never married white women in that category. In much the same way that greater disadvantage in marriage means more nonmarital pregnancies and higher fractions of nonmarital births, it also means that there is a higher abortion cost associated with black women's performance of elite motherhood. Figure 15 below indicates that black women with some college and with college degrees have terminated more than 20 percent of their pregnancies (see the black portion of the top two lines in the figure) while degreed Hispanic and white women have terminated around 15 percent of their pregnancies.

Not only do degreed black women terminate a greater portion of their pregnancies than similarly educated white and Hispanic women: they also abort a higher fraction of pregnancies than black women with no college experience who are similarly challenged in marriage. At roughly 14 percent of pregnancies terminated, black women with no college experience have abortion levels that are more similar to those of highly educated white and Hispanic women than to those of black women who have attended college. According to the argument of this chapter, abortion is most prevalent at the intersection of low racial and high educational status because it finds its greatest use on bodies that are highly vulnerable to racially stigmatizing nonmarital childbearing and among minds most steeped in the rhetoric and symbols that construct femininities and motherhoods as elite.[20] In other words, this book maintains that the management of stigmatizing nonmarital childbearing falls to those who are

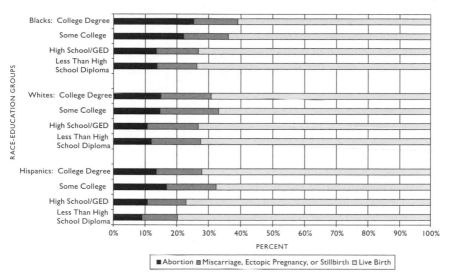

15 Percentage of pregnancies ending in abortion, in miscarriage, ectopic pregnancy, or stillbirth, and in live birth. Calculations are based on reproductive history data from the NSFG (NCHS 1995) and are found in table A17.

both marriage challenged and compelled to "speak" and be understood in settings and interactions where elites' race-sex meanings, interpretations, and evaluations dominate. Abortion is just one of the ways that stigma is managed.

The racial factors that support the need for degreed black women's involvement in the management of stigma for nonmarital childbearing include both an actual race-based disadvantage in marriage and a symbolic connection between black women's bodies and emblems of low sexual and maternal status. The former ensures that nonmarital pregnancy and childbearing are likely to constitute the familiar and even the intimately known in degreed black women's lives. The latter means that others will connect them to nonmarital childbearing and will hold them responsible for being familiar with, for intimately knowing, and for even explaining and representing it. Degreed black women's more frequent use of abortion to avoid racial stigma for nonmarital childbearing is just one kind of evidence of the way in which this stigma management around sex and reproduction amounts to racially unequal experiences in the achievement of elite love outcomes. The following descriptions of Deanna's, Sparkle's, and Ashley's experiences suggest that the tasks of explanation and representation that emerge wherever symbols and significations threaten to limit black women's access to elite love and money are another way in which the burden of stigma management generates racially unequal experiences.

Stigma management does not always take the form of the stigma-avoiding abortion. For as figure 14 indicates, not even half of the stigmatizing nonmarital pregnancies that degreed black women experience are resolved in abortion. When degreed black women decide to carry nonmarital pregnancies to term, like my subject Deanna did at the age of twenty-three, stigma management means dealing with the powerful and prevalent imagery linking one "social problem-generating" sexual or reproductive behavior to another and to black women. Below, Deanna manages stigma by using thoughts and words that fracture symbols and frustrate interpretive processes. She denies culpability for teen childbearing and the list of "social problems" typically associated with it, despite the symbolic links that she expects people to make between her situation and that of a pregnant teenager. She described her feelings during her pregnancy, saying, "I could see people thinking, 'Look at that, another teenager, pregnant!' But I'm sayin', 'I'm a woman!' I mean I wasn't a teenager; I was twenty-three. But I could just feel it, you know, so I was kinda—a little ashamed, like maybe a little embarrassed . . . Because I knew that they were thinkin' that, um, 'Here's a teenager, pregnant.'"

My argument in this chapter contends that Deanna's fear that she will be made culpable for her participation in the social problem of teen childbearing results from the fact that her black and pregnant body is a familiar signifier of socially problematic sexual and reproductive activity, and not from some rational estimation that nonmarital pregnancy catapults twenty-three-year-old women back to their teenaged years. She is therefore like Andrea, whose abortion apparently occurred amid worry that having a baby would make her a part of the social problem of financially impoverished, welfare-dependent parenting, despite her professional salary and private medical insurance coverage. Both women are responding to the symbol created by Moynihan (Office of Policy Planning and Research 1965) and his descendants when they racialized the link between black women's "pathological" sexual and reproductive behavior on the one hand, and poverty and its attendant social problems on the other. The symbol has coalesced around black women's single parenting but nonetheless contains and refracts multiple versions of a story in which problematic outcomes are associated with sexual and reproductive choices that have been "blackened."

Andrea's abortion of her nonmarital pregnancy avoids the stigmatizing actions, thoughts, and looks of others insofar as it distances her from the negatively cast sexual and reproductive behaviors that have typically been associated with lower-status black women. This avoidance activity leaves the racialized symbol of low-status motherhood intact; indeed, it may even reify the symbolic fusion of behavior, status, and racialized body—making it more real. In contrast, "stigma challenge" might be a more accurate way to describe what Deanna is involved in even if her dialogue only goes on inside of her own head. For she fractures the comfortable fusion between one "pathologized" behavior and another—for example, "But I'm a woman" (and not a teenager). In other words, she focuses on disrupting the notion that nonmarital childbearing and teen pregnancy are always found in the same dark bodies. In either case, a certain racial inequality in elite women's nonmarital childbearing is evidenced by the way degreed black women like Andrea and Deanna make decisions about single parenting that come to involve the management of stigma for all those transgressive activities that are symbolically associated with black women's pregnant bodies (for example, teen parenting, welfare-dependent motherhood) instead of the one transgressive behavior in which the women are actually involved (that of nonmarital childbearing).

Sparkle also discussed activity that I would describe as challenging a stigma. Although she was degreed, salaried, and married when the surprise pregnancy and the birth of her twins occurred, she still found herself responsible for explaining and justifying black women's nonmarital childbearing and, ultimately, for disrupting the processes in which race, single status, and pregnancy work together to attract stigma, scorn, and judgment to black women. Her description illustrates the intersectional aspects of the burden of stigma management as her class-based proximity to white insurance company co-workers led to incidents of "stigma challenge" years before she got pregnant with and delivered her babies. She explained,

Everybody who knew me knew "Sparkle don't do babies." I heard that
for nine months: "Not Miss-I-Don't-Do Babies is havin' a baby!" 'Cause
I was always known for sayin' that "I don't do babies, ya'll." So, no, it
[my pregnancy] was well received. The showers on—or shower on the
job was unbelievable, um. People were very happy for me. They knew
how much I love my husband. We were married five years before we
had the boys. So no, that was not a concern . . . It did bother me when I
knew they talked about the young black single mothers . . . Yeah, 'cause
I had to set 'em straight. You know, "Why would she bring another baby
into the world? She's not married." And I said, "She chooses to. She
wants children. It's not a choice I would have made. She chooses to.
It's not for any of ya'll to judge." . . . But I would see . . . how they would
comment on single black mothers, yes.

Sparkle's position at the intersection of low racial and high educational status has placed her between the nonmarital childbearing signifier of low-status black motherhood and elite whites' stigmatizing interpretations of the racial signs and symbols.[21] While she was married and
childless, this intersectional positioning nonetheless translated to responsibility for the management of stigma for racialized nonmarital childbearing. Sparkle's conversations with co-workers are thus directed at signification processes in cross-class and cross-race relations in her workplace
context. Her words challenge stigma by frustrating those interpretive
processes in which elite white persons create or maintain socioeconomic
status boundaries and distance out of single black women's pregnancy
and parenting. Her speech says that nonmarital childbearing reflects
more than the social problem-generating, low-status behavior that bolsters, stands against, and amplifies elites' own versions of motherhood.
Her talk says that the decision to have a child while single also reflects
black women's apparently reasonable desire for children (or, as I might
say, their apparently reasonable desire for love).[22]

Finally, Ashley described feelings that underscore the symbolic status
of black women's sexual and reproductive activity for economic class relations. But she spoke about the symbolic status of abortion rather than
childbearing, and, in doing so, suggested that black women's management
of stigma often means secrecy and silence as opposed to conversation and
speech. Ashley's concern about stigma and exclusion surfaced in response

to a question that I asked at the end of each of my fifty-eight interviews with the college-educated black women whom I sampled. It was then that I requested that the women tell me what they would change about their lives if they could. In this case, Ashley, a thirty-five-year-old former engineer and current homemaker, responded with, "My three abortions." When I asked her why, I expected her to begin once again speaking with me about the difficulties she had had getting pregnant after terminating these three pregnancies—difficulties that had lasted through six years of marriage and several failed attempts at adoption. But, instead, she communicated the discomfort and embarrassment she experienced when she visited doctors' offices and had to disclose these abortions as part of her medical history. She explained with the very brief statement, "I feel like I'm this professional who has had three abortions." In other words, Ashley invoked her class (and not, incidentally, her religion, her pro-life politics, her infertility treatments, or her race—all things she had discussed during prior moments in the interview) as that which she found to be inconsistent with abortion.

In addition to betraying her ignorance of national data that indicates that educated elites abort a higher percentage of their pregnancies than women whose educational achievements are too few to call themselves "professionals,"[23] Ashley's assumption that her three abortions are inconsistent with her elite professional status reflects her reliance on symbols that unite low-status motherhood with non-elite bodies and with the type of woman whose "irresponsible" or "out-of-control" sexual and reproductive activity implies the need for abortion. Given the myriad of scholars who have told us in numerous ways which women are likely to benefit from postponing fertility[24] and which women are likely to benefit from hastening it,[25] I argue that Ashley's incorrect assumptions cannot reflect her rational calculation of the likely costs and benefits of unplanned childbearing to women with respectively promising or bleak career futures. Instead, Ashley's regret over these abortions that she believes make her into a low-status imposter hiding out among "professionals" points to her expectation that her professional status-seeking ends should have been realized through and should be signified by outcomes in sex, reproduction, romance, and love as much as they are experienced through achievements in education, job, career trajectory, and money. The abortions are obviously linguistically inconsistent with communicating "professional" status even if they might be practically consistent with achieving that status.

Above, racial symbols joined one socially problematic sexual or reproductive behavior to another and to black women, compounding the stigma Deanna experienced during nonmarital pregnancy. Racial symbols also brought black bodies involved in nonmarital childbearing under the purview of a black woman's body that was not so involved at Sparkle's workplace. In Ashley's case, racial symbols make class standing into moral penalty and reward for group sexual and reproductive behavior and shape the framework that she uses to interpret and understand her own life. Moreover, I argue that it takes just that powerful a set of racial symbolic resources to turn abortions that delay childbearing and supposedly pave the way to Ashley's superior level of educational attainment into abortions that act as hostile forces lying in wait and threatening to "out" Ashley and compromise her elite status. Ashley carries the stigma management burden associated with her current performance of elite motherhood by keeping these abortions secret.

The turn, move, or shift from the "rational choice" abortion to the signifying abortion, which I am asking readers to make, not only highlights the role of racial symbols in the creation of degreed black women's burden of stigma management. It also summarizes the claims made in this chapter's argument about inequality and love. First, Ashley's focus on the signifying aspects as opposed to the practical aspects of her abortions reiterates this chapter's argument about degreed black women's elite identities and the ways in which their class achievements are tied to, achieved through, and signified by processes and outcomes in love (as well as money). Second, I rely on discussions of what pregnancy, childbearing, and abortion signify in the cross-class and cross-race relations that Ashley experiences to explain why black women's elite achievements (in this case, the achievement of an elite motherhood) require attention to racial matters including decisions and actions to avoid or manage racial stigma. And third, the turn from abortions based on rational choice to the secrets Ashley keeps about her signifying abortions illustrates important intersections between inequality structures—making the case that elite class identities are constituted by racial processes of stigmatization and exclusion and the gendering performance of motherhood (as well as women's use of abortion in support of particular versions of motherhood). This gendering perfor-

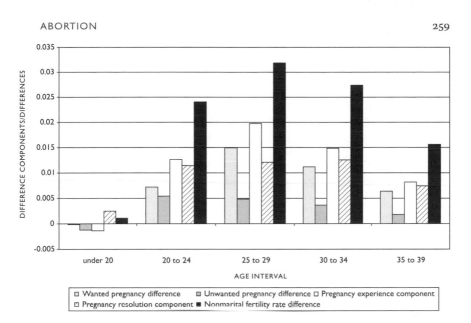

16   Wanted pregnancy experience, unwanted pregnancy experience, and pregnancy experience and
resolution components of nonmarital fertility rate differences between college-educated black
and white women. Results of decomposition analysis are based on reproductive history data
from the NSFG (NCHS 1995) and are found in table A18.

mance of motherhood is, in turn, reliant on the race-making and class-
constituting processes that currently define motherhood.

Signifying at Work, Signifying in Family

Despite their low level of involvement with marriage, degreed black
women keep pace with degreed Hispanic and white women's fertility
levels by relying on higher levels of nonmarital fertility (see chapter 2).
According to the decomposition analysis of racial differences in nonmarital fertility depicted in figure 16 above, they achieve these higher levels
of nonmarital fertility because they are more likely to get pregnant while
single than degreed white women are (a difference represented by the
solid white bars extending upward in each age interval) and because they
are more likely to carry the nonmarital pregnancies that they experience
to term than degreed white women are (note the slightly shorter bars
shaded in a striped pattern that stand to the right of the white bars). The
solid black bars in the figure depict the total difference between the non-

marital fertility rates of degreed black and white women: each one shows the sum of black women's numerical advantage in nonmarital pregnancy and their numerical advantage in nonmarital pregnancies resolved in births during the specified age interval (that is, the sum of the two prior bars).[26]

Thus, inasmuch as college-educated black women's achievement of similar fertility outcomes with college-educated Hispanic and white women depends on black women's higher nonmarital fertility, it is also dependent on higher nonmarital pregnancy (likely attributable to their relatively low rates of contraceptive use, as discussed in chapter 5 of this text)[27] and lower nonmarital abortion. This final section of the chapter maintains that this lower nonmarital abortion or, in other words, the more likely resolution of nonmarital pregnancy in birth is also related to degreed black women's identity performance and the signifying aspects of abortion and childbearing.

Despite the usefulness of abortion to elite status signification in the context of class and race relations, salient familial relations that are also associated with degree attainment lower degreed black women's use of abortion in cases of nonmarital pregnancy. Analysis of degreed black women's rationales for carrying unplanned nonmarital pregnancies to term does not indicate that higher valuation of motherhood or lower costs of motherhood to schooling and/or career separate these decision-making moments from those where abortion was the chosen outcome. Rather, the structure of familial relations and the definitions attached to abortion and nonmarital childbearing in the context of these relations support identity performances that do not unilaterally conflict with degreed black women's nonmarital childbearing in the ways that elite status signification typically does.

Above, I discussed the stigma management activity in which Deanna engaged as she carried her unplanned nonmarital pregnancy to term. But despite her concern about stigma and her belief that she needed to manage it throughout her pregnancy, she did not, during that time, really consider abortion. In addition to heightened fears about never being able to have a child that were based in her friendship during middle school and high school with a young woman who became sterile through illness, Deanna maintained that her decision to forgo abortion also had to do with her mother's encouragement to continue with the pregnancy. Her mother specifically advised her against having an abortion because she felt "ashamed or something like that." In other words, her mother specifically advised her against the stigma-avoiding abortion, all the while pointing out that Deanna could handle the challenge of single motherhood since she had "already finished school," had made a good career choice in the stable field of nursing, and had lots of support from her family. In my evaluation of the data, then, Deanna's familial relationships are social spaces in which nonmarital childbearing and abortion both signify quite different things than they do in the school and workplace interactions of middle-class professionals.

Deanna's choice of motherhood over abortion "because my mother told me to" is not so much a notion or an excuse as it is a matter of an identity or a series of life experiences and decisions in the context of a specific set of relationships. These contextualized experiences show individual women and those in their context who they are, how they would like others to see and understand them, and whether that self can comfortably include unplanned single motherhood. In chapter 1, I identified Deanna as a "prominent person pleaser" because the decision-making trajectory of her life indicated that she had done a number of things "because her mother told her to." The list included making preparations for and attending college, choosing a career as a nurse, guiding her younger sister through her own first days at the local university that their mother recommended that they attend because of its nursing program, and rejecting the idea of marrying the father of her baby only for the sake of legitimating the pregnancy and the couple's family status.

Deanna's securing of the college degree and professional career were directly attributable to the supportive relationship she enjoyed with her mother, her valuation of family relationships, and her consequent desire to please her mother. It is because she is a daughter who is supported by and who pleases her mother that she achieved elite professional status and chose single parenthood over abortion. Moreover, in the context of these familial relations, abortion and nonmarital childbearing shift in meaning: having an abortion means shame "or something like that" while childbearing demonstrates individual competence and economic success as well as strong family bonds and family functionality. Deanna shows how decisions in the language of love (rather than money) supported professional career achievement and single parenting (as opposed to professional career achievement and the frequently associated stigma-avoiding abortion).

Both prominent person pleasing (a type of action typically tied to familial relations) and elite status seeking (an activity recognizable because of its ties to economic relations) bring together love outcomes (for example, motherhood) with money outcomes (for example, nursing careers and professional salaries). But the configuration of the relationship between love and money is different in each of these cases. In the former, money and the job serve family building; in the latter, family building displays, demonstrates, and rewards class achievements. Thus, the reproductive relations that structure pleasing decisions frequently separate elite status attainment from the need to use stigma-avoiding abortion in cases of nonmarital pregnancy. And a woman like Deanna can perform a "pleasing" identity in the context of her familial relationships using, as opposed to negotiating around, the signal of nonmarital childbearing.

Aleah's "profiling" was also discussed in chapter 1. Described as a shallow version of status seeking, it accounted for her degree-attainment decisions by her temporary or inconsistent valuation of the rewards of status seeking and by her limited tolerance for rather than valuation of the lifestyle demands associated with status seeking. Above, I indicated that Aleah terminated her first pregnancy during her second year in college and then followed through with a second pregnancy that occurred the next year. The pregnancy termination was, like her first job in human resources, a "profile" of status-seeking careerism. It was replaced a bit more than a year later with a "profile" of an interest in homemaking and being the primary caretaker of a family headed by the fathering figure in both of her pregnancies.

Between the first and second pregnancy, Terrance, Aleah's boyfriend, who was two years ahead of her in school, had earned his degree and started an entry level position in industrial engineering. He supported Aleah's decision to follow through with the second pregnancy and promised that the couple would marry soon. His promise eventually came to pass, but was accompanied by Aleah's moves in and out of the labor market in pursuit of one career, then a break, then another career, and then a separation because she believed her husband to be manipulative and found their marriage to be too traditional and confining. Aleah was going through both a divorce and a career change at the time of our interview, and even now, after sifting through, reflecting on, and reading over our interview many times, it remains unclear to me what exactly she was profiling at that moment. But I know what it was not: it was neither elite professional status seeking nor traditional married femininity.

Aleah's differing resolutions of her first and second pregnancies are what one might expect to find with any profiler, whose goals fluctuate or are abandoned because the required tasks associated with their pursuit seem irrelevant, disconnected, or simply not worth the time, effort, or discomfort they demand. Abortion may be rejected and single motherhood and the school interruption it implies may be accepted because renewing a prescription for birth control pills "cost[s] too much" and because a pregnancy occurs at precisely the moment when childbearing could act as a resource for a traditional married femininity profile. Childbearing is here the means of achieving access to rewards in love and money (for example, in the form of access to male's professional wages and status) in a way that no longer requires her to complete her own college credentials. When love and money were configured around a profile of status seeking, nonmarital and teen childbearing were rejected. But once the combination existed in a profile of traditional married femininity, the meaning of childbearing changed from that which detracts from elites' educational credentialing to that which facilitates romantic coupling and the building of elite family status.

Jane also took the route of abortion before single motherhood. But her situation differed from Aleah's in a couple of ways. First, in Jane's case there were two terminations rather than one prior to the birth of a child. And second, the pregnancy terminations and the single motherhood were, for Jane, both communications of a single message to self and relevant others. For Aleah, in contrast, the two divergent actions of aborting and continuing with unplanned nonmarital pregnancy reflected fluctuating or unstable sets of relations, significations, and meanings.

Jane's single message is one of "insurgence." Sent to live with different sets of relatives during periods of her youth when her parents found her behavior particularly disruptive and, once again, when they found themselves in financial crises that involved large scale relocation, Jane has come to understand herself as the family rebel. Her practice of bucking institutional authority and reorganizing the ways in which things are done means that she tends to follow just enough rules to put her in a position to negotiate the breaking or changing of others. And this pattern of "insurgence," in which her degree was earned her own way (that is, at a slower pace and in educational settings of her own choosing) or, what her parents might call the hard way (that is, intermittently dropping out of and changing situations for times and places where she would garner less financial and emotional support from them), can be found in her reproductive decision making as well. In clipped dialogue and hushed tones used to ensure that she would not be overheard by the two young teens playing in her daughter's bedroom, Jane, the thirty-four-year-old business manager for two nonprofit organizations and a single mother, described her decision making on three pregnancies as follows:

JANE: Got p-g [pregnant] at age sixteen.

AVERIL: Mm hm.

JANE: Um, experimenting basically.

AVERIL: Mm hm.

JANE: There was probably nothing else to that but that.

AVERIL: Okay.

JANE: Um and then a-b'd [aborted].

AVERIL: Okay.

JANE: Um, p-g again at 18.

AVERIL: Mm hm.

JANE: My senior year in high school.

AVERIL: Mm hm.

JANE: And very much wanted to keep, but the dynamics were such that after having run away three times, not getting along with my stepmother, the said objective was that I was trying to ruin everybody's life—

AVERIL: Mm hm.

JANE: Basically. Instead of it being, "She's got some major problems and needs some help"—

AVERIL: Mm hm—

JANE: It's "she's trying to ruin everybody's life." So by the time this one came at twenty-one, no one really said anything to me because I didn't leave the doors open for conversation.

AVERIL: Okay.

JANE: I decided that the approach was, "Mom, Dad, I'm *having* a baby," and not "Mom, Dad, I'm p-g" because "Mom, Dad, I'm p-g" says that I wanna hear something that you've got to say, and I didn't want to hear anything that they had to say . . . The first time, no one forced me to do anything. I just woke up and said, "Oh no, you, not this, I know." Um, and therefore didn't tell anybody . . . or anything. Ah, stole the money from my stepmother . . .

AVERIL: Okay.

JANE: Um, and then got some from the guy to take care of that. The second time I felt very much forced and coerced because I didn't feel like I was—I wasn't as strong a person mentally maybe as I thought I was, and I thought that if I was told I would have no place to live, I didn't know how I'd be able to survive. And I thought that probably the only thing that I could do was what they said do . . . They felt very strongly that that's what was supposed to happen. There was disagreement about it. Um, and then it came down to "Well, you will have no place to live. How you gon' eat? Where you gon' sleep?"

Both abortions fit squarely within the animosity and rebelliousness in which Jane maintains that she lives: the first one was the victory of having acted independently, without her parents' consent while utilizing their resources; the second one was their victory over her and accusations about her trying to "ruin everyone else's life." When she carries her third pregnancy to term, she is able to get back at her parents. She was away from home and out of their control, and she did not return home until it was too late to terminate.

Chapter 1's conforming escape artists want to get away from their parents, but Jane and other insurgents want to stay close enough to fight theirs. In fighting for the right for daughters to control their own fertility and to simultaneously be able to access family support and resources, Jane communicates a message about what family is or should be (for example, a consensus-based or democratic organization rather than a parental- or authority-driven one) and about who she is in the context of this family (for example, the needed but mistreated member whose baby becomes another way of illustrating new rules for family inclusivity). Similar to

Deanna's pleasing above, money is meant to serve outcomes and significations in love. Furthermore, although one might need to follow the rules of elite status seeking at times when one needs money, the rules are not necessarily dominant or legitimate in the context of familial relations. They may therefore be subject to negotiation and change. Abortion or birth in cases of nonmarital pregnancy are both possible outcomes when the struggle in the reproductive arena is over independence and interdependence and the satisfaction of multiple and often conflicting interests in a single family.

Both the termination and continuation of pregnancies signify. But what do they say and to whom? Earlier in this chapter, I described the way in which they signify to would-be elite women's professional selves—the way they sound the operatic notes of a tragedy communicating one's own unworthiness to an elite status, an elite femininity, and an elite motherhood. Such notes must often be kept secret lest they announce to the wrong audiences that women like Ashley have had three too many abortions to be representative of the sexual control that she imagines (and that racialized and gendered symbols help us all to imagine) elite women to exhibit.

But the stigma-avoiding abortion and the carrying of nonmarital pregnancy to nonmarital birth might nonetheless simultaneously act as signifiers to family, potential family, and elite women's familial selves. Here, they may communicate to partners about the unworthiness of romantic partnerships or about the unsuitability of particular partners for marriage and/or partnered childbearing. They may be the words that Karie and Tracey do not have to say to an incompatible boyfriend or husband about their chances of a familial future, the decision that Deanna does not have to explain to her boyfriend about reliance on consanguinal rather than conjugal bonds for achievement in money and love, and the unspoken acknowledgment that Aleah makes to her partner that over the course of a single school year, his degree attainment, professional status, and promise of marriage can make her ready for parenting instead of or before completing school. Furthermore, when nonmarital abortions and births speak to families of origin, they might signal the willingness to solidify ties of interdependence (Deanna) or the struggle for distinctive identity within the family without the loss of privileges associated with familial membership (Jane).

Key to this book's argument here is that while love outcomes signify in the context of economic relations and can support or detract from the performance of class identities, teen pregnancy, welfare-dependent parenting, and nonmarital childbearing, because of their connection to racialized symbols of low status, are quite limited in their ability to support the performance of an elite motherhood. At the same time, *nonmarital childbearing means something different or is a different kind of sign in romantic and familial contexts, and it did support the performance of certain familial identities* among the women whom I sampled. Moreover, these familial identities are not necessarily in strict competition with the achievement and performance of elite identities, in the ways discussed by gender and family scholars who claim that individuals' investments in family and reproductive sector activities limit successful experiences and outcomes in the formal labor market.[28] Rather the one serves the other, as when Deanna's nursing degree and job security make nonmarital childbearing into an act reflecting both competence and confidence in family solidarity or when Ashley's prevention of nonmarital childbearing make her current performance of an elite married motherhood possible during all those moments when she is not discussing past abortions in doctors' offices.

This chapter's discussion of the factors that shape abortion and that account for race and class differences in the use of abortion returned readers to the very beginnings of this book. For it was there, in chapter 1, that I first discussed connections between experiences, meaning, activity, and outcomes. It was there that I began using evidence from degreed black women's decision-making activities to make the point that love was more than an incidental factor in inequality-making processes. In chapter 1, I maintained that familial relations and experiences and outcomes in love were often central factors in degreed black women's decisions to involve themselves in degree-seeking activities. And here, in this chapter, I have argued the inverse—that family formation activities are meaningful for the signification of economic class. Since racial symbols structure the definitions of elite motherhood and the signs and signifying activities with respect to elite feminine identities, degreed black women find themselves vulnerable to having their love read as money. Therefore, they terminate pregnancies based on codes that tie blackness, truncated education, welfare dependency, and single parenting to low status, and they are not alone in their propensity to rely on this code when interpreting and responding to the experience of nonmarital pregnancy. In short, where chapter 1 pointed out the love relations in the background of elite class achievements, this chapter foregrounds the love inequalities (for example, abortion, sexual and reproductive stigma, nonmarital childbearing) out of which elite status identities and elite similarities in fertility are constructed.

This chapter is also highly related to other chapters in this book. For in discussions of romantic relationships, sex, and contraception, chapters 3, 4, and 5 provide important evidence of degreed black women's challenges in achieving marriage and descriptions of the way in which these marital constraints change the meanings of and consequently access to sex and contraception. The marriage challenge reverberates throughout this book's arguments about degreed black women's sexual and reproductive decision making, culminating here in this chapter's assertions about the ways in which racial inequality in marriage and symbolic status leads to inequality in abortion and nonmarital childbearing experience: it is out of these inequalities that the elite class "similarity" in love outcomes is constituted.

Love matters. Love matters because it is the context that makes certain choices possible. This becomes clear as we think through the discussions and descriptions that fill the chapters of this book—as we think through Wanda's status as a thirty-four-year-old virgin (in the introduction), Karie's eleven-year-long series of returns to her incompatible romantic partner (in chapter 3's analysis of romantic relationships), Janet's celibacy after sexual initiation (in chapter 4's discussion of sex), Rose's antipathy toward contraception (in chapter 5), and, of course, the elevated levels of abortion experienced by the NSFG (NCHS 1995) sample of college-educated black women (in this chapter's argument). Black women's inability to realize their marital goals circumscribes the choices that they can make in each of these discussions. Contexts low on romantic love constrain choices in ways that create degreed black women's disadvantages vis-à-vis sexual satisfaction and with respect to feelings of legitimacy around sexual, contraceptive, and childbearing desires. The low-love context creates these disadvantages even as it constitutes apparently equivalent levels of fertility among degreed women across races. It is only because love matters that equivalent fertility levels can come to stand for such unequal experiences.

But love does not only matter to degreed black women, or to the racial inequalities of marriage and nonmarital childbearing discussed throughout this text. It also has relevance for the achievement, the understanding, the interpreting, the demonstrating, and the experiencing of class, gender, and racial identities, or alternatively, of an individual's class-gender-race status. Love is the material out of which degree-seeking activities, college-educated outcomes, and professional jobs are sometimes built. In chapter 1's narrative histories with regard to schooling, where familial love was either abundant or scarce, love was sometimes the motivating force behind the completion of college applications, the reason for adherence to parental disciplinary guidelines, and the inspiration to select particular professional careers. Furthermore, love gave these class achievements meaning and form. Such is the case when Imani (from the book's introduction) understands the income from her professional occupation as the means to her fertility end—an end in which her child's preexisting college fund is completely intertwined with the begetting of the child. Such is also the case when Andrea frames childbearing as a class achievement and Ashley frames abortion as a class signifier (as is the case here in chapter 6). Here, it becomes clear that love makes these black women into subjects whose class identities can be read. Moreover, these are gendered class identities. And they are gendered class identities that are defined against race-gender symbols of low status.

By moving love to the center stage of inequality analyses, this book illuminates the point that individuals respond to and engage in strategic activity to achieve outcomes that can best be described as configurations of love and money. In other words, it says that we want it all. Furthermore, it exposes the love behind money outcomes as resource inequities. In other words it shows us how qualitatively different experiences of familial love and qualitatively different desired love outcomes structure different responses to economic and romantic opportunities. And finally, this book's focus on love exposes the love in which money dresses itself. Here it points to constraints and opportunities in micro-level interactions that are implied by the class, racial, and gender identities with which our love outcomes label us. It is my sincere hope that these illuminations lead to greater awareness of and intellectual work on the generation, maintenance, and meanings of inequalities of love.

Love Notes

IN ADDITION TO being a researcher, I am a teacher. In this moment, I am a teacher who has just given her longest lecture ever, and I am conscious of the fact that my audience has comments and questions. I have anticipated at least three of these comments and made the "love notes" that make up this conclusion. Since my students routinely want to know what portion of the reading is the most important or which pieces of the lectures are actually going to be on the test, I constructed the first set of notes. They are akin to a set of lecture notes that touch on the highlights of what I have been saying about inequality, family, and college-educated black women.

The second and third love notes are guided by the comments and questions of the academic colleagues, friends, and acquaintances who have been responding to the research findings as I have been generating them and preparing this manuscript. I have found that these audience members at formal presentations and casual acquaintances at dinner parties tend to respond to this text's love inequalities in one of two ways. Some assert, "There just aren't enough black men!" And others recommend that degreed black women should be more "open"—both to the possibility of finding love and to men from other class and/or racial groups. The second and third love notes describe the areas of commonality between and point out the ways this book's conclusions deviate from, criticize, and improve upon these popular ideas about race, class, and black women's depressed marriage rates. My final notes at the end of the conclusion address those with an ongoing interest in these issues by summarizing what we have learned from the past and can learn from future research on love inequalities.

Lecture Notes for *Inequalities of Love*

In the introduction to this book, I said two things. First, I said that *love matters*. And second, I said that *race, class, and gender combine to create our inequality experiences and outcomes*. In between the introduction, where I said I would be making these arguments, and this conclusion, I have been presenting my research evidence for these two claims. That evidence is the in-depth story of college-educated African American women's romantic and family formation experiences; it is the comprehensive report on analyses of how these romantic and family formation experiences compare with the experiences of college-educated white and Hispanic women and less-educated black women; and it is the detailed illustrations of how these experiences reflect social disadvantage.

Degreed black women's romance and family formation story is one of deprivation and disadvantage in love. In the simplest terms, these women's level of romantic partnership, marriage, and voluntary sexual activity are low when compared to similarly educated white and Hispanic women. The racial inequalities in question here may be masked by the fact that my research subjects have equivalent fertility outcomes with other college-educated women, but nonetheless, degreed black women's route to the low-fertility outcomes that we expect among the professional middle-class includes less marriage, sex, and contraception as well as more abortion, unwanted pregnancy, and nonmarital childbearing than the routes of degreed women in other racial groups. Now although some black women may prefer to be single than married, those sampled here did not indicate disinterest in committed romantic partnerships. Using qualitative data from their romance narratives, I make the point that degreed black women desire and pursue more romantic partnership than they get. Moreover, I show that these women's constrained contraceptive use and their elevated unwanted pregnancy and abortion rates are tied to the extensive amount of time they spend single and the consequent efforts they make to avoid social sanction for involvement in "immoral" nonmarital sexual activity.

This story of college-educated black women—whose low fertility reflects deprivation in love and disadvantage in social interactions and settings where marital status has important consequences—functions as evidence in the book's two larger arguments. It is evidence, first of all, that love matters: more specifically, the romantic limitations that my research subjects experience matter. They matter because they constitute deprivation and constraint vis-à-vis desirable experiences of emotional exchange and intimacy. And they matter because they lead to other experiences that are disadvantageous and emotionally upsetting. These secondary experiences include discomfort with nonmarital sexual activity and with the acknowledgment of one's own contraceptive needs as well as a heightened exposure to unwanted nonmarital pregnancy and abortion.

Second, the story of degreed black women's romance and family formation experiences is also evidence for the relevance of social theory's intersectionality perspective on inequality—a perspective that stresses the importance of links between institutions and connections across race, gender, and class inequality-making processes in the creation of advantage and disadvantage. Thus, the chapters on marriage and sex (chapters 3 and 4) show how observed inequalities of love emerge through racial isolation and gender-biased rules of romance on predominantly white college campuses. In other words, these chapters demonstrate that degreed black women's racial status, strategies of class achievement, and gendered romantic relations are all simultaneously implicated in the specific love disadvantage that they experience. Similarly, in the book's last two chapters, subjects simultaneously negotiate for goals in multiple institutions (that is, education, labor, and family) and against multiple, interconnected, stratification processes (that is, race, class, and gender). The argument in this instance rests on the point that contemporary elite feminine identities are constructed against images of poor black women's "immoral," "irresponsible," and "manipulative" nonmarital sexual and childbearing behavior. It is focused on demonstrating that degreed black women's class identity performance involves distancing themselves from these images. Unmarried subjects who establish this distance through the performance of chastity are unwilling to premeditate and plan nonmarital sex, and they emerge as inconsistent users of contraception. In the event of pregnancy, abortions that hide nonmarital sexual activity and prevent nonmarital childbearing become part of their efforts to avoid racial stigma and claim elite status. It is in these decision-making moments—when women worry over what their contraceptive preparedness, pregnant bellies, and nonmarital parenting might say outside of familial contexts and inside of school, workplace, and other institutional contexts where class identities are salient—that this book observes inseparable symbolic links between sexual and family formation decision making, professional class identity performance, and the avoidance of racial stigma.

Thus, here, at the end of this book, I point to the importance of witnessing and learning from the journeys that black women take to their educational and family status outcomes. These data analyses do not teach us about the racial similarity in college-educated women's fertility outcomes. Instead, they tell us about the race-based inequality in the distribution of love that constrains the sexual and family formation choices of black women regardless of class. These women's journeys do not singly instruct us about a system of class stratification that dictates familial and other arena outcomes along the same lines as it structures a hierarchical wage distribution. They also point to class advantage that is generated and claimed in loving and, at times, not so loving, gender-restrictive familial relationships; they point to class credentials that are the consequences of collective racial struggle and avoidance of racial stigma. Finally, these journeys cannot be understood as school-to-work-to-family-formation transitions that were not "derailed" by precocious sexual activity or "thrown away" for an exceptionally high valuation of children and motherhood. Instead, they are best understood as a series of decision-making moments in which women must consider what their racialized and gendered bodies "say" in multiple settings even as they struggle to determine and achieve their desires in money and love.

Notes for Advisers of the Lovelorn

A myriad of "Dear Abbys," matchmakers, and well-meaning advisers in my research audience have responded to the love inequalities that this text describes by focusing on the practical. Instead of academic answers

to and explanations for black women's romantic disadvantage, these individuals offer their advice to degreed black women on how they can find
love. I am continually struck by the fact that so many of the people who
hear about the work I have done here respond to the analyses on this
purely personal level, even though my research anecdotes and reports are
not framed as a set of individual cries for help. I have thought a great deal
about the recommendations that these individuals make to my research
subjects, and I have to admit that the advice that they give shares territory
with this book, since we both *rely heavily on the symbolic realm*. But I have
also made these notes to criticize these advisers' *tendency to view signs
and language as entities devoid of particularized context*. In this latter regard, they miss one of the important aspects of the book's argument and
of the sociological perspective more broadly speaking.

The "Dear Abbys" of my research audience advise the lovelorn victims
whom I study to take stock of the signals they are sending or not sending
to potential suitors and to focus their energies on signifying or performing
more "openness" to love itself and to a larger racial and/or class variety of
potential partners, like, for example, white males or lower-income black
males. They further point out that degreed black women are supposed to
communicate better, which means that they should both be clearer with
men about what they want and pay closer attention to what men are saying about their own needs and desires. Here, women's leaving and staying
behavior in the context of particular romantic relationships is particularly
important since it tells men which women are willing to settle for substandard treatment and noncommittal romantic relations that are unlikely to lead to marriage and family building. But so too is black women's
ability to present or represent their "softer," less aggressive sides critical
to developing and maintaining the interest of potential partners. For these
softer, more feminine selves will help them to refrain from being so absolute in their assessments of men's behavior toward them, ending all possibilities of relations before actually getting to see these men's best qualities.
And finally, degreed black women must also develop skills at reading into
men's own meaning-filled gestures in order to achieve their family formation goals, since women skilled in these arenas will be able to locate their
own demands for commitment and transitions to marriage and motherhood in the moments and places where men are, respectively, most ready
and most approachable.

For now, let us imagine that it is besides the point that these match-making recommendations carry with them an assumed explanation for black women's challenges in the love arena—an explanation that not so subtly lays the romantic disadvantage they face at degreed black women's own feet. Instead, my notes here are concerned with two other things. The first is the attention that my advice givers appropriately pay to the symbolic realm. And the second is the inappropriate way in which their attention to the symbolic remains completely detached from the unequal social relations out of which these oh-so-important signs, symbols, and gestures arise.

What I believe we learn from this book is that signification is important to the creation of unequal outcomes, but it is not so much skill in signing and interpreting that is at issue. The language of love is far from being some disembodied tool applied in romantic interactions with varying degrees of talent, skill, and expertise. Instead, it acquires meaning in its use in interactions with embodied actors. In this study, the focus has been on the point that the actors have bodies that can carry race and gender, and that have the potential to carry class as well. Advice implying that black women's performance of "openness" to finding love will be read and responded to as simple interest in marriage ignores their potential suitors' familiarity with symbols that connect black women's sexual openness to images of animals rather than wives and honorable mothers; it ignores their familiarity with images of black female prostitutes and welfare cheats who supposedly use hypersexuality and excessive childbearing for economic gain rather than the expression of romantic or familial feeling and emotion.

In this text's in-depth observation of Janet's storied pursuit of romance and sexual satisfaction in chapter 4 or Rose's development of an antipathy toward contraception in chapter 5, we observe that the signifying aspect of sexual and reproductive action is, in and of itself, determinative of women's constraints and choices in family formation. In chapter 4, Janet finds her romantic opportunities on campus limited by past sexual activity and the degree to which this activity signifies her excessive sexual availability and her "low" sexual "value". Meanwhile, in chapter 5, Rose finds that forgoing contraceptive practice facilitates efforts to perform and communicate a chaste, nonsexual identity even as she remains sporadically sexually active. Their constraints and choices are in these instances related to concern over what their behaviors are saying and not over the achievement of a desired fertility outcome. Thus, evidence from this book confirms that advisers and counselors in my audience are correct in their sense that signification, signs, and the interpretation of signs is of great importance in the generation of differences in family formation outcomes. But still, it is not enough to know that communication and symbols matter to individuals' strategic decision making and the social outcomes that they achieve. It is also necessary to ask whether these signs and signifiers have the same result—the same connection to marital outcomes—no matter who signifies and who interprets.

Although my matchmakers' responses to romantic inequality acknowledge the relevance of women's communication through and interpretation of romantic signs, they fail to observe and account for the inequality of signifiers. They do not examine, address, or deal with qualitative differences in prevalent symbols—symbols that carry within them distinctive race- and gender-located meanings and that consequently might interpolate and corrupt the interpretations of black women's signifying action. And in this sense, they fail to study inequities in instances of signification and interpretation in specific encounters or settings, including those created by unequal symbols and by existing inequities between a given signifying body and a particular interpreting body.

Janet may or may not believe that her race and gender status influenced the degree to which her unveiled display of sexual interest came to mean that she was of "low" sexual "value" on her college campus, but evidence presented in this text suggests that it likely did. Rose may not connect the rejection of her own sexual self and the contraception that might support the realization of that self to the proliferation of limiting images of hypersexualized black women in the mass media, but other subjects I encountered while completing the research that supported this book did. Consider that it is not black but white female characters who get to believably parade the sets of *Sex and the City* performing professional workplace success and an openness to sex with multiple men, even as they retain their "high" sexual "value" or attractiveness on the marriage market. The signifying help offered to black women by certain vocal members of my research audience is given out as if signs and signification are read the same regardless of what body is doing the signing and what bodies are doing the interpreting. They carry on as if even their own assumptions that my degreed black subjects are not "open" to love, that they consistently reject white male suitors while giving a hard time to any lower-earning black suitor who looks their way, and that they have difficulty reading and accommodating their demands to men's signals are not also led by particular, prevalent images of black women.

The findings discussed in the foregoing chapters support further investigation of whether the embodied selves of men and women, Asian Americans and whites, youth and elders can communicate clearly about their sexual or family formation wants and have those communications read and understood equally. What does it mean for a black woman to pay close attention to the things men do, to take notice of the places they spend their time, to read the romantic and sexual desires they telegraph, and then to respond to these received communications by making her romantic interest and availability known to these men in some context where men and women comfortably gather? Is she more or less likely than a white woman or a gay black man to come away from such an encounter with a boyfriend, an engagement ring, a bad reputation, all, or none of the above? We cannot know why degreed black women or others are peculiarly disadvantaged or advantaged in love or money without more systematic investigation of signification processes and the use and negotiation of symbols in the context of relations in which inequalities are determined—without an understanding of the race-, class-, and gender-related boundaries of signing and signification in particular contexts.

Yes, the employment counselor's recommendation that a chronically unemployed black man wear a tie, show up on time, and look the interviewer directly in the eye while speaking clearly and confidently is probably good advice. But absent evidence of the unequal ways in which direct eye contact between blacks and whites has historically been viewed and data analyses pointing to white employers' susceptibility to criminalized images of young black men during employment interviews with such subjects,[1] these recommendations do more to obscure inequality and represent economic inequality-making processes as susceptible to disadvantaged workers' control than they do to illuminate or change processes that ensure that African Americans will be overrepresented among the nation's unemployed. Similarly, the analyses of degreed black women's romantic disadvantages reported on here indicate that such women require the understanding born of an inequality study that incorporates evaluation of unequal signs, symbols, and signifying bodies more than they need advice on how to flirt with white men.

Earlier, I suggested that we put aside the point that matchmakers' advice to degreed black women about performing openness implied that it was within their capability to overcome the romantic challenges that this book describes. However, this book disagrees with this assumption that underlies their advice. The study's findings indicate that the differences between degreed black, Hispanic, and white women's marital behavior and nonmarital childbearing outcomes arise out of institutionalized social arrangements and structural processes that generate social inequality rather than random individual variation. Evidence of the eminently social quality of the factors that generate the book's love inequalities includes the race-gender boundaries on love's language and the legacy of race-gender symbols that signifying black women must negotiate that I discussed above. But below I recall a second piece of the book's social evidence. In notes made for those members of my research audience who explain black women's romantic disadvantages by describing their limited romantic markets, I argue that this text's findings indicate that these "romantic market" analyses fail to go far enough.

Notes for Those Who See Love as a Numbers Game

I report on degreed black women who are highly likely to remain celibate, and some audience members recall statistics on young black males' disproportionately high unemployment, incarceration, and death rates. I describe black women's difficulty negotiating marital commitments from attractive partners, and some people point to the media's images of oppressed, criminalized, and endangered black men. When members of my research audience talk about shortages of "marriageable" black men, they are not speaking about individual attitudinal or communication problems. Rather, they are *offering a social explanation for differences in individual outcomes*. More specifically, they are applying the statistics and images associated with black men's experience of U.S. race-based inequality to the case of black women's limited marriage opportunities. In so many words, they are saying that college-educated black women's fertility is low, their marriage rates are depressed, and their nonmarital fertility is high because of factors outside of these women's immediate control—because of black men, their circumstances, and their outcomes.

At the end of my research presentations, these audience members who blame black men's numbers rather than black women's signs for the women's marital disadvantage ask me, "Why don't you explain these love inequalities by discussing the shortage of black men?" In their view, the book should point to Census 2000 data (or other data) that indicate that the sex ratio (that is, the ratio of males to females) in the community of degreed black individuals in the United States is low. This proves, they say, that even if all degreed black men marry, and even if they all marry degreed black women, the relative paucity of their numbers would mean that some degreed black women would not have partners in the black population.[2] Moreover, those who link black female marriage disadvantage to low sex ratios in the black community also express concern about black males' rate of marriage to non-black women. For the fact that they tend to "marry out" more so than black women exacerbates the low sex ratio issue. And finally, sex ratio explanation proponents stress the point that numbers determine "value." They argue that because there is an "over-supply" of degreed black women, these research subjects' marriage market "value" is low. In a situation where some black woman will typically be available and willing to accommodate their needs, black men, who are comparatively speaking relatively scarce, do not really have to make or maintain long-term commitments in order to have romantic companionship or children.

This book agrees with the use of social explanations to account for degreed black women's romantic challenges. But my notes below make the point that counting the numbers of black men unemployed and in jail does not go far enough in its description of social inequality. For these calculations accept and obscure the *long-term inequality-generating processes that are at play in the creation of contemporary unequal circumstances*—processes that "assign" black women to a pool of partners who have been racialized as black through their marginalization and exploitation. The calculations presuppose boundaries and exclusionary practices that are rarely described or accounted for.

Chapter 3 of this book argues that women like Jennifer, Sparkle, and Danielle are taught about their "undesirability" in their own romantic relationships with black men as well as in their observations of black men's romantic interactions with other black women, like their mothers or their friends. But the chapter is also clear on the point that a population with low numbers of black male romantic partners is not the only ingredient necessary for the social construction of black women's "undesirability"— or, as the sex ratio proponents would have it, their "low value." Those who ridicule and threaten men who cross the color line to date black women, or who otherwise police the border between non-black men and black women are also involved in this construction. So too are those who deploy the symbols of black women whose sexuality and motherhood are devalued and those whose analyses frame black fertility across the globe as excessive, cheap, illegitimate, and exploitable. In short, sex ratio explanations for race, class, or gender inequalities of love only become meaningful amid inequality-generating processes that ensure that racial (and class) boundaries around dating populations are maintained. They only become visible in the light of a racial inequality that makes an oversupply of "low-value" black women out of a race-gender group that ordinarily constitutes a relatively small minority of the students on U.S. college campuses.

This book reflects the results of a type of study that empirically investigates the prior social context factors, processes, and experiences that are presupposed in sex ratio explanations of black women's romantic challenge. It is a study designed with the understanding that knowledge that the sex ratio is low in a particular race-class category generates more questions than it answers about how individuals reach their unequal outcomes. For example, why are there fewer black men with degrees than black women? Are fewer black men born to black middle-class couples? Do black boys, regardless of parental class status, have greater difficulty than black girls when it comes to engaging with the educational system and achieving college degrees? Why are black males more likely to marry outside of their race than black females? Do non-black women give them more romantic access and opportunity than non-black men offer black women? And, ultimately, given the absence of legal barriers to interracial marriage, why does the paucity of African American males with college degrees amount to degreed black women's peculiar disadvantage in romantic partnership and marriage? In other words, why aren't all women or even all women with degrees equally affected by the relative shortage of degreed black men in the population? Shouldn't fewer men mean fewer partners for all women?

The questions I have listed above are all questions that rest on the notion of a complex inequality that evolves from an individual's life trajectory of constraints and decisions across multiple institutional arenas (for example, work, family, school) and from structured social relations in multiple social hierarchies (for example, gender, race, class). They are all the type of questions around which this book's study of case history data, individual decision-making moments, and specific proximate determinant routes to fertility ends is built. Because of this book's concern with *describing how inequalities come about*, it remains dissatisfied with the simple sex ratio answer to a complex marriage inequality question. It remains dissatisfied with an answer that obscures rather than illuminates the unequal arrangements that are presupposed by the answer.

Now it is not my contention that this book answers all the questions about the simultaneous evolution of an individual's life in different social arenas that I outlined above. But it is absolutely the case that its analyses are of a kind that pursues and finds understandings of how a complex inequality comes about. They do so by asking and answering questions about systematic differences in the ways women experience and resolve their constrained choices in romance and reproduction. And they do so by relying on data that reveal individuals' desires, understandings, and strategic action at a series of relevant decision-making junctures of their school, work, romantic, and reproductive lives. This is why chapter 3's discussion of the likely influence of the sex ratio on their marital outcomes occurs alongside a description of the moments in which the action or inaction of black and non-black men limited degreed black women to black male romantic partners. The book's analyses utilize women's trajectories of constrained choices to illuminate the prior understandings, deprivations, and privileges that inform and shape present inequalities and inequality-making processes with respect to class achievement and romantic and family formation activity. Analyses of this kind distinguish this book by supporting descriptions of the unequal experiences and understandings that are presupposed in more traditional causal arguments about unequal marriage outcomes.

The results of this study's efforts to diagram degreed black women's life trajectories of limitations, opportunities, deprivations, and privileges with respect to love and money suggest a slightly different course of action for scholars interested in black women's marriage market than that recommended by many in my research audience. For if the sex ratio among degreed black Americans is so important, then so too are the inequality-generating processes that make it so. Therefore, such analysts should consider expanding their research focus beyond the immediate circumstances of black women's most obvious partners and developing greater command of men's trajectories of constrained choices across racial and class categories. It is study of this kind that can inform of us how men in different race-class categories come to find themselves or not find themselves on the college campuses and in the work and leisure sites where they might meet degreed black women. Such study can tell us how these varied categories of men happen to simultaneously make the decisions that exclude black women from their world of romantic and marital partners. As yet, we know little about men's early family formation experiences or about their wants and strategic actions with respect to romance and family formation over the life course. Moreover, while stratification researchers have long been involved in assessing the influences of men's class origins on their economic achievements, they have yet to apply lessons from those scholars focused on relationships between youthful childbearing and schooling or between work life and family life to their evaluations of men's unfolding lives. So we are also ignorant of the scope of the intersections between men's romantic and economic life trajectories.

This book challenges inequality study's more or less exclusive focus on labor and the productive sector. Its findings about deprivation that is constituted by systematic differences in women's access to particular romantic and family formation experiences suggest that men's inequalities may also be constituted as such and that unequal gender relations may be linked to access to (as opposed to exploitation through) desirable sexual and reproductive experiences. Answers to questions about men's romantic and family formation decision making or to investigations of systematic differences in that decision making across racial and class groups do more than support more comprehensive explanations of degreed black women's low marriage rates. They also can speak to these more general issues about inequality and love that have remained largely unexplored by mainstream inequality scholars.

Final Notes

I have actually been quite pleased with the responses I have gotten to discussions of my research for this book. The fact that so many of them come in the form of advice and explanation suggests that those who hear the results of the study are engaging with one of the text's central themes; it suggests that the inequalities of love that I describe are being understood as important. There are many areas of social variation that inspire no such commentary, and I do not take it for granted that black women's marriage disadvantage and the difficulties that singles in their situations face with long- and short-term celibacy, with using contraception effectively, and with reliance on abortion seem to inspire concern. Nonetheless, I remain, as indicated above, somewhat disappointed about the specific questions asked and suggestions made by these respondents. I remain disappointed because, in the end, their answers do not truly engage with the questions of this book.

In the beginning, there were Ashley, Wanda, Imani, Maya, and Renae. Ashley told me a life that read like a fairytale—a rural, working-class girl turned elite, degreed, stay-at-home mother. But does her life still seem like a "hard work pays off even if you are black" fairytale now that we know that the "work" includes letting go of a shame-inspiring, factory-worker boyfriend, sporadically using contraceptives through her twenties, and having and hiding three abortions? What sort of love inequalities are implied in the creation of the outcome of an elite, feminine, black self?

Wanda was the introduction's trinity of "nevers": she had never had a child, she had never been married, and she had never had sex at the time of our interview. Coincidentally, she was also, at the age of thirty-four, still living in the housing project apartment with her mother and brother. If she is one of the few girls who listened to her parents' warnings about resisting sex and not needing contraception as she pursued her education and career as discussed in chapter 5, how come she ends up disadvantaged in love and money?

And finally, at the end of the introduction, there were the three women with single-daughter families. There was Imani, who wanted a "big-money" and "big-family" outcome and had to consistently postpone and risk the latter to get the former. There was Maya, who thought right up until her visit to the abortion clinic that she wanted no children. And there was Renae, who wanted another child of her own even as she had spent many of her reproductive years working to help the less-educated women in her family to support theirs. What does it mean when the similarly low fertility of a group of college-educated elites is not about a rational, systematic, consistent "reproduction for economic outcome" scheme but rather a chaotic set of constraints and performances in settings where both love and money goals are conventionally achieved? These are the questions asked in this book. And while I appreciate the work that my audiences and prior scholars have done to answer these questions using data from women, I think that it is time that we begin to ask these questions of men.

What does love have or not have to do with money? We have asked this question of poor, often black, women and maintained that too much love too early spoils their chances of money. We have asked it of older, elite, educated, professional, mostly white women and told them the reverse—that their early money, late love strategy may ultimately have cost them love. We have even asked it of heterosexual married couples and once again come up with a version of the story in which the one who concentrates on loving and reproductive care loses out where making money is concerned. Now, I have asked the question of degreed black women and argued that love may actually have less to do with money and more to do with race. I have claimed that access to love is an important resource in the performance of feminine, elite class identities, as well as in the achievement of desired sexual and family formation ends. If it is true that race, class, and gender are intertwined in these ways, it is time for a more systematic analysis of another side of the gender equation. So those of you who are audience respondents and are men, why don't you consider thinking through the questions in this book by throwing your own data in the ring? It could mean a walk-on role in the sequel to this "chick flick."

Table A1. Percentage of the population that is childless by race, age, and education level (number of women surveyed)

AGE AND EDUCATION LEVEL	BLACK WOMEN % (#)	HISPANIC WOMEN % (#)	WHITE WOMEN % (#)
Under 20			
Some college	93 (15)	100 (9)	97 (88)
HS diploma	62 (42)	89 (36)	89 (173)
< HS diploma	80 (235)	85 (167)	95 (595)
20 to 24			
College degree	92 (26)	67 (9)	94 (124)
Some college	72** (115)	71 (83)	86** (366)
HS diploma	32** (139)	41 (94)	51** (284)
< HS diploma	18** (74)	17** (70)	13** (70)
25 to 29			
College degree	65 (51)	50 (32)	76 (308)
Some college	30** (125)	37 (59)	48** (252)
HS diploma	19** (193)	22** (104)	27** (351)
< HS diploma	8** (75)	2** (93)	11** (57)

Table A1. *Continued*

AGE AND EDUCATION LEVEL	BLACK WOMEN % (#)	HISPANIC WOMEN % (#)	WHITE WOMEN % (#)
30 to 34			
College degree	41 (63)	33 (42)	43 (306)
Some college	19** (147)	18 (92)	26** (331)
HS diploma	14** (230)	9** (88)	17** (508)
< HS diploma	11** (82)	1** (90)	11** (104)
35 to 39			
College degree	23 (74)	21 (28)	29 (358)
Some college	16 (106)	15 (53)	19** (341)
HS diploma	6** (176)	6 (108)	16** (557)
< HS diploma	7** (83)	3* (94)	5** (91)
40 to 45			
College degree	23 (60)	27 (30)	24 (366)
Some college	13 (102)	14 (37)	18* (296)
HS diploma	9* (152)	8* (63)	14** (458)
< HS diploma	14 (76)	1** (71)	8** (87)

Source: Calculations are based on cross-sectional data from NSFG (NCHS 1995) respondents.

Notes: * Results from t-test indicate that the difference from same race, college-educated women is statistically significant at the .05 level.

** Results from t-test indicate that the difference from same race, college-educated women is statistically significant at the .01 level.

Table A2. Racial group differences in the percentage of women at the unmarried and never married marital statuses

	BLACK % (#)	DIFFERENCE BETWEEN BLACKS AND WHITES DIFFERENCE	HISP. % (#)	DIFFERENCE BETWEEN HISPANICS AND BLACKS DIFFERENCE	WHITE % (#)	DIFFERENCE BETWEEN WHITES AND HISPANICS DIFFERENCE
Women aged 14 to 19						
% Unmarried	.98		.94		.97	
(#)	(292)	.01	(213)	-.04*	(856)	.02
% Never married	.98		.94		.96	
(#)	(292)	.02*	(213)	-.04*	(856)	.02
Women aged 20 to 24						
% Unmarried	.90		.65		.71	
(#)	(354)	.19**	(256)	-.25**	(846)	.06
% Never married	.85		.59		.65	
(#)	(354)	.20**	(256)	-.26**	(846)	.06

Table A2. *Continued*

	BLACK % (#)	DIFFERENCE BETWEEN BLACKS AND WHITES: DIFFERENCE	HISP. % (#)	DIFFERENCE BETWEEN HISPANICS AND BLACKS: DIFFERENCE	WHITE % (#)	DIFFERENCE BETWEEN WHITES AND HISPANICS: DIFFERENCE
Women aged 25 to 29						
% Unmarried	.75	.33**	.41	-.34**	.42	.01
(#)	(444)		(286)		(961)	
% Never married	.61	.30**	.28	-.33**	.31	.03
(#)	(444)		(286)		(961)	
Women aged 30 to 34						
% Unmarried	.64	.36**	.29	-.36**	.29	-.05
(#)	(522)		(312)		(1250)	
% Never married	.41	.27**	.13	-.28*	.14	.05
(#)	(522)		(312)		(1250)	

Women aged 35 to 39

% Unmarried	.62	.38**	.36	-.26**	.24	-.11**
(#)	(439)		(284)		(1349)	
% Never married	.32	.24**	.14	-.18**	.0815	-.06**
(#)	(439)		(284)		(1349)	

Women aged 40 to 45

% Unmarried	.58	.32**	.35	-.19**	.26	-.13**
(#)	(395)		(202)		(1221)	
% Never married	.23	.16**	.10	-.12**	.0663	-.04
(#)	(395)		(202)		(1221)	

Source: Calculations are based on cross-sectional data from NSFG (NCHS 1995) respondents.

Notes: * Results from t-test indicate that the difference is statistically significant at the .05 level.

** Results from t-test indicate that the difference is statistically significant at the .01 level.

Table A3. Percentage of reproductive years lived at three marital statuses

	PERCENTAGE OF PERSON-YEARS MARRIED	PERCENTAGE OF PERSON-YEARS FORMERLY MARRIED*	PERCENTAGE OF PERSON-YEARS SINGLE**
Black women			
College degree	21.57	8.74	66.17
Some college	20.94	9.73	66.36
HS diploma/GED	21.59	10.90	64.57
< HS diploma	15.29	10.83	73.07
White women			
College degree	27.48	5.10	58.93
Some college	30.53	7.37	51.93
HS diploma/GED	35.07	9.63	41.55
< HS diploma	31.27	13.37	47.21
Hispanic women			
College degree	25.59	6.99	61.03
Some college	27.94	8.90	55.79
HS diploma/GED	30.29	10.02	50.89
< HS diploma	31.55	9.70	48.67

Source: Calculations are based on marriage histories of NSFG (NCHS 1995) respondents.

Notes: * Formerly married person-years are years during which NSFG respondents' marital status was either "divorced," "separated," or "widowed."

** Single person-years are years during which NSFG respondents' marital status was "never married."

Table A4. Percentage of births to women at three marital statuses

	PERCENTAGE MARITAL BIRTHS	PERCENTAGE POST-MARITAL* BIRTHS	PERCENTAGE NONMARITAL** BIRTHS
	Black women		
College degree	66.32	4.51	29.17
Some college	43.84	6.16	50.00
HS diploma/GED	33.39	7.18	59.43
< HS diploma	18.98	6.33	74.69
	White women		
College degree	96.45	.85	2.69
Some college	88.04	3.21	8.75
HS diploma/GED	84.71	4.19	11.10
< HS diploma	64.02	10.96	25.03
	Hispanic women		
College degree	85.79	4.92	9.29
Some college	79.11	6.34	14.55
HS diploma/GED	69.24	5.50	25.26
< HS diploma	61.69	7.85	30.46

Source: Calculations are based on reproductive histories of NSFG (NCHS 1995) respondents.

Notes: * Post-marital births are births to women whose marital status at the time of the birth was "divorced," "separated," or "widowed."
** Nonmarital births are births to women whose marital status at the time of the birth was "never married."

Table A5. Marital and childbearing components of education level differences in black fertility rates

AGE	COLLEGE DEGREE FERTILITY RATE	GED/HS DIPLOMA FERTILITY RATE	DIFFERENCE BETWEEN FERTILITY RATES
Under 20	.0144	.09462	−.08017
20 to 24	.0573	.153318	−.096
25 to 29	.0976	.111919	−.01432
30 to 34	.0690	.050335	.018642
35 to 39	.0390	.024285	.014727
40 and over	.0064	.007936	−.00156

Source: Fertility rate calculations are based on reproductive history data from 276 college-educated black women and 932 black women with high-school diplomas or GED certificates but no college experience who were sampled by the NSFG (NCHS 1995).

Notes: * Equation for marital component of difference between educational level fertility rates during each age interval:

$$M_i = \bar{m}_{iab} \cdot (q_{ia} - q_{ib}) + \bar{p}_{iab} \cdot (r_{ia} - r_{ib}) + \bar{n}_{iab} \cdot (s_{ia} - s_{ib}),$$

where $\bar{m}_{iab}$ = mean of the marital fertility rates for education groups "a" and "b" during the age interval i; q_i = proportion person-years spent married during age interval i by education group members; $\bar{p}_{iab}$ = mean of the post-marital fertility rates for education groups

MARITAL COMPONENT OF DIFFERENCE* (%)	CHILDBEARING COMPONENT OF DIFFERENCE** (%)	% OF DIFFERENCE EXPLAINED IN ANALYSIS†
−.00645	−.07373	100
(8.04)	(91.96)	
−.0144	−.08159	100
(15.00)	(85.00)	
.00478	−.01910	100
(−33.37)	(133.37)	
.00257	.01607	100
(13.76)	(86.24)	
.00089	.01383	100
(6.07)	(93.93)	
−.00041	−.00115	100
(26.23)	(73.77)	

"a" and "b" during the age interval i; r_i = proportion person-years spent separated, divorced, or widowed during age interval i by education group members; $\bar{n}_{iab}$ = mean of the nonmarital fertility rates for education groups "a" and "b" during the age interval i; and s_i = proportion person-years spent single (never married) during age interval i by education group members.

** Childbearing component of difference between educational level fertility rates in each age interval is calculated using an equation identified in table A6 below.

† Percentage of difference explained in analysis is calculated using an equation identified below in table A6.

Table A6. Marital and childbearing components of education level differences in Hispanic fertility rates

AGE	COLLEGE DEGREE FERTILITY RATE	GED/HS DIPLOMA FERTILITY RATE	DIFFERENCE BETWEEN FERTILITY RATES
Under 20	.0153	.0637	−.04842
20 to 24	.0620	.1616	−.09961
25 to 29	.1083	.1376	−.02936
30 to 34	.1185	.0927	.025783
35 to 39	.0599	.0326	.02729
40 and over	.0492	.0124	.036788

Source: Fertility rate calculations are based on reproductive history data from 141 college-educated Hispanic women and 493 Hispanic women with high-school diplomas or GED certificates but no college experience who were sampled by NSFG (NCHS 1995).

Notes: * Marital component of difference between educational level fertility rates during each age interval is calculated using an equation identified above in table A5.

** Equation for childbearing component of difference in educational level fertility rates in each age interval:

$$C_i = \bar{q}_{iab} \cdot (m_{ia} - m_{ib}) + \bar{r}_{iab} \cdot (p_{ia} - p_{ib}) + \bar{s}_{iab} \cdot (n_{ia} - n_{ib}),$$

where $\bar{q}_{iab}$ = mean of the proportion person-years spent married for education groups "a" and "b" during the age interval i; m_i = marital fertility rate of education group during the age interval i; $\bar{r}_{iab}$ = mean of the proportion person-years spent separated, divorced, or widowed for education groups

MARITAL COMPONENT OF DIFFERENCE* (%)	CHILDBEARING COMPONENT OF DIFFERENCE** (%)	% OF DIFFERENCE EXPLAINED IN ANALYSIS†
−.02177	−.02665	100
(44.97)	(55.04)	
−.04996	−.04965	100
(50.16)	(49.84)	
−.01524	−.01412	100
(51.90)	(48.09)	
.001012	.024772	100
(3.92)	(96.08)	
.001247	.026042	100
(4.57)	(95.43)	
−.00653	.043321	100
(−17.76)	(117.76)	

"a" and "b" during the age interval i; p_i = post-marital fertility rate of education group during the age interval i; $\bar{s}_{iab}$ = mean of the proportion person-years spent single (never married) for education groups "a" and "b" during the age interval i; and n_i = nonmarital fertility rate of education group during the age interval i.

† Equation for percent of difference explained in analysis:

$$\frac{M_i + C_i}{F_{ia} - F_{ib}}$$

where M_i = marital component of difference between fertility rates during age interval i; C_i = childbearing component of difference between fertility rates during age interval i; F_{ia} = the age specific fertility rate of educational group "a" during age interval i; and F_{ib} = the age specific fertility rate of educational group "b" during age interval i.

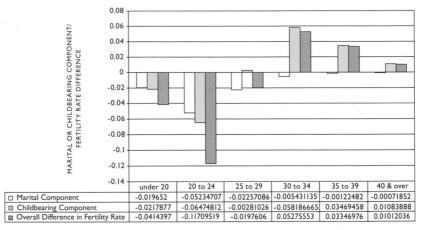

	under 20	20 to 24	25 to 29	30 to 34	35 to 39	40 & over
☐ Marital Component	-0.019652	-0.05234707	-0.02257086	-0.005431135	-0.00122482	-0.00071852
☐ Childbearing Component	-0.0217877	-0.06474812	-0.00281026	-0.058186665	0.03469458	0.01083888
▦ Overall Difference in Fertility Rate	-0.0414397	-0.11709519	-0.0197606	0.05275553	0.03346976	0.01012036

AGE INTERVAL

A₁ Marital and childbearing components of fertility rate differences between college-educated white women and white women with only a high-school diploma or GED. Results of decomposition analysis are based on reproductive history data from the NSFG (NCHS 1995).

Table A7. Percentage of black and white women's fertility rates attributable to nonmarital fertility

AGE	UNDER 20	20 TO 24	25 TO 29	30 TO 34	35 TO 39	40 AND OVER
			Black			
College degree fertility rate	.01445	.05732	.0976	.06898	.03901	.00638
Nonmarital percentage of college fertility*	83	43	18	16	11	0
HS diploma/GED fertility rate	.09462	.15332	.11192	.05034	.02429	.00794
Nonmarital percentage of HS fertility*	82	58	41	35	21	0
			White			
College degree fertility rate	.00288	.03044	.10201	.1129	.05735	.01557
Nonmarital percentage of college fertility*	41	6	2	1	1	0
HS diploma/GED fertility rate	.04432	.14754	.12177	.06014	.02388	.00545
Nonmarital percentage of HS fertility*	30	11	04	02	02	0

Source: Fertility rate calculations are based on reproductive history data from 276 college-educated black women, 1,465 college-educated white women, 932 high-school-educated (no college) black women, and 2,336 high-school-educated white (no college) women, all sampled by the NSFG (NCHS 1995).

Notes: * Equation for nonmarital percentage of fertility rate:

$$\frac{n_{ia} \times s_{ia}}{(m_{ia} \times q_{ia}) + (p_{ia} \times r_{ia}) + (n_{ia} \times s_{ia})} \times 100,$$

where n_{ia} = nonmarital fertility rate for race-education group "a" during age interval i; s_{ia} = proportion person-years spent single (never married) during age interval i by race-education group members; m_{ia} = marital fertility rate for race-education group "a" during age interval i; q_{ia} = proportion person-years spent married during age interval i by race-education group members; p_{ia} = post-marital fertility rate for race-education group "a" during the age interval i; and r_{ia} = proportion person-years spent separated, divorced, or widowed during age interval i by race-education group members.

Table A8. Racial differences in the mean age at first voluntary sex
(between white and Hispanic women)

	# IN SAMPLE	MEAN	DIFFERENCE FROM WHITE WOMEN	T	P<
Hispanic women			*White mean-Hispanic mean*		
College degree	134	20.16	−.96**	−2.90	.004
Some college	305	18.67	−.94**	−4.62	.000
HS diploma	465	18.20	−1.08**	−6.94	.000
< HS diploma	502	17.33	−1.80**	−10.44	.000

Source: Data for the above calculations are taken from the NSFG (NCHS 1995). Sample sizes for whites were as follows: 1,408 for college degree; 1,566 for some college; 2,246 for high-school diploma/GED; and 661 for less than high-school diploma.

Note: ** T-test indicates that the difference from the mean age at first voluntary sex for white women is significant at the .01 level.

Table A9. Percentage of virgins, celibate women, and women reporting
intercourse during the past three months

	# IN SAMPLE	PERCENT VIRGINS	PERCENT CELIBATE NON-VIRGINS	PERCENT HAVING INTERCOURSE
		Black women		
College degree	276	2.9	23.9	73.2
Some college	598	2.8	15.4	81.8
HS diploma	890	1.5	12.1	86.4
< HS diploma	390	0	9.7	90.3
		White women		
College degree	1465	3.9	12.2	83.9
Some college	1588	5	11.3	83.7
HS diploma	2163	2	8.8	89.2
< HS diploma	411	.5	10	89.5
		Hispanic women		
College degree	141	5	17	78
Some college	324	7.4	15.4	77.2
HS diploma	457	3.5	10.3	86.2
< HS diploma	419	.7	14.8	84.5

Source: Data for the above calculations are taken from NSFG (NCHS 1995) respondents who are over the age of nineteen.

Table A10. Racial differences in the mean number of months of celibacy three years prior to interview (between white and Hispanic women)

	# IN SAMPLE	MEAN	DIFFERENCE FROM WHITE WOMEN	T	P<
Hispanic women			*White mean-Hispanic mean*		
College degree	134	6.63	−.3347	−.351	.726
Some college	300	5.98	−.3870	−.626	.531
HS diploma/GED	441	4.80	−.7321	−1.50	.135
< HS diploma	416	5.48	−1.5585*	−2.26	.024

Source: Data for the above calculations are taken from NSFG (NCHS 1995) respondents over the age of nineteen who have ever had voluntary sex. Sample sizes for white women are as follows: 1,415 for college degree; 1,511 for some college; 2,121 for high school diploma/GED; and 409 for less than high school diploma.

Note: * Indicates that the difference from the mean number of months of celibacy for white women is significant at the .05 level.

Table A11. Percentage of unmarried respondents who are virgins, celibate women, and women reporting intercourse during the past three months

	# IN SAMPLE	PERCENT VIRGINS	PERCENT CELIBATE NON-VIRGINS	PERCENT HAVING INTERCOURSE
Black women				
College degree	159	5	40.9	54.1
Some college	392	4.3	22.2	73.5
HS diploma	612	2.1	15.7	82.2
< HS diploma	326	0	11	89
White women				
College degree	516	10.9	29.3	59.9
Some college	656	12.2	24.8	63
HS diploma	682	6.5	23.9	69.6
< HS diploma	159	1.3	22.6	76.1
Hispanic women				
College degree	51	13.7	43.1	43.1
Some college	148	16.2	33.1	50.7
HS diploma	180	8.9	21.7	69.4
< HS diploma	177	1.7	33.3	65

Source: Data for the above calculations were taken from NSFG (NCHS 1995) respondents who are over the age of nineteen and whose marital status is separated, divorced, widowed, or never married.

Table A12. Mean differences between the age at first family formation events and the age at first voluntary sex

	FIRST MARRIAGE-FIRST VOLUNTARY SEX		FIRST BIRTH-FIRST VOLUNTARY SEX	
	# IN SAMPLE	MEAN DIFFERENCE	# IN SAMPLE	MEAN DIFFERENCE
Black women				
College degree	174	6.5	161	7.2075
Some college	328	6.61677	419	4.9123
HS diploma	483	5.412	766	4.105
< HS diploma	160	6.2188	388	2.922
White women				
College degree	1084	4.9557	789	8.699
Some college	1129	4.0363	954	6.4689
HS diploma	1865	3.3807	1706	5.3861
< HS diploma	368	3.1304	405	3.7832
Hispanic women				
College degree	108	3.6296	91	5.9596
Some college	223	2.8969	215	4.7173
HS diploma	351	2.6239	380	3.3666
< HS diploma	337	2.0564	424	2.5262

Source: Data for above calculations are taken from the NSFG (NCHS 1995).

Table A13. Percentage of respondents who did not attempt to use any contraception* at last intercourse during the three months prior to interview

	BLACK		WHITE		HISPANIC	
	# IN SAMPLE	%	# IN SAMPLE	%	# IN SAMPLE	%
Currently married						
College degree	112	63.7	895	55.7	84	59.6
Some college	188	78.0	871	66.3	162	67.3
HS diploma/GED	269	80.4	1382	75.2	264	74.9
< HS diploma	58	89.5	242	82.7	234	73.1
Never married						
College degree	93	40.7	353	17.7	27	37.9
Some college	270	43.1	506	23.0	98	33.3
HS diploma/GED	416	60.8	448	36.0	127	59.9
< HS diploma	422	69.5	587	40.6	233	62.7

Source: Data for the above calculations are taken from NSFG (NCHS 1995) respondents who are not sterile, sterilized, pregnant, or postpartum.

Note: * Contraception includes chemical contraception (including birth control pills, Norplant, Depo-Provera shot, and the morning after pill), barrier contraception (including male and female condom, diaphragm, cervical cap, IUD, sponge, foam, suppository, and jelly, or cream w/out diaphragm), or natural contraception (including natural family planning, calendar rhythm, withdrawal, and "other" forms of contraception).

Table A14. Racial differences in the mean ratio of unwanted† to total pregnancies (between white and Hispanic women)

	# IN SAMPLE	MEAN	DIFFERENCE FROM WHITE WOMEN	T	P<
			Hispanic women		
College degree	101	.3581	−.0356	−.904	.366
Some college	245	.4033	−.0162	−.604	.546
HS diploma/GED	411	.4223	−.0270	−1.35	.179
< HS diploma	451	.3910	.1240**	5.03	.000

Source: Data for the above calculations are taken from NSFG (NCHS 1995) respondents. Sample sizes for white women are as follows: 951 for college degree; 1,102 for some college; 1,873 for high school diploma/GED; and 457 for less than high school diploma.

Notes: † Includes pregnancies classified as "unwanted," "mistimed (too early)," or "not sure" by NSFG respondents; other possible classifications were "on time," "overdue," or "indifferent."

** T-test indicates that the difference from the mean ratio of unwanted to total pregnancies for white women is significant at the .01 level.

Table A15. Mean number of unwanted* pregnancies and mean number of pregnancies experienced by women of different fertility levels

# BIRTHS EXPERI- ENCED	BLACK WOMEN		WHITE WOMEN		HISPANIC WOMEN	
	# IN SAMPLE	MEAN	# IN SAMPLE	MEAN	# IN SAMPLE	MEAN
Unwanted pregnancies						
Parity 0	654	.3196	2456	.2052	400	.2150
Parity 1	511	1.0900	1077	.7103	266	.7632
Parity 2	569	1.5729	1482	.8758	350	1.0257
Parity 3	309	2.2330	734	1.319	242	1.4959
Total pregnancies						
Parity 0	638	.4483	2387	.3146	385	.3065
Parity 1	495	1.8020	1047	1.7259	257	1.7276
Parity 2	544	2.8456	1429	2.6305	340	2.6294
Parity 3	296	3.8074	714	3.6597	240	3.6125

Source: Data for the above calculations are taken from NSFG (NCHS 1995) respondents.

Note: * Includes pregnancies classified as "unwanted," "mistimed (too early)," or "not sure" by NSFG respondents; other possible classifications were "on time," "overdue," or "indifferent."

Table A16. Percentage of pregnancies to single (never married) women ending in abortion, in miscarriage, ectopic pregnancy, or stillbirth, and in live birth

	# IN SAMPLE	NUMBER NON-MARITAL PREGNANCIES†	PERCENT ABORTION	PERCENT MISCARRIAGE, ETC.	PERCENT LIVE BIRTH
Black women					
College degree	169	175	45.7	9.1	45.1
Some college	435	674	30.0	12.8	57.3
HS diploma	747	1314	17.0	13.9	69.2
< HS diploma	366	897	14.9	11.8	73.2
White women					
College degree	853	283	77.7	10.6	11.7
Some college	981	464	54.7	15.3	30.0
HS diploma	1655	846	36.6	20.2	43.1
< HS diploma	395	368	23.4	17.7	59.0

Hispanic women

College degree	84	33	39.4	12.1	48.5
Some college	225	144	45.1	13.2	41.7
HS diploma	367	291	23.0	10.3	66.7
< HS diploma	402	432	15.0	9.7	75.2

Source: The calculations above are based on reproductive history data from NSFG (NCHS 1995) respondents who had resolved at least one pregnancy by the time of interview. Women who were pregnant for the first time at interview and women who have never been pregnant are excluded from the analysis.

Note: † Number of respondent pregnancies resolved while respondents' marital status was single (never married).

Table A17. Percentage of respondent pregnancies ending in abortion, in miscarriage, ectopic pregnancy, or stillbirth, and in live birth

	# IN SAMPLE*	NUMBER PREGNANCIES†	PERCENT ABORTION	PERCENT MISCARRIAGE, ETC.	PERCENT LIVE BIRTH
Black women					
College degree	169	229	25.2	13.8	61.0
Some college	435	589	22.1	14.0	63.9
HS diploma	747	1027	13.5	13.3	73.3
< HS diploma	366	1353	13.7	12.6	73.7
White women					
College degree	853	1138	14.9	15.9	69.2
Some college	981	4449	14.7	18.5	66.9
HS diploma	1655	2531	10.6	16.1	73.3
< HS diploma	395	2031	12.0	15.6	72.5

Hispanic women

College degree	84	428	13.5	14.4	72.1
Some college	225	1204	16.8	15.6	67.6
HS diploma	367	2075	10.7	12.2	77.1
< HS diploma	402	1225	9.0	11.2	79.7

Source: The calculations above are based on reproductive history data from NSFG (NCHS 1995) respondents who have resolved at least one pregnancy by the time of interview. Women who were pregnant for the first time at interview and women who have never been pregnant are excluded from the analysis.

Note: † Number of respondent pregnancies that have been resolved by the time of interview.

Table A18. Wanted pregnancy experience, unwanted pregnancy experience, and pregnancy experience and resolution components of nonmarital fertility rate differences between college-educated black and white women†

AGE	BLACK RATE	WHITE RATE	DIFFERENCE BETWEEN NONMARITAL FERTILITY RATES	WANTED PREGNANCY DIFFERENCE
Under 20	.0025	.0014	.0011	−.0002
20 to 24	.0259	.0018	.0241	.0072
25 to 29	.0349	.0031	.0319	.0149
30 to 34	.0350	.0076	.0274	.0112
35 to 39	.0184	.0028	.0156	.0064

Source: Fertility rate calculations are based on reproductive history data from 250 college-educated black women and 1,335 college-educated white women who were sampled by the NSFG (NCHS 1995).

Notes: * Equation for pregnancy experience component of racial difference in nonmarital fertility rates:

$$E_i = \bar{x}_{ibg} \cdot (w_{ib} - w_{ig}) + \bar{y}_{ibg} \cdot (u_{ib} - u_{ig}),\text{w}$$

where $\bar{x}_{ibg}$ = mean proportion of wanted pregnancies that are resolved in live births by never married women in racial groups "*b*" and "*g*" during the age interval *i*;

UNWANTED PREGNANCY DIFFERENCE	PREGNANCY EXPERIENCE COMPONENT OF DIFFERENCE* (%)	PREGNANCY RESOLUTION COMPONENT OF DIFFERENCE** (%)
−.0012	−.0014 (−123%)	.0025 (223%)
.0054	.0126 (53%)	.0114 (47%)
.0048	.0198 (62%)	.0121 (38%)
.0037	.0148 (54%)	.0125 (46%)
.0018	.0082 (52%)	.0074 (48%)

w_i = rate at which never married women in racial group "b" or "g" experience wanted pregnancies during the age interval i; $\bar{y}_{ibg}$ = mean proportion of unwanted pregnancies that are resolved in live births by never married women in racial groups "b" and "g" during the age interval i; $\bar{u}_i$ = rate at which never married women in racial group "b" or "g" experience unwanted pregnancies during the age interval i. ** Pregnancy resolution component of racial difference in non-marital fertility rates in each age interval is calculated using an equation identified below in table A19.

Table A19. Wanted pregnancy experience, unwanted pregnancy experience, and pregnancy experience and resolution components of nonmarital fertility rate differences between college-educated white and Hispanic women

AGE	WHITE RATE	HISPANIC RATE	DIFFERENCE BETWEEN NONMARITAL FERTILITY RATES	WANTED PREGNANCY DIFFERENCE
Under 20	.0014	.0096	−.0083	−.0009
20 to 24	.0018	.0019	−.0001	−.0007
25 to 29	.0031	.0132	−.0101	−.0080
30 to 34	.0076	.0245	−.0170	−.0007
35 to 39	.0028	.0513	−.0485	−.0228

Source: Fertility rate calculations are based on reproductive history data from 1,335 white women and 118 Hispanic women sampled by the NSFG (NCHS 1995).

Notes: * See Table A18 above for the equation for the pregnancy experience component of the racial difference in nonmarital fertility rates.

** Equation for pregnancy resolution component of racial difference in nonmarital fertility rates:

$$R_i = \bar{w}_{ibg} \cdot (x_{ib} - x_{ig}) + \bar{u}_{ibg} \cdot (y_{ib} - y_{ig}),$$

where $\bar{w}_{ibg}$ = mean rate at which never married women in racial groups "*b*" or "*g*" experience wanted pregnancies during the age interval *i*; x_i = proportion wanted

UNWANTED PREGNANCY DIFFERENCE	PREGNANCY EXPERIENCE COMPONENT OF DIFFERENCE* (%)	PREGNANCY RESOLUTION COMPONENT OF DIFFERENCE** (%)
−.0006	−.0015 (18.5%)	−.0067 (81.5%)
−.0002	−.0005 (606.2%)	−.0004 (-506.2%)
−.0002	−.0078 (76.7%)	−.0024 (23.3%)
−.0005	−.0012 (7.3%)	−.0157 (92.7%)
−.0100	−.0328 (67.7%)	−.0156 (32.3%)

pregnancies that are resolved in live births during age interval i by members of racial group "b" or "g"; $\bar{u}_{ibg}$ = mean rate at which never married women in racial groups "b" or "g" experience unwanted pregnancies during the age interval i; y_i = proportion unwanted pregnancies that are resolved in live births during age interval i by members of racial group "b" or "g."

Introduction. Inequality

1 While the term "chick flick" may be offensive to some, I have elected to use it because of the way in which it conveys a dismissive attitude toward interests, concerns, or objects that have been gendered as female. I am trying to move love from the periphery to the center of inequality scholarship, and I believe that the term "chick flick" helps to emphasize this point.

2 This name (Ashley) is a pseudonym for one of my informants. All the informants referenced in the text have been promised anonymity, and so the names that I use to refer to them are pseudonyms. In addition, I have omitted or disguised other identifying information (including places of residence and upbringing, the names of schools attended, and the names of significant others).

3 Hayes and Miller (1993) criticize the "conventionalist" and "functionalist" expectation that women's class identities and class-based actions will follow that of their husbands or fathers. They join Acker (1973, 1980), Haug (1973), and Hayes and Jones (1992) in an effort to come up with more "modern" methods of measuring women's class, including using their own educational and career achievements. The expectation that a husband's or a father's class is an effective measure of an individual woman's own class status has been articulated by Goldthorpe (1983, 1984), who bases this claim on the argument that men have greater opportunity and

commitment with respect to the labor market and on the stratification researcher's interest in studying economic and occupational structures.

4 Snarey and Vaillant (1985) make this point in their study of the psychological factors that support upward mobility.

5 In a study explaining the importance of racial attitudes and race and class identities in audiences' appreciation of NBC's sitcom *The Cosby Show*, which aired in the 1980s and 1990s, Jhally and Lewis (1992) document and present scholarship on the overrepresentation of middle-class individuals in entertainment television.

6 Some notable exceptions would include books on youth and childrearing, such as Bettie 2003, Lareau 2003, and Pattillo-McCoy 1999. The latter emphasizes middle-class black individuals' proximity to lower-class black persons (in terms of actual class outcome as well as familial and neighborhood relations) as a central factor in the decision making and unfolding choices of black middle-class youth. With the exception of Lacy 2007, other books about the black middle class or black individuals' middle-class status achievement (for example, Bowser 2007; Cose 1994; Feagin and Sykes 1994; Oliver and Shapiro 1995; Price 2004; St. Jean and Feagin 1998) are books about racial disadvantage in which middle-class black individuals' constraints and decision making are observed for the window they provide on racially inferior rather than class superior outcomes. Similarly, scholarship on elite women (for example, A. Hochschild 1989, 1997; Holland and Eisenhart 1990) has located such study in analyses of women's gender disadvantages and not their elite privilege. McCall (2000a and 2001) makes this critique of gender scholarship.

7 Following Blau and Duncan (1967) and Sewell, Haller, and Portes (1969), stratification researchers like Ainsworth and Roscigno (2005), Biblarz, Bengston, and Bucur (1996), Biblarz and Raftery (1993), Biblarz, Raftery, and Bucur (1997), Breen (2000), Hout (1984, 1986), Kerckhoff (1989), Sewell and Hauser (1972), and Sewell, Hauser, and Wolf (1980) are concerned with explaining differences in occupational status outcomes. In contrast, Budig and England (2001), England (1982, 1984), England, Budig, and Folbre (2002), Maxwell and D'Amico (1986), McCall (1998, 2000a, 2000b, 2001), Royster (2003), Waldfogel (1997, 1998a, 1998b), and Western and Pettit (2005) explain differences in wages and income. And still others (including Correll, Benard, and Paik 2007; D'Amico and Maxwell 1995; Holzer 1998a, 1998b; McCreary, England, and Farkas 1989; Moss and Tilly 1995; Ridgeway and Correll 2004; Royster 2003) focus on differences in the likelihood of being employed. Oliver and Shapiro (1995) are known for their study of wealth inequality, which evaluates and explains differences in savings, inheritance, and other capital accumulation regardless of source. And Price (2004) chose to investigate debt rather than wealth accumulation.

8 Stratification researchers often rely on a rather well-known status attainment model (Ainsworth and Roscigno 2005; Blau and Duncan 1967; Sewell, Haller,

and Portes 1969) to explain job status differences. The model indicates that individual and parental aspirations influence a person's educational attainment and that education then influences the first job, which, in turn, influences the last job. The model has been criticized by Kerckhoff (1989) and Jacobs, Karen, and McClelland (1991) for ignoring the possibility that aspirations might change in accordance with specific experiences in school and the labor market. Nonetheless, even those stratification researchers that do not use this model find that education is an important predictor of productive sector outcomes and that the importance of education has only grown over time. See, for example, Breen 2000; and Grusky and DiPrete 1990.

9 Inequality analysts expect that workers' occupational status and wages will rise as their age and labor force experience rise, but ageist discrimination can lower the returns a worker gets from his or her experience. Duncan and Lorretto (2004) found that U.K. survey respondents of all ages perceived age discrimination, but that the youngest and oldest were the most likely to report age bias in interaction around employment. In work that considers the restructuring of the American economy in and around the millennium, Roscigno, Mong, Byron, and Tester (2007) focus on the particular vulnerability of workers over the age of fifty to discrimination while Sum, Khatiwada, and Palma (2005) report that jobs going to teens consistently declined between 2000 and 2004.

10 See Appold, Siengthai, and Kasarda 1998; Dex, Ward, and Joshi 2008; DiPrete and Soule 1988; Grusky and Diprete 1990; Hotchkiss and Pitts 2007; Joy 2003; Konstantopoulos and Constant 2008; Mandel and Semyonov 2005; Manning and Swaffield 2008; McCall 1998; McDonald and Thornton 2007; Noonan, Corcoran, and Courant 2005; Roksa 2005; Rosenfeld and Kalleberg 1991; Sewell, Hauser, and Wolf 1980; Wright, Baxter, and Birkelund 1995; and Wu 2007.

11 Work by Budig and England (2001), Casper, McLanahan, and Garfinkel (1994), Christopher, England, Smeeding, and Phillips (2002), Correll, Benard, and Paik (2007), McLanahan, Sorensen, and Watson (1989), Okamoto and England (1999), Ridgeway and Correll (2004), Sewell, Hauser, and Wolf(1980), Trappe and Rosenfeld (2000), and Waldfogel (1997, 1998a, 1998b) establishes the employment, wage, and occupational status penalties associated with parenthood or familial responsibilities for women. Some studies indicate that men may actually benefit in the labor market from marriage and parenthood. See, for example, Correll, Benard, and Paik 2007; Lundberg and Rose 2002; and Trappe and Rosenfeld 2000.

12 Status attainment researchers, including Ainsworth and Roscigno (2005), Biblarz, Bengston, and Bucur (1996), Biblarz and Raftery (1993), Biblarz, Raftery, and Bucur (1997), Blau and Duncan (1967), Breen (2000), Grusky and DiPrete (1990), Pascarella, Smart, and Stoecker (1989), and Sewell, Haller, and Portes (1969), have developed and/or applied models for estimating the influence of

family origins, educational aspirations and attainment, and first jobs on occupational status outcomes. The focus of such work is on explaining the distribution of productive sector outcomes, showing why one individual's occupational status might be higher or lower than another's. In other instances, stratification studies investigate whether employment and income inequality between class, racial, or gender groups is located in workers' proximity to jobs or other differences in the structure of local labor markets (Baganha 1991; McCall 1998, 2001; Wilson 1978/1980, 1996). Biblarz, Bengston, and Bucur 1996; Kalleberg and Rosenfeld 1990; Kerckhoff, Campbell, Trott, and Kraus 1989; Kerckhoff, Campbell, and Winfield-Laird 1985; and Rosenfeld and Kalleberg 1991 are among the studies that test whether inequality is based in broad features of national labor markets. But whether at the individual, socioeconomic group, or national level, the focus is on money and other outcomes associated with employment in the formal economy.

13 For scholarship confirming this explanation for wage inequality, see Bayard, Hellerstein, Neumark, and Troske 2003; Cohen and Huffman 2003a, 2003b; Dex, Ward, and Joshi 2008; DiPrete and Soule 1988; England, Budig, and Folbre 2002; England, Farkas, Kilbourne, and Dou 1988; England, Herbert, Kilbourne, Reid, and Megdal 1994; England, Reid, and Kilbourne 1996; Groshen 1991; Kilbourne, England, and Beron 1994; Kilbourne, Farkas, Beron, Weir, and England 1994; Korkeamaki and Kyyra 2006; Petersen and Morgan 1995; Polavieja 2008; Reskin and Bielby 2005; and Shauman 2006.

14 Group size explanations for racial differences in employment maintain that discrimination increases as the subordinate group increases in size and is perceived as a greater threat (Blalock 1956, 1957), or as the subordinate group reaches a size that would ensure that whites would gain from subordinate groups' positioning behind them in a "queue" for the best jobs (Lieberson 1980), or from exploitation of the subordinate group (N. Glenn 1963). See Beggs, Villemez, and Arnold 1997; P. Cohen 1998; Tigges and Tootle 1993; and Tolnay 2001 for findings in support of these propositions. Some argue that the effect of group size reverses in regions in which subordinate groups are large enough to constitute a demographic majority—that in these regions, discrimination goes down as group size increases. McCreary, England, and Farkas (1989) observe both trends in their study of variance in young black males' employment. Note that regional differences in the influence of race on employment or wage outcomes might also be explained by more place-based theses, including hypotheses about the history of unionization and the current strength of unions in these places, as in McCall's (2001) analyses.

15 Social network explanations for inequality often argue that the strength or weakness of an individual's ties account for employment or occupational status. Here the point is that those with whom we have only weak ties are more likely to have information about jobs that we do not already have; thus, they are in a position to support a more expansive and productive job-search (Gra-

novetter 1973, 1974/1995, 1983). See Lin (2000) for articles documenting the network limitations of nonwhite workers including Elliott (1999) and Green, Tigges, and Diaz (1999). Alternatively, predominantly white networks of labor may collude to limit the resources and opportunities of non-white workers to whom they are "weakly" tied because the enhancement of such ties is not seen as important or beneficial. Such was the case in Royster's (2003) study.

16 England and Browne (1992) maintain that sex differentials in occupational choices are in part due to childhood socialization differences, the effects of which persist to later life and shape occupational preferences.

17 Studies aimed at explaining inequality as a function of the time-dependent conditions of the national economy, such as Biblarz, Bengston, and Bucur 1996, have data that cover over one hundred years of human experience but little or no variance across race or gender. The processes and variables that differentiate white men in different eras from one another might be quite different from the variables that differentiate contemporary young adult workers in the ways that Ainsworth and Roscigno 2005 report.

18 Browne and England 1997 and England 1999 criticize this conceptual apparatus. Their argument indicates that an inequality sociology that amasses evidence of ongoing social constraints faced by members of subordinate groups and that simultaneously rejects the idea that some unequal outcomes may be caused by the choices that subordinated individuals make unnecessarily exaggerates a distinction between a social constraint and an individual choice. Rather, inequality scholarship can avoid blaming the victims of gender oppressive systems for problematic choices by challenging those arguments that indicate that such victims should be blamed for choices that result from internalized gender socialization that happened early in the life course. An experimental study by Correll (2004) provides some evidence that gender differentials in career aspirations are indeed influenced by individuals' socialization to beliefs about women's and men's different areas of job-related competence.

19 Higginbotham and Weber (1992) maintain in their cross-racial study of college-educated women's status attainment that the use of subjective experience data to understand working-class white male's upward mobility went out of vogue in the 1970s. They point out that their quantitative treatment is one of a number of subjective experience studies (beginning in the late 1980s and the early 1990s) that signaled the beginning of a new era of status attainment literature. Studies like Bettie 2003; Carter 2005; Holland and Eisenhart 1990; Kao and Tienda 1998; MacLeod 1995; Newman 1999/2000; O'Connor 1999; Sullivan 1989; Venkatesh 1994, 2006; and Young 2004 use qualitative data to study males and females of color, as well as white men and women, with respect to their achievement (or lack thereof) in school and work.

20 Examples of ethnographers who observe in schools and talk formally and informally with students, parents, and school-based personnel in order to make their conclusions about inequality include R. Cohen (1998), Fine (1991), Hol-

land and Eisenhart (1990), Horvat and Antonio (1999), Lopez (2003), Mac-
Leod (1995), Tyson (2002, 2003), Tyson, Darity, and Castellino (2005), and
Willis (1977), the last of which reports on inequalities in British males' school
and school-to-work transition experiences.

21 Worksite ethnographies typically rely on data from scholars who observe and
often participate as workers in specific spaces of economic production. They
include the classic study based on data from a factory floor by Burawoy (1979)
and more recent work by Bourgois (1995), Sullivan (1989), and Venkatesh
(2006) on work in underground or informal economies, by Rollins (1985) on
domestic workers, by Salzinger (2003) on Mexican factory workers, and by
Sherman (2007) on luxury hotel workers.

22 There are also ethnographers who spend some observation time in relevant
worksites or in organizations that provide workers with employment support in order to recruit subjects with whom they conduct formal and informal
interviews about their work challenges, capacities, and experiences. In some
cases, they might also shadow some of these subjects and observe them in
other settings of their lives. Examples of this type of study include A. Hochschild 1997; Newman 1988/1999, 1999/2000; Venkatesh 1994, 2006; and Young
2004. Lareau 2003; MacLeod 1995; O'Connor 1997, 1999; and Shaw and Coleman 2000 are among the works that use shadowing and open-ended interviewing to collect data on individuals' subjective experience of school and
school-related activities and interactions.

23 This is the classic social reproduction argument articulated in the theoretical claims of Pierre Bourdieu (Bourdieu 1977a, 1977b; Bourdieu and Passeron
1977/1990; Bourdieu and Wacquant 1992) and in the empirical and theoretical
work on education that comprises Bourdieu's legacy (for example, Carrington
1986; Carter 2005; Fine 1991; Giroux 1981; Holland and Eisenhart 1990; Horvat and Antonio 1999; Lamont and Lareau 1988; Lareau 2003; MacLeod 1995;
Solomon 1992; and Willis 1977). Incorporating varying amounts of human
agency, the argument usually maintains that disadvantaged youth (whether
they are lower-class males or lower- and middle-class females and whether
they are of one race or of varied racial backgrounds) are discouraged or negatively sanctioned in their creative attempts to succeed in an educational system that is biased against their linguistic and aesthetic contributions. Whether
they recognize the bias and rebel or continue trying to master a set of cultural
codes that is the native tongue of elites but that they only get to practice during school hours, they are unlikely to succeed or to compete effectively with
the more advantaged students. Ultimately, this "symbolic violence" that they
experience (Bourdieu 1977a; Bourdieu and Waquant 1992) can be observed
in a couple of ensuing scenarios. In some cases, disadvantaged students reject school and the education-based status seeking that demands a "cultural
capital" they do not possess (that is, the knowledge, dispositions, pastimes,

tastes, and appreciations of class elites and/or dominant status groups). Alternatively, students gradually lower their aspirations in benign acceptance of the system's mediocre assessment of the cultural attributes they have to offer. In either case, relatively few of these students manage to escape the material disadvantage of their youth. Those that do tend to achieve lower educational and economic outcomes than their more advantaged peers and do so at some psychic and/or emotional cost. Although the empirical examples listed above are qualitative, Bourdieu and other scholars writing about social reproduction have also relied on quantitative data. Bowles and Gintis (1976) used quantitative data on schools' differential performance with respect to advantaged and disadvantaged youth to support their arguments about social reproduction. DiMaggio 1982 and DiMaggio and Mohr 1985 also rely on empirical models to demonstrate relationships between cultural capital and educational and marital achievement. Price's (2004) report on the higher levels of student loan debt of lower-class and minority race college graduates is also a quantitative study framed and executed in this theoretical tradition. Furthermore, studies that use survey data on students' levels of belief in traditional achievement ideology (that is, the idea that hard work pays off for everyone) and on their assessments about the prevalence of race, class, or gender-based discrimination in models predicting academic success are confirming hypotheses associated with social reproduction theory. See, for example, Felice 1981; Ford and Harris 1996; Marchant 1991; Mickelson 1990; and Taylor, Casten, Flickinger, Roberts, and Fulmore 1994.

24 The argument that black, Latino, and Native American children eschew success in school, are ridiculed or marginalized by peers for striving to conform to an ostensibly white cultural institution, and feel disloyal and disconnected from families, communities, and their racial identities when they succeed in school has most consistently been put forth by John Ogbu (Fordham and Ogbu 1986; Ogbu 1978, 1990, 1991, 1992, 2003; Ogbu and Simons 1998). Other works that discuss black and Latino students' distance from the dominant educational culture and/or their disbelief that their successes will be rewarded in educational and economic spaces dominated by whites and or white culture disagree about what these cultural factors mean for students of color. Some agree with Ogbu's thesis and find that the cultural factors hinder students' academic achievement (for example, Gibson 1991; Matute-Bianchi 1991; Taylor, Casten, Flickinger, Roberts, and Fulmore 1994). Others find that to the extent that these factors exist across populations of "involuntary minorities," they reflect structural inequalities in or beyond the educational system that are consequently more important factors in student achievement (for example, Massey, Charles, Lundy, and Fischer 2003; Portes and Zhou 1994; Tyson 2002; Tyson, Darity and Castellino 2005). And still others argue that ethnic identities and awareness of racial discrimination only potentially com-

promise, and possibly support, the achievement experiences of students of color (for example, Bettie 2003; Carter 2005; O'Connor 1997; Taylor, Casten, Flickinger, Roberts, and Fulmore 1994). Class-based arguments about white students who demonstrate these kinds of rebellious or "oppositional" relationships to school culture come from Bettie 2003; MacLeod 1995; Tyson, Darity, and Castellino 2005; and Willis 1977.

25 Beginning with the earliest population scholars (for example, Malthus 1798/1965, 1872), observed associations between early and high fertility, on the one hand, and low socioeconomic status, on the other, have often, although not always, been subject to the interpretation that these family formation behaviors caused or limited escape from poverty. During eras and in settings where women have raised children that they bore out of wedlock, nonmarital childbearing has joined the list of family formation causes of poverty. See Furstenberg 1976; Hofferth and Moore 1979; McLanahan 1985; McLanahan and Booth 1989; Stier and Tienda 2001: Teti and Lamb 1989; and Trussell 1976 for scholarly work identifying early, high, and nonmarital fertility as a cause of poverty.

26 Scholarly work that discusses limited economic opportunity as a marriage constraint and/or the economic barriers to marriage as a reason for elevated levels of nonmarital childbearing include Bennett, Bloom, and Craig 1989; Brien 1997; Carlson, McLanahan, and England 2004; Goldstein and Kenney 2001; Hughes 2003; Lichter, LeClere, and McLaughlin 1991; Lichter, McLaughlin, and Ribar 2002; Lloyd and South 1996; Manning and Smock 1995; Neal 2004; Oppenheimer 1988, 1994; Oppenheimer, Kalmijn, and Lim 1997; Raley 1996; Sassler and Schoen 1999; Testa, Astone, Krogh, and Neckerman 1989; Tucker and Taylor 1989; and Wilson and Neckerman 1987.

27 Research attempting to explain rather than simply document racial disparities in health most often discusses socioeconomic differentials in access to health care and health supportive environments as primary causal factors. Such is the case when Gwynn and Thurston (2001) try to explain racial differences in disease experience associated with exposure to air pollution. Although language barriers may be introduced as parts of the discussion, such barriers rarely trump economic class disadvantage. Another example is the work of Rogers, Hummer, Nam, and Peters (1996), who explain racial groups' disproportionate levels of disease experience by their relative socioeconomic advantage or their health and risk behavioral differences.

28 David Williams and his colleagues (Schulz, Williams, Israel, and Lempert 2002; Williams and Collins 1995; Williams, Lavizzo-Mourey, and Warren 1994) represent a branch of health disparities scholarship that is critical of analyses that "reduce" race and racially organized structural inequality to a list of apparently unrelated socioeconomic status variables. This book takes cues from this more "authentic" treatment of the race variable in inequality study.

29 The much love-little money or much money-little love association that is described by demographers tends to emerge in two kinds of empirical reports. It undergirds the discussions in which fertility behavior is understood as a cause of women's poor or affluent socioeconomic outcomes. And it is at the foundation of claims about women's high educational and occupational achievements being tied to their postponement and limitation of fertility. Both the literature that argues that poor women are poor at least in part because they chose to have children as teenagers or as singles (Beutel 2000; Billy and Moore 1992; Budig and England 2001; Casper, McLanahan, and Garfinkel 1994; Christopher, England, Smeeding, and Phillips 2002; Dillard and Pol 1982; Driscoll, Hearn, Evans, Moore, Sugland, and Call 1999; Furstenberg 1976; Hofferth and Moore 1979; Hoffman, Foster, and Furstenberg 1993; Stier and Tienda 2001; and Waite and Gallagher 2000) and the literature that maintains that elite women's willingness to postpone or forgo childbearing accounts for their superior educational and occupational achievements (Bloom and Trussell 1984; Blossfeld and Huinink 1991; Caldwell and Schindlmayr 2003; Forest, Moen, and Dempster-McLain 1995; Lehrer and Nerlove 1986; S. Morgan 1991, 2003; Rindfuss, Bumpass, and St. John 1980; Rindfuss, Morgan, and Offutt 1996; Schoen, Kim, Nathanson, Fields, and Astone 1997; Swicegood, Bean, Stephen, and Opitz 1988; Wilkie 1981) frame fertility or love as a causal variable in the achievement of economic outcomes. In contrast, discussions of poor young women's limited educational and employment futures as the explanations for the early onset of their fertility (Anderson 1989; Edin and Kefalas 2005; Geronimus 1997; Kaplan 1997; Luker 1996)—claims that more often come from inequality ethnographers than they do from demographers—frame fertility as the consequence of economic determinants.

30 Some demographers' observations of the low fertility of highly educated or higher-class black women and professional white women have linked this cross-racial similarity in childbearing or childlessness to declining racial inequality, the black community's social and economic gains, and black women's consequent social acculturation and assimilation to white middle-class norms. See, for example, Boyd 1989; N. Davis 1982; Grindstaff 1976; McFalls 1973; and McFalls and Masnick 1981. In this way, characteristics of white middle-class women's feminist liberation become measures of racial equality, racial group assimilation and acculturation, and black women's increasing choice.

31 An important caveat to demographic research's relentless documentation of the inverse relationship between love and money through study of fertility inequality is scholarly work demonstrating the economic decline of women who experience divorce. Here, the loss of love relationship or marriage, or, in some cases, the lack of love or marriage is shown to have a negative effect on money outcomes as well. See Bianchi, Subaiya, and Kahn 1999; Holden and Smock 1991; L. Morgan 1991; Neumark and Korenman 1994; Peterson 1996;

Popenoe 1996; Smock 1993, 1994; Smock, Manning, and Gupta 1999; Stirling 1989; Waite 1995; and Waite and Gallagher 2000 for empirical studies confirming the increased economic benefits that accrue to the married relative to those in other marital statuses (for example, never married, divorced, and remarried).

32 Note that although the book focuses on nonproductive sector inequities, there is evidence that marriage is associated with increases in wage income. (See, for example, Budig and England 2001; Neumark and Korenman 1994; Waite 1995; Waite and Gallagher 2000; and Waldfogel 1997.) Thus, black women's deprivation in love may be reflected in decreased productive sector outcomes as well.

33 Thus, the book's arguments challenge the assumptions made by analysts like Boyd (1989), N. Davis (1982), Grindstaff (1976), or McFalls (McFalls 1973; McFalls and Masnick 1981) about the relationship between higher class status and black women's fertility choices. Where they see increases in class leading to voluntary fertility limitation, I identify racial inequality and involuntary limitation in love.

34 See Snarey and Vaillant 1985 for discussion of this point. Notable exceptions to ethnography's focus on poor or working-class status attainment include Lareau's (2003) comparison of poor and middle-class youth and their families, Higginbotham and Weber's (1992) and Holland and Eisenhart's (1990) examinations of the middle-class and/or degree attainment processes of women from different race and class origins, A. Hochschild's (1997) description of the work and family decision making of employees at multiple levels of a firm, and Pattillo-McCoy's (1999) and Ogbu's (2003) analyses of the decisions of black middle-class youth. Studies of lower-class individuals' perceptions of the opportunity structure include Bettie 2003; Carter 2005; R. Cohen 1998; Lopez 2003; MacLeod 1995; Newman 1999/2000; O'Connor 1999; Shaw and Coleman 2000; and Young 2004.

35 Quantitative analyses in chapter 2 and elsewhere in the book rely on data from the National Survey of Family Growth. These data were collected by the National Center for Health Statistics (NCHS), using in-home interviews with non-institutionalized, civilian, U.S. women ages fifteen to forty-four. The interviews took place from January to August 1995. Covering detailed questions about women's sexual, contraceptive, abortion, pregnancy, marriage, and childbearing experiences, as well as demographic and background questions, the survey is the fifth and last of such surveys (spread between 1973 and 1995) focused on these substantive areas and sampling only women. (The 2002 survey and the continuous survey design that has run from 2006 through 2010 sampled both women and men.) The 10,847 women interviewed in 1995 were chosen using a multi-stage probability sample meant to support estimations about women's behavior that can be generalized to women of reproductive age in the U.S. population. The sample also reflects oversamples of Hispanic and non-Hispanic black subjects so that these groups are each large enough

to make generalizations about the behaviors of women from these groups and to compare them to the larger white population.

36 Boyd 1989 uses similar evidence (for example, high rates of childlessness among black women of high socioeconomic status, and black women's high rates of marital disruption) to argue the point that late eighteenth- and early nineteenth-century black and white women had similar reasons for an observed spike in rates of childlessness. Boyd challenges the point that black increases in childlessness during the period were largely involuntary and due to higher rates of sexually transmitted disease and disease-related infecundity and infertility. Alongside Grindstaff 1976; McFalls 1973; and McFalls and Masnick 1981, Boyd's article focuses on the experiences of black women across multiple arenas (for example, economy, marriage, health) in order to explain their achievement of higher rates of childlessness. In this regard, it is similar to the analysis in this book, but the argument in this book departs from Boyd's in terms of its assumptions about the degree to which class status signifies greater choice with respect to fertility.

37 Building on earlier work by Davis and Blake (1956), Bongaarts and Potter (1983) develop a model to estimate more precisely the amount of fertility change over time or the amount of fertility difference between groups that is directly caused by change or difference in action around one of seven "proximate determinants" to fertility. This list of directly influential variables through which any social cause must work in order to influence fertility outcomes includes age at entry into marriage, age at menopause, fecundity or frequency of intercourse, contraceptive use, incidence of miscarriage or spontaneous abortion, incidence of induced abortion, and the length of postpartum infecundability associated with breastfeeding or abstinence.

38 Created by the Office of Policy Planning and Research (1965), this report presented contemporary data on the prevalence of female headship in black families and linked that prevalence to the black community's history of exploitation. The report was controversial and has since its publication acquired a certain infamy for its framing of black families as pathological.

39 See endnote 25 for a list of studies describing black women's fertility as the problematic cause of poor socioeconomic outcomes.

40 In work on occupational sex segregation Okamoto and England (1999) find that black women in general and black mothers in particular work in occupations with a higher percentage of male employees than women of other races. They understand these findings as evidence of black women's "prioritization of earnings in choice of jobs" (571)—behavior that they link to these women's inability to rely on marriage to support childrearing. Here, in my book, racial deprivation in marriage emerges from the sidelines of a discussion of gender inequality in occupation and earnings in order to occupy center stage.

41 Malthus's (1798/1965, 1872) reasoning undergirds these analyses of poverty based on these sexual and reproductive arenas. Malthus argued that individu-

als' inability to exercise a "moral restraint" that would delay sexual activity and family formation and, thereby, limit fertility consigned them to social lives characterized by overpopulation, poverty, and starvation.

42 Oscar Lewis (1959, 1968) first described what he saw as a culture of poverty in a Mexican community. He maintained that some of the listed cultural practices were developed as individual and community level adaptations to life under significant material disadvantage. But he indicated that over time the practices and values take on a life of their own and become self-sustaining. Others (for example, Office of Policy Planning and Research 1965; Wilson 1978/1980) have continued to use the phrase "culture of poverty" in their descriptions of low-income African American communities.

43 Documentation of women's disproportionately high share of household labor even in cases where they work full time in the formal labor market is accomplished by a large tradition of scholarship, including Bittman, England, Folbre, Sayer, and Matheson 2003; and A. Hochschild 1989, 1997. Bittman, England, Folbre, Sayer, and Matheson 2003 investigates several theoretical explanations for women's consignment to higher shares of household labor. It includes specialization and efficient time use models (see Becker, 1973, 1974, 1981), exchange theory (Edwards 1969), and game theoretic models, all of which say that women do more household labor because they earn less money in the formal labor market than their husbands, whose negotiating power in household decision making is consequently higher. Also included is the idea that gender inequity in the division of household labor emerges from individuals' and couples' beliefs in and/or adherence to traditional gender norms and from women's and men's respective performance of femininity and masculinity in ways that make their behaviors and choices intelligible and understandable to those around them (Berk 1985; Coltrane 1989, 2000; West and Zimmerman 1987).

44 In particular, women's low occupational status, employment, and labor-related income is associated with their status as mothers, as indicated by Budig and England 2001; Casper, McLanahan, and Garfinkel 1994; Christopher, England, Smeeding, and Phillips 2002; McLanahan, Sorensen, and Watson 1989; Waldfogel 1997, 1998a, 1998b; and Williams 2000.

45 Some feminist analyses go beyond discussions of gender as an aspect of individuals' lives in order to describe the ways in which gender functions as an organizing principle of social institutions—institutions that thereby imply a division of roles by sex and inequities in the distribution of responsibilities and rewards along gender lines. For a discussion of this "third stage" of gender research, see England 1999 and E. Glenn 2002.

46 Paula England and her colleagues (England, Budig, and Folbre 2002; England, Farkas, Kilbourne, and Dou 1988; England, Reid, and Kilbourne 1996; Kilbourne, Farkas, Beron, Weir, and Englandal 1994) have given significant attention to discussing and establishing the veracity of empirical models maintain-

ing that individuals who work in jobs dominated by women experience a wage penalty. In addition, England, Budig, and Folbre 2002, and Kilbourne, Farkas, Beron, Weir, and England 1994 demonstrate that individuals who do jobs that can be categorized generally as interactive service work and more specifically as care work experience a wage penalty as well.

47 Kenkel 1985 finds that young women's desire for childlessness is associated with higher than average educational and career aspirations.

48 Important scholarship with respect to the evaluation of the economic benefits of marriage has been completed by Pamela Smock and her colleagues (Holden and Smock 1991; Smock 1993, 1994; Smock, Manning, and Gupta 1999). Because they use specific regression techniques to account for measured and unmeasured differences between women who divorce and women who remain married, they feel confident in their conclusion that marriage has large and significant benefits to women's economic well-being. Statements from Smock and her colleagues, like the point that the women who remained married would have fared as badly as the women who divorced if they had divorced or the point that remarriage is the best route to economic recovery for divorced women, reinforce the arguments made by other studies about the importance of the marital status variable for economic outcomes (including Bianchi, Subaiya, and Kahn 1999; L. Morgan 1991; Popenoe 1996; Stirling 1989; and Waite 1995).

49 Edin and Kefalas's (2005) work on the utility their subjects gain from motherhood, despite the economic hardship that may be related to the timing and circumstances of parenting, makes this point with regard to poor women in general and poor women of color in particular. Middle-class and/or high-achieving women's desires in this regard are described in Hertz 2006 and Hewlett 2002. On a more general note, England 1999 might place the argument set forth in Edin and Kefalas 2005, the studies of Hertz 2006 and Hewlett 2002, and the claims about Imani's family formation desires that are being made here in the cultural feminist tradition of gender study. It is in this tradition of gender scholarship that we find analyses that question social valuation of those interests and goals that are understood to be "male" and the devaluation of aspects of social life and individual agendas that are attended to and/or focused on by women.

50 See endnote 48 above for a summary of scholarship discussing the improvement of class outcomes associated with marriage. Also see Blee 1985 for discussion of the ways women who achieved class mobility through marriage differ in political and class orientations from those who were occupationally mobile.

51 This finding of racial limitation and racial difference despite apparent childbearing outcome similarity across races contrasts with theoretical claims about middle-class black individuals' growing similarities with whites and about racially unequal outcomes being concentrated among low-income Afri-

can Americans whose disadvantages are based on class. These claims have been organized and articulated in work by William Julius Wilson (1978/1980, 1987, 1996).

52 The earliest trends in intersectionality scholarship focus on describing the ways the experiences of women of color differ from those of white women. The theoretical implications of this work—that gender systems and their outcomes influence and are influenced by the specific evolution of other sets of unequal social relations like race and class in these social settings—have been outlined by scholars of color like P. Collins (1991, 2004) and E. Glenn (2002). Empirical precursors to this text's discussion of the interconnectedness of gender, race, and class on degreed black women's experiences and outcomes in love and money include Higginbotham and Weber's (1992) discussion. They found socially mobile black women's greater sense of obligation to kin and community, black families' greater interest in preparing daughters for the breadwinning role, and upwardly mobile black women's likelihood of shocking co-workers' and others with their elite status as such areas of difference.

53 In an article on his grandmother, Margaret Sanger (credited with founding and leading the early twentieth-century feminist movement to improve poor women's access to birth control), Alexander Sanger (2007) discusses the dangers of a more or less exclusive focus on childbearing as the space within which women can exert the kind of control that will lead to the improvement of their own lives and the overall health and "fitness" of society. This focus on poor women's gender disadvantage and women's "slavery" to reproductive labor as the central mechanism of inequality maintenance has historically fit all too well with movements that deny women the right to bear children and deny women and their children the right to basic food, shelter, and health care because of their low racial and class status.

54 E. Glenn's (2002) discussion of the way U.S. citizenship and the system of free labor in the United States developed as a set of race-gender privileges is an example of the way in which representation works alongside micro-level interactions and macro-structural organization in the creation of institutionalized inequality and unequal lives. E. Glenn 2002 includes a theoretical chapter in which she describes how these three simultaneously operating processes are foundational to the generation and maintenance of an intersecting race-gender inequality. Brodkin's (1999) observation of Jews in the mid-twentieth century United States makes similar claims about the tandem workings of representation (e.g., in the work of Jewish public intellectuals and Hollywood producers) and structural change (e.g., increasing access to educational, economic, and residential opportunities for Jewish veterans) in the accomplishment of Jewish upward mobility. Here again, representations (e.g., of Jewish women occupying gender appropriate roles in homemaking rather than formal sector employment and of Jewish women appearing distinct from African American mothers in their cultural practices) are important for class

mobility in a scholarly argument about the ways privilege and disadvantage are constituted in intersecting race, class, and gender inequality making processes.

55 There are a number of intersectionality analyses of the U.S. welfare system and/or its recent welfare reform that discuss the importance of racial representations or symbols (including imagery regarding the "welfare queen") and beliefs about moral and ethical differences between black and non-black welfare recipients to the acceptability of some of the more class exploitative aspects of that system. These aspects include the low levels of funding allocation to homemaking women, the imposition of time limits and work requirements on mothering recipients, and policies designed to restrict recipients' fertility and reproductive freedom. These analyses can be found in work by Brodkin (1999), P. Collins (1991, 2004), Hays (2003), Quadagno (1994), Roberts (1997, 2002), and Solinger (2001).

56 Studies focused on documenting discrimination in everyday interactions and experiences (for example, applying for jobs; purchasing homes; shopping and accessing services from state agencies, private enterprises, and medical organizations; and routine or informal interactions with police and justice system agents) include Feagin and Sykes 1994; Massey and Denton 1993; Pager 2003, 2007; Pager and Quillian 2005; Roscigno 2007; St. Jean and Feagin 1998; and Thorburn and Bogart 2005a.

57 Bobo and Kluegel (1993), Bobo and Zubrinsky (1996), Bonilla-Silva (2003), Moss and Tilly (1996), Pager (2007), Pager and Quillian (2005), Wilson (1996), and Zubrinsky and Bobo (1996) are among those researchers who study the racial attitudes of black individuals' would-be employers, neighbors, colleagues and co-workers, political supporters, and even spouses. They tell us that those individuals' rejection of race-neutral or anti-racist action can be tied to their negative views of African Americans. Their collective work also indicates that their research subjects usually represent themselves as more race-neutral or race-blind than they actually are, which means that scholarly descriptions of the influence of racist imagery and attitudes on the constraints black individuals face in their everyday interactions probably underestimate that influence.

58 Both Carr 1997 and Bonilla-Silva 2003 use the term colorblind racism to describe whites' use of race-neutral terms and the language of inarticulateness and confusion to describe and at the same time mask what is essentially racist action.

59 See, for example, Omi and Winant's (1994) discussion of racial formations in which individuals and communities rearticulate the language of "equal rights" in order to oppose the racially integrative busing of children out of highly segregated neighborhood schools or the use of affirmative action to hire and grant college admission to underrepresented minorities. Here, as in Bonilla-Silva's (2003) work, behavior aimed at limiting or reversing racial

gains made by African Americans in the civil rights movement is disguised by race-neutral frames (like support for local community integrity or opposition to reverse discrimination).

Chapter 1. School

1 Bourdieu (Bourdieu 1977b, 1984; Bourdieu and Passeron 1977/1990) used the concept of "habitus" to describe the "lasting and transposable dispositions" that individuals carry with them into the different arenas in which they travel over the life course. He maintained that these dispositions are based in former actions and experiences and that individuals' future actions are determined by an intersection between these dispositions of their past and the structures of opportunity they face in particular "fields" or arenas of social life. The argument in this chapter runs parallel to this theoretical treatment of the relationship between experience and action, making a specific claim about the relevance of experiences with families and the racial structure and women's educational decision making. Bourdieu's description of individuals' constrained choice as an interaction between habitus and opportunity within fields is usually used to discuss or explain how persons with different experiences in the same field (for example, family) develop different dispositions and thereby end up with different class outcomes—that is, their different dispositions produce different interactions and outcomes with the educational and economic fields. But here different dispositions are developed across different fields and these experiences are linked to similar class or education level outcomes. The analysis thereby suggests that single class groups—or persons with similar class statuses—might depend upon and be constituted by the logic, actions, dispositions, and experiences of different social arenas.

2 In 53 percent of the cases, a preponderance of the sampled woman's degree-supporting decisions could be classified using just one of my types. Thus each of these women is classified using a single label corresponding to one of the seven logics of degree attainment. Just about 95 percent of the sample carries two or fewer labels.

3 Cultural constructions around gender and work specifically support females' provision of valuable care and service work to households and family members for no monetary remuneration but rather because they are motivated by love. See England, Budig, and Nancy Folbre 2002; England and Folbre 1999; Folbre and Nelson 2000; Macdonald and Merrill 2002; and Nelson 1999 for more detailed theoretical discussions of this idea. The behaviors and family services that prevent the rebellious escape of the girls and young women who here emerge as conforming escape artists may constitute the kind of performance of femininity or "doing" of gender in the familial context that has been theorized by West and Fenstermaker (1993, 1995) and West and Zimmerman (1987), and discussed by Coltrane (1989, 2000). Bettie (2003) finds that the

performance of this reproductive labor for parents and younger siblings can be limiting even as it constrains poor and working-class girls from the more self-destructive rebellious behavior or acting out that characterizes their brothers and male cousins; for she indicates that such girls may be prevented from going away to colleges because there is no one to continue performing these supportive roles for younger siblings.

4 Wharton and Thorne's (1997) quantitative study offers some support for the finding regarding conforming escape artists in this book. Their investigation of the predictive power of class and the experience of upward mobility on the closeness of the mother-daughter tie argues that the negative association between upward mobility and daughters' closeness to their mothers may not mean that establishing distance between one's family and oneself is a necessary strategy of class improvement. Rather, they say that the association may mean that an already weak mother-daughter bond motivates upward mobility.

5 Shaw and Coleman's (2000) study of black females attending community colleges argues that subjects "choose" to maintain relationships with even those family members who frustrate their progress in school (including mothers who believe that study time encroaches on family time and husbands or male partners who believe that the woman's educational attainment creates the stress of a status differential in the romantic relationship). At the same time, Shaw and Coleman's subjects drop friends and peers who threaten to hold them back in the educational arena. Concluding that this is a way in which working-class females (across race) differ from scholarly reports on the experiences of working-class males, they indicate that the relevant area of gender difference in upward mobility lies in the differential choices made by women. I argue here that what appears more relevant with respect to conforming escape artists is the gender constraints embedded in the structure of families—constraints that indicate that daughters are more tightly confined to the home by parents and that they are more likely to be compelled to stand in for mothers in reproductive labor roles than are boys. With respect to this portion of my sampled subjects, these gender constraints generated conformism rather than rebellious escape from these families of upbringing.

6 Higginbotham and Weber (1992) and Lareau (2003) also study familial influences on women's or girls' achievement in school on their way to middle-class status. The former focus on women's ongoing attachment to family during social mobility processes, and the latter focuses on the family's transmission of appropriate or inappropriate class style to youth who are expected respectively to perform well and poorly in school and the status attainment game. Both works privilege discussions of whether and how individuals' relationships with families are oriented toward class achievements. The analyses in this book differ from these works in that educational decision making and class achievements are here based in the development of "family actors" who come to value and work toward love relationships with specific quali-

ties. School and work thus remain byproducts of a different set of relations and different sets of personal aims. Although Bettie (2003) indicates that the few working-class female subjects poised for upward mobility in her sample included a sub-sample of girls whose desire to give their parents less trouble than their truant brothers motivated school success, family obligation and duty to a poor or working-class family tended to cause feelings of ambivalence and even detract from upward mobility projects in her study.

7 The presentation of these two love logics of degree attainment contrasts with most scholarly descriptions of middle-class attainment and the influence of the family on the process. The status attainment literature (Ainsworth and Roscigno 2005; Blau and Duncan 1967; Campbell 1983; Cote 1997; Fairlie and Meyer 2000; Henretta 1984; Jacobs, Karen, and McClelland 1991; Jencks, Crouse, and Mueser 1983; Kalmijn 1994; Kerckhoff, Campbell, and Trott 1982; Looker and McNutt 1989; Looker and Pineo 1983; Rumberger 1983; Sewell, Haller, and Portes 1969; Sewell and Hauser 1972; Sewell, Hauser, and Wolf 1980; Steelman and Powell 1991; Tachibanaki 1979) often forgoes consideration of the family beyond the parental aspirations for the child and parental occupational and income resource measures. Their predictive models might capture the positive influence of pleaser parents' aspirations on their daughters' outcomes but would likely miss those of the escape artists. Neither this model nor Merton's (1957) typology addresses love as a relevant value with respect to economic status attainment. Furthermore, while Bourdieu's discussion of the socializing power of "fields" indicates that individuals' experiences in love and family are likely to be relevant forces in determining the habitus and individuals' future action (Bourdieu 1977b, 1984; Bourdieu and Passeron 1977/1990), it remains unclear, in the logic of this discussion, why such disparate experiences in the family would lead to the similar class outcomes displayed here. This is because this theoretical understanding of families focuses more or less exclusively on behaviors and practices that arise out of families' material constraints and opportunities. In this book, families are organized around more than their material existence; and their organization around and for the distribution of love relations can and does affect individual members' educational and professional class outcomes.

8 Both quantitative (Eitle and Eitle 2004; Felice 1981; Jencks and Phillips 1998; Kao and Thompson 2003; Kao and Tienda 1998; Massey, Charles, Lundy, and Fischer 2003; Mickelson 1990; Orr 2003; Steele 1997; Steele and Aronson 1995; Steele and Davies 2003; Stier and Tienda 2001; Taylor, Casten, Flickinger, Roberts, and Fulmore 1994) and qualitative (Carter 2005; Fine 1991; Fordham and Ogbu 1986; Lareau and Horvat 1999; Lopez 2003; Matute-Bianchi 1991; Ogbu 1991, 1992, 2003; Tyson 2003) scholars have dedicated analytical effort toward explaining black and Latino underachievement in schools.

9 Literature offering theoretical and empirical explanations for racial inequality in wages and the depressed employment and income of African Americans

relative to whites includes Allen and Farley 1986; Boardman and Field 2002; Bound and Freeman 1992; Cancio, Evans, and Maume 1996; P. Cohen 1998; D'Amico and Maxwell 1995; Fairlie and Sundstrom 1999; Farkas and Vicknair 1996; Grodsky and Pager 2001; Holzer 1998b; Maume 2004; Moss and Tilly 1995, 1996; Pager 2003; Pager and Quillian 2005; Royster 2003; Sakamoto, Wu, and Tzeng 2000; Stoll, Holzer, and Ihlanfeldt 2000; and Tigges and Tootle 1993.

10 Bettie (2003), Horvat and Antonio (1999), and MacLeod (1995) all suggest that students may engage with the opportunities made available by affirmative action legislation and programming without being fooled into thinking that such programming constitutes a definitive end to race-based exclusion or predicts the progression of U.S. racial groups toward greater and greater equality in future generations.

11 Patricia Hill Collins (Collins 1991, 2004) is part of a tradition of scholarship (for example, Glenn 2002; St. Jean and Feagin 1998) that argues that imagery supports racist policy and practice. Her theoretical work describes specific stereotypical images like "black bitches," "mammies," and "bad boys" and analyzes their historical evolution from stereotypes of black men and women that prevailed in earlier eras. The imagery evolves over time because racist exploitation and oppression have taken different forms in different eras. In one era, a black bitch is a dog incapable of controlling her sexuality and the "litters" of puppies that she bears. She exists to encourage black women's reproduction and provision of cheap agricultural labor during the antebellum and Jim Crow eras. Under Collins's "new racism," a new version of the black bitch emerges. This one aggressively manipulates her sexuality, producing children that the state must support. She exists to legitimate policies to repress black women's reproductive freedom through coerced sterilization, semi-permanent contraceptive devices (for example, Norplant and Depo-Provera), and limitations on cash available from welfare to support additional children. Brodkin's (1999) description of the Jewish American transition to whiteness, Hays's (2003) discussion of women's and families' experience of the welfare reform of 1996, and Solinger's (2001) investigation of the relationship between evolving adoption, abortion, and welfare policies all include analyses that use data from the media and historical records to point out that particular representations of black women and men support political processes and outcomes. The connection between the representation of black women as welfare dependent "queens" and U.S. policy to contract welfare program benefits is raised in each of these texts and in Gilens 1999; Quadagno 1994; and Thomas 1998. These and other texts in this tradition (for example, Collins 2004; Nagel 2003) might also show connections between images of violent and sexually aggressive black men and repressive social control regimes like lynching and contemporary mass incarceration.

12 This book's discussion of stigma avoidance is distinct from scholarly treat-

ments of racism and representation in which symbols play a role in macro-level politics (see endnote 11 above). For the work in this text constitutes direct observation of individuals' micro-level interactions around racist symbolic representations. In the tradition of Steele's (Steele 1997; Steele and Aronson 1995; Steele and Davies 2003) stereotype threat thesis, it reports on individuals' response to the macro-level framing and deployment of images like the "welfare queen" or "bad boy." Horvat and Antonio's (1999) study of African American girls in an elite white prep school reports that success in this setting required that students shed their own culture or at least perform the elite white culture, although her discussion does not rely on student engagement with particular stereotypical symbols.

13 Nonetheless, it is possible that a general sample of African Americans might contain a greater proportion of persons whose more invariant experience of institutional racism means that stigma avoidance and mediocre school performance become their modus operandi. The set of experiences and associated values that I am calling stigma avoidance may mirror what Ogbu (Fordham and Ogbu 1986; Ogbu 1990, 1992, 2003; Ogbu and Simons 1998) has observed among larger populations of African Americans in urban and suburban school settings. He and his colleagues argue that black students eschew success in school as a means of avoiding the accusation that they are "acting white." Above, I argue that when racist exclusion familiarizes black people with the hostility of a pointing finger, they may seek to avoid it no matter where it comes from. Ogbu's use of the term "acting white," although it may appear to be appropriately drawn from insiders to his ethnographic setting, may also imprecisely narrow or particularize the students' behavior and the social dynamics from which those behaviors emerge. What is actually avoidance of the spotlight in fear of the pointing finger in general becomes an avoidance of the academic spotlight and the pointing fingers of fellow black students in a setting with clearly marked racial sides.

A study of race- and class-varied high-school settings (Tyson, Darity, and Castellino 2005) criticizes Ogbu's interpretation of his data with the finding that lower-class white students in higher academic tracks sought to avoid being accused of "acting uppity" by class-similar schoolmates who were disproportionately located in lower-level academic tracks. The authors of this study argue that disadvantaged students' understanding that "acting white" or "acting uppity" equates with superior academic performance is likely based in a structure of schooling that routinely places advantaged students in higher level academic tracks than disadvantaged students and that, in so doing, associates high academic achievement with certain ascribed social statuses (for example, class origins and race). My argument here is that structural location and experience among the stigmatized sensitizes individuals to the pointing finger and stigmatization even when it comes from those who are similarly marginalized. Furthermore, I am also suggesting that in those situations where stigma avoidance leads to poor academic performance, problematic performance may not reflect a desire to do poorly in school but rather a failed attempt at mediocre achievement.

14 Most of the literature on educational aspirations (Campbell 1983; Konstantopoulos, Modi, and Hedges 2001; Okagaki and Frensch 1998; Sewell, Haller, and Portes 1969; Stryker 1981; Tachibanaki 1979; Turrittin, Anisef, and MacKinnon 1983; Wong 1990) predicts that those with high educational aspirations end up with higher educational and occupational achievements. Although Jacobs, Karen, and McClelland (1991) expected to find that high-achieving racial minority group members have higher aspirations than comparable whites, they observed rather small racial and class differences among men in the National Longitudinal Survey of Young Men. They expected and found that men in subordinate groups (for example, lower classes and minority races) were more likely to experience a decline in aspirations as they encountered unemployment, low wages, and low career advancement—a finding that they maintain is consistent with Bourdieu's (1977b) claim that individuals' aspirations would adjust based on their experience in social "fields."

15 Note that the claims being made about racial logics of degree attainment are meant to be more comprehensive in scope than those made in work that documents the additional burdens associated with social mobility or status attainment among women and/or individuals of color (for example, R. Cohen 1998; Cose 1994; Feagin and Sykes 1994; Higginbotham and Weber 1992; Horvat and Antonio 1999; Lopez 2003; MacLeod 1995; Massey 2007; Massey, Charles, Lundy, and Fischer 2003; Massey and Denton 1993; Pager 2003; Roscigno 2007; Royster 2003; St. Jean and Feagin 1998; M. Sullivan 1989). Here the claim is that race defines the terms of decisions that make status attainment possible. In this sense, race is more analogous to the habitus that Bourdieu (Bourdieu 1977b, 1984; Bourdieu and Passeron 1977/1990) describes, as it outfits women with ways of being that make sense for a particular set of racial challenges and opportunities. Scholars who have argued that degree attainment in communities of color is predicted by individuals' ability to engage with both the assimilationist and resistance-oriented meanings attached to academic success and upward mobility (Bettie 2003; Gandara 1995; Gibson 1988; Mehan, Hubbard, and Villanueva 1994; O'Connor 1997, 1999) are closer to my arguments in this book about recruitment and stigma avoidance. For such scholars acknowledge that racial and interracial communities give degree-supporting actions meanings that support or detract from individuals' likelihood of seeing these actions as activities that make sense for persons such as themselves.

16 Paul DiMaggio (DiMaggio 1982; DiMaggio and Mohr 1985) joins Pierre Bourdieu (Bourdieu 1977a; Bourdieu and Passeron 1977/1990) in evaluating whether and to what extent class membership is constituted by individuals' participation or lack of participation in certain forms of high culture, including art, music, literature, and film. Their findings include conclusions about

participation in high culture supporting the achievement of higher class (that is, educational and occupational) outcomes and about participation in high culture being more prevalent among elites. While these studies point to the ways lifestyle supports and signifies elite class membership, Michele Lamont's (1992) investigation of a slightly different question found that upper-middle-class white men in the United States were more likely to use moral and socio-economic boundaries than cultural ones when distinguishing between "them" and "us." This book's discussion of status seeking as a set of experiences that generate certain values and motivate action directed at those values is closest in its conclusions to theoretical and empirical work suggesting that middle-class status is associated with a notoriety and prestige that commands emulation by individuals in lower classes. Other work that relies on empirical data to evaluate and elaborate upon claims about status identities being produced by participation in and display of culture and lifestyle includes work on voting by Clifford and Heath (1993), Lipset and Bendix (1959), and Weakliem (1992). (But these voting studies have more recently rejected the idea that voting is relevant to status identity building.) Also included is work on media participation and/or consumption by Jhally and Lewis (1992), Press (1991), Schor (1998), and Veblen (1953). Here the scholars have continued to maintain that identification with the middle and upper middle classes is developed and reinforced by ongoing observation of media representations of elites and emulation of the observed taste and consumption patterns.

17 While early status attainment literature suggested that aspirations were created on the home front by families (for example, Sewell, Haller, and Portes 1969; Campbell 1983), later criticisms of this literature argue that aspirations may really be shaped by parents' and children's realistic assessments of their probabilities of success (for example, Kerckhoff 1989; Jacobs, Karen, and McClelland 1991) and would therefore adjust when individuals confront racially discriminatory and exclusionary practices. Jacobs, Karen, and McClelland 1991 and MacLeod 1995 disagree about aspirations in a post–civil rights climate—with the former quantitative study finding high aspirations across racial and class groups and arguing that they are due to populous belief in a newer more open society and the latter qualitative investigation of lower-class males reporting that only the minority group members' aspirations were elevated by the post–civil rights climate. Mickelson's (1990) and Kao and Tienda's (1998) investigations find that the educational aspirations of minority youth are high in the abstract, but that these abstract attitudes are less meaningful for achievement than their concrete attitudes about the likelihood of racial exclusion or their specific knowledge about and expectations for completing the tasks and processes associated with qualifying for high-status careers. In this book, status seekers' valuation of those educational credentials and professional careers that are open to them and that do not appear racially restrictive mirrors scholarly findings indicating that individuals of color may strive

toward high achievement in schools and workplaces despite observations of racist exclusion as long as such students have the sense that the racial barriers may be challenged or are negotiable. In this regard, see Carter 2005; Mehan, Hubbard, and Villanueva 1994; and O'Connor 1997. The idea that perceptions about the openness of American society are based in observations of cross-racial rather than cross-class inclusion is discussed by Erikson and Goldthorpe (1985) and by Ogbu and his colleagues in their work on voluntary and involuntary minorities (Fordham and Ogbu 1986; Ogbu 1990, 1992, 2003; Ogbu and Simons 1998).

18 The scholarly discussion of educational aspirations and the aspirations-achievement gap among black and Latino students (Kao and Tienda 1998; Mickelson 1990) is in agreement with this analysis. That discussion suggests that "profiling"—or the development of superficial interest in middle-class educational and occupational outcomes rather than specific goals and practical realizable plans for the achievement of the same—reflects structural disadvantage. Whether students of color are unsure of college financing, are lacking in social connections to mentors who have navigated the college admissions and matriculation processes, or are doubtful that a racially discriminatory labor market will fairly reward hard-working college graduates of color, the lower level of educational attainment associated with these conditions can—in the words of these studies—first be observed in their high but abstract aspirations. Profilers included in my study are not, by virtue of their degree attainment, in the population of "underachievers" typically identified by scholars of educational inequality. Capable and culturally sensitized to many of the larger signposts associated with the status-seeking game, they are unaware of or unengaged with many of that game's basic rules because of their disadvantages. As Gandara (1995) finds in her study of degreed Chicanos in high-status professions, they often end up in the spaces and places associated with degree attainment by happenstance rather than design.

19 Horvat and Antonio (1999) argue that Bourdieu's (Bourdieu 1977a and Bourdieu and Wacquant 1992) concept of "symbolic violence" appropriately describes the experience of the six African American girls in their study. They maintain that the process "others" the girls in the context of their elite independent school and demonstrates to them that their natural predispositions and culture are less than those of the dominant wealthy whites who own that space. These young girls respond by performing or changing their own "habitus" in order to "fit in" and thereby gain social mobility via entrance into selective colleges. Randi's insurgence is here described as the individuals' attempt to use access to such settings not to "fit in" but rather to change the terms of inclusion and exclusion. R. Cohen's (1998) article on special status students at Smith College contains a more involved description of the process by which isolation and the possession of a minority viewpoint develop into decisions and activities in support of structural change.

Chapter 2. Family

1 For example, see Ainsworth and Roscigno 2005; Blau and Duncan 1967; D'Amico and Maxwell 1995; Kilbourne, England, and Beron 1994; McCall 1998, 2000a; Sewell, Haller, and Portes 1969; Sewell, Hauser, and Wolf 1980— all studies that either directly or indirectly consider the occupational and earnings differentials associated with individuals' educational credentials.

2 Writing on health inequality that indicates that class, socioeconomic status, and/or education differences lead to health and mortality outcome differences includes Gwynn and Thurston 2001; Rogers, Hummer, Nam, and Peters 1996; Williams and Collins 1995; and Williams, Lavizzo-Mourey, and Warren 1994.

3 The finding that a woman's education lowers her likelihood of experiencing divorce is reported in Martin and Bumpass 1989; Moore and Waite 1981; Ono 1998; Rankin and Maneker 1985; South and Spitze 1986; and Tzeng 1992. Bruce Western's (Pettit and Western 2004; Western 2007; Western, Kleykamp, and Rosenfeld 2006) descriptions of the recent turn of the century increases in U.S. incarceration maintain that educational disadvantage increases an individual's likelihood of experiencing incarceration and that the importance of education as a determinative factor in incarceration experience has grown in the recent era.

4 Since William Julius Wilson's (1978/1980) *The Declining Significance of Race* called on inequality scholarship to focus on the class-based rather than race-based origins of urban black disadvantage, a number of racial inequality specialists have completed analyses maintaining that racial discrimination remains a powerful and important determinant of disadvantage in the United States. Such scholars—including Lawrence Bobo and his co-authors (Bobo and Kluegel 1993; Bobo and Zubrinsky 1996; Zubrinsky and Bobo 1996), Douglas Massey and his co-authors (Massey and Denton 1989, 1993; Massey 2007), Joe Feagin and his co-authors (Feagin and Sykes 1994; Feagin and Vera 1995; St. Jean and Feagin 1998), Mary Pattillo-McCoy (1999), and Devah Pager and her colleagues (Grodsky and Pager 2001; Pager 2007; Pager and Quillian 2005)—have often, although not exclusively, relied on data on middle-class black individuals' experiences and outcomes in order to make this point.

5 Based on the results of a historical study of persistent high fertility in the southern region of the United States, Tolnay and Glynn (1994) support scholarly exploration of multiple causes for demographic outcomes and scholars' identification of diverse mechanisms associated with the achievement of such outcomes. This recommendation is based on research findings that identify racial differences in the explanations for high fertility in the black and white populations prior to the baby boom. This book focuses on low rather than high fertility, but it argues that a description of the racial differences in the underlying processes of fertility achievement is an important finding associated with this study as well.

6 Studies that discuss or examine the veracity of claims about economically advantaged women's low fertility as an outcome of the competition between their fertility desires and the benefits they receive from the pursuit of emotionally and materially rewarding educational and professional opportunities include Bloom and Trussell 1984; Blossfeld and Huinink 1991; Caldwell and Schindlmayr 2003; Forest, Moen, and Dempster-McClain 1995; Lehrer and Nerlove 1986; S. Morgan 1991, 2003; Rindfuss, Bumpass, and St. John 1980; Rindfuss, Morgan, and Offutt 1996; Schoen, Kim, Nathanson, Fields, and Astone 1997; Swicegood, Bean, Stephen, and Opitz 1988; Torr and Short 2004; and Wilkie 1981.

7 Here, I refer to the largely economic underpinnings of what is commonly known as demographic transition theory, describing Europe's historical transition from high to low fertility. (See Weeks 2007 for a description of the development of and intellectual contributors to demographic transition theory.) In short the theory maintains that couples' demand for children declined as societies and individuals transitioned from agricultural to urban industrial economies. Urban industrial economies imply lower infant and child mortality, and, with the increasing importance of education, they change surviving children's roles from that of youthful agricultural workers to long-term dependents in need of scarce urban housing and schooling. Furthermore, urbanization means increased employment options for women and thereby raises the opportunity cost of childbearing and childrearing. It also allows for the diffusion of elites' contraceptive know-how to those in classes below them. Demographers have elaborated upon as well as evaluated and found support for demographic transition theory in historical analyses of now industrialized regions (for example, Coale 1969; K. Davis 1963; Galloway, Hammel, and Lee 1994; Hajnal 1965; Sklar 1974; van de Walle 1980) and in observations of unindustrialized and industrializing areas of the globe (Cleland and Rodriguez 1988; Swicegood, Bean, Stephen, and Opitz 1988; Tuladhar, Stoeckel, and Fisher 1982; Weinberger, Lloyd, and Blanc 1989). Ongoing criticism of this theory of fertility decline has relied on the same two sources of data. In most cases, problems with demographic transition theory's expectation that fertility decline is necessarily tied to economic "development" are at the foundation of these criticisms. Critics have used their analyses to highlight societal transitions to low fertility in which contraceptive knowledge and new ideologies about children as recipients of familial wealth happen despite relatively low levels of industrialization or "development" (for example, Caldwell 1980; Cleland and Rodriguez 1988; Nassirpour 1985).

8 Arguments that maintain that there are fertility pattern causes of women's poor socioeconomic status tend to link these poor socioeconomic outcomes to the early or teenaged pattern of childbearing (Beutel 2000; Dillard and Pol 1982; Furstenberg 1976; Hofferth and Moore 1979; Hoffman, Foster, and Furstenberg 1993; Trussell 1976) and/or to the nonmarital pattern of child-

bearing (Billy and Moore 1992; Driscoll, Hearn, Evans, Moore, Sugland, and Call 1999; McLanahan and Sandefur 1994; Popenoe 1996; Stier and Tienda 2001; and Waite and Gallagher 2000).

9 Economic explanations of regions' or nations' relatively high, moderate, or low fertility that come from analyses linking macro-level economic conditions (for example, levels of economic development, urbanization, production for export, educational and employment opportunities for women) to the early or late timing of women's first births or to the average number of children that women have can be found in Cleland and Rodriguez 1988; Kirk and Pillet 1998; Swicegood, Bean, Stephen, and Opitz 1988; Tuladhar, Stoeckel, and Fisher 1982; van de Walle 1980; and Weinberger, Lloyd, and Blanc 1989. In these studies, high levels of economic prosperity, production, development, and the like are linked to later childbearing and low fertility, while lower economic indicators are associated with the earlier and higher fertility patterns.

10 The individual level variable that most distinguishes women or groups with high and low fertility is women's education. In demographic inquiries covering a wide cross-section of societies (Aassve and Altankhuyag 2002; Ainsworth, Beegle, and Nyamete 1996; Axinn 1993; Axinn and Barber 2001; Benefo and Schultz 1996; Caldwell, Orubuloye, and Caldwell 1992; Dreze and Murthi 2001; Fennelly, Cornwell, and Casper 1992; Gertler and Molyneaux 1994; Gupta and Leite 1999; Jain 1981; Kirk and Pillet 1998; Lavely and Freedman 1990; London 1992; Martin and Juarez 1995; Remez 1998; Rindfuss, Morgan, and Offutt 1996; Singh 1998; Swicegood, Bean, Stephen, and Opitz 1988; Tawiah 1984; Weinberger 1987; Weinberger, Lloyd, and Blanc 1989), individual women with more education and educational opportunity and communities or ethnic groups with more highly educated women have lower or "classier" fertility than those with less education. It has been documented that some of education's depressing effects on fertility are related to the education that women give or expect to give to their children rather than the education of the women themselves (Axinn 1993; Axinn and Barber 2001; Caldwell 1980; Sweetman and Dicks 1999). Women with high incomes and status also have lower fertility than those with little or no income and low status (for example, Martin and Juarez 1995; Remez 1998; Sathar, Crook, Callum, and Kazi 1988), although income differences seem to have smaller and less consistent effects on fertility outcomes than educational differences.

11 S. Morgan's (1991) investigation of childlessness in the United States during the nineteenth century suggests that even then childlessness began with women's incentives to postpone marriage and childbearing within marriage. Maintaining that childlessness in the contemporary era is typically explained the same way, he points out that education and work-related postponement are likely to involve women in lifestyles that continue to compete with childbearing even as they age and the reproductive window closes. Hewlett (2002)

dedicates her text to an in-depth exploration of women's education-led and elite employment-led progression toward childlessness.

12 As indicated in the above class analyses and despite the importance of "classy" fertility logic in fertility study, racial differentials in fertility at the different education levels are observed and studied. Articles in this tradition report on the investigation of persistent racial differentials in fertility once income and/ or education are taken into account (for example, Spanier, Roos, and Shockey 1985; St. John 1982; R. Sullivan 2005). Of particular interest here are those studies that focus on identifying interactions between minority status and class—studies that typically evaluate whether racial differentials in fertility are smaller or minority group fertility is uncharacteristically lower than that of whites among education or income elites. The findings with regard to a race and class interaction are mixed, with some studies observing few or no differences between the fertility constraints, choices, and behaviors of the different racial groups at elite educational or income statuses (Boyd 1989; N. Davis 1982; Grindstaff 1976; Johnson 1979; Johnson and Lean 1985; Lehrer 1992; McFalls 1973; McFalls and Masnick 1981; Spanier, Roos, and Shockey 1985). Others observe the minority status effect and offer it as evidence of the greater constraints and larger fertility sacrifices associated with status attainment and fertility decision making in racial minority populations (Feinberg, Larsen, Catherino, Zhang, and Armstrong 2006; Goldscheider and Uhlenberg 1969; Johnson and Lean 1985). The "classy fertility" tradition underlies both of these categories of research findings, as each highlights the depressed childbearing of educated elites and the upwardly mobile.

13 In 1995, Tucker and Mitchell-Kernan dedicated an edited volume to essays focusing on the causes and consequences of marriage decline in the black community. Many others have advanced and tested theoretical explanations for the decline or identified associated variables and precipitating experiences in articles (for example, Bennett, Bloom, and Craig 1989; Graefe and Lichter 2002; Kiecolt and Fossett 1995; Lopoo and Western 2005; Manning and Smock 1995; Michael and Tuma 1985; Sassler and Schoen 1999; Spanier and Glick 1980; Tucker and Taylor 1989) and even in a full-length text (Guttentag and Secord 1983).

14 Some scholars argue that the low rates of marriage among African Americans are related to the large proportion of African Americans who are lower class and who therefore cannot afford to marry (for example, Raley 1996; Sassler and Schoen 1999; Teachman, Polonko, and Leigh 1987; Testa and Krogh 1995; Tucker and Taylor 1989; Wilson 1996; Wilson and Neckerman 1987). In their consideration of the local economy, wage rates or education levels of males and females, and the size of welfare benefits alongside sex ratios, scholars in the marriage market research tradition (Bennett, Bloom, and Craig 1989; Blau, Kahn, and Waldfogel 2000; Brien 1997; Goldman, Westoff, and Hammer-

slough 1984; Lichter, LeClere, and McLaughlin 1991; Lichter, McLaughlin, Kephart, and Landry 1992) also assess whether black-white marriage differences are really proxies for family formation differences based in class.

15 The literature on divorce contains consistent evidence of African Americans' higher rates of marital dissolution, including Martin and Bumpass 1989; Moore and Waite 1981; and South and Spitze 1986.

16 Based on the significance tests in table A2 in the appendix, the differences in the unmarried percentage and in the never married percentage between black and white women and between black and Hispanic women are significant at the .01 level in each age interval but the first. In contrast, the differences between white and Hispanic women are only statistically significant at the end of the reproductive period.

17 The percentages depicted in figure 3 measure marital experience as a fraction or part of women's reproductive years lived. The total number of reproductive years that the specified group of individuals has lived at a particular marital status forms the numerators of these fractions. And the total reproductive years lived by women in the specific race-education group form the denominators. This measure is clearly different from the measures used in studies focused on identifying and explaining marriage rates, the percentage of black or white women in a specific region who are currently married, or differences in marriage timing (for example, Brien 1997; Lichter, LeClere, and McLaughlin 1991; Lopoo and Western 2005; Manning and Smock 1995; Raley 1996; Sassler and Schoen 1999). However, I have elected this measure as well as this graph because it enables readers to simultaneously appreciate the importance of race's influence on both the time women live as singles (never married) and as formerly married individuals.

18 Other scholars have also observed the changing relationship between education and marriage as one moves across racial groups. Specifically, Bennett, Bloom, and Craig 1989 found (as I have here) that high levels of education are associated with being married among black women but that more education lowers the likelihood that white women will marry. In Teachman, Polonko, and Leigh's (1987) study, being in school and higher socioeconomic status meant delayed marriage for white women but had no significant effects on black women's likelihood of marrying. Goldstein and Kenney's (2001) study predicts that for younger cohorts among both black and white women, college educations will switch from being a disadvantage to being an advantage with respect to the likelihood of marrying. And Hewlett (2002) reports on the survey "High-Achieving Women 2001," in which respondents earned wages in the top 10 percent of women in their age group (either ages twenty-eight to forty or ages forty-one to fifty-five), held doctorate degrees, or held the professional degree for medicine, law, or dentistry. Sixty percent of the high-achieving respondents in the older age group were married, while just 33 percent of the sample's African American subjects were married at the time of the survey.

19 As indicated in the text's introduction, the framework set forth in Bongaarts and Potter 1983 indicates that all social influences, including the time it takes to earn a college degree or the high cost of an unpaid maternity leave to a woman who works in a well-paying professional occupation, must act through these proximate determinants to influence the amount of children a woman eventually has. Thus, for example, schooling associated with degree attainment might lower women's fertility by motivating contraceptive use and abortion in the case of an unplanned pregnancy or by turning a hot and heavy high school romance that might have led to marriage into a long-distance love affair destined for certain breakup.

20 Driscoll, Hearn, Evans, Moore, Sugland, and Call 1999; Hoffman and Foster 2000; McLanahan and Sandefur 1994; Popenoe 1996; Stier and Tienda 2001; and Waite and Gallagher 2000 are all studies that document the relationship between nonmarital childbearing and decreased educational and economic outcomes.

21 Stier and Tienda (2001, 3) maintain that nonmarital childbearing is one of the two mechanisms (along with premature school leaving) "that perpetuate economic and social disadvantage over the life course" In Waite and Gallagher's (2000, 110–11) apologetic on the benefits of marriage, the chapter on the relative wealth of spouses when compared with singles opens with the suggestion that unwed childbearing is one of the "important" differences between one woman who experiences welfare dependency and a life characterized by extreme material disadvantage and a second research subject who is a struggling low-income mother with steadily improving financial circumstances.

22 Smith, Morgan, and Koropeckyj-Cox (1996) decomposed the changes in nonmarital fertility ratios that occurred between 1960 and 1992 in the black and white communities. They found that increases in the fraction of black births that occurred out of wedlock across the entire period were predominantly due to increases in the proportion of black women who are single in each reproductive age interval. During the last decade of their observation, increases in single women's childbearing also played a role in raising black nonmarital childbearing ratios, but marriage differences remain the predominant source of the change in the black community. Among white women, the early increases in nonmarital fertility ratios were associated with lower childbearing rates among married women; but after 1975 increases in single women's childbearing rates (of primary importance) and in the fraction of women of reproductive age who were single (of secondary importance) were responsible for these elevations. Describing the mid- to late 1990s, Ventura and Bachrach (2000) maintain that the percentage of nonmarital births in the United States stabilized because of two competing trends—continued increases in the fractions of unmarried women of reproductive age and increases in married women's birth rates. In a related argument, Akerlof, Yellen, and Katz's (1996) summary of the research measuring the prevalence of "shotgun" mar-

riages maintains that more than half of the increases in nonmarital childbearing among white and black women in the late 1960s and the late 1980s are associated with a decline in romantic couples' deciding to marry in order to prevent a nonmarital pregnancy from becoming a nonmarital birth.

23 According to Smith, Morgan, and Koropeckyj-Cox (1996), the black nonmarital fertility ratio for women aged fifteen to forty-four increased from approximately 24 percent of births in 1960 to just under 69 percent of births in 1992. The comparable figures for white births are 2 percent in 1960 and 22 percent in 1992.

24 See Billy and Moore 1992 for empirical documentation of the increases in nonmarital childbearing associated with singleness, low male to female sex ratios, and other variables reflecting communities' low marriage likelihoods. Other work offering discussions of and empirical evidence for the relationship between marriage challenge and single parenting include Darity and Myers 1995; Neal 2004; Smith, Morgan, and Koropeckyj-Cox 1996; Upchurch, Lillard, and Panis 2002; Willis and Haaga 1996.

25 Note that Hewlett 2002 describes gender differences in childlessness and marriage associated with women's high levels of educational and professional achievements. Her study asks a similar question about why high-status careers require women of all racial stripes to sacrifice the love of spouses and children to a greater degree than similarly career-oriented men. The reliance on "classy fertility" logic is the main difference between her work and this book, for her work takes as its starting point the idea that it is women's different experiences of career success that account for their depressed marital and childbearing outcomes relative to that of men. Differences in love outcomes by occupational status reported from her survey data analyses further underscore the book's salient message—that gender inequality (even a gender inequality of love) is ultimately tied to the productive sector.

Chapter 3. Marriage

1 Here, I am speaking about theory and research that explains why some women marry early in the life course and others marry later or not at all (Blau, Kahn, and Waldfogel 2000; Brien, Dickert-Conlin, and Weaver 2004; Carlson, McLanahan, and England 2004; Gibson-Davis, Edin, and McLanahan 2005; Graefe and Lichter 2002; Guttentag and Secord 1983; Lichter, LeClere, and McLaughlin 1991; Lichter, McLaughlin, Kephart, and Landry 1992; Lichter, McLaughlin, and Ribar 2002; Loughran 2002; Oppenheimer 1988, 1994; Oppenheimer, Kalmijn, and Lim 1997; Sassler and Schoen 1999; South and Lloyd 1992; South and Trent 1988; Tucker and Taylor 1989) and about scholarly literature that tells us why individuals choose partners with one set of demographic characteristics and reject partners who lack such traits (Becker 1981; Carlson, McLanahan, and England 2004; Schoen and Weinick 1993;

Schoen and Wooldredge 1989; South 1991; Spanier and Glick 1980; Waller and McLanahan 2005).

2 William Julius Wilson (Wilson and Neckerman 1987) is the author most known for linking the decline in marriage in the African American community to the economic misfortunes of poor urban communities. Lengthy periods of unemployment, severely depressed wages, dependence on the illegal drug trade for income, and the cycles of incarceration that this dependence usually implies make men "unmarriageable" as they remain unable to offer consistent support to dependents. Scholarly investigations of the veracity of this marriageable male hypothesis can be found in Lichter, LeClere, and McLaughlin 1991; Lichter, McLaughlin, and Ribar 1992; Lopoo and Western 2005; Loughran 2002; Sassler and Schoen 1999; Testa, Astone, Krogh, and Neckerman 1989; Testa and Krogh 1995; and Wood 1995.

3 Studies that examine the traits of married couples make these determinations by looking at unions where the traits of spousal couples do not match (that is, heterogamous unions). The understanding is that the preponderance of heterogamous unions in which husbands have higher incomes and education levels than their wives demonstrates the importance of these traits to women. Examples of such studies include Schoen and Weinick 1993 and Schoen and Wooldredge 1989.

4 Waite and Gallagher (2000) summarize research on the better health, wealth, and happiness of those who are married when they are compared with those in the single and divorced statuses. Studies that show that individuals and couples are more likely to marry as their wages and employment activity go up (for example, Blau, Kahn, Waldfogel 2000; Lloyd and South 1996; Oppenheimer 1994; Testa, Astone, Krogh, and Neckerman 1989) also account for these trends.

5 This dichotomy has a number of permutations, including that of the feminist/career woman and the traditional woman/homemaker. Furthermore, the racial and class dimensions of these permutations are such that the latter half of the dichotomy ceases to retain honor or to be cast as a defensible choice for individual women when non-white and/or poor women are the subjects under discussion. Thus Evelyn Nakano Glenn (2002), Sharon Hays (2003), Dorothy Roberts (1997, 2002), and Rickie Solinger (2001) all discuss the ways non-white women's roles as exploited laborers and conditions of material disadvantage have limited their ability to opt into the role of full-time mother or homemaker without enduring discriminatory treatment as well as public criticism and scorn.

6 Gender scholarship typically phrases this argument in terms of a structural dichotomy between home and work (Brodkin 1999; Hochschild 1989, 1997; Williams 2000) and/or an institutional separation of reproductive and productive labor (Ridgeway and Correll 2004; Waldfogel 1997, 1998a), of women's and men's occupations (Bayard, Hellerstein, Neumark, and Troske 2003; England

and Folbre 1999; England, Herbert, Kilbourne, Reid, and Megdal 1994; Jacobs 1995; Joy 2003; Lehrer 1992; Peterson and Morgan 1995; Reskin and Bielby 2005; Shauman 2006), and of the bodies or embodied subjects that perform these distinct forms of labor (Berk 1985; Coltrane 1989, 2000).

7 For example, Bettie (2003), Edin and Kefalas (2005), Freeman and Rickels (1993), Geronimus (1986, 1987), Kaplan (1997), Luker (1996), and Zelnick and Kantner (1980) all conclude in their studies that young women with poor educational and occupational prospects (and in some cases, those who have already dropped out or become disengaged from school) are the ones with high likelihoods of carrying their teenage pregnancies to term. Thus, in one of sociology study's classic chicken and egg questions, these authors are focused on evidentiary arguments that suggest that poverty and educational constraints precipitate young women's decisions to mother early in the life course.

8 Beutel (2000), Dillard and Pol (1982), Freeman and Rickels (1993), Furstenberg (1976), Hofferth and Moore (1979), Hoffman, Foster, and Furstenberg (1993), and Trussell (1976) all use their empirical analyses to make claims about the economic and educational limitations associated with teen childbearing.

9 Blossfeld and Huinink (1991) use quantitative data from Germany to report on a related finding. In an event history analysis designed to study the processes in which women's educational and employment achievements influence their family formation outcomes, the authors reject the new home economics model's claims about women's growing economic independence being responsible for their delayed marriage and childbearing behavior. Instead, they maintain that it is women's long-term participation in schooling (rather than the particular quality of their human capital investments and their promising career futures) that constitutes their lack of readiness for marriage. Their interpretation of the data is that German women are conforming to norms indicating that young women who are in school are not ready for marriage as opposed to deciding that marriage is less urgent or necessary as long as they have the education and training to take care of themselves financially. Thus, without investigating the specific romantic relationship experiences in which these women are engaged, the authors suggest, as this book has, that normative guidelines communicated through institutional involvements (rather than certain women's ongoing choice of money over love) account for the depressed family formation outcomes of highly educated women.

10 See, for example, Holland and Eisenhart's (1990) description of the ways in which the romantic culture of college campuses as well as the dating activity in which young female students become involved circumscribes educational striving toward high status, male-dominated career fields. Hewlett's (2002) description of the dating difficulties and the family formation postponement associated with her subjects' achievement of high wages and high-status careers uses a negative case to make the same point about the existence of an inverse relationship between reproductive and productive labor.

11 When academic writing points to the lower likelihoods of pregnancy and childbearing that exist among stronger students with higher educational aspirations (for example, Geronimus 1997; Geronimus and Korenman 1992; Luker 1996) or describes the high valuation of motherhood and children that exists in the cultural outlooks of young women in poor neighborhoods (for example, Anderson 1989; Edin and Kefalas 2005), it contributes to the idea that distinctive outlooks and approaches to romance and family formation exist among women who originate in and are destined for the different positions in the class hierarchy.

12 Scholars who debate about whether the limited educational and economic outcomes of women who have children at an early age mean that teen childbearing causes poverty (see endnote 8 above) or that teen childbearing is the intentional action of young women who want babies and who estimate that they will be adequately supported by family members and partners if they continue with a pregnancy at this time (see endnote 7 above) are essentially debating about whether youths' involvement in romance and sexual activity and their decision making in family planning clinics amounts to irrational, misguided, and ill-considered action or to the rational behavior of teens who are unlikely to achieve lots of education and good jobs even if they postpone childbearing. I am arguing that it is difficult for scholars making the first of these arguments to account for the behavior of those women in my sample who enter speedy climax relationships (that is, who take an "irrational" fast track to family formation) after having demonstrated that their approach to family formation is deliberate, rational, and calculating. Scholars making the latter argument are consistent with this book's point here—that women who want babies and/or marriage adopt a speedy climax approach at whatever time they have the opportunity to do so.

13 Arguing that nothing could stop the "passion between the sexes," Malthus believed that an inability to exercise the "moral restraint" of marriage delay and premarital abstinence resulted in overpopulation in the lower classes. His understanding was, further, that the starvation, disease, and high mortality that plagued lower-class settings acted as a "check" on population growth.

14 This is the thrust of much of the literature that points out the negative consequences of teenaged childbearing (see endnote 8 above)—that changing the behavior (that is, waiting until later to have children) will eliminate or significantly improve those outcomes. According to Weeks (2007), Dumont discussed a principle that he named "social capillarity," as far back as 1890. He used this term to describe the social phenomenon in which the postponement and limitation of childbearing supposedly works as a strategy for upward mobility.

15 Scholarship discussing the educational and occupational status gains associated with fertility postponement includes Bloom and Trussell 1984; Blossfeld and Huinink 1991; Caldwell and Schindlmayr 2003; Lehrer and Nerlove

1986; S. Morgan 1991, 2003; Rindfuss, Bumpass, and St. John 1980; Rindfuss, Morgan, and Offutt 1996; Schoen, Kim, Nathanson, Fields, and Astone 1997; Swicegood, Bean, Stephen, and Opitz 1988.

16 In this regard, Hewlett's (2002) description of the marriage and fertility costs associated with the creation of women's high-status careers compares women in a young cohort (ages twenty-eight to forty) to those in an older cohort (ages forty-one to fifty-five). She finds that women in the young cohort expect to have plenty of time to have children later in their reproductive lives. This belief is in no small part due to their observation of media coverage of successful medical interventions allowing women of advanced ages to bear children.

17 As is the case with scholarship on marriage in general, scholarship on interracial marriage does not usually deal much with pre-marital romantic or dating relations. But see a recent article by Feliciano, Robnett, and Komaie (2009) for further evidence of the point that white individuals' race-based rejections of romantic partners is gendered. Their study of Internet dating found that African American women were the most likely rejects of white men, while the most likely rejects of white women were Asian men. Where marriage is concerned, there is some disagreement in the literature about how much gender affected African Americans' likelihood of marrying outside of their race prior to World War II, with the historian Renee Romano (2003) maintaining that African American men and women had relatively equivalent rates of marrying white spouses and Tucker and Mitchell-Kernan (1990) indicating that, with the exception of a few states and a few special locations, black men were consistently more likely to marry outside of their race than women. However, there is scholarly agreement that since the civil rights era, African American males have had a clear "advantage" in out-marriage (Kalmijn 1998). The more recent investigations indicate that black men are more than two times as likely to marry outside of their race than black women (Kalmijn 1993; Tucker and Mitchell-Kernan 1990). This gender imbalance has been explained by the fact that traditional gender roles permit black men with high wages and occupational status to offer these attractive economic traits to white women of lesser means in a "trade" for their more highly valued racial traits. The traditional male as breadwinner, female as homemaker model of marriage precludes highly educated black women from making the same trade (Kalmijn 1998). Gender imbalances in interracial marriage among other groups have also been linked to opportunity—with Asian American females' higher rates of out-marriage being to some degree explained by white males' presence at military bases in Japan and Korea and with some abatement in the Asian gender imbalance in out-marriage when Asian war brides are excluded from analyses (Kalmijn 1998; Labov and Jacobs 1986). Opportunity is not a relevant explanation for the gender imbalance in African Americans' out-dating discussed in Sparkle's and Sierra's descriptions of campus life since both black

men and women are exposed to non-black potential dating partners on these campuses.

18 To the extent that one believes that the things I am here calling black women's "romantic desirability," black male's "advantage" in romantic settings, or even "marriage challenge" and "marital attraction" can be quantified and objectively measured, then work by Lichter, LeClere, and McLaughlin 1991; Lichter, McLaughlin, Kephart, and Landry 1992; Schoen and Wooldredge 1989; and South 1991 illustrates black women's low level of "desirability" and black males' "advantage" in romantic markets. Using data on sex ratios, population size of race-gender groups, average earnings of males and females in local areas, availability of cash from welfare in those same areas, and individuals' spousal preferences, these authors make assessments about the numbers of potential partners that are available to black women (as well as individuals in other race-gender groupings), about the degree to which men in their and other racial groups find them attractive as marital partners, about their own preferences for marriage partners, and about the degree to which they might compromise on those preferences because they are challenged in marriage. While Schoen and Wooldredge's (1989) calculations indicate that black women in their study emerged as the least attractive marriage partners (that is, given their size in the local population, they were the least often chosen as marriage partners), and Lichter and colleagues (Lichter, LeClere, and McLaughlin 1991; Lichter, McLaughlin, Kephart, and Landry 1992) indicate that black women face disadvantageous sex ratios and pools of employed and salaried potential partners, South (1991) maintains that these women's responses to survey questions demonstrate that they remain less willing to marry men with non-normative traits or of low status than white women. South's conclusion argues that black women's marital expectations are out of line with the demographic realities that they face. This book's point with respect to these quantifications and measures is that they underestimate the degree to which preferences and dating and marriage behavior are constantly being constructed and reconstructed by the race-maintaining behaviors and actions of others.

19 See, for example, Roberts 1997, 2002; and Solinger 2001.

20 Glenn (2002) links the more contemporary processes discussed by Brodkin (1999) and P. Collins (2004) to the construction of "free labor" and "U.S. citizenship" during the nineteenth century. It was here that white men's privileges in labor and their more or less exclusive right to vote was constructed by restricting non-whites and women from these privileges based on race- and gender-ascribed characteristics. In this moment, black women's lack of dependent femininity maintained their status as exploitable labor and constrained their access to support as mothers and dependents.

21 Edin and Kefalas's (2005) study of marriage—or rather, non-marriage—among

low-income women repeatedly suggests that the women in their sample indicate that male partners are more interested in marrying than the women themselves are. These women's marriage challenge lies in the unattractive characteristics and behaviors of their partners (for example, violent behavior, unemployment and minimal economic resources, cheating behavior) and in the high prerequisites to marriage (for example, stable income, independent home) that they impose upon themselves. In contrast, the data on relationship progress in this book indicates that significant portions of the sample of highly educated black women have a history of romantic relationships in which their partners have demonstrated low interest in committing to marrying them. Anderson (1989) blames lack of interest in marriage among men in his sample on their lower-class status and the conditions in poor black communities. In a few cases, women in my sample were in relationships with poor young men residing in poor communities, but there were several romantic relationships where men who were not poor and did not reside in poor communities remained uninterested in committed romantic partnerships with my subjects.

Chapter 4. Sex

1 According to investigators of young women's sexual and contraceptive behavior (for example, Manlove and Terry-Humen 2007; Manning, Longmore, and Giordano 2000), younger ages at first sex are associated with a lower likelihood of using contraceptives at first sex and an increased risk of sexually transmitted infection and adolescent pregnancy and childbearing.

2 In a quantitative study assessing the relative importance of school-based norms and parents for adolescents' involvement in sexual activity, Castronova (2004) finds that a higher level of familial interaction and the presence of both parents in the household can lower the likelihood that a girl has sex by almost one half (that is, from 32 to 18 percent). This effect was significantly more important than attendance at a school with a permissive or restrictive norm environment. Castronova's claims that children are responding to parental wishes that they delay sexual activity and that parental rules or moments when they transmit their conservative values to their children may be more important than peer influence in determining youth sexual activity seem to conflict with my discussion of Janet's experiences here. However, the study does underscore the point that the moment of sexual initiation is likely to be perceived as a moment of emancipation from parental influence. Other studies that indicate that parental attachment reduces the likelihood of early sexual initiation include Pearson, Muller, and Frisco 2006 and L'Engle and Jackson 2008, both of whose findings are mostly relevant for white as opposed to African American youth. Hahm, Lahiff, and Barreto 2006 finds that less acculturated Asian American women (but not men) as well as those women (not men)

with medium levels of attachment to parents were less likely to have sexual experience.

3 Also see Warren, Santelli, Everett, Kann, Collins, Cassell, Morris, and Kolbe 1998, a study that supports the racial differences in age at sexual initiation found here. Of the high-school students studied, African Americans were the most likely to be sexually experienced. Similarly Browning, Leventhal, and Brooks-Gunn (2004) found that African Americans in their study of youth in Chicago neighborhoods had lower ages at sexual initiation than whites and Latinos. (No significant differences between whites and Latinos in age at sexual debut were observed in this study.) Moreover, they were able to explain the racial difference that remained after demographic, peer, and family effects were controlled in their model by including neighborhood-level concentrated poverty in their model. According to Pearson, Muller, and Frisco (2006) and L'Engle and Jackson (2008), African Americans appear less susceptible to the types of parental and school influences that delay white youths' sexual debuts. Although Ompad, Strathdee, Celentano, Latkin, Poduska, Kellam, and Ialongo (2006) share the early African American initiation finding with the aforementioned scholarly works, the authors also found that white women were the earliest to perform oral sex.

4 Data from this sample as well as other qualitative and quantitative research supports the point that college-bound and non-college-bound black teens are more likely to have contact with and influence on one another than are white and black youth who share high educational tracks and/or high academic achievement. Ethnographers of the school-based peer group (for example, Bettie 2003; Fordham and Ogbu 1986; Ogbu 2003; Ogbu and Simons 1998) and of youth experiences in black middle-class communities (for example, Pattillo-McCoy 1999), as well as quantitative scholars of the influence of race on college matriculation (for example, Massey, Charles, Lundy, and Fischer 2003), indicate that racial status, racially segregated residential settings, and tracked schools or classroom settings facilitate interactions and influences among students of color that cut across class and academic achievement levels in ways that are distinctive from the ways in which whites are "shielded" from their same-race peers who are of a lower class or who "perform" educational underachievement. Teitler and Weiss (2000) maintain that school effects on sexual initiation are larger than neighborhood effects and that school effects are tied to the racial composition of schools, with predominantly black schools having lower ages at initiation than schools where the student body is largely white. Moreover, there is much more white variation in type of school attendance (public versus private) than there is black variation. The explanation of some of the racial differences between blacks and non-blacks regarding the age at virginity loss by black youths' greater experience of concentrated neighborhood poverty (see Browning, Leventhal, and Brooks-

Gunn 2004) lends support to the idea that blacks' cues about sexual initiation come from their frequent interaction with other youth in African American communities.

5 Massey and Denton's (1993) work on segregation indicates that poor white individuals live under much less segregated circumstances than those who are black and those who are black and poor.

6 Massey, Charles, Lundy, and Fischer (2003) find this exact ratio in their study comparing black, Latino, Asian, and white students at selective colleges and universities. In their study, they also found that Latino women outnumbered Latino men at selective colleges, but the relative size of Latino women in the population of Latino college students is smaller than the relative size of black women in the population of black college students. Moreover, college enrollment of white men is currently declining when compared to the enrollment of white women, but male to female ratios among whites have not gotten as small as those that exist among black and Latino college matriculates.

7 Bogle (2008) indicates that women face difficulty establishing emotionally intimate relationships with men as well as losses of status for unconcealed interest in sex. With respect to the latter, she contrasts the loss of status and power within heterosexual relations that women experience with the low penalties males receive for similar behaviors.

8 Waite and Gallagher (2000) summarize data indicating that sex is more frequent among the married and cohabiting.

9 In qualitative descriptions of white college students' "hooking up" for single evenings of physical intimacy that may just include kissing but may also proceed as far as oral sex and/or intercourse, Bogle (2008) and Stepp (2007) describe women's low power to turn a "hookup" into a more long-term committed romantic partnership. Their works suggest that the practice of hooking up and women's inability to push for long-term romance on contemporary college campuses is at least in part related to white women's new majority status in these settings and to a pressure to delay serious romance and family formation that is implied by women's newfound access to the high-status careers traditionally reserved for men. The first of these issues (that is, majority status in their respective racial groups) should affect African American and Hispanic women on college campuses more so than white women, since there is evidence that the proportion of women in these ethnic and racial categories is actually higher than it is among white students. If female-dominated gender imbalances presage women's limited power to negotiate for committed romantic partnerships, then black (and Hispanic) ethno-racial status exacerbates this problem. But note that neither of these writers indicates that such a straightforward relationship between sex ratios, racial communities, and the practice of hooking up exists: both authors maintain that they found little or no evidence of African American participation in the hookup culture. Since graduation signaled white males' and females' return to a pattern of dating

and courtship in which heterosexual partners get to know one another for a while before entering committed romantic relationships and intercourse, then white women's campus-based gender disadvantage in romance seems to reflect their educational and class status achievement and recent higher educational gains relative to white men. However, the high levels of celibacy among black women in the NSFG (NCHS 1995), the qualitative data from this study's sample, and the books on hooking up discussed here all indicate that racial status lowers black women's sexual activity—whether it is "hookup" sex or otherwise—and that there is little reason to expect processes that increase white women's involvement in committed romantic partnerships after college to operate similarly for black women.

10 For a related finding, see Marin, Kirby, Hudes, Coyle, and Gomez 2006, which finds that sexual initiation and involvement among youth are highly related to both past and present romantic involvement with boyfriends or girlfriends.

11 According to East 1998, Hispanic girls fully expect to make transitions into first sex, marriage, and motherhood at early ages and in rapid succession.

12 Scholars utilizing the Fragile Families and Child Wellbeing survey (for example, Waller and McLanahan 2005) are investigating the degree to which nonmarital childbearing leads to later marriage in the contemporary era.

13 This is the logic of writing that argues that young women with high educational and career aspirations are the likely users of contraception and abortion (for example, Abma, Martinez, Mosher, and Dawson 2004; Abma and Sonenstein 2002; Edin and Kefalas 2005; Luker 1996). Such writing implies and outwardly exclaims that these women are delaying or trying to circumvent the attachment to reproductive labor that would limit their achievement of educational and occupational goals.

Chapter 5. Contraception

1 Historical study in demography (for example, Coale 1969; K. Davis 1963; Hajnal 1965) reports that this is the method of fertility limitation that was employed in western Europe (as well as other areas of the industrialized world) prior to the advent of widespread use of modern birth control methods.

2 Demographers discussing breastfeeding (for example, Becker and Ahmed 2001; Palloni and Kephart 1989) are convinced enough of its efficacy in limiting fertility through child spacing that they expect the introduction of modern contraception to have the short-term effect of raising fertility. This is because the changes in patterns of breastfeeding and postpartum celibacy that accompany modernization might proceed at a faster pace than the practice of skilled contraceptive use. Note that Bledsoe, Banja, and Hill 1998 indicates that as modern birth control devices have become more acceptable in these contexts, their use has not in all cases signaled the advent of more planning behavior. Instead, birth control pills might be used after a "reproductive mis-

hap" (miscarriage, stillbirth, or infant death) in order to "rest" the body and rebuild its capacity to produce more successful pregnancies. The earlier prevalence of long-term breastfeeding and/or postpartum celibacy as methods of child spacing was supported by a similar logic about the body's capacity.

3 In some literature on teen childbearing, both abortion and childbearing are discussed as the "problematic" or accidental outcomes resulting from insufficient control of or plans to address teens' sexual impulses. In this regard, the team of authors (led by Elise Jones) that produced *Teenage Pregnancy in Industrialized Countries* (1988) makes an argument about the ambivalence of U.S. policy with regard to adolescent sexual activity. They maintain that the elevated rates of both teen childbearing and abortion in the United States relative to other industrialized nations can be explained by this ambivalence about providing teens with and encouraging their use of contraception.

4 For documentation of communist Eastern Europe's profuse use of abortion in the face of a limited supply of contraceptive products see, for example, Okolski 1983.

5 Weeks's (2007) introductory population studies textbook references Dumont and describes his social capillarity concept.

6 Demographic studies making this observation include Caldwell and Ware 1977; Chaudhury 1978; Cleland and Rodriguez 1988; Prada and Ojeda 1987; Shah, Shah, and Radovanovic 1998; Shapiro and Tambashe 1994; and Weinberger, Lloyd, and Blanc 1989.

7 A list of studies reporting on the influence of education (including educational achievement, grades or school success, educational aspirations, attitudes toward school, and parental education) finds that those students with higher achievement and grades, as well as more positive attitudes about school and higher educational aspirations, are more likely to use contraception. Included in this list are Abma, Martinez, Mosher, and Dawson 2004; Abma and Sonenstein 2002; Culwell and Feinglass 2007; Dawson 1986; Heavey, Moysich, Hyland, Druschel, and Sill 2008; Manlove and Terry-Humen 2007; Manlove, Ryan, and Franzetta 2003; Manning, Longmore, and Giordano 2000; Shah, Shah, and Radovanovic 1998; Shapiro and Tambashe 1994; and Weinberger, Lloyd, and Blanc 1989.

8 Alexander Sanger's (2007) article on the eugenic aspects of his grandmother Margaret Sanger's family planning activism explains how her early twentieth-century efforts to enable women with reproductive services and the ability to control their fertility were supposed to work. Contraceptives were meant to support women's improvement of their economic circumstances by allowing them to plan their fertility around or forgo fertility during moments of material disadvantage. He points out that his grandmother claimed that women were "natural eugenicists"—that given adequate access to birth control information and products, they themselves would prevent their children from being born into poverty or a diseased condition. Inequality in contra-

ceptive knowledge and access between elites and women of lower status remain in the contemporary era. For example, Foster, Ralph, Arons, Brindis, and Harper 2007 found that despite increases in Californian women's knowledge of emergency contraception between 1999 and 2004, disparities between social groups with respect to knowledge about this newer method remained. Foreign-born Hispanic women, women below the poverty level, and women without high-school diplomas were the least likely to know about emergency contraception. Other studies that discuss educational and class disparities in women's contraceptive knowledge include Foster, Harper, Bley, Mikanda, Induni, Saviano, and Stewart 2004; and Jackson, Schwarz, Freedman, and Darney 2000.

9 In this regard, see discussions of adolescent pregnancy that cover subjects' beliefs or assessments that postponing childbearing is undesirable and makes little sense (for example, Edin and Kefalas 2005; Geronimus 1997; Geronimus and Korenman 1992; Luker 1996; Trussell 1988), since it is unlikely to significantly alter their educational and economic futures or since it may threaten their access to networks of support available during their youth.

10 Among the reasons Mia lists for forgoing contraception is a distrust of hormonal birth control that requires prescriptions from physicians. Using survey data from a national, random sample of African Americans, Thorburn and Bogart 2005b found that females' non-use of birth control requiring healthcare provider contact and males' non-use of birth control of any kind were associated with individuals' belief in the idea that the delivery of birth control to African Americans was part of a genocidal conspiracy or the racist use of untested or unsafe birth control methods on African Americans. Although the study mentioned that the prevalence of these beliefs was relatively high, Mia was my only subject who brought up this issue specifically in her discussion of her own contraceptive decision making.

11 "Fecundable" denotes capable of becoming pregnant.

12 Racial differences in contraceptive use are not a new finding. Studies observing that black and Hispanic women have lower contraceptive usage rates than whites include Abma, Martinez, Mosher, and Dawson 2004; Ford, Sohn, and Lepkowski 2001; Manlove, Ryan, and Franzetta 2003; Manning, Longmore, and Giordano 2000; Milan, Ethier, Lewis, Kershaw, Niccolai, and Ickovics 2006; and Stephen, Rindfuss, and Bean 1988. But these differences tend to remain (sometimes as necessary controls in an explanatory model) largely unexplained by theoretical discussion in the study. The exceptions are cases where the racial differences that remain after class has been controlled are explicitly or implicitly framed as reflective of the aspects of class that are unobserved in the particular study. For example, remaining racial differences might be due to the lower or working-class backgrounds of black and Hispanic women who have equivalent education and income to the white women to whom they are being compared.

13 Luker's (1975) study of the "contraceptive risk-taking" that leads to abortion finds that contraceptive inconsistency can be linked to women's inability to assess the quality of and likely direction of romantic relationships. In the cases that she describes, women end up in abortion clinics because their pregnancies forced partners into critical conversations; these critical conversations enabled the women's discoveries that their relationships were not proceeding toward greater commitment or in the direction that they would like. Thus, in this formulation, it is women's lack of power or ability to negotiate for romantic commitments or desired romantic outcomes in day-to-day relations with partners that leads to inconsistent contraceptive practice. Furthermore, research regarding women's negotiations with partners for condom use reports similar findings. Studies reporting lower likelihood of condom or contraceptive use among individuals with partners who are different from them in terms of age (for example, Ford, Sohn, and Lepkowski 2001; Manlove and Terry-Humen 2007) also support the idea that inconsistency is related to the differing interests, concerns, and/or power of partners in heterosexual romantic relationships.

14 Luker (1996) has indicated that it is difficult to measure how wanted a pregnancy is, especially retrospectively where an unwanted or unintended pregnancy may have resulted in a wanted child. She maintains that surveys prior to the 1988 cycle of the NSFG have asked the questions in a way that made it difficult for women to describe pregnancies as wanted if they were not planned or intended. The choices offered in this cycle of the NSFG are a bit better, allowing individuals to say that they wanted a child but had imagined they would have it later (for example, mistimed, too early), and that they were unsure or indifferent about it. They seem to allow for the range of possibilities observed by Luker and by Edin and Kefalas (2005), who argued that their study's poorer, single mothers also were not planning but were often indifferent about pregnancies or wanted them a bit later than they came. At the same time, these new survey answer options do not solve the problems with retrospective data collection. Here, I have used an expanded definition of wantedness with unwanted, mistimed, and unsure pregnancies all being placed in the numerator because of my focus on educated elites and my exploration of theoretical and empirical claims about their planning behavior. While readers might dispute the notion that an answer of "unsure" should classify a pregnancy as "unwanted," it seems unlikely that the "unsure" answer should place it in the category of a "planned" pregnancy.

15 Reports on the contraceptive success stories associated with sex education programming include Christopher 1995; Dawson 1986; Frost and Forrest 1995; Kirby, Barth, Leland, and Fetro 1991; Mueller, Gavin, and Kulkarni 2008.

16 Aspy, Vesely, Oman, Rodine, Marshall, Fluhr, and McLeroy 2006; and Hutchinson and Cooney 1998 are studies that have these conflicting findings: parental

conversations about sex and pregnancy had positive, negative, and no effect on contraceptive usage.

17 Use effectiveness is measured with failure rates under the actual conditions that individuals use contraceptive devices and includes failures associated with improper use or even with individuals' inconsistent use of an adopted method. This contrasts with effectiveness measured by failure rates under conditions of "perfect" use (for example, leaving out the experiences of subjects who forget to take pills or who sometimes remove diaphragms sooner after intercourse than the directions recommend). In this regard, Trussell's (2004) calculations of contraceptive failure rates distinguish between "typical use" and "perfect use."

18 See Trussell 2004 on the point that prescription methods that require ongoing contact with health-care providers (and that are consequently not "silent" methods) are more effective than nonprescription methods under both actual and perfect use conditions.

19 Heavey, Moysich, Hyland, Druschel, and Sill (2008) are responsible for the finding that African Americans preferred the "invisible" injectables over other hormonal contraceptive methods like the pill. But note that African Americans still remain less likely than whites and Hispanics to choose prescription methods that require contact with health-care providers. (See, for example, Culwell and Feinglass 2007.)

20 Although quantitative study indicates that women's contraceptive practice improves (in terms of use, consistency of use, and skill) with age (see Glei 1999; the summary in Luker 1996; Warren, Powell, Morris, Jackson, and Hamilton 1988; and Zelnick and Kantner 1980), in my sample, I have found that where contraceptive inconsistency was based in women's rejection of their own non marital sexual activity or their desire to present chaste sexual selves, it did not tend to disappear with age. At the same time, there were cases like Marie's where contraceptive use improved once the women were married and thereby "legitimate" sexual actors. Glei (1999) finds that both age and relationship stability (as in cohabitation or marriage versus being single) improve the odds of consistent use of effective contraceptive methods.

21 Zimmerman, Noar, Feist-Price, Dekthar, Cupp, Anderman, and Lock (2007) are among the scholars studying condom use for disease prevention who find that the taking of preparatory steps prior to intercourse is a strong predictor of condom use among black and white males and females. Their research argues that impulsivity is the problem barring individuals from more consistent use of contraception. Trussell 1988 and Glei 1999 are other studies pointing to low contraceptive use among those who fail to anticipate or plan intercourse. But the explanation for contraceptive inconsistency offered above suggests that the degreed black women are not so much impulsively involved in sexual acts as they are planning not to plan sex. In contrast to the negative finding

of Zimmerman, Noar, Feist-Price, Dekthar, Cupp, Anderman, and Lock 2007 where the effect of impulsivity is concerned, this book's findings suggest that the opposite of planning is not impulsivity, but rather strategic action that would both minimize sexual activity and enable individuals to represent any sexual activity that actually occurred as unplanned.

22 Although studies indicating that religiosity delays sexual initiation but lowers the contraceptive use of these delayed initiators (Bruckner and Bearman 2005; Cooksey, Rindfuss, and Guilkey 1996) generally support the findings discussed here, I have not invoked them in the discussion above because I believe that religion in these articles remains a bit too narrow in its scope of influence. These studies distinguish between the religious like Tamika and the non-religious like Terri too radically, indicating that individual belief or voluntary ritual participation and self-segregation are ultimately at issue in sexual and contraceptive decision making and not gendered norms around chastity imposed (perhaps in part but not exclusively because of institutionalized religion) on a more broad cross-section of the population of degreed black women.

23 Furstenberg 1976 and Manning, Longmore, and Giordano 2000 both found that those in casual sexual relationships are less likely to use contraception than those who are involved in committed relationships. The opposite trend is observable in a study of condom use to prevent disease by Ku, Sonenstein and Pleck (1994): condom use declined over the course of long-term relationships; and men appeared more likely to use condoms in relationships that ended before cohabitation, engagement, or marriage.

24 In a summary of research findings explaining why teenagers fail to use contraception, Luker (1996, chapter 6) lists unpredictability of intercourse as one of the risk factors for inconsistent contraceptive use.

25 I talk with the students about this example because it is an impressive example from one of the textbooks that I have used—*Statistics* by Freedman, Pisani, Purves, and Adhikari (1998, 16–19).

26 In *Promises I Can Keep*, Edin and Kefalas (2005) spend a great deal of data-describing time and energy trying to convince readers that black, Hispanic, and white women in poor neighborhoods want their early pregnancies, want motherhood early in the life course and earlier in the life course than marriage, and cannot imagine their lives without the children that they have.

Chapter 6. Abortion

1 Edin and Kefalas (2005) use data from black, Hispanic, and white women residing in poor neighborhoods in Camden, New Jersey and Philadelphia, Pennsylvania to make the argument that such women highly value motherhood and see little reason to postpone it until later in the life course or after marriage. The authors' explanation for early childbearing in poor urban contexts

links this strong desire for children to sampled women's concomitant belief that their futures prior to pregnancy were bleak with respect to education and employment. Thus, this description communicates the point that for these subjects, motherhood is both high in value and low in cost. Similarly, Luker's (1996) discussion of teen childbearing as well as scholarship from Anderson (1989), Freeman and Rickels (1993), Geronimus (1987, 1997), Kaplan (1997), and Zelnick and Kantner (1980) suggest that the willingness to follow through with early pregnancies is tied to young women's own estimation that postponement of childbearing is unlikely to change their disadvantaged circumstances and may even limit the availability of support for childbearing and childrearing.

2 Hertz (2006) maintains that compulsory motherhood—or the hegemonic belief that all women want to become mothers—lies behind her unmarried subjects' desire to pursue motherhood. Exacerbated by the contemporary era's proliferation of reproductive enhancement technologies, compulsory motherhood maintains its hold on women even as alternative, productive sector roles have become available to them. Moreover, Hertz maintains, as I have here, that motherhood defines women as women in ways that high-status careers or other accomplishments in the productive sector, in and of themselves, cannot. She argues that motherhood "has always been a critical status worthy achievement" (5). Hewlett (2002) describes a similar longing for motherhood or drive to mother that plagues the childless career achievers in her study. And S. Morgan's (2003) claim that "low fertility" is a "problem we want to have" as opposed to a "crisis" (600) is buttressed by descriptions of analyses suggesting that despite large scale economic and social changes, individuals continue to desire first, second, and even third births for the purpose of establishing and building loving familial relationships. Here again, the findings from this book's study confirm that women with professional status in modern societies are interested in this type of family building to produce these love outcomes.

3 In this regard, see Brodkin 1999; E. Glenn 2002; Roberts 1997, 2002; and Solinger 2001, all of which make the claim that esteemed motherhood and this kind of femininity are racial privileges of whiteness. They are denied to women of color who work at jobs in low levels of the productive sector and who "produce" or give birth to children who constitute the exploitable labor pool.

4 Moreover, Goffman (1963) would describe such inappropriate behaviors as "discrediting," in that they communicate to others that a person that they perceived to be normal or worthy of a certain amount of esteem might actually belong to a "discredited" group. These behaviors thereby invite stigma and constitute failure at managing the "spoiled identity."

5 In *Dubious Conceptions*, Luker (1996) describes the way in which teen childbearing garnered the attention of policymakers' negative sanctioning, even as young women in sectors of the population that used to be able to respond to

teen pregnancy by marrying their boyfriends struggled with rising inequality, rising divorce rates, increases in the availability of birth control and abortion, and women's large scale involvement in the labor force. Scholars whose documentation of the educational and employment costs associated with teen childbearing constitutes one aspect of the chorus sanctioning that behavior include Beutel (2000), Dillard and Pol (1982), Freeman and Rickels (1993), Furstenberg (1976), Hofferth and Moore (1979), Hoffman, Foster, and Furstenberg (1993), and Trussell (1976).

6   There is a strand of the literature on teen childbearing that sets young women up as rational actors—as individuals pursuing their desire for children and doing so while incurring as few costs as possible. The authors of these studies maintain that the circumstances of young women who bear children as teens are characterized by such limitation that early childbearing costs them little in terms of education and employment and may even gain them some parenting support from elder kin who remain healthy and alive during their early reproductive years. See endnote 1 above.

7   Not only have I taught and advised students in day and evening programs who are in exactly that situation, but Luker (1996) maintains that in the contemporary period, high schools with programs for teens with children have become a much more visible and utilized aspect of the social landscape.

8   Here, the scholars making these suggestions are those who argue that early childbearing limits young women's educational and economic achievements (see endnote 5 above) and those who link high-achieving women's late and limited fertility to education- and career-related family formation postponement (for example, Bloom and Trussell 1984; Blossfeld and Huinink 1991; Caldwell and Schindlmayr 2003; Forest, Moen, and Dempster-McClain 1995; Lehrer and Nerlove 1986; S. Morgan 1991, 2003; Rindfuss, Bumpass, and St. John 1980; Rindfuss, Morgan, Offutt 1996; Schoen, Kim, Nathanson, Fields, and Astone 1997; Swicegood, Bean, Stephen, and Opitz 1988; Torr and Short 2004; and Wilkie 1981).

9   The title of this section contains the title of and an adaptation of some of the words from Gwen Guthrie's hit song of 1986, "Ain't Nothin' Goin' on but the Rent." It was written and produced by Guthrie and released as a single on Polydor Records.

10 Joan Williams's (2000) text, entitled *Unbending Gender*, is about the organization of the productive labor market around domesticity. This means that good jobs that are economically rewarding and interesting and/or challenging are structured around the expectation that the workers who fill them can work excessively long hours each week because they have wives who take care of the labor in the home, particularly the labor associated with the care of the workers' children. Williams's argument is that this gendered organization of the labor market accounts for women's depressed labor market outcomes with

respect to employment and income and for the relatively low labor market outcomes of male and female workers who assume responsibility for meeting their children's day-to-day needs. To the extent that Williams's analysis is correct, Cheryl's pregnant belly, set off by her naked ring finger, makes it clear to potential employers that she is not what Williams refers to as an "ideal worker." Other authors who discuss the depressing effects of women's status as mothers on their employment outcomes include Budig and England (2001), Casper, McLanahan, and Garfinkel (1994), Christopher, England, Smeeding, and Phillips (2002), Correll, Benard, and Paik (2007), McLanahan, Sorensen, and Watson (1989), Okamoto and England (1999), Ridgeway and Correll (2004), Sewell, Hauser, and Wolf (1980), Trappe and Rosenfeld (2000), and Waldfogel (1997, 1998a, 1998b).

11 In discussions of the social factors supporting the movement of national populations from high fertility to low fertility regimes, Caldwell (1976, 1980) argued that change in the direction of the intergenerational flow of wealth is a key causal factor in this transition. In other words, he makes the point that when children change from being free laborers who provide wealth to family enterprises (for example, farms) to being luxury goods requiring extensive financial commitments to rear, educate, and allow them to develop to their full potential, this is the point at which fertility declines. Here, a similar argument is being made about abortion being more likely in situations where women see performances of motherhood as legitimate only insofar as these performances can reflect parental ability to finance the specific tasks associated with elite motherhood.

12 Ventura and Bachrach (2000) found that a third of all U.S. births in 1999 were to unmarried women. Although there has been little change in this figure since 1994, the 1994 and 1999 figures reflect consistent increases during the prior half century, with such rates starting in 1940 at just under 4 percent. In the more recent period (between 1980 and 1999), Ventura and Bachrach show increases in the proportions of births to single women across black, Hispanic, and white populations. For black women, births to single women were already the majority of births (56 percent) in 1980 but nonetheless increased to 69 percent in 1999. Among Hispanic women, the fraction of births to single women went from 24 to 42 percent over the period, and among white women, the movement was from 9 to 22 percent. White nonmarital childbearing rates (that is, the rate at which unmarried women decide to have children) have been rising for most of this period. Despite stabilization of these rates in the mid- to late 1990s, the percentage of births to single white women has gone up because there were higher fractions of single women in the population. In contrast, most of the recent period has reflected a relative decline in black nonmarital childbearing rates; it reflects a decline that remains masked (when the measure is the fraction of births to single women) by declines in both mar-

riage and marital childbearing rates among black women. Thus, Hertz's (2006) study of mostly white women's decisions to bear children while single emerges as an investigation of significant change in white family formation patterns— for example, a more than doubling of the fraction of births to unmarried white women.

13 Hertz (2006) and Hewlett (2002) both maintain that women have not let go of the dream of and responsibility for family, despite a women's movement that allowed for their participation in the traditionally more lucrative "male" careers. Indeed, Hertz's claim is that this holding on to family has produced the voluntary single motherhood of a myriad of financially independent women—some of whom are more career accomplished than others, but all of whom assume a responsibility for family that goes beyond taking care of one that exists but also demands that one be brought into existence. Here, I am agreeing that professional elite women, whether married or not, maintain an interest in family. But I am also arguing that the elite motherhood that they desire often implies the use of abortion.

14 Here, it is Edin and Kefalas's (2005) work that is instructive. Although they do not go so far as to maintain that particular motherhood meanings predict early nonmarital motherhood among the poor, they do dedicate a chapter of their book to these women's descriptions of a version of motherhood that centers on the idea of sacrifice. Thus, I am drawing attention to the intimate ties that exist between particular understandings of motherhood and decisions to follow through with pregnancies.

15 Analyses of differences in abortion experience, between those who do and those who do not attain college degrees, are limited because of the way in which data on abortion is collected and because of the relatively high incidence of abortion to youth who might eventually complete a college degree but who do not at the time of abortion hold one. Nonetheless, when class measures are available, those women of higher status tend to be more likely to terminate pregnancies: this is especially true early in the reproductive life course. For example, using neighborhood income as a measure of class, South and Baumer (2001) find that adolescents in low-income neighborhoods are less likely to terminate pregnancies than those in wealthier neighborhoods. In this study, as well as in a study by Cooksey (1990), youth with more highly educated parents were more likely to terminate their pregnancies than those whose parents' educational achievement was low. Furthermore, in an investigation of the influence of legal restrictions and provider availability on abortion, Gius (2007) reports that those who have completed high school are more likely to terminate pregnancies than those who have not. Trent and Powell-Griner (1991) reported that among the unmarried, rates of pregnancy termination went up as education level increased, but no such effect was observable among married women. They also found that among the childless, women

were the likeliest to abort if they were college educated and the least likely to abort if they had a high-school education or less. Finally, although Medoff (2000) finds that black women with college degrees have a lower "demand" for abortion than those with less education, the demand measure is not conditional on pregnancy (as are the measures in this book and the aforementioned studies): thus, Medoff's interpretation of this finding is that education raises degreed women's contraceptive use (lowering their pregnancy rates) to a greater extent than it raises their demand for abortion.

16 Several analyses of family policy including investigations of adoption, abortion, contraception, and foster care policy (Luker 1996; Roberts 1997, 2002: and Solinger 2001), analyses of Welfare and Welfare Reform (Hays 2003; Katz 1989), and even exploration of the disbursal of employment, housing, and educational benefits to military veterans (Brodkin 1999) include discussions of the representations of black women who are mothers and/or mothers-to-be, who are at the same time financially impoverished and unmarried or abandoned by spouses, and who depend upon the state. The blackness of these images informs the racial aspects of the arguments and conclusions in these texts. More generalized discussion of the proliferation of these images and their diffuse affects in localized spaces have been authored by Collins (1991, 2004), Nagel (2003), and St. Jean and Feagin (1998).

17 In addition to Luker's (1996, 86) text, this suggestion is made in work by Brodkin (1999), Hays (2003), and Katz (1989).

18 *Dubious Conceptions*, Luker's (1996) analysis of the way in which teen pregnancy becomes a social problem on the U.S. national radar and of the way in which teen women become the blameworthy culprits of debilitating family poverty and expanding welfare rolls, contains the most comprehensive explication of the way in which a myriad of social problems can and do coalesce around a symbolic black woman. However Katz's (1989) description of the federal shift from warring on poverty to warring on welfare also connects race-gender symbols to macro-level policy. The analyses in this book attempt to bring discussions like these down to the micro-level by illustrating the effects of such symbols on micro-level interactions and individuals' decisions. As Jhally and Lewis's (1992) and Bonilla-Silva's (2003) analyses connect white and black individuals' beliefs about African Americans to their acceptance or rejection of certain anti-racist and anti-poverty policies, so too does this book attempt to show black women's responses to race-gender representations. Moreover, it undertakes this project around arenas formerly understood as personal (for example, childbearing) rather than public (for example, politics, employment).

19 Race making is a term that is only meaningful if one accepts the point that race is socially constructed. The above definition of socially constructed race is an attempt to summarize Cornell and Hartmann's (2007) much longer and more

systematic articulation of race and its distinction from ethnicity. My project
relies on data from women who self-identified into black, white, and "other"
racial categories and indicated "yes" or "no" on an Hispanic ethnicity question on the NSFG (NCHS 1995) survey. The analyses compare non-Hispanic
black women to women placed in the non-Hispanic white category and to
those placed in the Hispanic category. Nonetheless, the project treats race
as constructed within the three societal levels articulated by Evelyn Nakano
Glenn (2002): these are institutional structures, day-to-day, micro-level interactions, and representations of reality. Thus, as Brodkin (1999) systematically
describes in her own tale of *How Jews Became White Folks and What That Says
about Race in America*, mass media, scientific, or policy-making descriptions
of reality that link black women to poverty through nonmarital childbearing
(that is, representation) play as important a role in race making as do laws intended to support single parent families headed by white widows with higher
levels of financial assistance than those headed by women who became single
mothers through nonmarital childbearing (that is, structure); and they play as
important a role in race making as human resource officers who suspect that a
black woman who is a single parent might turn out to be a more irresponsible
worker than a white man whose family status is unknown (that is, micro-level
interaction).

20 Numerous analyses document black women's elevated level of involvement
with abortion. Hamilton and Ventura (2006) describe racial differences in the
use of abortion between 1960 and 2002. Noting that data on abortions tend
to be of lower quality than that of fertility, they report that a cohort of black
women who experienced the year 2000's abortion rates during their lifetimes
would have experienced about 1.75 abortions per woman. This compares to almost 0.9 of an abortion per Hispanic woman and almost 0.4 of an abortion per
non-Hispanic white woman. These figures reflect reductions in abortion since
1980. Using data from U.S. women of reproductive age, from abortion clinics,
and from abortion patients, Jones, Singh, Finer, and Frohwirth's (2006) investigation of repeat abortions in the United States finds that African American
women are overrepresented among abortion patients. In their study, black
women make up less than 15 percent of the population of women of reproductive age but are almost 33 percent of the abortion patients and almost 38
percent of those receiving repeat abortions; white women's representation is
about 30 percent lower among abortion and repeat abortion patients than it
is in the population of women of reproductive age. (Hispanic women were
also overrepresented among abortion patients, but these distributional differences were not statistically significant.) Furthermore, in Jones, Singh, Finer,
and Frohwirth's (2006) model predicting the incidence of repeat abortions
and controlling for age, education, poverty level, and marital status, black
racial status is associated with statistically significant increases in the odds of

being an abortion patient who has had prior abortions. The documentation of these racial differences notwithstanding, neither of these analyses examines the possible effects of an interaction between race and education on abortion as this book attempts to do here. With respect to education level differences, the study by Jones, Singh, Finer, and Frohwirth (2006) shows that it is those in the middle of the educational distribution—that is, those with high-school diplomas but no college degrees (and not those with degrees or, for that matter, high-school dropouts)—who have statistically significant increased odds of repeat abortions.

21 I expect that in their reading of this narrative, my audience of students, scholars, and armchair analysts has likely made the same presumption that I have made. That is that the black workers whom Sparkle defends are lower-status workers than Sparkle and than the white employees who are criticizing their decisions to become unmarried parents. I argue that our collective presumption relies on our knowledge of and facility with interpreting symbols uniting race, gender, sex, and reproduction with class outcomes. Symbols and language that tell us that single parenting is the incomprehensible behavior of low-status black women help with this presumption even though none of Sparkle's words actually provides the evidence that would allow us to make an evidentiary-based conclusion that that is who these women are. I draw attention to my and the readers' likely presumptions here not to discuss how problematic they are but to provide another illustration of our dependence on race- and gender-based symbols in our communication about reproduction and inequality.

22 This analysis of degreed black women's management of racial stigma, in general, and of Sparkle's conversations with her white co-workers, in particular, shares important territory with both Cohen's (1999) and Pattillo's (2007) theorizing of the "middle." Both Cohen's *The Boundaries of Blackness* and Pattillo's *Black on the Block* describe the ways in which members of the black middle class exist between the more politically and economically powerful white middle-class citizens and poorer and often disenfranchised lower-class black citizens. They both make the point that gains by middle-class blacks are often predicated on their ability to manage, represent, buffer, and even act as social control agents vis-à-vis lower-class black individuals, communities, and constituencies. Each text focuses on public processes and outcomes—as in local and national politics—and on racial group and/or race-class group activities. In this book, Sparkle and the other subjects often exist in the "middle," but their management of race-sex stigma takes on a decidedly private and personal cast. The behaviors under study are traditionally understood as private rather than public behaviors, as is the case in Cohen's and Pattillo's analyses. Furthermore, the management of stigma may involve representing lower-class black women's sexual and reproductive activity to white co-workers, but as

the material in this and other chapters shows, it more often involves managing, hiding, altering, and/or representing their own behavior. As such, this book's contribution to Cohen's and Pattillo's intersectional race-class theoretical work is focused on emphasizing the significance of privatized, personal, micro-level activities in these race-class relations.

23 See endnote 15 for a discussion of education level differences in abortion among younger (and for the most part single women).

24 Here, I am referring to lessons from scholarship on the relationship between higher-class outcomes and postponed fertility (for example, Bloom and Trussell 1984; Hewlett 2002; Rindfuss, Bumpass, and St. John 1980; Rindfuss, Morgan, and Offutt 1996; and Wilkie 1981).

25 Here, I am referring to the scholarly claims about poor women who are supposedly motivated to have children by the prospect of cash assistance from welfare. The research findings in this regard are divided, with some (for example, Anderson 1989; Hoffman and Foster 2000; and Rosenzweig 1999) arguing that cash assistance increases fertility and others (for example, Blau, Kahn, and Waldfogel 2004; Kearney 2004) disagreeing with this claim. Others indicate that poor, urban youth may be motivated to have their children early because of increased availability of kin support during their youth (Geronimus 1987, 1997; Geronimus and Korenman 1992) and because of cultural values and strategies that surround motherhood in these communities (Edin and Kefalas 2005).

26 A comparable analysis of differences between degreed white and Hispanic women's nonmarital fertility rates (see table A19 in the appendix) shows the greater similarity between these two groups with respect to their nonmarital pregnancy, pregnancy termination, and childbearing experiences between ages 20 and 35. At the very beginning of the reproductive period (when most women remain unmarried) and at the very end of the reproductive period, college-educated Hispanic women's nonmarital fertility rates are higher than both white and black women with degrees.

27 Data analyses in chapter 4 show that these higher rates of nonmarital pregnancy are unlikely to be attributable to racial differences in sexual activity: these analyses indicate that degreed black women have the highest incidence of celibacy among all race-education groups.

28 With respect to this competition, see, for example, Hochschild's (1997) and Williams's (2000) discussions of the time demands of high-status and more financially rewarding employment and how parents without stay-at-home spouses have difficulty meeting those time demands. See endnote 10 above for a list of studies documenting the lower employment outcomes of mothers when compared to men and women without children and to fathers.

Conclusion. Love Notes

1 Consider, for example, studies indicating that employers respond negatively to black males' racial status and what that racial status supposedly says about their likely criminal involvement when they make hiring decisions (for example, Moss and Tilly 1996; Pager 2003).

2 According to Census 2000 data, the ratio of degreed black men to degreed black women in the U.S. population is .7—a figure that is considerably lower than the ratio observed among degreed whites (1.06) and Hispanics (.94). These figures tend to go down when calculations are confined to the younger ages and when foreign-born persons are excluded from each population. For example, ratios in the fifteen to forty-four age group in the black, white, and Hispanic populations are respectively .68, .93, and .86; black natives have a ratio of .65 while white natives' ratio is 1.06 and Hispanic natives' ratio is .88. Note that the Census data treats Hispanic status differently than the National Survey of Family Growth (NSFG [NCHS 1995]) does and consequently than I do throughout the text. Individuals surveyed by the Census answer a Hispanic ethnicity question separately from the question about race. Thus persons might be both Hispanic and black, both Hispanic and white, or both Hispanic and some other race. Since the Census made a "non-Hispanic white" category available, the white sex ratios in this note were calculated using individuals who identified solely as white, but the Hispanic ratios represent a multiracial group of Hispanics that includes some of the individuals who are also in the "black" or "white" categories. In contrast, in this text's analyses using NSFG data there was no overlap between white, black, and Hispanic categories. Finally, the African American community's low sex ratios when compared to other racial groups are confirmed in more refined marriage difference analyses cited earlier in this text (for example, Bennett, Bloom and Craig 1989; Blau, Kahn, and Waldfogel 2000; Brien 1997; Lichter, LeClere, and McLaughlin 1991; Lichter, McLaughlin, Kephart, and Landry 1992).

Aassve, Arnstein, and Gereltuya Altankhuyag. 2002. Changing patterns of Mongolian fertility at a time of social and economic transition. *Studies in Family Planning* 33(2): 165–72.

Abma, Joyce C., Gladys M. Martinez, William D. Mosher, and Brittany S. Dawson. 2004. Teenagers in the United States: Sexual activity, contraceptive use, and childbearing, 2002. *Vital and Health Statistics* 23(24): 1–87.

Abma, Joyce C., and Freya L. Sonenstein. 2002. Sexual activity and contraceptive practices among teenagers in the United States, 1988 and 1995. *Vital and Health Statistics* 23(21): 1–88.

Acker, Joan. 1973. Women and social stratification: A case of intellectual sexism. *American Journal of Sociology* 78(4): 936–45.

———. 1980. Women and stratification: A review of recent literature. *Contemporary Sociology* 9(1): 25–35.

———. 1990. Hierarchies, jobs, bodies: A theory of gendered organizations. *Gender and Society* 4(2): 139–58.

Ainsworth, James W., and Vincent J. Roscigno. 2005. Stratification, school-work linkages, and vocational education. *Social Forces* 84(1): 259–86.

Ainsworth, Martha, Kathleen Beegle, and Andrew Nyamete. 1996. The impact of women's schooling on fertility and contraceptive use: A study of fourteen sub-Saharan African countries. *World Bank Economic Review* 10(1): 85–122.

Akerlof, George A., Janet L. Yellen, and Michael L. Katz. 1996. An analysis of out-of-wedlock childbearing in the United States. *Quarterly Journal of Economics* 111(2): 277–317.

Allen, Walter R., and Reynolds Farley. 1986. The shifting social and economic tides of black America. *Annual Review of Sociology* 12: 277–306.

Anderson, Elijah. 1989. Sex codes and family life among poor inner-city youths. *Annals of the American Academy of Political and Social Science* 501 (The ghetto underclass: social science perspectives): 59–78.

Appold, Stephen J., Sununta Siengthai, and John D. Kasarda. 1998. The employment of women managers and professionals in an emerging economy: Gender inequality as an organizational practice. *Administrative Science Quarterly* 43(3): 538–65.

Aspy, Cheryl B., Sara K. Vesely, Roy F. Oman, Sharon Rodine, LaDonna Marshall, Janene Fluhr, and Ken McLeroy. 2006. Youth-parent communication and youth sexual behavior: Implications for physicians. *Family Medicine* 38(7): 500–504.

Axinn, William G. 1993. The effect of children's schooling on fertility limitation. *Population Studies* 47(3): 481–93.

Axinn, William G., and Jennifer S. Barber. 2001. Mass education and fertility transition. *American Sociological Review* 66(4): 481–505.

Baganha, Maria Ioannis Benis. 1991. The social mobility of Portuguese immigrants in the United States at the turn of the nineteenth century. *International Migration Review* 25(2): 277–302.

Bayard, Kimberly, Judith Hellerstein, David Neumark, and Kenneth Troske. 2003. New evidence on sex segregation and sex differences in wages from matched employee-employer data. *Journal of Labor Economics* 21(4): 887–922.

Becker, Gary S. 1973. A theory of marriage: Part I. *The Journal of Political Economy* 81(4): 813–46.

———. 1974. A theory of marriage: Part II. *The Journal of Political Economy* 82: S11–S26.

———. 1981. *A treatise on the family*. Cambridge: Harvard University Press.

Becker, Stan, and Saifuddin Ahmed. 2001. Dynamics of contraceptive use and breastfeeding during the post-partum period in Peru and Indonesia. *Population Studies* 55: 165–79.

Beggs, John J., Wayne J. Villemez, and Ruth Arnold. 1997. Black population concentration and black-white inequality: Expanding the consideration of place and space effects. *Social Forces* 76(1): 65–91.

Benefo, Kofi, and T. Paul Schultz. 1996. Fertility and child mortality in Côte d'Ivoire and Ghana. *World Bank Economic Review* 10(1): 123–58.

Bennett, Neil G., David E. Bloom, and Patricia H. Craig. 1989. The divergence of black and white marriage patterns. *American Journal of Sociology* 95(3): 692–722.

Berk, Sarah Fenstermaker. 1985. *The gender factory: The apportionment of work in American households.* New York: Plenum.

Bettie, Julie. 2003. *Women without class: Girls, race, and identity.* Berkeley: University of California Press.

Beutel, Ann M. 2000. The relationship between adolescent nonmarital childbearing and educational expectations: A cohort and period comparison. *Sociological Quarterly* 41(2): 297–314.

Bianchi, Suzanne M., Lekha Subaiya, and Joann R. Kahn. 1999. The gender gap in the economic well-being of nonresident fathers and custodial mothers. *Demography* 36(2): 195–203.

Biblarz, Timothy J., Vern L. Bengston, and Alexander Bucur. 1996. Social mobility across three generations. *Journal of Marriage and Family* 58(1): 188–200.

Biblarz, Timothy J., and Adrian E. Raftery. 1993. The effects of family disruption on social mobility. *American Sociological Review* 58(1): 97–109.

Biblarz, Timothy J., Adrian E. Raftery, and Alexander Bucur. 1997. Family structure and social mobility. *Social Forces* 75(4): 1319–41.

Billy, John O. G., and David E. Moore. 1992. A multi-level analysis of marital and nonmarital fertility in the U.S. *Social Forces* 70(4): 977–1011.

Bittman, Michael, Paula England, Nancy Folbre, Liana Sayer, and George Matheson. 2003. When does gender trump money? Bargaining and time in household work. *American Journal of Sociology* 109(1): 186–214.

Blalock, H. M., Jr. 1956. Economic discrimination and Negro increase. *American Sociological Review* 21(5): 584–88.

———. 1957. Percent nonwhite and discrimination in the South. *American Sociological Review* 22(6): 677–82.

Blau, Francine D., and Andrea H. Beller. 1992. Black-white earnings over the 1970s and 1980s: Gender differences in trends. *Review of Economics and Statistics* 74(2): 276–86.

Blau, Francine D., Lawrence M. Kahn, Jane Waldfogel. 2000. Understanding young women's marriage decisions: The role of labor and marriage market conditions. *Industrial and Labor Relations Review* 53(4): 624–47.

———. 2004. The impact of welfare benefits on single motherhood and headship of young women: Evidence from the census. *Journal of Human Resources* 39(2): 382–404.

Blau, Peter M., and Otis Dudley Duncan. 1967. *The American occupational structure.* New York: John Wiley and Sons.

Bledsoe, Caroline, Fatoumatta Banja, and Allan G. Hill. 1998. Reproductive mishaps and western contraception: An African challenge to fertility theory. *Population and Development Review* 24(1): 15–57.

Blee, Kathleen M. 1985. Mobility and political orientation: An analysis of sex differences. *Sociological Perspectives* 28(3): 385–400.

Bloom, David E., and James Trussell. 1984. What are the determinants of delayed childbearing and permanent childlessness in the United States? *Demography* 21(4): 591–611.

Blossfeld, Hans-Peter, and Johannes Huinink. 1991. Human capital investments or norms of role transition? How women's schooling and career affect the process of family formation. *American Journal of Sociology* 97(1): 143–68.

Boardman, Jason D., and Samuel H. Field. 2002. Spatial mismatch and race differentials in male joblessness: Cleveland and Milwaukee 1990. *Sociological Quarterly* 43(2): 237–55.

Bobo, Lawrence, and James R. Kluegel. 1993. Opposition to race-targeting: Self-interest, stratification ideology, or racial attitudes? *American Sociological Review* 58(4): 443–64.

Bobo, Lawrence, and Camille L. Zubrinsky. 1996. Attitudes on residential integration: Perceived status differences, mere in-group preference, or racial prejudice? *Social Forces* 74(3): 883–909.

Bogle, Kathleen A. 2008. *Hooking up: Sex, dating, and relationships on campus.* New York: New York University Press.

Bongaarts, John, and Robert G. Potter. 1983. *Fertility, biology, and behavior: An analysis of the proximate determinants.* New York: Academic Press.

Bonilla-Silva, Eduardo. 2003. *Racism without racists: Color-blind racism and the persistence of racial inequality in the United States.* New York: Rowman and Littlefield.

Bound, John, and Richard B. Freeman. 1992. What went wrong? The erosion of relative earnings and employment among young black men in the 1980s. *Quarterly Journal of Economics* 107(1): 201–32.

Bourdieu, Pierre. 1977a. Cultural reproduction and social reproduction. In *Power and ideology in education*, ed. J. G. Richardson, 487–511. New York: Greenwood.

———. 1977b. *Outline of a theory of cultural practice.* Trans. Richard Nice. New York: Cambridge University Press.

———. 1984. *Distinction: A social critique of the judgment of taste.* Trans. Richard Nice. Cambridge: Harvard University Press.

Bourdieu, Pierre, and Jean-Claude Passeron. 1977/1990. *Reproduction in education, society and culture.* London: Sage.

Bourdieu, Pierre, and Loic J. D. Wacquant. 1992. *An invitation to reflexive sociology.* Chicago: University of Chicago Press.

Bourgois, Phillippe. 1995. *In search of respect: Selling crack in El Barrio.* Cambridge: Cambridge University Press.

Bowles, Samuel, and Herbert Gintis. 1976. *Schooling in capitalist America: Educational reform and the contradictions of economic life.* New York: Basic Books.

Bowser, Benjamin P. 2007. *The black middle class: Social mobility—and vulnerability*. Boulder, Colo.: Lynne Rienner.

Boyd, Robert L. 1989. Racial differences in childlessness: A centennial review. *Sociological Perspectives* 32(2): 183–99.

Breen, Richard. 2000. Class inequality and social mobility in Northern Ireland, 1973–1996. *American Sociological Review* 65(3): 392–406.

Brien, Michael J. 1997. Racial differences in marriage and the role of marriage markets. *Journal of Human Resources* 32(4): 741–78.

Brien, Michael J., Stacy Dickert-Conlin, and David Weaver. 2004. Widows waiting to wed? (Re)Marriage and economic incentives in social security widow benefits. *Journal of Human Resources* 39(3): 585–623.

Brodkin, Karen. 1999. *How Jews became white folks and what that says about race in America*. New Brunswick: Rutgers University Press.

Browne, Irene, and Paula England. 1997. Oppression from within and without in sociological theories: An application to gender. *Current Perspectives in Social Theory* 17: 77–104.

Browning, Christopher R., Tama Leventhal, and Jeanne Brooks-Gunn. 2004. Neighborhood context and racial differences in early adolescent sexual activity. *Demography* 41(4): 697–720.

Bruckner, Hannah, and Peter Bearman. 2005. After the promise: The STD consequences of adolescent virginity pledges. *Journal of Adolescent Health* 36: 271–78.

Budig, Michelle J., and Paula England. 2001. The wage penalty for motherhood. *American Sociological Review* 66(2): 204–25.

Burawoy, Michael. 1979. *Manufacturing consent: Changes in the labor processes under monopoly capitalism*. Chicago: University of Chicago Press.

Caldwell, John C. 1976. Toward a restatement of demographic transition theory. *Population and Development Review* 2(3/4): 321–66.

——. 1980. Mass education as a determinant of the timing of fertility decline. *Population and Development Review* 6(2): 225–55.

Caldwell, John C., I. O. Orubuloye, and Pat Caldwell. 1992. Fertility decline in Africa: A new type of transition? *Population and Development Review* 18(2): 211–42.

Caldwell, John C., and Thomas Schindlmayr. 2003. Explorations of the fertility in crisis in modern societies: A search for commonalities. *Population Studies* 57(3): 241–63.

Caldwell, J. C., and Helen Ware. 1977. The evolution of family planning in an African city: Ibadan, Nigeria. *Population Studies* 31(3): 487–507.

Campbell, Richard T. 1983. Status attainment research: End of the beginning or beginning of the end? *Sociology of Education* 56(1): 47–62.

Cancio, A. Silvia, T. David Evans, and David Maume Jr. 1996. Reconsidering the declining significance of race: Racial differences in early career wages. *American Sociological Review* 61(4): 541–56.

Carlson, Marcia, Sara McLanahan, and Paula England. 2004. Union formation in fragile families. *Demography* 41(2): 237–61.

Carr, Leslie G. 1997. *Color-blind racism*. Thousand Oaks, Calif.: Sage.

Carrington, Bruce. 1986. Social mobility, ethnicity and sport. *British Journal of Sociology of Education* 7(1): 3–18.

Carter, Prudence L. 2005. *Keepin' it real: School success beyond black and white.* New York: Oxford University Press.

Casper, Lynne M., Sara S. McLanahan, and Irwin Garfinkel. 1994. The gender-poverty gap: What we can learn from other countries. *American Sociological Review* 59(4): 594–605.

Castronova, Edward. 2004. Social norms and sexual activity in U.S. high schools. *Journal of Human Resources* 39(4): 912–37.

Chaudhury, Rafiqul Huda. 1978. Female status and fertility behaviour in a metropolitan urban area of Bangladesh. *Population Studies* 32(2): 261–73.

Christopher, F. Scott. 1995. Adolescent pregnancy prevention. *Family Relations* 44(4): 384–91.

Christopher, Karen, Paula England, Timothy M. Smeeding, and Karen Ross Phillips. 2002. The gender gap in poverty in modern nations: Single motherhood, the market, and the state. *Sociological Perspectives* 45(3): 219–42.

Cleland, John, and German Rodriguez. 1988. The effect of parental education on marital fertility in developing countries. *Population Studies* 42(3): 419–42.

Clifford, P., and A. F. Heath. 1993. The political consequences of social mobility. *Journal of the Royal Statistical Society*, Series A (*Statistics in Society*) 156(1): 51–61.

Coale, Ansley J. 1969. The decline of fertility in Europe from the French Revolution to World War II. In *Fertility and family planning: A world view*, ed. S. J. Behrman, Leslie Corsa Jr., and Ronald Freedman, 3–24. Ann Arbor: University of Michigan Press.

Cohen, Cathy. 1999. *The boundaries of blackness: AIDS and the breakdown of black politics*. Chicago: University of Chicago Press.

Cohen, Philip N. 1998. Black concentration effects on black-white and gender inequality: Multilevel analysis for U.S. metropolitan areas. *Social Forces* 77(1): 207–29.

Cohen, Phillip N., and Matt L. Huffman 2003a. Occupational segregation and the devaluation of women's work across U.S. labor markets. *Social Forces* 81(3): 881–908.

———. 2003b. Individuals, jobs, and labor markets: The devaluation of women's work. *American Sociological Review* 68(3): 443–63.

———. 2007. Working for the woman? Female managers and the gender wage gap. *American Sociological Review* 72(5): 681–704.

Cohen, Rosetta Marantz. 1998. Class consciousness and its consequences: The impact of an elite education on mature, working-class women. *American Educational Research Journal* 35(3): 353–75.

Collins, Patricia Hill. 1991. *Black feminist thought: Knowledge, consciousness, and the politics of empowerment*. New York: Routledge.

———. 2004. *Black sexual politics: African Americans, gender, and the new racism*. New York: Routledge.

Collins, Randall. 1986. *Weberian sociological theory*. New York: Cambridge University Press.

Coltrane, Scott. 1989. Household labor and the routine production of gender. *Social Problems* 36(5): 473–90.

———. 2000. Research on household labor: Modeling and measuring the social embeddedness of routine family work. *Journal of Marriage and Family* 62(4): 1208–33.

Cooksey, Elizabeth C. 1990. Factors in the resolution of adolescent premarital pregnancies. *Demography* 27(2): 207–18.

Cooksey, Elizabeth C., Ronald R. Rindfuss, and Ronald K. Guilkey. 1996. The initiation of adolescent sexual and contraceptive behavior during changing times. *Journal of Health and Social Behavior* 37(1): 59–74.

Cornell, Stephen, and Douglas Hartmann. 2007. *Ethnicity and race: Making identities in a changing world*. 2nd ed. Thousand Oaks, Calif.: Pine Forge.

Correll, Shelley. 2004. Constraints into preferences: Gender, status, and emerging career aspirations. *American Sociological Review* 69(1): 93–113.

Correll, Shelley, Stephen Benard, and In Paik. 2007. Getting a job: Is there a motherhood penalty? *American Journal of Sociology* 112(5): 1297–1338.

Cose, Ellis. 1994. *The rage of a privileged class: Why are middle-class blacks angry? Why should America care?* New York: Harper Collins.

Cote, Guy L. 1997. Socio-economic attainment, regional disparities, and internal migration. *European Sociological Review* 13(1): 55–77.

Culwell, Kelly R., and Joe Feinglass. 2007. Changes in prescription contraceptive use, 1995–2002: The effect of insurance status. *Obstetrics and Gynecology* 110(6): 1371–78.

D'Amico, Ronald, and Nan L. Maxwell. 1995. The continuing significance of race in minority male joblessness. *Social Forces* 73(3): 969–91.

Darity, William A., Jr., and Samuel L. Myers. 1995. Family structure and the marginalization of black men: Policy implications. In *The Decline in marriage among African Americans*, ed. M. Belinda Tucker and Claudia Mitchell-Kernan, 263–308. New York: Russell Sage Foundation.

Davis, Kingsley. 1963. Theory of change and response in modern demographic history. *Population Index* 29(4): 345–66.

Davis, Kingsley, and Judith Blake. 1956. Social structure and fertility: An analytic framework. *Economic Development and Cultural Change* 4(3): 211–35.

Davis, Nancy J. 1982. Childless and single-childed women in early twentieth-century America. *Journal of Family Issues* 3(4): 431–58.

Dawson, Deborah Anne. 1986. The effects of sex education on adolescent behavior. *Family Planning Perspectives* 18(4): 162–70.

Dex, Shirley, Kelly Ward, and Heather Joshi. 2008. Gender differences in occupational wage mobility in the 1958 cohort. *Work, Employment and Society* 22(2): 263–80.

Dillard, K. Denise, and Louis G. Pol. 1982. The individual economic costs of teenage childbearing. *Family Relations* 31(2): 249–59.

DiMaggio, Paul. 1982. Cultural capital and school success: The impact of status culture participation on the grades of U.S. high school students. *American Sociological Review* 47(2): 189–201.

DiMaggio, Paul, and John Mohr. 1985. Cultural capital, educational attainment, and marital selection. *American Journal of Sociology* 90(6): 1231–61.

DiPrete, Thomas A., and Whitman T. Soule. 1988. Gender and promotion in segmented job ladder systems. *American Sociological Review* 53(1): 26–40.

Dreze, Jean, and Mamta Murthi. 2001. Fertility, education, and development: Evidence from India. *Population and Development Review* 27(1): 33–63.

Driscoll, Anne K., Gesine K. Hearn, V. Jeffrey Evans, Kristin A. Moore, Barbara W. Sugland, and Vaughn Call. 1999. Nonmarital childbearing among adult women. *Journal of Marriage and the Family* 61(1): 178–87.

Duncan, Colin, and Wendy Lorretto. 2004. Never the right age? Gender and age-based discrimination in employment. *Gender, Work and Organization* 11(1): 95–115.

East, Patricia L. 1998. Racial and ethnic differences in girls' sexual, marital, and birth expectations. *Journal of Marriage and the Family* 60(1): 150–62.

Edin, Kathryn, and Maria Kefalas. 2005. *Promises I can keep: Why poor women put motherhood before marriage.* Berkeley: University of California Press.

Edwards, J. N. 1969. Familial behavior as social exchange. Journal of Marriage and Family 31: 518–26.

Eitle, Tamela McNulty, and David James Eitle. 2004. Inequality, segregation, and the overrepresentation of African Americans in school suspensions. *Sociological Perspectives* 47(3): 269–87.

Elliott, James R. 1999. Social isolation and labor market insulation: Network and neighborhood effects on less-educated urban workers. *Sociological Quarterly* 40(2): 199–216.

Ellwood, David, and Jonathan Crane. 1990. Family change among black Americans: What do we know? *Journal of Economic Perspectives* 4(4): 65–84.

England, Paula. 1982. The failure of human capital theory to explain occupational sex segregation. *Journal of Human Resources* 17(3): 358–70.

———. 1984. Wage appreciation and depreciation: A test of neoclassical economic explanations of occupational sex segregation. *Social Forces* 62(3): 726–49.

———. 1999. The impact of feminist thought on sociology. *Contemporary Sociology* 28(3): 263–68.

England, Paula, and Irene Browne. 1992. Trends in women's economic status. *Sociological Perspectives* 35(1): 17–51.

England, Paula, Michelle Budig, and Nancy Folbre. 2002. Wages of virtue: The relative pay of care work. *Social Problems* 49(4): 455–73.

England, Paula, George Farkas, Barbara Stanek Kilbourne, and Thomas Dou. 1988. Explaining occupational sex segregation and wages: Finding a model with fixed effects. *American Sociological Review* 53(4): 544–58.

England, Paula, and Nancy Folbre. 1999. The cost of caring. *Annals of the American Academy of Political and Social Science* 561: 39–51.

England, Paula, Melissa S. Herbert, Barbara Stanek Kilbourne, Lori L. Reid, and Lori McCreary Megdal. 1994. The gendered valuation of occupations and skills: Earnings in 1980 census occupations. *Social Forces* 73(1): 65–100.

England, Paula, Lori L. Reid, and Barbara Stanek Kilbourne. 1996. The effect of the sex composition of jobs on starting wages in an organization: Findings from the NLSY. *Demography* 33(4): 511–21.

Erikson, Robert, and John H. Goldthorpe. 1985. Are American rates of social mobility exceptionally high? New evidence on an old issue. *European Sociological Review* 1(1): 1–22.

Fairlie, Robert W., and Bruce D. Meyer. 2000. Trends in self-employment among white and black men during the twentieth century. *Journal of Human Resources* 35(4): 643–69.

Fairlie, Robert W., and William A. Sundstrom. 1999. The emergence, persistence, and recent widening of the racial unemployment gap. *Industrial and Labor Relations Review* 52(2): 252–70.

Farkas, George, Paula England, Kevin Vicknair, and Barbara Stanek Kilbourne. 1997. Cognitive skill, skill demands of jobs, and earnings among European American, African American, and Mexican American workers. *Social Forces* 75(3): 913–38.

Farkas, George, and Kevin Vicknair. 1996. Appropriate tests of racial wage discrimination require controls for cognitive skill: Comment on Cancio, Evans, and Maume. *American Sociological Review* 61(4). 557–60.

Feagin, Joe R., and Melvin P. Sykes. 1994. *Living with racism: The black middle-class experience.* Boston: Beacon.

Feagin, Joe R., and Hernan Vera. 1995. *White racism: The basics.* New York: Routledge.

Feinberg, Eve C., Frederick W. Larsen, William H. Catherino, Jun Zhang, and Alicia Y. Armstrong. 2006. Comparison of assisted reproductive technology utilization and outcomes between Caucasian and African American patients in an equal-access-to-care setting. *Fertility and Sterility* 85(4): 888–94.

Felice, Lawrence G. 1981. Black student dropout behavior: Disengagement from school rejection and racial discrimination. *Journal of Negro Education* 50(4): 415–24.

Feliciano, Cynthia, Belinda Robnett, and Golnez Komaie. 2009. Gendered racial exclusion among white internet daters. *Social Science Research* (38): 39–54.

Fennelly, Katherine, Gretchen Cornwell, and Lynne Casper. 1992. A comparison

of the fertility of Dominican, Puerto Rican, and mainland Puerto Rican adolescents. *Family Planning Perspectives* 24(3): 107–10, 134.

Fenstermaker, Sarah, and Candace West, eds. 2002. *Doing gender, doing difference: Inequality, power, and institutional exchange*. New York: Routledge.

Fine, Michelle. 1991. *Framing dropouts: Notes on the politics of an urban public
high school*. Albany: State University of New York Press.

Folbre, Nancy, and Julie A. Nelson. 2000. For love or money—or both? *Journal
of Economic Perspectives* 14(4): 123–40.

Ford, Donna Y., and J. John Harris III. 1996. Perceptions and attitudes of black
students toward school, achievement, and other educational variables. *Child
Development* 67(3): 1141–52.

Ford, Kathleen, Woosung Sohn, and James Lepkowski. 2001. Characteristics of
adolescents' sexual partners and their association with use of condom and
other contraceptive methods. *Family Planning Perspectives* 33(3): 100–105,
132.

Fordham, Signithia, and John U. Ogbu. 1986. Black students' school success:
Coping with the burden of acting white. *Urban Review* 18: 176–206.

Forest, Kay B., Phyllis Moen, and Donna Dempster-McClain. 1995. Cohort differences in the transition to motherhood: The variable effects of education
and employment before marriage. *Sociological Quarterly* 36(2): 315–36.

Foster, Diana G., Cynthia C. Harper, Julia J. Bley, John J. Mikanda, Marta Induni,
Elizabeth C. Saviano, and Felicia H. Stewart. 2004. Knowledge of emergency
contraception among women aged 18 to 44 in California. *American Journal of
Obstetrics and Gynecology* 191: 150–56.

Foster, Diana G., Lauren J. Ralph, Abigail Arons, Claire D. Brindis, and Cynthia
Harper. 2007. Trends in knowledge of emergency contraception among
women in California, 1999–2004. *Women's Health Issues* 17: 22–28.

Freedman, David, Robert Pisani, Roger Purves, and Ani Adhikari. 1998. *Statistics*. 2nd ed. New York: W. W. Norton.

Freeman, Ellen W., and Karl Rickels. 1993. *Early childbearing: Perspectives of
black adolescents on pregnancy, abortion, and contraception*. Newbury Park,
Calif.: Sage.

Frost, Jennifer J., and Jacqueline Darroch Forrest. 1995. Understanding the
impact of effective teenage pregnancy prevention programs. *Family Planning
Perspectives* 27(5): 188–95.

Furstenberg, Frank F., Jr. 1976. The consequences of teenage parenthood. *Family
Planning Perspectives* 8(4): 148–64.

Galloway, Patrick R., Eugene A. Hammel, and Ronald D. Lee. 1994. Fertility
decline in Prussia, 1875–1910: A pooled cross-section time series analysis.
Population Studies 48(1): 135–58.

Gandara, Patricia. 1995. *Over the ivy walls*. Albany: State University of New York
Press.

Geronimus, Arline T. 1986. The effects of race, residence, and prenatal care on the relationship of maternal age to neonatal mortality. *American Journal of Public Health* 76(12): 1416–21.

———. 1987. On teenage childbearing and neonatal mortality in the United States. *Population and Development Review* 13(2): 245–79.

———. 1997. Teenage childbearing and personal responsibility: An alternative view. *Political Science Quarterly* 112(3): 405–30.

Geronimus, Arline T., and Sanders Korenman. 1992. The socioeconomic consequences of teen childbearing reconsidered. *Quarterly Journal of Economics* 107(4): 1187–1214.

Gertler, Paul J., and John W. Molyneaux. 1994. How economic development and family planning programs combined to reduce Indonesian fertility. *Demography* 31(1): 33–63.

Gibson, Margaret A. 1988. *Accommodation without assimilation: Sikh immigrants in an American high school*. Ithaca: Cornell University Press.

———. 1991. Ethnicity, gender and social class: The school adaptation patterns of West Indian youths. In *Minority status and schooling: A comparative study of immigrant and involuntary minorities*, ed. Margaret A. Gibson and John U. Ogbu, 169–203. New York: Garland.

Gibson, Margaret A., and John U. Ogbu, eds. 1991. *Minority status and schooling: A comparative study of immigrant and involuntary minorities*. New York: Garland

Gibson-Davis, Christina M., Kathryn Edin, and Sara McLanahan. 2005. High hopes but even higher expectations: The retreat from marriage among low income couples. *Journal of Marriage and Family* 67: 1301–12.

Gilens, Martin. 1999. *Why Americans hate welfare: Race, media, and the politics of antipoverty policy*. Chicago: University of Chicago Press.

Giroux, Henry A. 1981. *Ideology, culture, and the process of schooling*. Philadelphia: Temple University Press.

Gius, Mark Paul. 2007. The impact of provider availability and legal restrictions on the demand for abortions by young women. *Social Science Journal* 44: 495–506.

Glauber, Rebecca. 2008. Race and gender in families and at work: The fatherhood wage premium. *Gender and Society* 22(1): 8–30.

Glei, Dana A. 1999. Measuring contraceptive use patterns among teenage and adult women. *Family Planning Perspectives* 31(2): 73–80.

Glenn, Evelyn Nakano. 2002. *Unequal freedom: How face and gender shaped American citizenship and labor*. Cambridge: Harvard University Press.

Glenn, Norval D. 1963. Occupational benefits to whites from the subordination of Negroes. *American Sociological Review* 28(3): 443–48.

Goffman, Erving. 1963. *Stigma: Notes on the management of spoiled identity*. New York: Simon and Schuster.

Goldman, Noreen, Charles F. Westoff, and Charles Hammerslough. 1984. Demography of the marriage market in the United States. *Population Index* 50(1): 5–25.

Goldscheider, Calvin, and Peter R. Uhlenberg. 1969. Minority group status and fertility. *American Journal of Sociology* 74(4): 361–72.

Goldstein, Joshua R., and Catherine T. Kenney. 2001. Marriage delayed or marriage foregone? New cohort forecasts of first marriage for U.S. women. *American Sociological Review* 66(4): 506–19.

Goldthorpe, John H. 1983. Women and class analysis: In defence of the conventional view. *Sociology* 17(4): 465–88.

———. 1984. Women and class analysis: A reply to the replies. *Sociology* 18(4): 491–99.

Graefe, Deborah Roempke, and Daniel T. Lichter. 2002. Marriage among unwed mothers: Whites, blacks, and Hispanics compared. *Perspectives on Sexual and Reproductive Health* 34(6): 286–93.

Granovetter, Mark. 1973. The strength of weak ties. *American Journal of Sociology* 78(6): 1360–80.

———. 1974/1995. *Getting a job: A study of contacts and careers.* 2nd ed. Chicago: University of Chicago Press.

———. 1983. The strength of weak ties: A network theory revisited. *Sociological Theory* 1: 201–33.

Green, Gary Paul, Leann M. Tigges, and Daniel Diaz. 1999. Racial and ethnic differences in job-search strategies in Atlanta, Boston, and Los Angeles. *Social Science Quarterly* 80(2): 263–78.

Grindstaff, Carl F. 1976. Trends and incidence of childlessness by race: Indicators of black progress over three decades. *Sociological Focus* 9(3): 265–84.

Grodsky, Eric, and Devah Pager. 2001. The structure of disadvantage: Individual and occupational determinants of the black-white wage gap. *American Sociological Review* 66(4): 542–67.

Groshen, Erica L. 1991. The structure of the female/male wage differentials: Is it who you are, what you do, or where you work? *Journal of Human Resources* 26(3): 457–72.

Grossbard-Schectman, Shoshana. 1993. *On the economics of marriage: A theory of marriage, labor, and divorce.* Boulder, Colo.: Westview.

Grusky, David B., ed. 1994. *Social stratification in sociological perspective.* Boulder, Colo.: Westview.

Grusky, David B., and Thomas A. DiPrete. 1990. Recent trends in the process of stratification. *Demography* 27(4): 617–37.

Gupta, Neeru, and Iuri da Costa Leite. 1999. Adolescent fertility behavior: Trends and determinants in northeastern Brazil. *International Family Planning Perspectives* 25(3): 125–30.

Guttentag, Marcia, and Paul F. Secord. 1983. *Too many women? The sex ratio question.* Beverly Hills: Sage.

Gwynn, R. Charon, and George D. Thurston. 2001. The burden of air pollution: Impacts among racial minorities. *Environmental health perspectives* 109(4): 501–6.

Hahm, Hyeouk Chris, Maureen Lahiff, and Rose M. Barreto. 2006. Asian American adolescents' first sexual intercourse: Gender and acculturation differences. *Perspectives on Sexual and Reproductive Health* 38(1): 28–36.

Hajnal, John. 1965. European marriage patterns in perspective. In *Population in history*, ed. D. V. Glass and D. E. C. Everly, 101–43. London: Edward Arnold.

Hamilton, Brady E., and Stephanie J. Ventura. 2006. Fertility and abortion rates in the United States. *International Journal of Andrology* 29: 34–45.

Haug, Marie R. 1973. Social class measurement and women's occupational roles. *Social Forces* 52(1): 86–98.

Hayes, Bernadette C., and F. L. Jones. 1992. Class identification among Australian couples: Are wives' characteristics irrelevant? *British Journal of Sociology* 43(3): 463–83.

Hayes, Bernadette C., and Robert L. Miller. 1993. The silenced voice: Female social mobility patterns with particular reference to the British Isles. *British Journal of Sociology* 44(4): 653–72.

Hays, Sharon. 2003. *Flat broke with children: Women in the age of welfare reform.* New York: Oxford University Press.

Heavey, Elizabeth J., Kirsten B. Moysich, Andrew Hyland, Charlotte Druschel, and Michael W. Sill. 2008. Differences in contraceptive choice among female adolescents at a state-funded family planning clinic. *Journal of Midwifery and Women's Health* 53(1): 45–52.

Henretta, John C. 1984. Parental status and child's home ownership. *American Sociological Review* 49(1): 131–40.

Hertz, Rosanna. 2006. *Single by chance, mothers by choice: How women are choosing parenthood without marriage and creating the new American family.* New York: Oxford University Press.

Hewlett, Sylvia Ann. 2002. *Creating a life: Professional women and the quest for children.* New York: Talk Miramax Books.

Higginbotham, Elizabeth, and Lynn Weber. 1992. Moving up with kin and community: Upward social mobility for black and white women. *Gender and Society* 6(3): 416–40.

Hochschild, Arlie Russell. 1989. *The second shift.* New York: Avon Books.

———. 1997. *The time bind: When work becomes home and home becomes work.* New York: Henry Holt.

Hochschild, Jennifer L. 1995. *Facing up to the American dream: Race, class, and the soul of the nation.* Princeton: Princeton University Press.

Hofferth, Sandra L., and Kristin A. Moore. 1979. Early childbearing and later economic well-being. *American Sociological Review* 44(5): 784–815.

Hoffman, Saul D., and E. Michael Foster. 2000. AFDC benefits and nonmarital births to young women. *Journal of Human Resources* 35(2): 376–91.

Hoffman, Saul D., Michael Foster, and Frank F. Furstenberg Jr. 1993. Reevaluating the costs of teenage childbearing. *Demography* 30(1): 1–13.

Holden, Karen C., and Pamela J. Smock. 1991. The economic costs of marital dissolution: Why do women bear a disproportionate cost? *Annual Review of Sociology* 17: 51–78.

Holland, Dorothy C., and Margaret A. Eisenhart. 1990. *Educated in romance: Women, achievement, and college culture.* Chicago: University of Chicago Press.

Holzer, Harry J. 1998a. Why do small establishments hire fewer blacks than large ones? *Journal of Human Resources* 32(4): 896–914.

———. 1998b. Employer skill demands and labor market outcomes for blacks and women. *Industrial and Labor Relations Review* 52(1): 82–98.

Horvat, Erin McNamara, and Anthony Lising Antonio. 1999. "Hey, those shoes are out of uniform": African American girls in an elite high school and the importance of habitus. *Anthropology and Education Quarterly* 30(3): 317–42.

Hotchkiss, Julie L., and M. Melinda Pitts. 2007. The role of labor market intermittency in explaining gender wage differentials. *AEA Papers and Proceedings* 97(2): 417–21.

Hout, Michael. 1984. Occupational mobility of black men: 1962–1973. *American Sociological Review* 49(3): 308–22.

———. 1986. Opportunity and the minority middle class: A comparison of blacks in the United States and Catholics in northern Ireland. *American Sociological Review* 51(2): 214–23.

Hughes, Mary Elizabeth. 2003. Home economics: Metropolitan labor and housing markets and domestic arrangements in young adulthood. *Social Forces* 81(4): 1399–1429.

Hutchinson, M. Katherine, and Teresa M. Cooney. 1998. Patterns of parent-teen sexual risk communication: Implications for intervention. *Family Relations* 47(2): 185–94.

Jackson, Rebecca, Eleanor Bimla Schwarz, Lori Freedman, and Philip Darney. 2000. Knowledge and willingness to use emergency contraception among low-income post-partum women. *Contraception* 61: 351–57.

Jacobs, Jerry A. 1995. Gender and academic specialties: Trends among recipients of college degrees in the 1980s. *Sociology of Education* 68(2): 81–98.

Jacobs, Jerry A., David Karen, and Katherine McClelland. 1991. The dynamics of young men's career aspirations. *Sociological Forum* 6(4): 609–39.

Jain, Anrudh K. 1981. The effect of female education on fertility: A simple explanation. *Demography* 18(4): 577–95.

Jencks, Christopher, James Crouse, and Peter Mueser. 1983. The Wisconsin model of status attainment: A national replication with improved measures of ability and aspiration. *Sociology of Education* 56(1): 3–19.

Jencks, Christopher, and Meredith Phillips, eds. 1998. *The black-white test score gap.* Washington: Brookings Institution Press.

Jhally, Sut, and Justin Lewis. 1992. *Enlightened racism: "The Cosby show," audiences, and the myth of the American dream.* Boulder, Colo.: Westview.

Johnson, Nan E. 1979. Minority-group status and the fertility of black Americans, 1970: A new look. *American Journal of Sociology* 84(6): 1386–1400.

Johnson, Nan E., and Suewen Lean. 1985. Relative income, race, and fertility. *Population Studies* 39(1): 99–112.

Jones, Elise F., Jacqueline Darroch Forrest, Noreen Goldman, Stanley Henshaw, Richard Lincoln, Jeannie I. Rosoff, Charles F. Westoff, and Deirdre Wulf. 1988. *Teenage pregnancy in industrialized countries: A study sponsored by the Alan Guttmacher Institute.* New Haven: Yale University Press.

Jones, Rachel K., Susheela Singh, Lawrence B. Finer, and Lori F. Frohwirth. 2006. Repeat abortion in the United States. Occasional Report no. 29. New York: Guttmacher Institute.

Joy, Lois. 2003. Salaries of recent male and female college graduates: Educational and labor market effects. *Industrial and Labor Relations Review* 56(4): 606–21.

Kalleberg, Arne L., and Rachel A. Rosenfeld. 1990. Work in the family and in the labor market: A cross-national, reciprocal analysis. *Journal of Marriage and the Family* 52(2): 331–46.

Kalmijn, Matthijs. 1993. Trends in black/white intermarriage. *Social Forces* 72(1): 119–46.

———. 1994. Mother's occupational status and children's schooling. *American Sociological Review* 59(2): 257–75.

———. 1998. Intermarriage and homogamy: Causes, patterns, trends. *Annual Review of Sociology* 24: 395–421.

Kao, Grace, and Jennifer S. Thompson. 2003. Racial and ethnic stratification in educational achievement and attainment. *Annual Review of Sociology* 29: 417–42.

Kao, Grace, and Marta Tienda. 1998. Educational aspirations of minority youth. *American Journal of Education* 106(3): 349–84.

Kaplan, Elaine Bell. 1997. *Not our kind of girl: Unraveling the myths of black teenage motherhood.* Berkeley: University of California Press.

Katz, Michael B. 1989. *The undeserving poor: From the war on poverty to the war on welfare.* New York: Pantheon Books.

Kearney, Melissa Schettini. 2004. Is there an effect of incremental welfare benefits on fertility behavior? A look at the family cap. *Journal of Human Resources* 39(2): 295–325.

Kenkel, Willliam F. 1985. The desire for voluntary childlessness among low-income youth. *Journal of Marriage and Family* 47(2): 509–12.

Kerckhoff, Alan C. 1989. On the social psychology of social mobility processes. *Social Forces* 68(1): 17–25.

Kerckhoff, Alan C., Richard T. Campbell, and Jerry M. Trott. 1982. Dimensions of educational and occupational attainment in Great Britain. *American Sociological Review* 47(3): 347–64.

Kerckhoff, Alan C., Richard T. Campbell, Jerry M. Trott, and Vered Kraus. 1989. The transmission of socioeconomic status and prestige in Great Britain and the United States. *Sociological Forum* 4(2): 155–77.

Kerckhoff, Alan C., Richard T. Campbell, and Idee Winfield-Laird. 1985. Social mobility in Great Britain and the United States. *American Journal of Sociology* 91(2): 281–308.

Kiecolt, K. Jill, and Mark A. Fossett. 1995. Mate availability and marriage among African Americans: Aggregate- and individual-level analyses. In *The decline in marriage among African Americans*, ed. M. Belinda Tucker and Claudia Mitchell-Kernan, 121–35. New York: Russell Sage Foundation.

Kilbourne, Barbara, Paula England, and Kert Beron. 1994. Effects of individual, occupational, and industrial characteristics on earnings: Intersections of race and gender. *Social Forces* 72(4): 1149–76.

Kilbourne, Barbara Stanek, George Farkas, Kert Beron, Dorothea Weir, and Paula England. 1994. Returns to skill, compensating differentials, and gender bias: Effects of occupational characteristics on the wages of white women and men. *American Journal of Sociology* 100(3): 689–719.

Kirby, Douglas, Richard P. Barth, Nancy Leland, and Joyce Fetro. 1991. Reducing the risk: Impact of a new curriculum on sexual risk taking. *Family Planning Perspectives* 23(6): 253–63.

Kirk, Dudley, and Bernard Pillet. 1998. Fertility levels, trends, and differentials in sub-Saharan Africa in the 1980s and 1990s. *Studies in Family Planning* 29(1): 1–22.

Konstantopoulos, Spyros, and Amelie Constant. 2008. The gender gap reloaded: Are school characteristics linked to labor market performance? *Social Science Research* 37: 374–85.

Konstantopoulos, Spyros, Manisha Modi, and Larry V. Hedges. 2001. Who are America's gifted? *American Journal of Education* 109(3): 344–82.

Korkeamaki, Ossi, and Tomi Kyyra. 2006. A gender wage gap decomposition for matched employer-employee data. *Labour Economics* 13: 611–38.

Ku, Leighton, Freya L. Sonenstein, and Joseph H. Pleck. 1994. The dynamics of young men's condom use during and across relationships. *Family Planning Perspectives* 26(6): 246–51.

Labov, Teresa, and Jerry A. Jacobs. 1986. Intermarriage in Hawaii, 1950–1983. *Journal of Marriage and Family* 48: 79–88.

Lacy, Karyn R. 2007. *Blue-chip black: Race, class, and status in the new black middle class*. Berkeley: University of California Press.

Lamont. Michele. 1992. *Money, morals, and manners: The culture of the French and the American upper-middle class*. Chicago: University of Chicago Press.

Lamont, Michele, and Annette Lareau. 1988. Cultural capital: Allusions, gaps and glissandos in recent theoretical developments. *Sociological Theory* 6(2): 153–68.

Lareau, Annette. 2003. *Unequal childhoods: Class, race, and family life.* Berkeley: University of California Press.

Lareau, Annette, and Erin McNamara Horvat. 1999. Moments of social inclusion and exclusion: Race, class, and cultural capital in family-school relationships. *Sociology of Education* 72(1): 37–53.

Lavely, William, and Ronald Freedman. 1990. The origins of Chinese fertility decline. *Demography* 27(3): 357–67.

Lehrer, Evelyn L. 1992. The impact of children on married women's labor supply: Black-white differentials revisited. *Journal of Human Resources* 27(3): 422–44.

Lehrer, Evelyn, and Marc Nerlove. 1986. Female labor force behavior and fertility in the United States. *Annual Review of Sociology* 12: 181–204.

L'Engle, Kelly Ladin, and Christine Jackson. 2008. Socialization influences on early adolescents' cognitive susceptibility and transition to sexual intercourse. *Journal of Adolescent Research* 18(2): 353–78.

Lewis, Oscar. 1959. *Five families.* New York: Basic Books.

———. 1968. *La vida.* New York: Alfred A. Knopf.

Lichter, Daniel T., Felicia B. LeClere, and Diane K. McLaughlin. 1991. Local marriage markets and the marital behavior of black and white women. *American Journal of Sociology* 96(4): 843–67.

Lichter, Daniel T., Diane K. McLaughlin, George Kephart, and David J. Landry. 1992. Race and the retreat from marriage: A shortage of marriageable men? *American Sociological Review* 57(6): 781–99.

Lichter, Daniel T., Diane K. McLaughlin, and David C. Ribar. 2002. Economic restructuring and the retreat from marriage. *Social Science Research* 31: 230–56.

Lieberson, Stanley. 1980. *A piece of the pie: Blacks and white immigrants since 1980.* Berkeley: University of California Press.

Lin, Nan. 2000. Inequality in social capital. *Contemporary Sociology* 29(6): 787–95.

Lipset, Seymour Martin, and Reinhard Bendix. 1959. *Social mobility in industrial society.* Berkeley: University of California Press.

Lloyd, Kim M., and Scott J. South. 1996. Contextual influences on young men's transition to first marriage. *Social Forces* 74(3): 1097–1119.

London, Bruce. 1992. School-enrollment rates and trends, gender, and fertility: A cross-national analysis. *Sociology of Education* 65(4): 306–16.

Looker, E. Dianne, and Karen L. McNutt. 1989. The effect of occupational expectations on the educational attainment of males and females. *Canadian Journal of Education* 14(3): 352–67.

Looker, E. Dianne, and Peter C. Pineo. 1983. Social psychological variables and their relevance to the status attainment of teenagers. *American Journal of Sociology* 88(6): 1195–1219.

Lopez, Nancy. 2003. *Hopeful girls, troubled boys: Race and gender disparity in urban education.* New York: Routledge.

Lopoo, Leonard M., and Bruce Western. 2005. Incarceration and the formation and stability of marital unions. *Journal of Marriage and Family* 67: 721–34.

Loughran, David S. 2002. The effect of male wage inequality on female age at first marriage. *Review of Economics and Statistics* 84(2): 237–50.

Luker, Kristin. 1975. *Taking chances: Abortion and the decision not to contracept.* Berkeley: University of California Press.

———. 1996. *Dubious conceptions: The politics of teenage pregnancy.* Cambridge: Harvard University Press.

Lundberg, Shelly, and Elaina Rose. 2002. The effects of sons and daughters on men's labor supply and wages. *Review of Economics and Statistics* 84(2): 251–68.

MacDonald, Cameron Lynne, and David A. Merrill. 2002. "It shouldn't have to be a trade": Recognition and redistribution in care work advocacy. *Hypatia* 17(2): 67–83.

MacLeod, Jay. 1995. *Ain't no makin' it: Aspirations and attainment in a low-income neighborhood.* Boulder, Colo.: Westview.

Malthus, Thomas Robert. 1798/1965. *An essay on population.* New York: Augustus Kelley Bookseller.

———. 1872. *An essay on the principle of population.* 7th ed. London: Reeves and Turner.

Mandel, Hadas, and Moshe Semyonov. 2005. Family policies, wage structures, and gender gaps: Sources of earnings inequality in 20 countries. *American Sociological Review* 70(6): 949–67.

Manlove, Jennifer, Suzanne Ryan, and Kerry Franzetta. 2003. Patterns of contraceptive use within teenagers' first sexual relationships. *Perspectives on Sexual and Reproductive Health* 35(6): 246–55.

Manlove, Jennifer, and Elizabeth Terry-Humen. 2007. Contraceptive use patterns within females' first sexual relationships: The role of relationships, partners, and methods. *Journal of Sex Research* 44(1): 3–16.

Manlove, Jennifer S., Elizabeth Terry-Humen, Erum N. Ikramullah, and Kristin A. Moore. 2006. The role of parent religiosity in teens' transition to sex and contraception. *Journal of Adolescent Health* 39: 578–87.

Manning, Alan, and Joanna Swaffield. 2008. The gender gap in early-career wage growth. *Economic Journal* 118: 983–1024.

Manning, Wendy D., Monica A. Longmore, and Peggy C. Giordano. 2000. The relationship context of contraceptive use at first intercourse. *Family Planning Perspectives* 32(3): 104–10.

Manning, Wendy D., and Pamela J. Smock. 1995. Why marry? Race and the transition to marriage among cohabitors. *Demography* 32(4): 509–20.

Marchant, Gregory J. 1991. A profile of motivation, self-perception, and achievement in black urban elementary students. *Urban Review* 23(2): 83–99.

Marin, Barbara VanOss, Douglas B. Kirby, Esther S. Hudes, Karen K. Coyle, and

Cynthia A. Gomez. 2006. Boyfriends, girlfriends and teenagers' risk of sexual involvement. *Perspectives on Sexual and Reproductive Health* 38(2): 76–83.

Martin, Teresa Castro, and Larry L. Bumpass. 1989. Recent trends in marital disruption. *Demography* 26(1): 37–51.

Martin, Teresa Castro, and Fatima Juarez. 1995. The impact of women's education on fertility in Latin America: Searching for explanations. *International Family Planning Perspectives* 21(2): 52–57, 80.

Massey, Douglas S. 2007. *Categorically unequal: The American stratification system.* New York: Russell Sage Foundation.

Massey, Douglas S., Camille Z. Charles, Garvey F. Lundy, and Mary J. Fischer. 2003. *The source of the river: The social origins of freshmen at America's selective colleges and universities.* Princeton: Princeton University Press.

Massey, Douglas S., and Nancy A. Denton. 1989. Hypersegregation in U.S. metropolitan areas: Black and Hispanic segregation along five dimensions. *Demography* 26(3): 373–91.

———. 1993. *American apartheid: Segregation and the making of the underclass.* Cambridge: Harvard University Press.

Matute-Bianchi, Maria Eugenia. 1991. Situational ethnicity and patterns of school performance among immigrant and non-immigrant Mexican-descent students. In *Minority status and schooling: A comparative study of immigrant and involuntary minorities,* ed. Margaret A. Gibson and John U. Ogbu, 205–47. New York: Garland.

Maume, David J., Jr. 2004. Wage discrimination over the life course: A comparison of explanations. *Social Problems* 51(4): 505–27.

Maxwell, Nan L., and Ronald J. D'Amico. 1986. Employment and wage effects of involuntary job separation: Male-female differences. *American Economic Review* 76(2): 373–77.

McCall, Leslie. 1998. Spatial routes to gender wage (in)equality: Regional restructuring and wage differentials by gender and education. *Economic Geography* 74(4): 379–404.

———. 2000a. Gender and the new inequality: Explaining the college/non-college wage gap. *American Sociological Review* 65(2): 234–55.

———. 2000b. Explaining levels of within group wage inequality in U.S. labor markets. *Demography* 37(4): 415–30.

———. 2001. *Complex inequality: Gender, class and race in the new economy.* New York: Routledge.

McCreary, Lori, Paula England, and George Farkas. 1989. The employment of central city male youth: Nonlinear effects of racial composition. *Social Forces* 68(1): 55–75.

McDonald, Judith A., and Robert J. Thornton. 2007. Do new male and female college graduates receive unequal pay? *Journal of Human Resources* 42(1): 32–48.

McFalls, Joseph A., Jr. 1973. Impact of VD on the fertility of the U.S. black population, 1880–1950. *Social Biology* 20(1): 2–29.

McFalls, Joseph A., Jr., and George S. Masnick. 1981. Birth control and the fertility of the U.S. black population, 1880 to 1980. *Journal of Family History* 6(1): 89–106.

McLanahan, Sara. 1985. Family structure and the reproduction of poverty. *American Journal of Sociology* 90(4): 873–901.

McLanahan, Sara, and Karen Booth. 1989. Mother-only families: Problems, prospects, and politics. *Journal of Marriage and Family* 51(3): 557–80.

McLanahan, Sara, and Gary Sandefur. 1994. *Growing up with a single parent: What hurts, what helps.* Cambridge: Harvard University Press.

McLanahan, Sara, Annette Sorensen, and Dorothy Watson. 1989. Sex differences in poverty, 1950–1980. *Signs* 15(1): 102–22.

McRoberts, Hugh A. 1985. Mobility and attainment in Canada: The effects of origin. In *Ascription and achievement: Studies in mobility and status attainment in Canada*, ed. Monica Boyd, John Goyder, Frank E. Jones, Hugh A. McRoberts, Peter C. Pineo, and John Porter, 67–100. Ottawa: Carleton University Press.

Medoff, Marshall H. 2000. Black abortion on demand. *Review of Black Political Economy* 28(1): 29–36.

Mehan, Hugh, Lea Hubbard, and Irene Villanueva. 1994. Forming academic identities: Accommodation without assimilation among involuntary minorities. *Anthropology and Education Quarterly* 25(2): 91–117.

Merton, Robert K. 1957. *Social theory and social structure.* New York: Free Press.

Michael, Robert T., and Nancy Brandon Tuma. 1985. Entry into marriage and parenthood by young men and women: The influence of family background. *Demography* 22(4): 515–44.

Mickelson, Roslyn Arlinn. 1990. The attitude-achievement paradox among black adolescents. *Sociology of Education* 63(1): 44–61.

Milan, Stephanie, Kathleen Ethier, Jessica Lewis, Trace Kershaw, Linda Niccolai, and Jeannette Ickovics. 2006. Reproductive health of urban adolescents: Differences in the behaviors, cognitions, and social context of African-American and Puerto Rican females. *Journal of Youth Adolescence* 35: 959–67.

Moore, Kristin A., and Linda J. Waite. 1981. Marital dissolution, early motherhood and early marriage. *Social Forces* 60(1): 20–40.

Morgan, Leslie A. 1991. *After marriage ends: Economic consequences for midlife women.* Newbury Park, Calif.: Sage.

Morgan, S. Philip. 1991. Late nineteenth and early twentieth century childlessness. *American Journal of Sociology* 97(3): 779–807.

———. 2003. Is low fertility a twenty-first-century demographic crisis? *Demography* 40(4): 589–603.

Morris, Martina, and Bruce Western. 1999. Inequality in earnings at the close of the twentieth century. *Annual Review of Sociology* 25: 623–57.

Moss, Philip, and Chris Tilly. 1995. Skills and race in hiring: Quantitative findings from face-to-face interviews. *Eastern Economic Journal* 21(3): 357–74.

———. 1996. "Soft" skills and race: An investigation of black men's employment problems. *Work and Occupations* 23(3): 252–76.

Mueller, Trisha E., Lorrie E. Gavin, and Aniket Kulkarni. 2008. The association between sex education and youth's engagement in sexual intercourse, age at first intercourse, and birth control use at first sex. *Journal of Adolescent Health* 42: 89–96.

Nagel, Joane. 2003. *Race, ethnicity, and sexuality: Intimate intersections, forbidden frontiers.* New York: Oxford University Press.

Nassirpour, Mehdi. 1985. The effect of oil revenue on the fertility pattern in Iran, 1952–1976. *Journal of Marriage and the Family* 47(3): 785–96.

NCHS (National Center for Health Statistics). 1995. National Survey of Family Growth, Cycle V (machine-readable data). Hyattsville, MD; public use data files. ftp://ftp.cdc.gov/pub/Health_Statistics/NCHS/Datasets/NSFG/spss/1995FemRespSetup.sps.

Neal, Derek. 2004. The relationship between marriage market prospects and never-married motherhood. *Journal of Human Resources* 39(4): 938–57.

Nelson, Julie. 1999. Of markets and martyrs: Is it ok to pay well for care? *Feminist Economics* 5(3): 43–49.

Neumark, David, and Sanders Korenman. 1994. Sources of bias in women's wage equations: Results using sibling data. *Journal of Human Resources* 29(2): 379–405.

Newman, Katherine S. 1988/1999. *Falling from grace: Downward mobility in the age of affluence.* New York: Vintage Books (a division of Random House) and Russell Sage Foundation.

———. 1999/2000. *No shame in my game: The working poor in the inner city.* New York: Vintage Books (a division of Random House) and Russell Sage Foundation.

Noonan, Mary C., Mary E. Corcoran, and Paul N. Courant. 2005. Pay differences among the highly trained: Cohort differences in the sex gap in lawyers' earnings. *Social Forces* 84(2): 853–72.

O'Connor, Carla. 1997. Dispositions toward (collective) struggle and educational resilience in the inner city: A case analysis of six African-American high school students. *American Educational Research Journal* 34(4): 593–629.

———. 1999. Race, class, and gender in America: Narratives of opportunity among low-income African American youths. *Sociology of Education* 72: 137–57.

Office of Policy Planning and Research. 1965. *The Negro family: The case for national action.* Washington, D.C.: United States Department of Labor.

Ogbu, John U. 1978. *Minority education and caste: The American system in cross-cultural perspective.* New York: Academic Press.

————. 1990. Minority education in comparative perspective. *Journal of Negro Education* 59(1): 45–57.

————. 1991. Immigrant and involuntary minorities in comparative perspective. In *Minority status and schooling: A comparative study of immigrant and involuntary minorities*, ed. Margaret A. Gibson and John U. Ogbu, 3–33. New York: Garland.

————. 1992. Adaptation to minority status and impact on school success. *Theory into Practice* 31(4): 287–95.

————. 2003. *Black American students in an affluent suburb: A study of academic disengagement*. Mahwah, N.J.: Lawrence Erlbaum Associates.

Ogbu, John U., and Herbert D. Simons. 1998. Voluntary and involuntary minorities: A cultural-ecological theory of school performance with some implications for education. *Anthropology and Education Quarterly* 29(2): 155–88.

Okagaki, Lynn, and Peter A. Frensch. 1998. Parenting and children's school achievement: A multiethnic perspective. *American Educational Research Journal* 35(1): 123–44.

Okamoto, Dina, and Paula England. 1999. Is there a supply side to occupational sex segregation? *Sociological Perspectives* 42(4): 557–82.

Okolski, Marek. 1983. Abortion and contraception in Poland. *Studies in Family Planning* 14(11): 263–74.

Oliver, Melvin L., and Thomas M. Shapiro. 1995. *Black wealth/white wealth: A new perspective on racial inequality*. New York: Routledge.

Omi, Michael, and Howard Winant. 1994. *Racial formation in the United States: From the 1960s to the 1990s*. 2nd ed. New York: Routledge.

Ompad, Danielle C., Steffanie A. Strathdee, David D. Celentano, Carl Latkin, Jeanne M. Poduska, Sheppard G. Kellam, and Nicholas S. Ialongo. 2006. Predictors of early initiation of vaginal and oral sex among urban young adults in Baltimore, Maryland. *Archives of Sexual Behavior* 35(1): 53–65.

Ono, Hiromi. 1998. Husbands' and wives' resources and marital dissolution. *Journal of Marriage and the Family* 60(3): 674–89.

Oppenheimer, Valerie Kincade. 1988. A theory of marriage timing. *American Journal of Sociology* 94(3): 563–91.

————. 1994. Women's rising employment and the future of the family in industrial societies. *Population and Development Review* 20: 293–342.

Oppenheimer, Valerie Kincade, Matthijs Kalmijn, and Nelson Lim. 1997. Men's career development and marriage timing during a period of rising inequality: Economic aspects of marriage and cohabitation. *Demography* 34(3): 311–30.

Orr, Amy J. 2003. Black-white differences in achievement: The importance of wealth. *Sociology of Education* 76(4): 281–304.

Pager, Devah. 2003. The mark of a criminal record. *American Journal of Sociology* 108(5): 937–75.

————. 2007. *Marked: Race, crime, and finding work in an era of mass incarceration*. Chicago: University of Chicago Press.

Pager, Devah, and Lincoln Quillian. 2005. Walking the talk? What employers say versus what they do. *American Sociological Review* 70: 355–80.

Palloni, Alberto, and George Kephart. 1989. The effects of breastfeeding and contraception on the natural rate of increase: Are there compensating effects? *Population Studies* 43(3): 455–78.

Pascarella, Ernest T., John C. Smart, and Judith Stoecker. 1989. College race and the early status attainment of black students. *Journal of Higher Education* 60(1): 82–107.

Pattillo, Mary. 2007. *Black on the block: The politics of race and class in the city*. Chicago: University of Chicago Press.

Pattillo-McCoy, Mary. 1999. *Black picket fences: Privilege and peril among the black middle class*. Chicago: University of Chicago Press.

Pearson, Jennifer, Chandra Muller, and Michelle L. Frisco. 2006. Parental involvement, family structure, and adolescent sexual decision making. *Sociological Perspectives* 49(1): 67–90.

Petersen, Trond, and Laurie A. Morgan. 1995. Separate and unequal: Occupation-establishment sex segregation and the gender wage gap. *American Journal of Sociology* 101(2): 329–65.

Peterson, Richard R. 1996. A re-evaluation of the economic consequences of divorce. *American Sociological Review* 61(3): 528–36.

Pettit, Becky, and Bruce Western. 2004. Mass imprisonment and the life course: Race and class inequality in U.S. incarceration. *American Sociological Review* 69(2): 151–69.

Polavieja, Javier G. 2008. The effect of occupational sex-composition on earnings: Job-specialization, sex-role attitudes and the division of domestic labour in Spain. *European Sociological Review* 24(2): 199–213.

Popenoe, David. 1996. *Life without Father: Compelling new evidence that fatherhood and marriage are indispensable for the good of children and society*. Cambridge: Harvard University Press.

Portes, Alejandro, and Min Zhou. 1994. Should immigrants assimilate? *Public Interest* 116: 18–33.

Prada, Elena, and Gabriel Ojeda. 1987. Selected findings from the demographic and health survey in Colombia, 1986. *International Family Planning Perspectives* 13(4): 116–20.

Press, Andrea L. 1991. *Women watching television: Gender, class, and generation in the American television experience*. Philadelphia: University of Pennsylvania Press.

Price, Derek V. 2004. *Borrowing inequality: Race, class, and student loans*. Boulder, Colo.: Lynne Rienner.

Quadagno, Jill. 1994. *The Color of welfare: How racism undermined the war on poverty*. New York: Oxford University Press.

Rainwater, Lee. 1969. *And the poor get children: Sex, contraception, and family planning in the working class*. Chicago: Quadrangle Books.

Raley, R. Kelly. 1996. A shortage of marriageable men? A note on the role of cohabitation in black-white differences in marriage rates. *American Sociological Review* 61(6): 973–83.

Rankin, Robert P., and Jerry S. Maneker. 1985. The duration of marriage in a divorcing population. *Journal of Marriage and the Family* 47(1): 43–52.

Remez, L. 1998. In Turkey, women's fertility is linked to education, employment and freedom to choose a husband. *International Family Planning Perspectives* 24(2): 97–98.

Reskin, Barbara F., and Denise D. Bielby. 2005. A sociological perspective on gender and career outcomes. *Journal of Economic Perspectives* 19(1): 71–86.

Ridgeway, Cecilia L., and Shelley J. Correll. 2004. Motherhood as a status characteristic. *Journal of Social Issues* 60(4): 683–700.

Rindfuss, Ronald R., Larry Bumpass, and Craig St. John. 1980. Education and fertility: Implications for the roles women occupy. *American Sociological Review* 45(3): 431–47.

Rindfuss, Ronald R., S. Philip Morgan, and Kate Offutt. 1996. Education and the changing age pattern of American fertility: 1963–1989. *Demography* 33(3): 277–90.

Roberts, Dorothy. 1997. *Killing the black body: Race, reproduction and the meaning of liberty*. New York: Vintage Books.

———. 2002. *Shattered bonds: The color of child welfare*. New York: Basic Civitas Books.

Rogers, Richard G., Robert A. Hummer, Charles B. Nam, and Kimberly Peters. 1996. Demographic, socioeconomic, and behavioral factors affecting ethnic mortality by cause. *Social Forces* 74(4): 1419–38.

Roksa, Josipa. 2005. Double disadvantage or blessing in disguise? Understanding the relationship between college major and employment sector. *Sociology of Education* 78(3): 207–32.

Rollins, Judith. 1985. *Between women: domestics and their employers*. Philadelphia: Temple University Press.

Romano, Renee C. 2003. *Race mixing: Black-white marriage in postwar America*. Cambridge: Harvard University Press.

Roscigno, Vincent J. 2007. *The face of discrimination: How race and gender impact work and home lives*. Lanham, Md.: Rowman and Littlefield.

Roscigno, Vincent J., Sherry Mong, Reginald Byron, and Griff Tester. 2007. Age discrimination, social closure, and employment. *Social Forces* 86(1): 313–34.

Rosenfeld, Rachel A., and Arne Kalleberg. 1991. Gender inequality in the labor market: A cross-national perspective. *Acta Sociologica* 34(3): 207–25.

Rosenzweig, Mark R. 1999. Welfare, marital prospects, and nonmarital childbearing. *Journal of Political Economy* 107(6 Part 2):S3-S32.

Royster, Deirdre A. 2003. *Race and the invisible hand: How white networks exclude black men from blue collar jobs*. Berkeley: University of California Press.

Rumberger, Russell W. 1983. The influence of family background on education, earnings, and wealth. *Social Forces* 61(3): 755–73.

Sakamoto, Arthur, Huei-Hsia Wu, and Jessie Tzeng. 2000. The declining significance of race among American men during the latter half of the twentieth century. *Demography* 37(1): 41–51.

Salzinger, Leslie. 2003. *Genders in production: Making workers in Mexico's global factories*. Berkeley: University of California Press.

Sanger, Alexander. 2007. Eugenics, race, and Margaret Sanger revisited: Reproductive freedom for all. *Hypatia* 22(2): 210–17.

Sassler, Sharon, and Robert Schoen. 1999. The effect of attitudes and economic activity on marriage. *Journal of Marriage and the Family* 61(1): 147–59.

Sathar, Zeba, Nigel Crook, Christine Callum, and Shahnaz Kazi. 1988. Women's status and fertility change in Pakistan. *Population and Development Review* 14(3): 415–32.

Schoen, Robert, Young J. Kim, Constance A. Nathanson, Jason Fields, and Nan Marie Astone. 1997. Why do Americans want children? *Population and Development Review* 23(2): 333–58.

Schoen, Robert, and Robin M. Weinick. 1993. Partner choice in marriages and cohabitation. *Journal of Marriage and the Family* 55(2): 408–14.

Schoen, Robert, and John Wooldredge. 1989. Marriage choices in North Carolina and Virginia, 1969–1971 and 1979–1981. *Journal of Marriage and the Family* 51(2): 465–81.

Schor, Juliet B. 1998. *The overspent American: Upscaling, downshifting, and the new consumer*. New York: Basic Books.

Schulz, Amy J., David R. Williams, Barbara A. Israel, and Lora Bex Lempert. 2002. Racial and spatial relations as fundamental determinants of health in Detroit. *Milbank Quarterly* 80(4): 677–707.

Sewell, William H., Archibald O. Haller, and Alejandro Portes. 1969. The educational and early occupational attainment process. *American Sociological Review* 34(1): 82–92.

Sewell, William H., and Robert M. Hauser. 1972. Causes and consequences of higher education: Models of the status attainment process. *American Journal of Agricultural Economics* 54(5): 851–61.

Sewell, William H., Robert M. Hauser, and Wendy C. Wolf. 1980. Sex, schooling, and occupational status. *American Journal of Sociology* 86(3): 551–83.

Shah, Nasra, Makhdoom A. Shah, and Zoran Radovanovic. 1998. Patterns of desired fertility and contraceptive use in Kuwait. *International Family Planning Perspectives* 24(3): 133–38.

Shapiro, David, and B. Oleko Tambashe. 1994. The impact of women's employment and education on contraceptive use and abortion in Kinshasa, Zaire. *Studies in Family Planning* 25(2): 96–110.

Shauman, Kimberlee A. 2006. Occupational sex segregation and the earnings of occupations: What causes the link among college-educated workers? *Social Science Research* 35: 577–619.

Shaw, Kathleen M., and Ashaki B. Coleman. 2000. Humble on Sundays: Family, friends, and faculty in the upward mobility experiences of African American females. *Anthropology and Education Quarterly* 31(4): 449–70.

Sherman, Rachel. 2007. *Class acts: Service and inequality in luxury hotels.* Berkeley: University of California Press.

Singh, Susheela. 1998. Adolescent childbearing in developing countries: A global review. *Studies in Family Planning* 29(2): 117–36.

Sklar, June L. 1974. The role of marriage behaviour in the demographic transition: The case of Eastern Europe around 1900. *Population Studies* 28(2): 231–47.

Smith, Herbert L., S. Philip Morgan, and Tanya Koropeckyj-Cox. 1996. A decomposition of trends in the nonmarital fertility ratios of blacks and whites in the United States, 1960–1992. *Demography* 33(2): 141–51.

Smock, Pamela J. 1993. The economic costs of marital disruption for young women over the past two decades. *Demography* 30(3): 353–71.

———. 1994. Gender and the short-run economic consequences of marital disruption. *Social Forces* 73(1): 243–62.

Smock, Pamela J., Wendy D. Manning, and Sanjiv Gupta. 1999. The effect of marriage and divorce on women's economic well-being. *American Sociological Review* 64(6): 794–812.

Snarey, John R., and George E. Vaillant. 1985. How lower- and working-class youth become middle-class adults: The association between ego defense mechanisms and upward social mobility. *Child Development* 56(4): 899–910.

Solinger, Rickie. 2001. *Beggars and choosers: How the politics of choice shapes adoption, abortion, and welfare in the United States.* New York: Hill and Wang.

Solomon, R. Patrick. 1992. *Black resistance in high school: Forging a separatist culture.* Albany: State University of New York Press.

South, Scott J. 1991. Sociodemographic differentials in mate selection preferences. *Journal of Marriage and the Family* 53(4): 928–40.

South, Scott J., and Eric P. Baumer. 2001. Community effects on the resolution of adolescent premarital pregnancy. *Journal of Family Issues* 22: 1025–43.

South, Scott J., and Kim M. Lloyd. 1992. Marriage opportunities and family formation: Further implications of imbalanced sex ratios. *Journal of Marriage and the Family* 54(2): 440–51.

South, Scott J., and Glenna Spitze. 1986. Determinants of divorce over the marital life course. *American Sociological Review* 51(4): 583–90.

South, Scott J., and Katherine Trent. 1988. Sex ratios and women's roles: A cross-national analysis. *American Journal of Sociology* 93(5): 1096–1115.

Spanier, Graham B., and Paul C. Glick. 1980. Mate selection differentials between whites and blacks in the United States. *Social Forces* 58(3): 707–25.

Spanier, Graham B., Patricia A. Roos, and James Shockey. 1985. Marital trajectories of American women: Variations in the life course. *Journal of Marriage and the Family* 47(4): 993–1003.

Stack, Carol. 1974. *All our kin.* New York: Basic Books.

Staples, Robert. 1991. Social inequality and black sexual pathology: The essential relationship. *Black Scholar* 21(3): 29–37.

Steele, Claude M. 1997. A threat in the air: How stereotypes shape intellectual identity and performance. *American Psychologist* 52(6): 613–29.

Steele, Claude M., and J. Aronson. 1995. Stereotype threat and the intellectual test performance of African Americans. *Journal of Personality and Social Psychology* 69: 797–811.

Steele, Claude M., and Paul G. Davies. 2003. Stereotype threat and employment testing: A commentary. *Human Performance* 16(3): 311–26.

Steelman, Lala Carr, and Brian Powell. 1991. Sponsoring the next generation: Parental willingness to pay for higher education. *American Journal of Sociology* 96(6): 1505–29.

Stephen, Elizabeth Hervey, Ronald R. Rindfuss, and Frank D. Bean. 1988. Racial differences in contraceptive choice: Complexity and implications. *Demography* 25(1): 53–70.

Stepp, Laura Sessions. 2007. *Unhooked: How young women pursue sex, delay love and lose at both.* New York: Riverhead Books.

Stier, Haya, and Marta Tienda. 2001. *The color of opportunity: Pathways to family, welfare, and work.* Chicago: University of Chicago Press.

Stirling, Kate J. 1989. Women who remain divorced: The long-term economic consequences. *Social Science Quarterly* 70(3): 549–61.

St. Jean, Yanick, and Joe R. Feagin. 1998. *Double burden: Black women and everyday racism.* Armonk, N.Y.: M. E. Sharpe.

St. John, Craig. 1982. Race differences in age at first birth and the pace of subsequent fertility: Implications for the minority group status hypothesis. *Demography* 19(3): 301–14.

Stoll, Michael A., Harry J. Holzer, and Keith R. Ihlanfeldt. 2000. Within cities and suburbs: Racial residential concentration and the spatial distribution of employment opportunities across sub-metropolitan areas. *Journal of Policy Analysis and Management* 19(2): 207–31.

Stryker, Robin. 1981. Religio-ethnic effects on attainments in the early career. *American Sociological Review* 46(2): 212–31.

Sullivan, Mercer. 1989. *Getting paid: Youth, crime, and work in the inner city.* Ithaca: Cornell University Press.

Sullivan, Rachel. 2005. The age pattern of first-birth rates among U.S. women: The bimodal 1990s. *Demography* 42(2): 259–73.

Sum, Andrew, Ishwar Khatiwada, and Sheila Palma. 2005. The age twist in employment rates, 2000–2004. *Challenge* 48(4): 51–68.

Sweetman, Arthur, and Gordon Dicks. 1999. Education and ethnicity in Canada: An intergenerational perspective. *Journal of Human Resources* 34(4): 668–96.

Swicegood, Gray, Frank D. Bean, Elizabeth Hervey Stephen, and Wolfgang Opitz. 1988. Language usage and fertility in the Mexican-origin population of the United States. *Demography* 25(1): 17–33.

Tachibanaki, Toshiaki. 1979. Models for educational and occupational achievement over time. *Sociology of Education* 52(3): 156–62.

Tawiah, E. O. 1984. Determinants of cumulative fertility in Ghana. *Demography* 21(1): 1–8.

Taylor, Ronald D., Robin Casten, Susanne M. Flickinger, Debra Roberts, and Cecil D. Fulmore. 1994. Explaining the school performance of African-American adolescents. *Journal of Research on Adolescence* 4(1): 21–44.

Teachman, Jay D., Karen A. Polonko, and Geoffrey K. Leigh. 1987. Marital timing: Race and sex comparisons. *Social Forces* 66(1): 239–68.

Teitler, Julien O., and Christopher C. Weiss. 2000. Effects of neighborhood and school environments on transitions to first sexual intercourse. *Sociology of Education* 73(2): 112–32.

Testa, Mark, Nan Marie Astone, Marilyn Krogh, and Katheryn M. Neckerman. 1989. Employment and marriage among inner-city fathers. *Annals of the American Academy of Political and Social Science* 501 (The ghetto underclass: Social science perspectives): 79–91.

Testa, Mark, and Marilyn Krogh. 1995. The effect of employment on marriage among black males in inner-city Chicago. In *The decline in marriage among African Americans*, ed. M. Belinda Tucker and Claudia Mitchell-Kernan, 59–95. New York: Russell Sage Foundation.

Teti, Douglas M., and Michael E. Lamb. 1989. Socioeconomic and marital outcomes of adolescent marriage, adolescent childbirth, and their co-occurrence. *Journal of Marriage and the Family* 51(1): 203–12.

Thomas, Susan L. 1998. Race, gender, and welfare reform: The antinatalist response. *Journal of Black Studies* 28(4): 419–46.

Thorburn, Sheryl, and Laura M. Bogart. 2005a. African American women and family planning services: Perceptions of discrimination. *Women and Health* 42(1): 23–39.

———. 2005b. Conspiracy beliefs about birth control: Barriers to pregnancy prevention among African Americans of reproductive age. *Health Education and Behavior* 32(4): 474–87.

Tigges, Leann M., and Deborah M. Tootle. 1993. Underemployment and racial competition in local labor markets. *Sociological Quarterly* 34(2): 279–98.

Tolnay, Stewart E. 2001. African Americans and immigrants in northern cities: The effects of relative group size on occupational standing in 1920. *Social Forces* 80(2): 573–604.

Tolnay, Stewart E., and Patricia J. Glynn. 1994. The persistence of high fertility in the American south on the eve of the baby boom. *Demography* 31(4): 615–31.

Torr, Berna Miller, and Susan E. Short. 2004. Second births and the second shift: A research note on gender equity and fertility. *Population and Development Review* 30(1): 109–30.

Trappe, Heike, and Rachel A. Rosenfeld. 2000. How do children matter? A comparison of gender earnings inequality for young adults in the former East Germany and the former West Germany. *Journal of Marriage and Family* 62(2): 489–507.

Trent, Katherine, and Eve Powell-Griner. 1991. Race, marital status, and education among women obtaining abortions. *Social Forces* 69(4): 1121–41.

Trussell, James. 1976. Economic consequences of teenage childbearing. *Family Planning Perspectives* 8(4): 184–90.

———. 1988. Teenage pregnancy in the United States. *Family Planning Perspectives* 20(6): 262–72.

———. 2004. Contraceptive failure in the United States. *Contraception* 70: 89–96.

Tucker, M. Belinda, and Claudia Mitchell-Kernan. 1990. New trends in black American interracial marriage: The social structural context. *Journal of Marriage and the Family* 52(1): 209–18.

———. 1995. *The Decline in marriage among African Americans: Causes, consequences, and policy implications.* New York: Russell Sage Foundation.

Tucker, M. Belinda, and Robert Joseph Taylor. 1989. Demographic correlates of relationship status among black Americans. *Journal of Marriage and the Family* 51(3): 655–65.

Tuladhar, J. M., J. Stoeckel, and A. Fisher. 1982. Differential fertility in rural Nepal. *Population Studies* 36(1): 81–85.

Turrittin, Anton H., Paul Anisef, and Neil J. MacKinnon. 1983. Gender differences in educational achievement: A study of social inequality. *Canadian Journal of Sociology* 8(4): 395–419.

Tyson, Karolyn. 2002. Weighing in: Elementary-age students and the debate on attitudes toward school among black students. *Social Forces* 80(4): 1157–89.

———. 2003. Notes from the back of the room: Problems and paradoxes in the schooling of young black students. *Sociology of Education* 76(4): 326–43.

Tyson, Karolyn, William Darity Jr., and Domini R. Castellino. 2005. It's not "a black thing": Understanding the burden of acting white and other dilemmas of high achievement. *American Sociological Review* 70(4): 582–605.

Tzeng, Meei-Shenn. 1992. The effects of socioeconomic heterogamy and changes on marital dissolution for first marriages. *Journal of Marriage and the Family* 54(3): 609–19.

Udry, J. Richard. 1988. Biological predisposition and social control in adolescent sexual behavior. *American Sociological Review* 53(5): 709–22.

Upchurch, Dawn M., Lee A. Lillard, and Constantijn W. A. Panis. 2002. Nonmarital childbearing: Influences of education, marriage, and fertility. *Demography* 39(2): 311–29.

van de Walle, Francine. 1980. Education and demographic transition in Switzerland. *Population and Development Review* 6(3): 463–72.

Veblen, Thorstein. 1953. *The theory of the leisure class: An economic study of institutions*. New York: New American Library.

Venkatesh, Sudhir Alladi. 1994. Getting ahead: Social mobility among the urban poor. *Sociological Perspectives* 37(2): 157–82.

———. 2000. *American project: The rise and fall of a modern ghetto*. Cambridge: Harvard University Press.

———. 2006. *Off the books: The underground economy of the urban poor*. Cambridge: Harvard University Press.

Ventura, Stephanie J., and Christine A. Bachrach. 2000. Nonmarital childbearing in the United States, 1940–1999. *National Vital Statistics Report* 48(16): 1–39.

Waite, Linda J. 1995. Does marriage matter? *Demography* 32(4): 483–507.

Waite, Linda J., and Maggie Gallagher. 2000. *The case for marriage: Why married people are happier, healthier, and better off financially*. New York: Broadway Books.

Waldfogel, Jane. 1997. The effect of children on women's wages. *American Sociological Review* 62(2): 209–17.

———. 1998a. Understanding the "family gap" in pay for women with children. *Journal of Economic Perspectives* 12(1): 137–56.

———. 1998b. The family gap for young women in the United States and Britain: Can maternity leave make a difference? *Journal of Labor Economics* 16(3): 505–45.

Waller, Maureen, and Sara S. McLanahan. 2005. "His" and "her" marriage expectations: Determinants and consequences. *Journal of Marriage and Family* 67: 53–67.

Warren, Charles W., Dorian Powell, Leo Morris, Jean Jackson, and Pansy Hamilton. 1988. Fertility and family planning among young adults in Jamaica. *International Family Planning Perspectives* 14(4): 137–41.

Warren, Charles W., John S. Santelli, Sherry A. Everett, Laura Kann, Janet L. Collins, Carol Cassell, Leo Morris, and Lloyd J. Kolbe. 1998. Sexual behavior among U.S. high school students, 1990–1995. *Family Planning Perspectives* 30(4): 170–200.

Weakliem, David L. 1992. Does social mobility affect political behaviour? *European Sociological Review* 8(2): 153–65.

Weeks, John R. 2007. *Population: An introduction to concepts and issues*. Belmont, Calif.: Wadsworth.

Weinberger, Mary Beth. 1987. The relationship between women's education and fertility: Selected findings from the world fertility surveys. *International Family Planning Perspectives* 13(2): 35–46.

Weinberger, Mary Beth, Cynthia Lloyd, and Ann Klimas Blanc. 1989. Women's education and fertility: A decade of change in four Latin American countries. *International Family Planning Perspectives* 15(1): 4–14, 28.

West, Candace, and Sarah Fenstermaker. 1993. Power, inequality, and the accomplishment of gender: An ethnomethodological view. In *Theory on gender/feminism on theory*, ed. Paula England, 151–74. New York: Aldine De Gruyter.

———. 1995. Doing difference. *Gender and Society* 9(1): 8–37.

West, Candace, and Don H. Zimmerman. 1987. Doing gender. *Gender and Society* 1(2): 125–51.

Western, Bruce. 2002. The impact of incarceration on wage mobility and inequality. *American Sociological Review* 67(4): 526–46.

———. 2007. Mass imprisonment and economic inequality. *Social Research* 74(2): 509–32.

Western, Bruce, and Katherine Beckett. 1999. How unregulated is the U.S. labor market? The penal system as a labor market institution. *American Journal of Sociology* 104(4): 1030–60.

Western, Bruce, Meredith Kleykamp, and Jake Rosenfeld. 2006. Did falling wages and employment increase U.S. imprisonment? *Social Forces* 84(4): 2291–2311.

Western, Bruce, and Becky Pettit. 2002. Beyond crime and punishment: Prisons and inequality. *Contexts* 1(3): 37–43.

———. 2005. Black-white wage inequality, employment rates, and incarceration. *American Journal of Sociology* 111(2): 553–78.

Wharton, Amy S., and Deborah K. Thorne. 1997. When mothers matter: The effects of social class and family arrangements on African American and white women's perceived relations with their mothers. *Gender and Society* 11(5): 656–81.

Wilkie, Jane Riblett. 1981. The trend toward delayed parenthood. *Journal of Marriage and the Family* 43(3): 583–91.

Williams, David R., and Chiquita Collins. 1995. U.S. socioeconomic and racial differences in health: Patterns and explanations. *Annual Review of Sociology* 21: 349–86.

Williams, David R., Risa Lavizzo-Mourey, and Reuben C. Warren. 1994. The concept of race and health status in America. *Public Health Reports (1974–)* 109(1): 26–41.

Williams, Joan. 2000. *Unbending gender: Why family and work conflict and what to do about it*. New York: Oxford University Press.

Willis, Paul. 1977. *Learning to labor: How working class kids get working class jobs*. New York: Columbia University Press.

Willis, Robert J., and John G. Haaga. 1996. Economic approaches to understanding nonmarital fertility. *Population and Development Review* 22 (suppl., Fertility in the United States: New patterns, new theories): 67–86.

Wilson, William Julius. 1978/1980. *The declining significance of race: Blacks and changing American cities*. Chicago: University of Chicago Press.

―――. 1987. *The truly disadvantaged: The inner city, the underclass, and public policy*. Chicago: University of Chicago Press.

―――. 1996. *When work disappears: The world of the new urban poor*. New York: Alfred A. Knopf.

Wilson, William Julius, and Katheryn Neckerman. 1987. Poverty and family structure: The widening gap between evidence and public policy issues. In *The truly disadvantaged: The inner city, the underclass, and public policy*, 63–92. Chicago: University of Chicago Press.

Wong, Morrison G. 1990. The education of white, Chinese, Filipino, and Japanese students: A look at "High school and beyond." *Sociological Perspectives* 33(3): 355–74.

Wong, Yin-Ling Irene, Irwin Garfinkel, and Sara McLanahan. 1993. Single-mother families in eight countries: Economic status and social policy. *Social Service Review* 67(2): 177–97.

Wood, Robert G. 1995. Marriage rates and marriageable men: A test of the Wilson hypothesis. *Journal of Human Resources* 30(1): 163–93.

Wright, Erik Olin, Janeen Baxter, and Gunn Elisabeth Birkelund. 1995. The gender gap in workplace authority: A cross-national study. *American Sociological Review* 60(3): 407–35.

Wu, Huoying. 2007. Can the human capital approach explain life-cycle wage differentials between races and sexes? *Economic Inquiry* 45(1): 24–39.

Young, Alford A. 2004. *The minds of marginalized black men: Making sense of mobility, opportunity, and future life chances*. Princeton: Princeton University Press.

Zelizer, Viviana. 2002. Intimate transactions. In *The new economic sociology: Developments in an emerging field*, ed. Mauro Gullen, Randall Collins, Paula England, and Marshall Meyer, 274–300. New York: Russell Sage.

Zelnick, Melvin, and John F. Kantner. 1980. Sexual activity, contraceptive use and pregnancy among metropolitan-area teenagers 1971–1979. *Family Planning Perspectives* 12(5): 230–37.

Zimmerman, Rick S., Seth M. Noar, Sonja Feist-Price, Olga Dekthar, Pamela K. Cupp, Eric Anderman, and Sharon Lock. 2007. Longitudinal test of a multiple domain model of adolescent condom use. *Journal of Sex Research* 44(4): 380–94.

Zubrinsky, Camille L., and Lawrence Bobo. 1996. Prismatic metropolis: Race and residential segregation in the city of angels. *Social Science Research* 25: 335–74.

AVERIL Y. CLARKE is an independent scholar.

Library of Congress Cataloging-in-Publication Data

Clarke, Averil Y. (Averil Yvette)
Inequalities of love : college-educated black women and the barriers to romance
and family / Averil Y. Clarke.
p. cm.—(Politics, history, and culture)
Includes bibliographical references and index.
ISBN 978-0-8223-4995-2 (cloth : alk. paper)
ISBN 978-0-8223-5008-8 (pbk. : alk. paper)
1. African American women—Family relationships.
2. African American women—Education.
3. Love.
4. Marriage.
5. Man-woman relationships.
I. Title. II. Series: Politics, history, and culture.
E185.86.C557 2011
305.48'896073—dc22   2010054447